Oh My Goddess!

ああ女神さま

Childhood's End

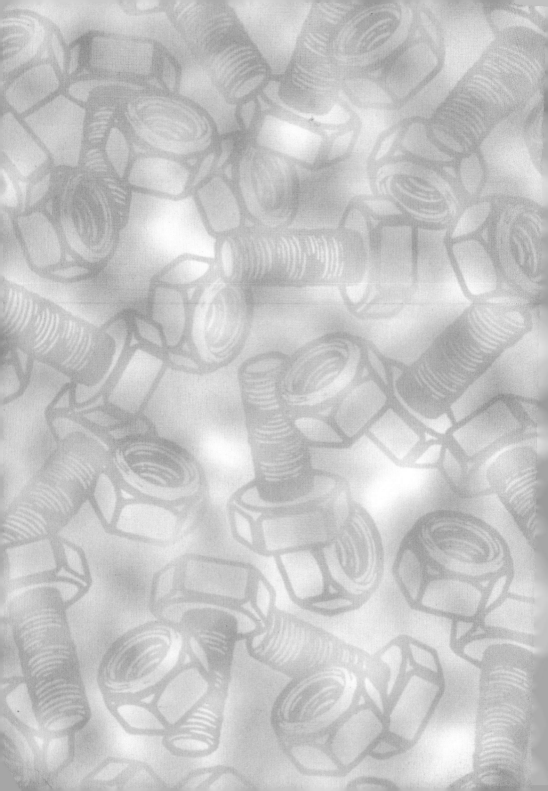

Oh My Goddess!

ああ女神さお

Childhood's End

STORY AND ART BY

Kosuke Fujishima

TRANSLATION BY

Dana Lewis & Toren Smith

LETTERING AND RETOUCH BY

Susie Lee & PC Orz

DARK HORSE COMICS®

PUBLISHER
Mike Richardson

SERIES EDITOR
Mike Hansen

COLLECTION EDITOR
Chris Warner

COLLECTION DESIGNER
Amy Arendts

ART DIRECTOR
Mark Cox

English-language version produced by Studio Proteus
for Dark Horse Comics, Inc.

OH MY GODDESS! Volume XIII: Childhood's End

This volume collects issues one through six of the Dark Horse comic-book series *Oh My Goddess! Part VIII.*

Published by
Dark Horse Comics, Inc.
10956 SE Main Street
Milwaukie, OR 97222

www.darkhorse.com

To find a comics shop in your area, call the Comic Shop
Locator Service toll-free at 1-888-266-4226

First edition: March 2002
ISBN: 1-56971-685-4

3 5 7 9 10 8 6 4 2
Printed in Canada

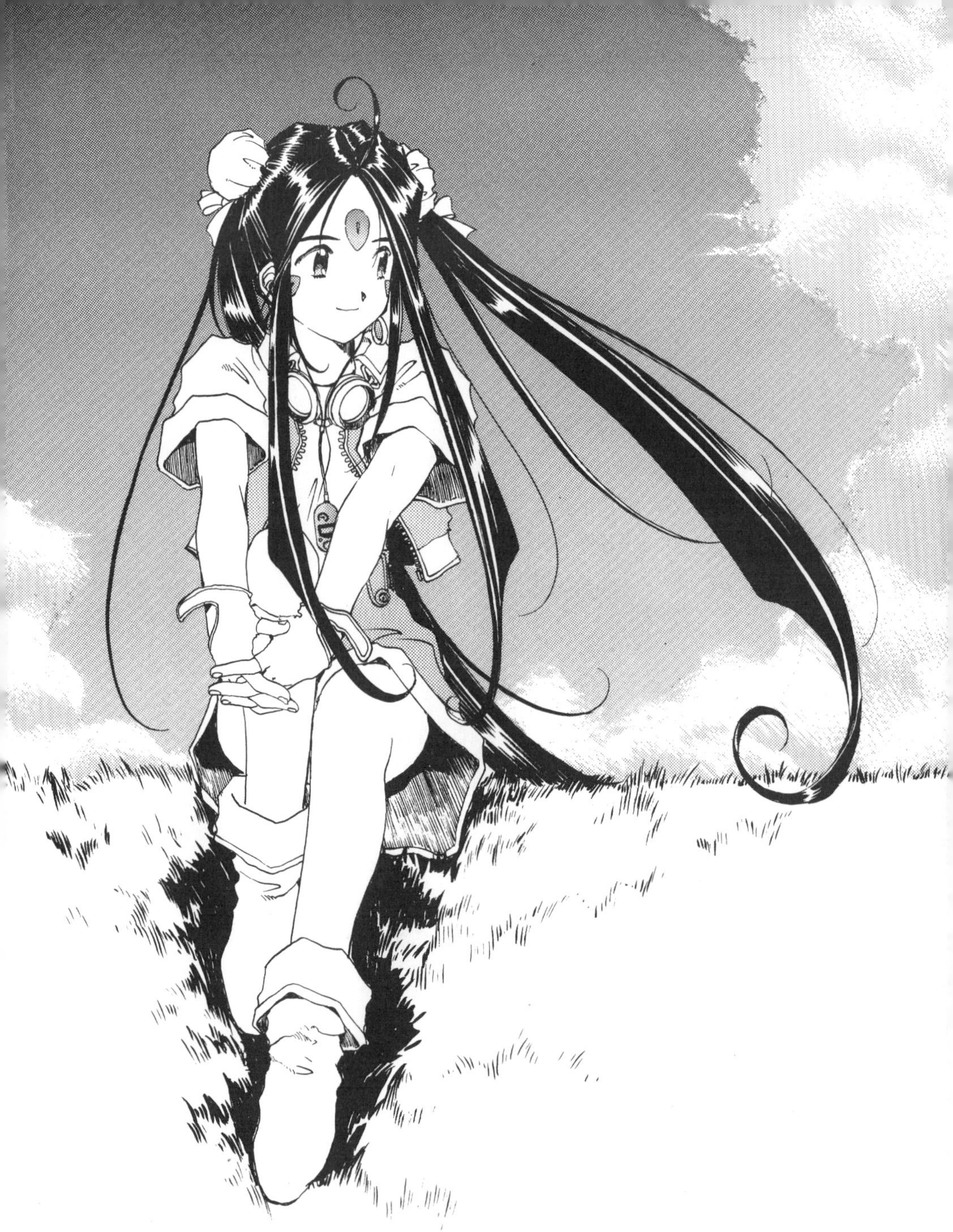

Childhood's End

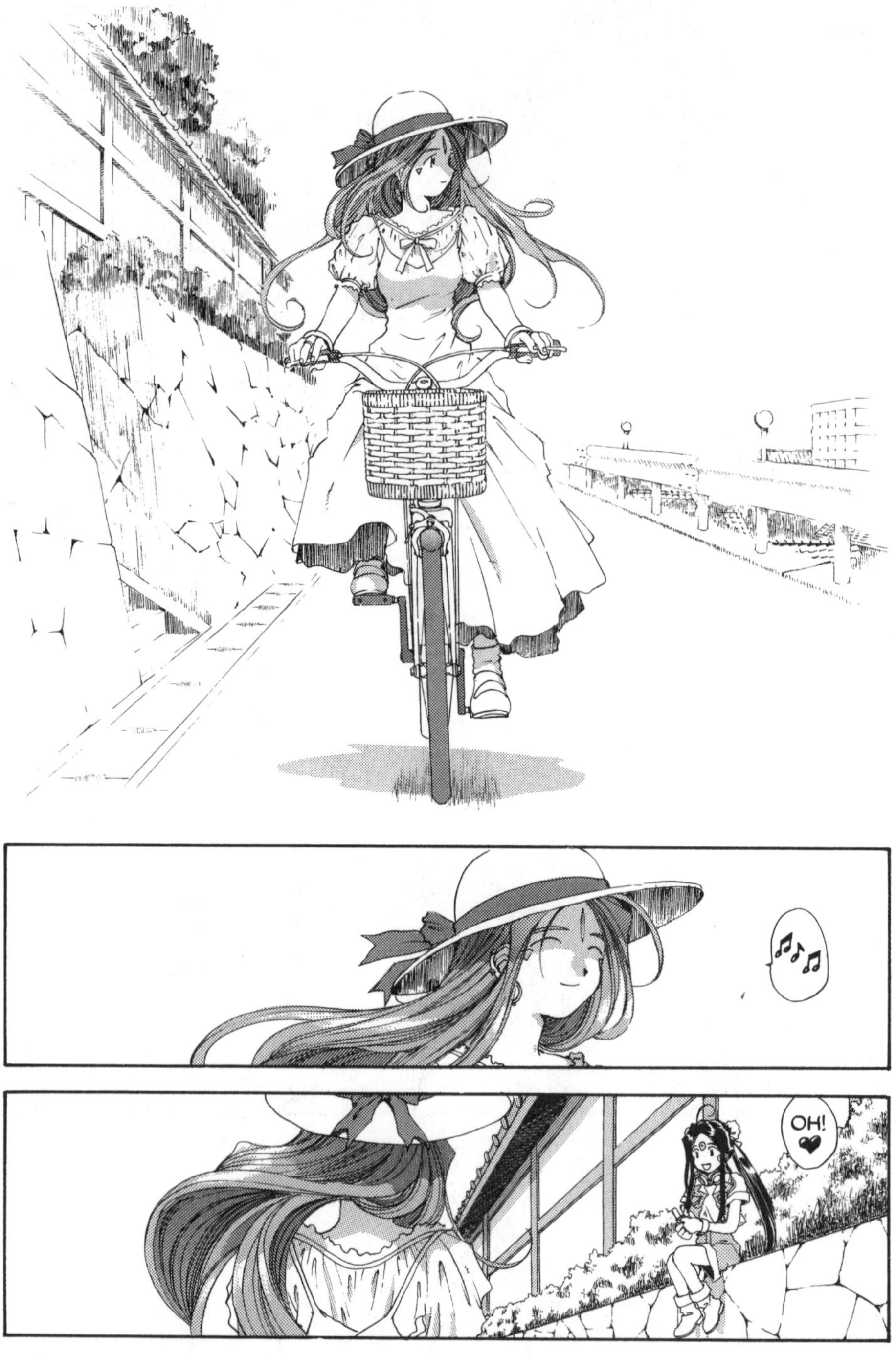
OH!

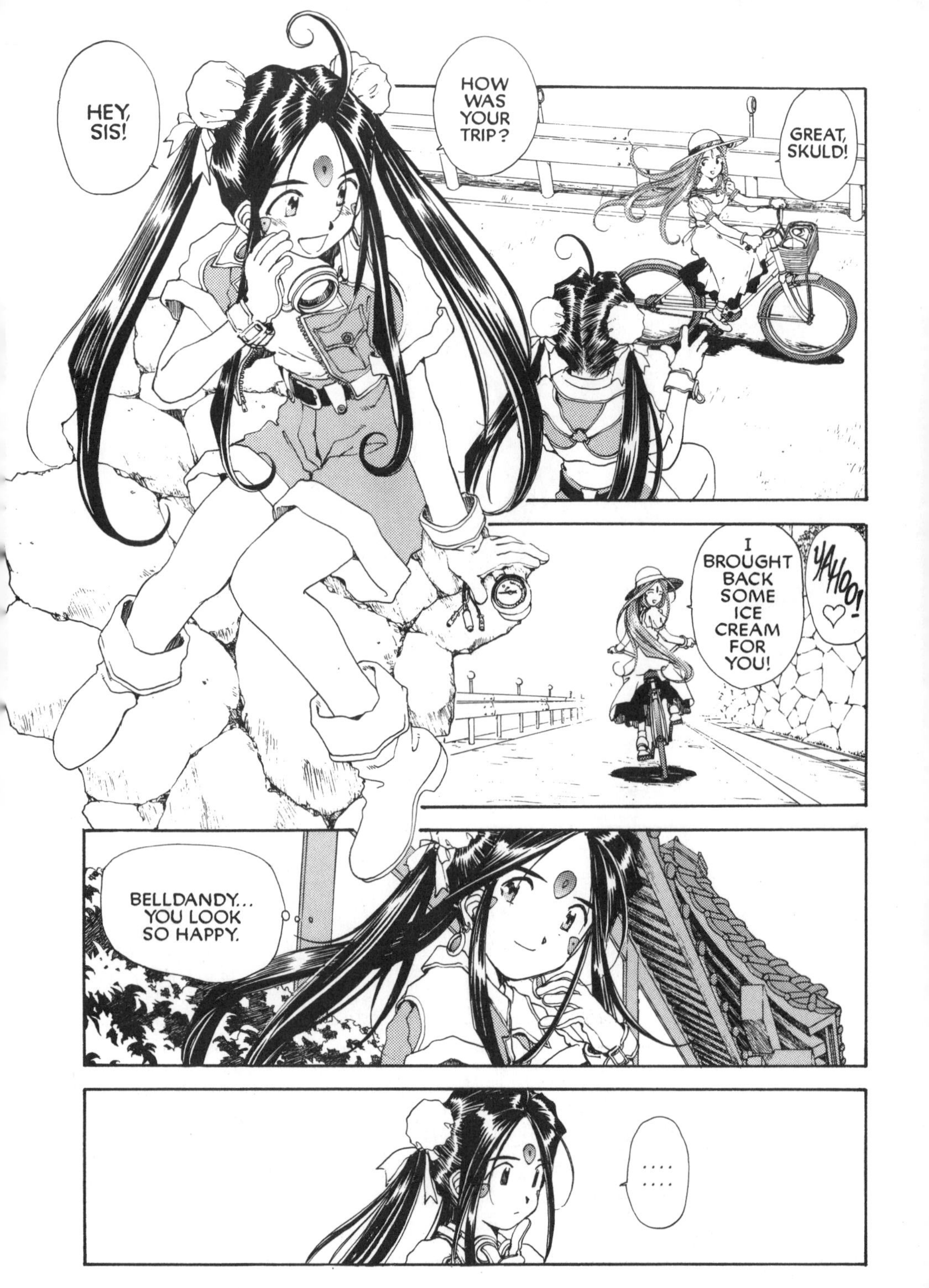
HEY, SIS!
HOW WAS YOUR TRIP?
GREAT, SKULD!
I BROUGHT BACK SOME ICE CREAM FOR YOU!
YAHOO!
BELLDANDY... YOU LOOK SO HAPPY.
....

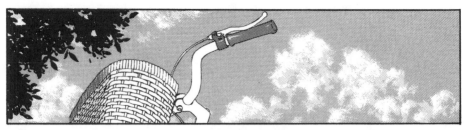

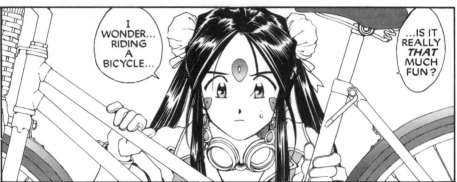

I WONDER... RIDING A BICYCLE...
...IS IT REALLY *THAT* MUCH FUN?
LET'S SEE-- WHEN YOU ROTATE THESE PEDALS...
...THE CHAIN TRANSMITS THE LEVERAGE TO THE SPROCKET AND AXLE AT THE REAR OF THE BIKE.
AND...
SQUEEZING THIS BRAKE LEVER...
...CAUSES THESE PADS TO MAKE CONTACT WITH THE WHEEL, CONVERTING ANGULAR MOMENTUM TO HEAT.
NO SHOCK ABSORBERS, BUT IN THEIR PLACE, AIR-BLADDER TIRES AND A SPRING SUSPENSION FOR THE SEAT.
I WONDER WHY THE FRAME ISN'T MORE PERFECTLY TRIANGULAR? STRANGE.
NOW, *THIS* JOINT COULD USE SOME IMPROVEMENT.
HMM. EXTREME SIMPLICITY, YET STRANGELY LOGICAL.

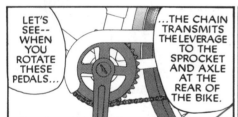

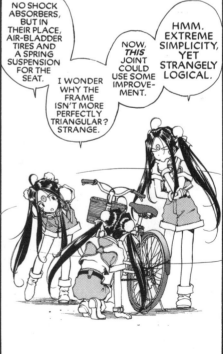

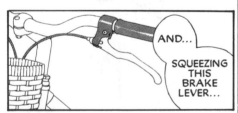

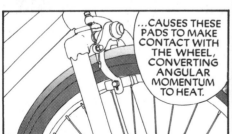

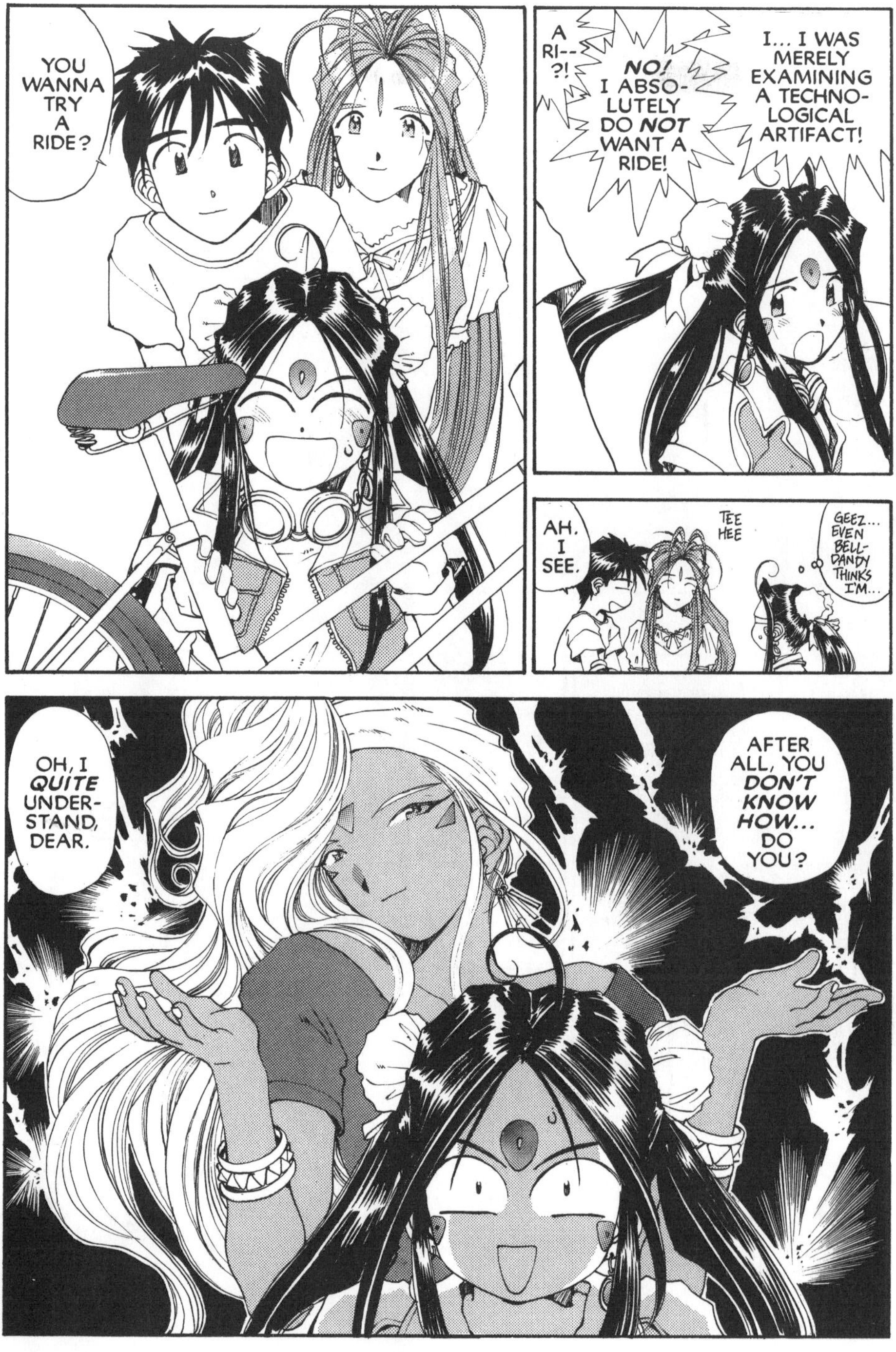
YOU WANNA TRY A RIDE?
A RI--?!
NO! I ABSOLUTELY DO NOT WANT A RIDE!
I... I WAS MERELY EXAMINING A TECHNOLOGICAL ARTIFACT!
AH. I SEE.
TEE HEE
GEEZ... EVEN BELLDANDY THINKS I'M...
OH, I QUITE UNDERSTAND, DEAR.
AFTER ALL, YOU DON'T KNOW HOW... DO YOU?

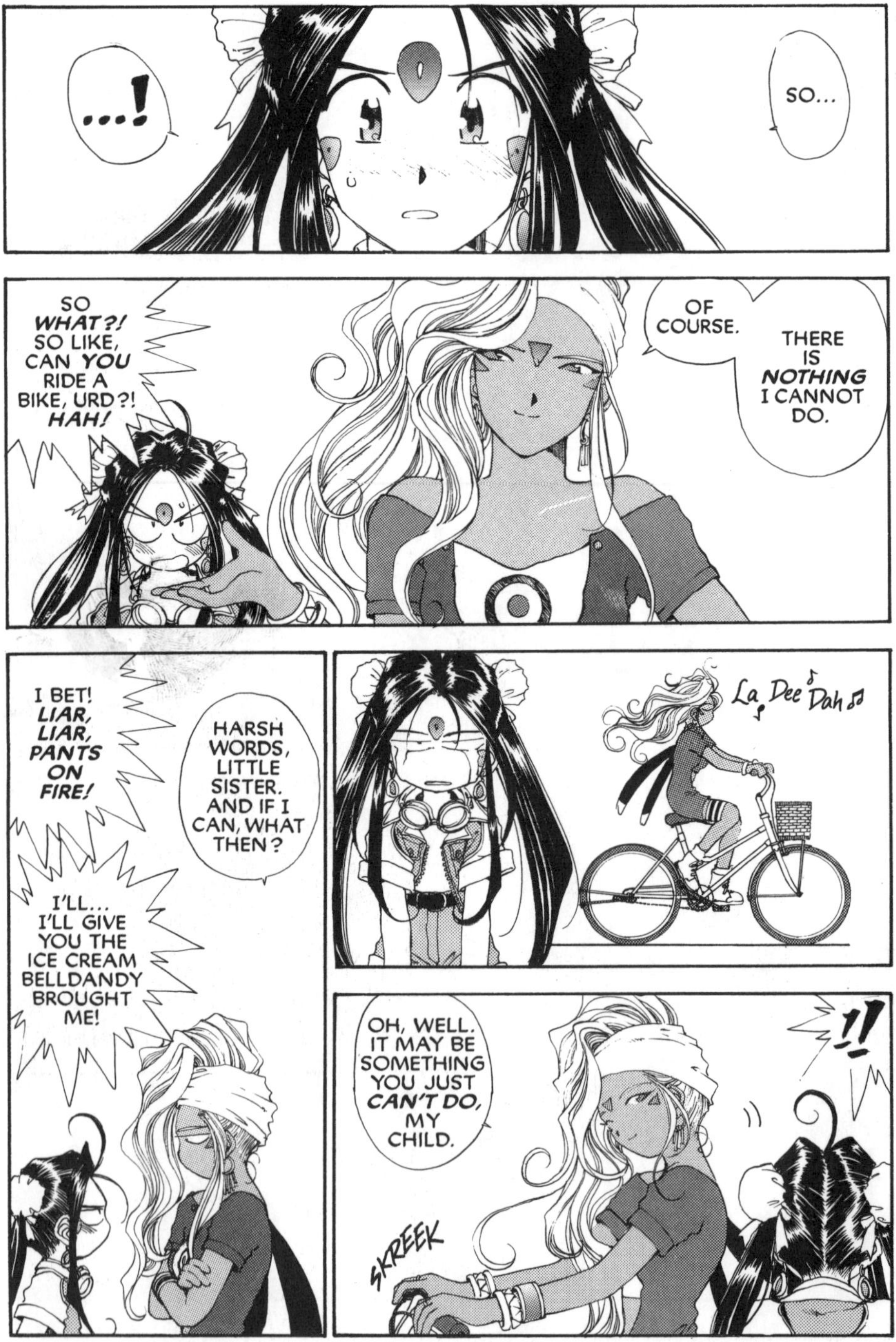
...!
SO...
SO WHAT?! SO LIKE, CAN YOU RIDE A BIKE, URD?! HAH!
OF COURSE.
THERE IS NOTHING I CANNOT DO.
I BET! LIAR, LIAR, PANTS ON FIRE!
HARSH WORDS, LITTLE SISTER. AND IF I CAN, WHAT THEN?
I'LL... I'LL GIVE YOU THE ICE CREAM BELLDANDY BROUGHT ME!
La Dee Dah
OH, WELL. IT MAY BE SOMETHING YOU JUST CAN'T DO, MY CHILD.
!!
SKREEK

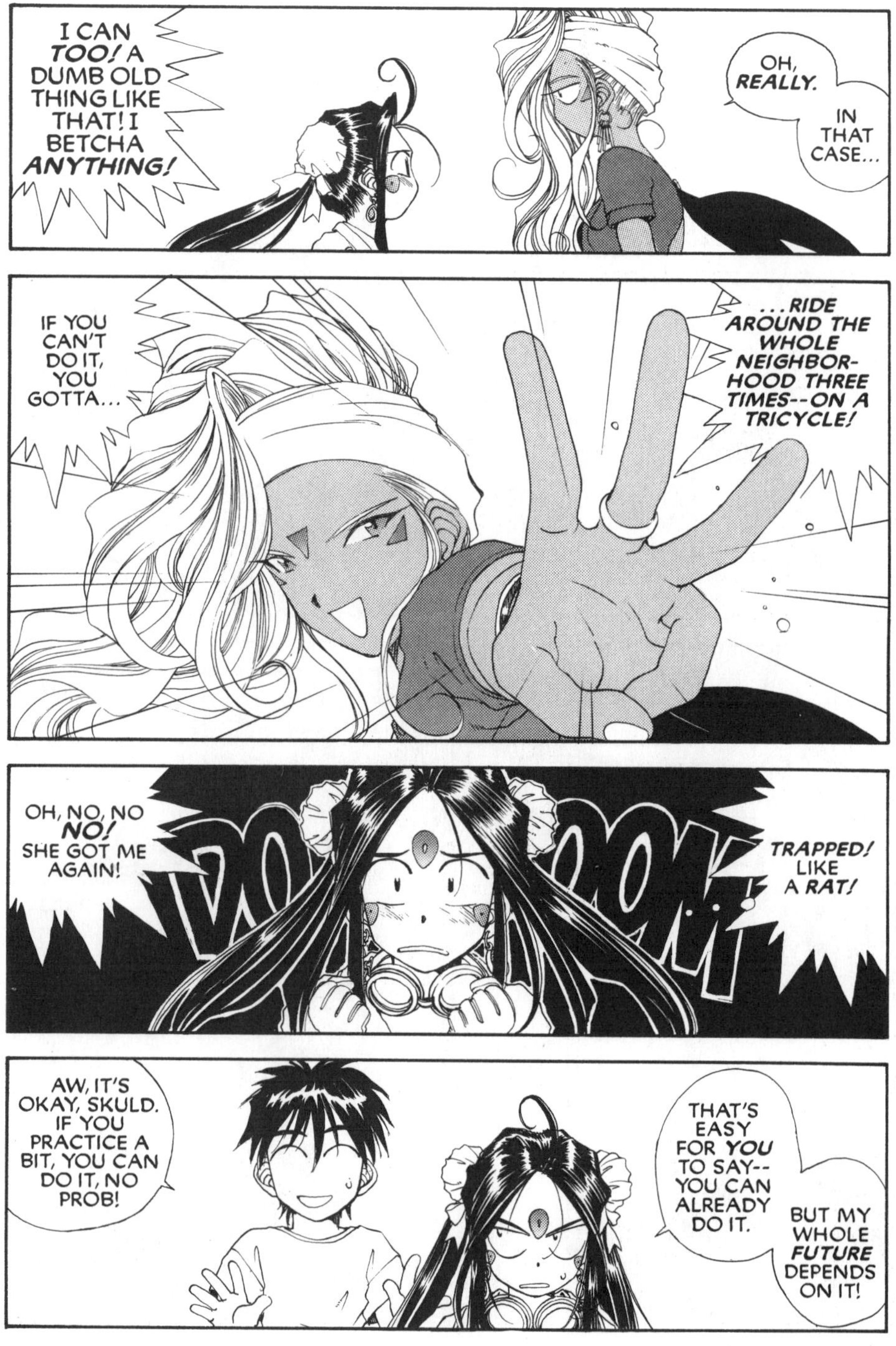
I CAN *TOO!* A DUMB OLD THING LIKE THAT! I BETCHA *ANYTHING!*
OH, *REALLY.*
IN THAT CASE...
IF YOU CAN'T DO IT, YOU GOTTA...
...RIDE AROUND THE WHOLE NEIGHBOR-HOOD THREE TIMES--ON A TRICYCLE!
OH, NO, NO *NO!* SHE GOT ME AGAIN!
TRAPPED! LIKE A *RAT!*
AW, IT'S OKAY, SKULD. IF YOU PRACTICE A BIT, YOU CAN DO IT, NO PROB!
THAT'S EASY FOR *YOU* TO SAY-- YOU CAN ALREADY DO IT.
BUT MY WHOLE *FUTURE* DEPENDS ON IT!

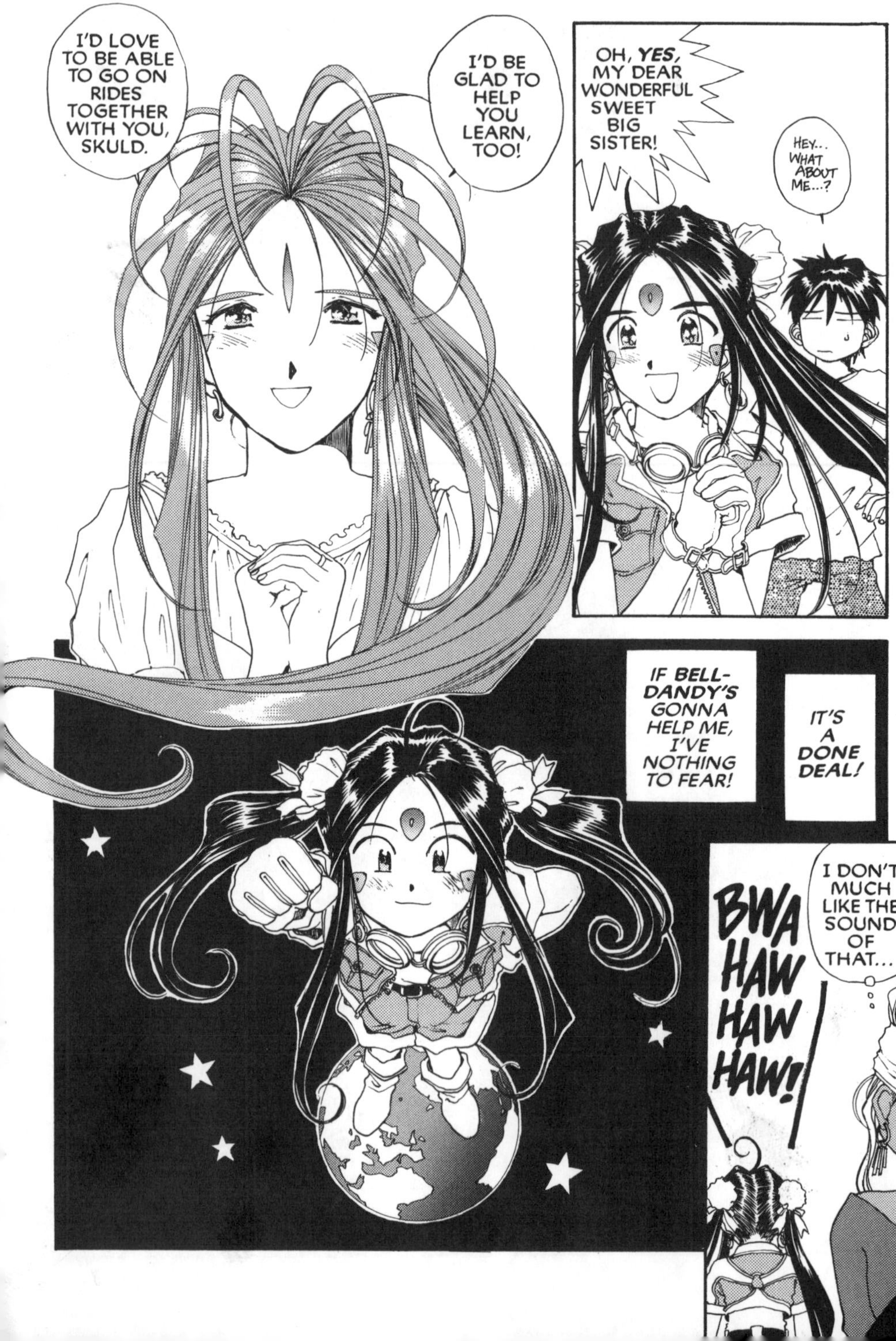
I'D LOVE TO BE ABLE TO GO ON RIDES TOGETHER WITH YOU, SKULD.
I'D BE GLAD TO HELP YOU LEARN, TOO!
OH, *YES*, MY DEAR WONDERFUL SWEET BIG SISTER!
HEY... WHAT ABOUT ME...?
IF BELL-DANDY'S GONNA HELP ME, I'VE NOTHING TO FEAR!
IT'S A DONE DEAL!
BWA HAW HAW HAW!
I DON'T MUCH LIKE THE SOUND OF THAT...

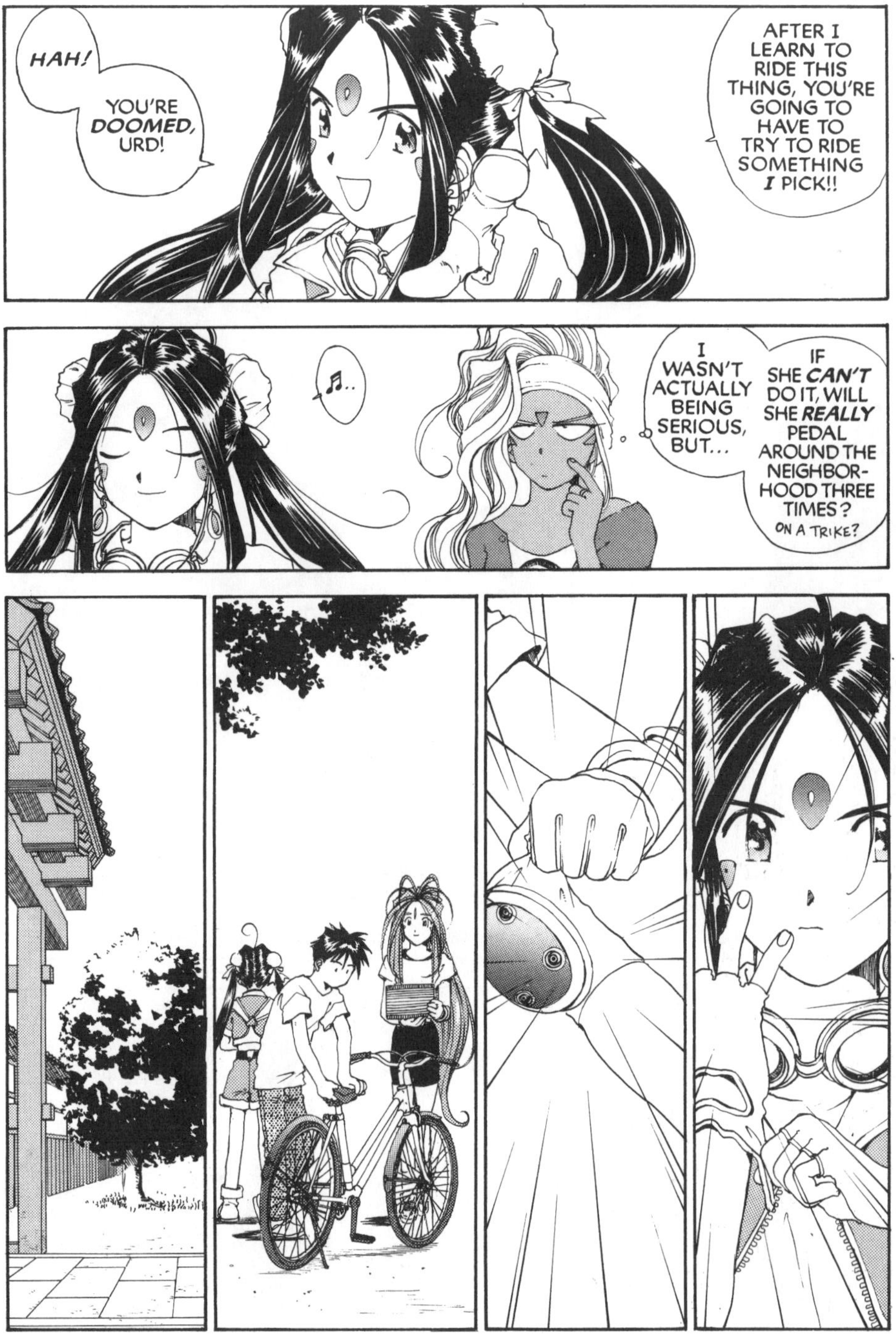
HAH!
YOU'RE DOOMED, URD!
AFTER I LEARN TO RIDE THIS THING, YOU'RE GOING TO HAVE TO TRY TO RIDE SOMETHING I PICK!!
♫..
I WASN'T ACTUALLY BEING SERIOUS, BUT...
IF SHE CAN'T DO IT, WILL SHE REALLY PEDAL AROUND THE NEIGHBOR-HOOD THREE TIMES?
ON A TRIKE?

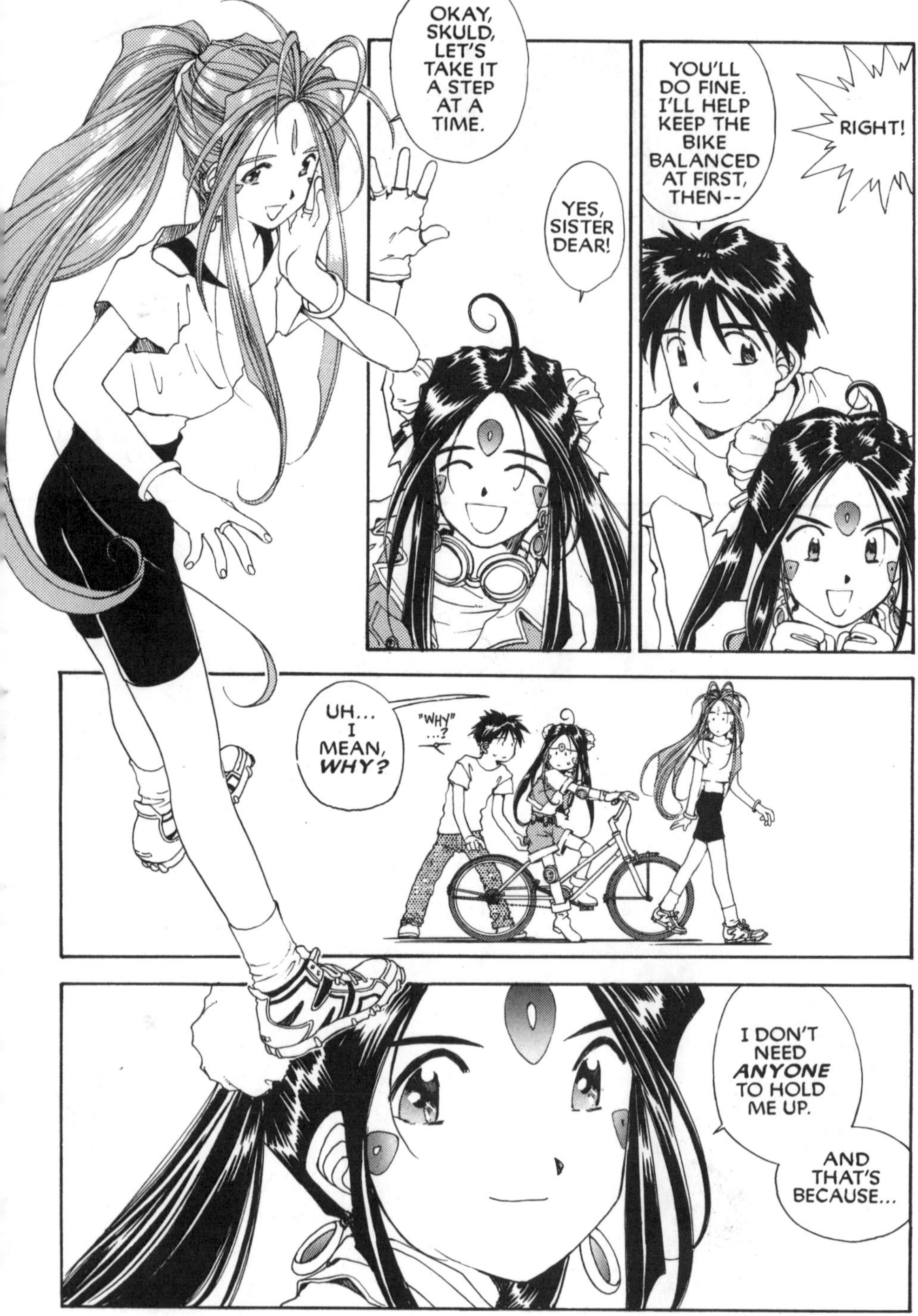
OKAY, SKULD, LET'S TAKE IT A STEP AT A TIME.
YES, SISTER DEAR!
YOU'LL DO FINE. I'LL HELP KEEP THE BIKE BALANCED AT FIRST, THEN--
RIGHT!
UH... I MEAN, *WHY?*
"WHY" ...?
I DON'T NEED *ANYONE* TO HOLD ME UP.
AND THAT'S BECAUSE...

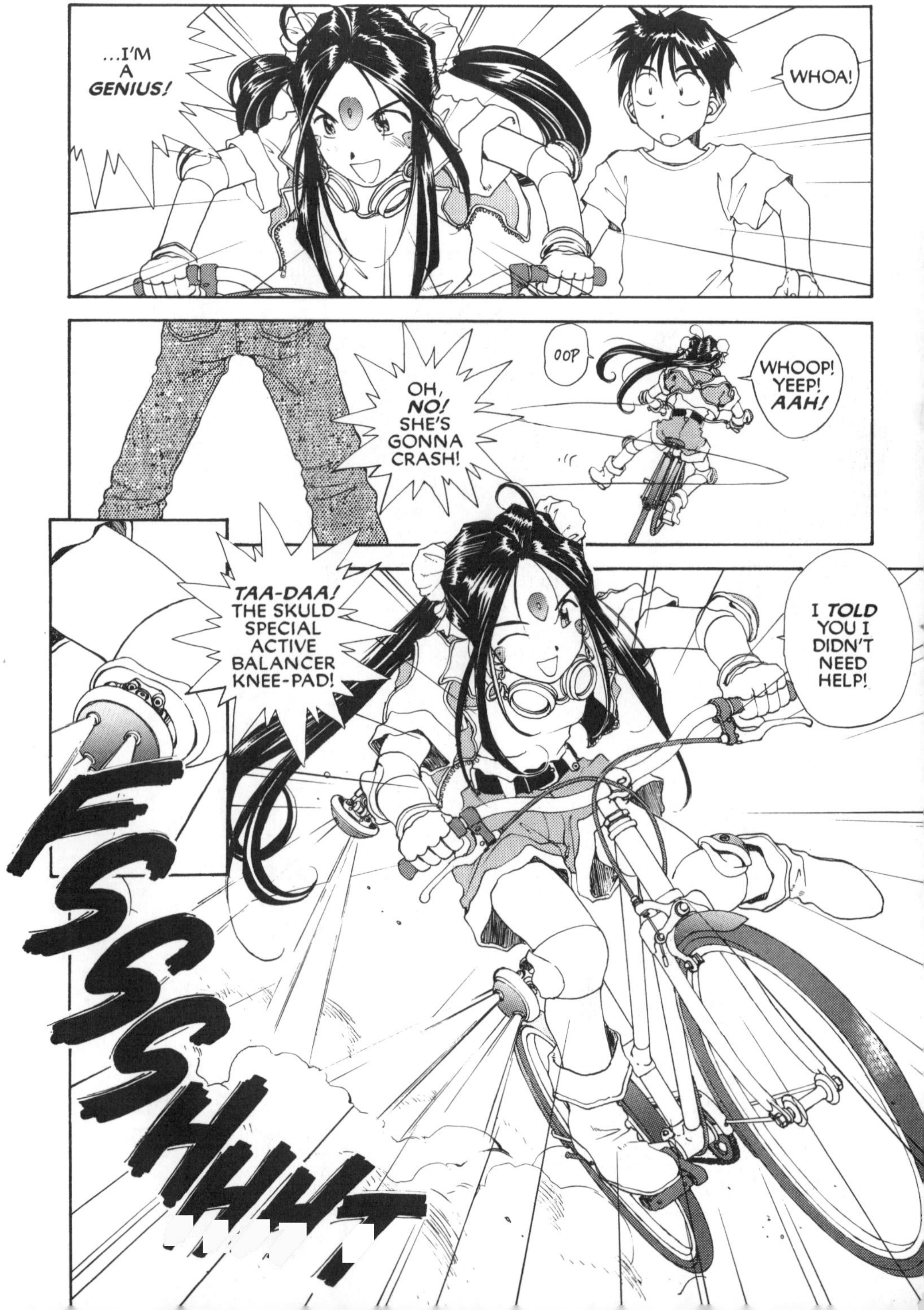
...I'M A GENIUS!
WHOA!
OH, NO! SHE'S GONNA CRASH!
OOP
WHOOP! YEEP! AAH!
TAA-DAA! THE SKULD SPECIAL ACTIVE BALANCER KNEE-PAD!
I TOLD YOU I DIDN'T NEED HELP!
FSSSHHT

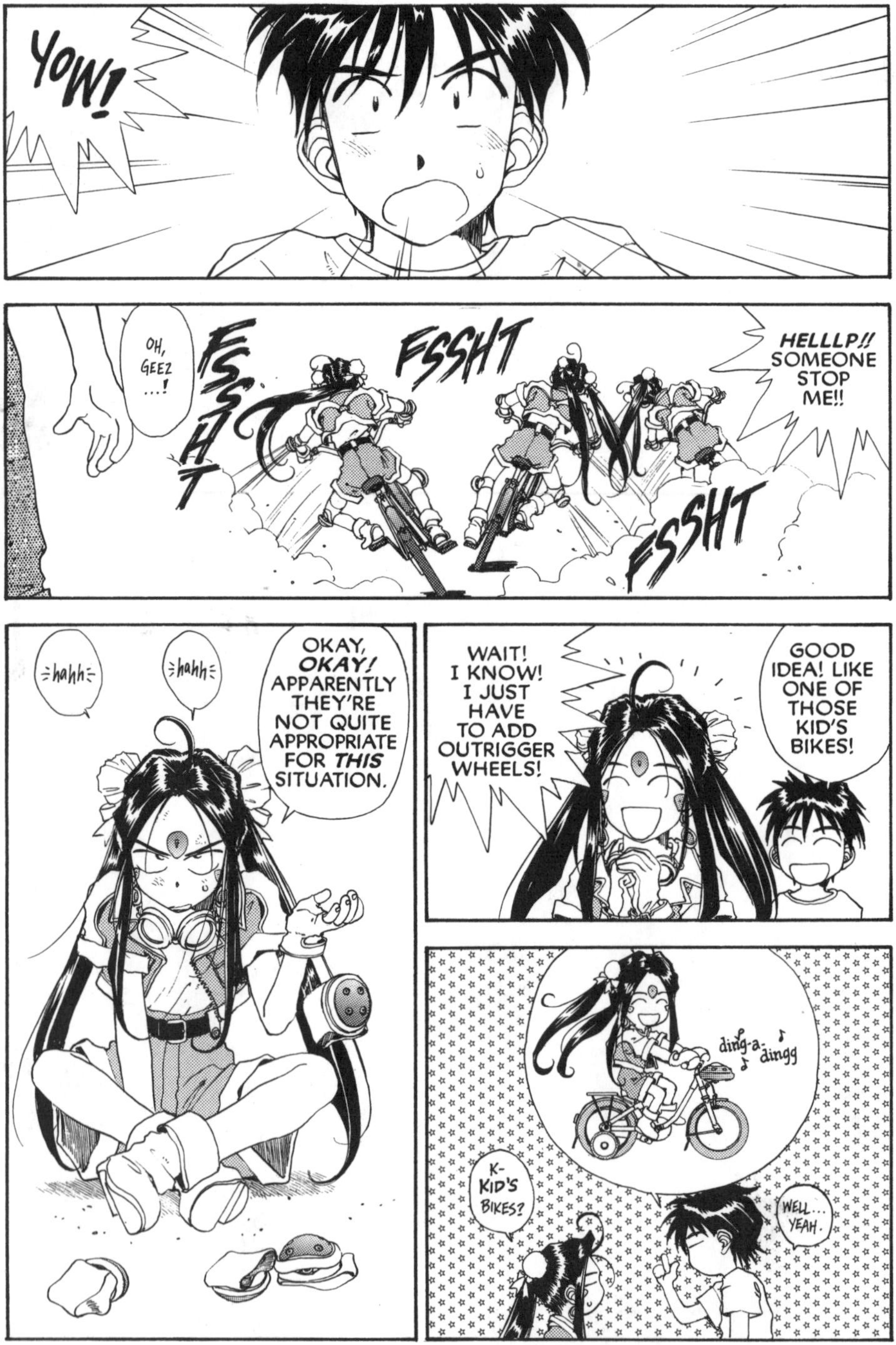
YOW!
OH, GEEZ ...!
FSSHT
FSSHT
HELLLP!! SOMEONE STOP ME!!
FSSHT
≡hahh≡
≡hahh≡
OKAY, OKAY! APPARENTLY THEY'RE NOT QUITE APPROPRIATE FOR THIS SITUATION.
WAIT! I KNOW! I JUST HAVE TO ADD OUTRIGGER WHEELS!
GOOD IDEA! LIKE ONE OF THOSE KID'S BIKES!
ding-a-dingg
K-KID'S BIKES?
WELL... YEAH.

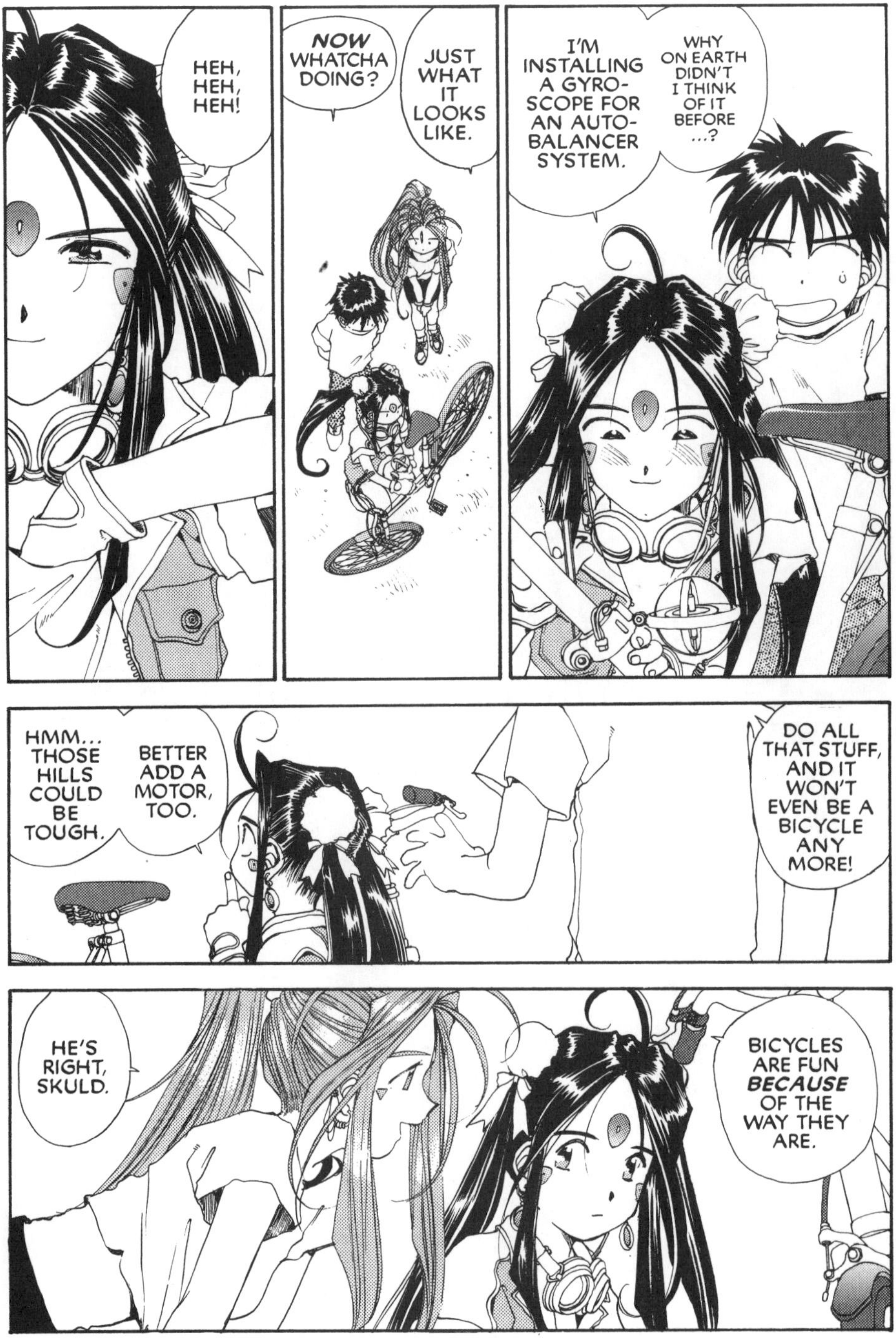
HEH, HEH, HEH!
NOW WHATCHA DOING?
JUST WHAT IT LOOKS LIKE.
I'M INSTALLING A GYRO-SCOPE FOR AN AUTO-BALANCER SYSTEM.
WHY ON EARTH DIDN'T I THINK OF IT BEFORE ...?
HMM... THOSE HILLS COULD BE TOUGH.
BETTER ADD A MOTOR, TOO.
DO ALL THAT STUFF, AND IT WON'T EVEN BE A BICYCLE ANY MORE!
HE'S RIGHT, SKULD.
BICYCLES ARE FUN ***BECAUSE*** OF THE WAY THEY ARE.

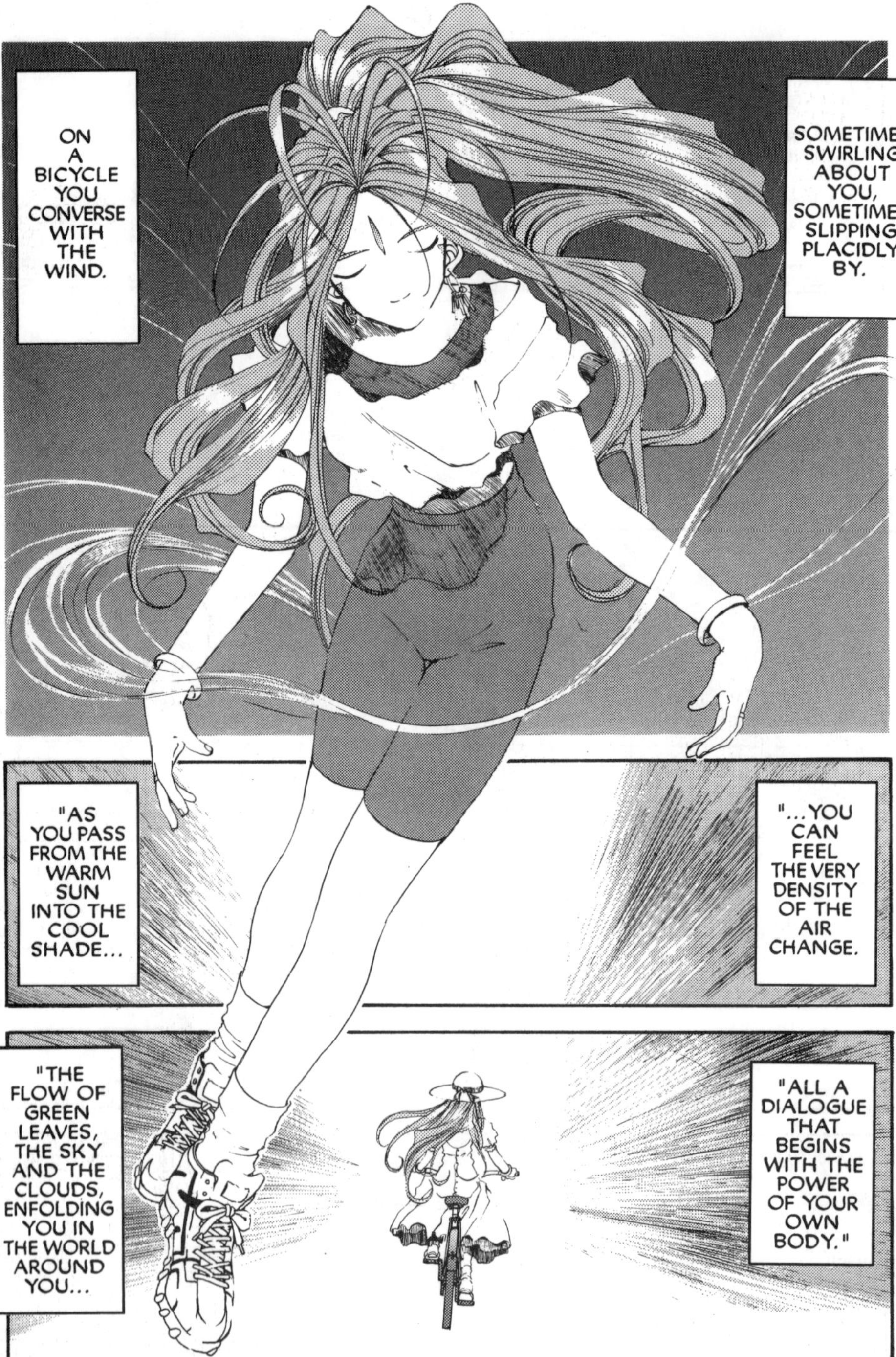

ON A BICYCLE YOU CONVERSE WITH THE WIND.
SOMETIMES SWIRLING ABOUT YOU, SOMETIMES SLIPPING PLACIDLY BY.
"AS YOU PASS FROM THE WARM SUN INTO THE COOL SHADE...
"...YOU CAN FEEL THE VERY DENSITY OF THE AIR CHANGE.
"THE FLOW OF GREEN LEAVES, THE SKY AND THE CLOUDS, ENFOLDING YOU IN THE WORLD AROUND YOU...
"ALL A DIALOGUE THAT BEGINS WITH THE POWER OF YOUR OWN BODY."

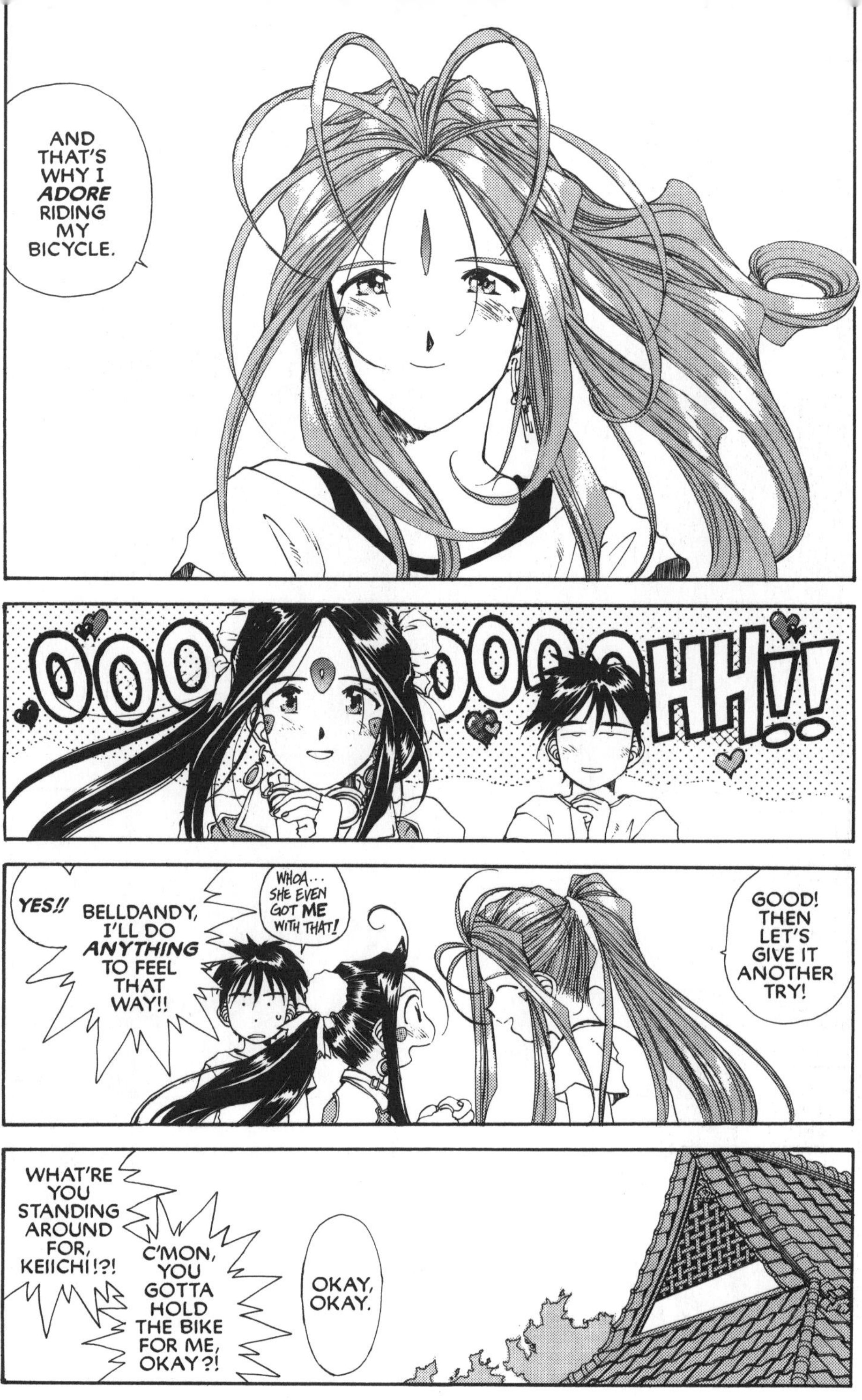
AND THAT'S WHY I ADORE RIDING MY BICYCLE.
OOOOOOOOHH!!
YES!!
BELLDANDY, I'LL DO ANYTHING TO FEEL THAT WAY!!
WHOA... SHE EVEN GOT ME WITH THAT!
GOOD! THEN LET'S GIVE IT ANOTHER TRY!
WHAT'RE YOU STANDING AROUND FOR, KEIICHI!?!
C'MON, YOU GOTTA HOLD THE BIKE FOR ME, OKAY?!
OKAY, OKAY.

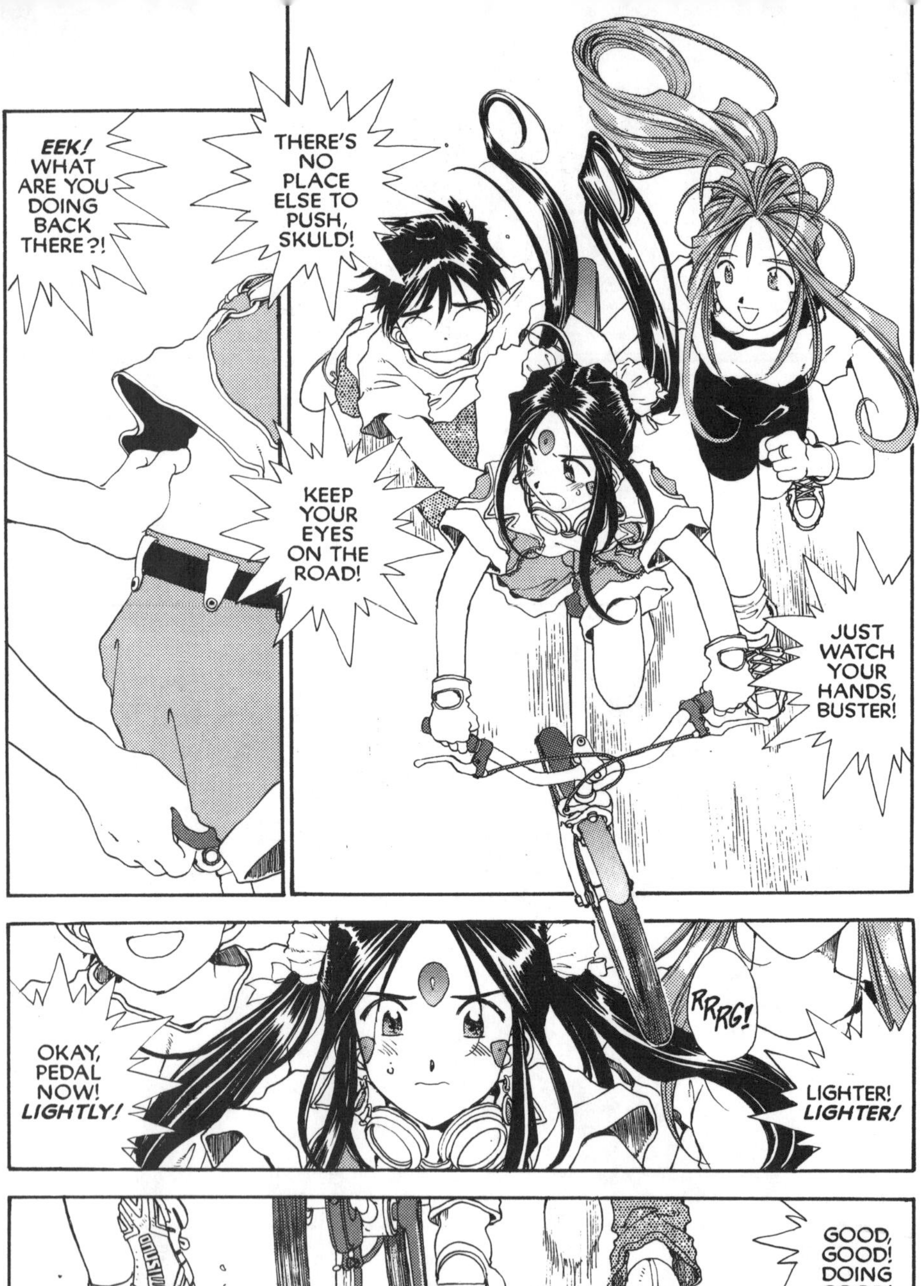
EEK! WHAT ARE YOU DOING BACK THERE?!
THERE'S NO PLACE ELSE TO PUSH, SKULD!
KEEP YOUR EYES ON THE ROAD!
JUST WATCH YOUR HANDS, BUSTER!
OKAY, PEDAL NOW! LIGHTLY!
RRRG!
LIGHTER! LIGHTER!
GOOD, GOOD! DOING GOOD!

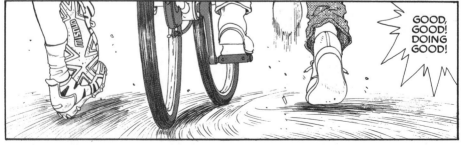

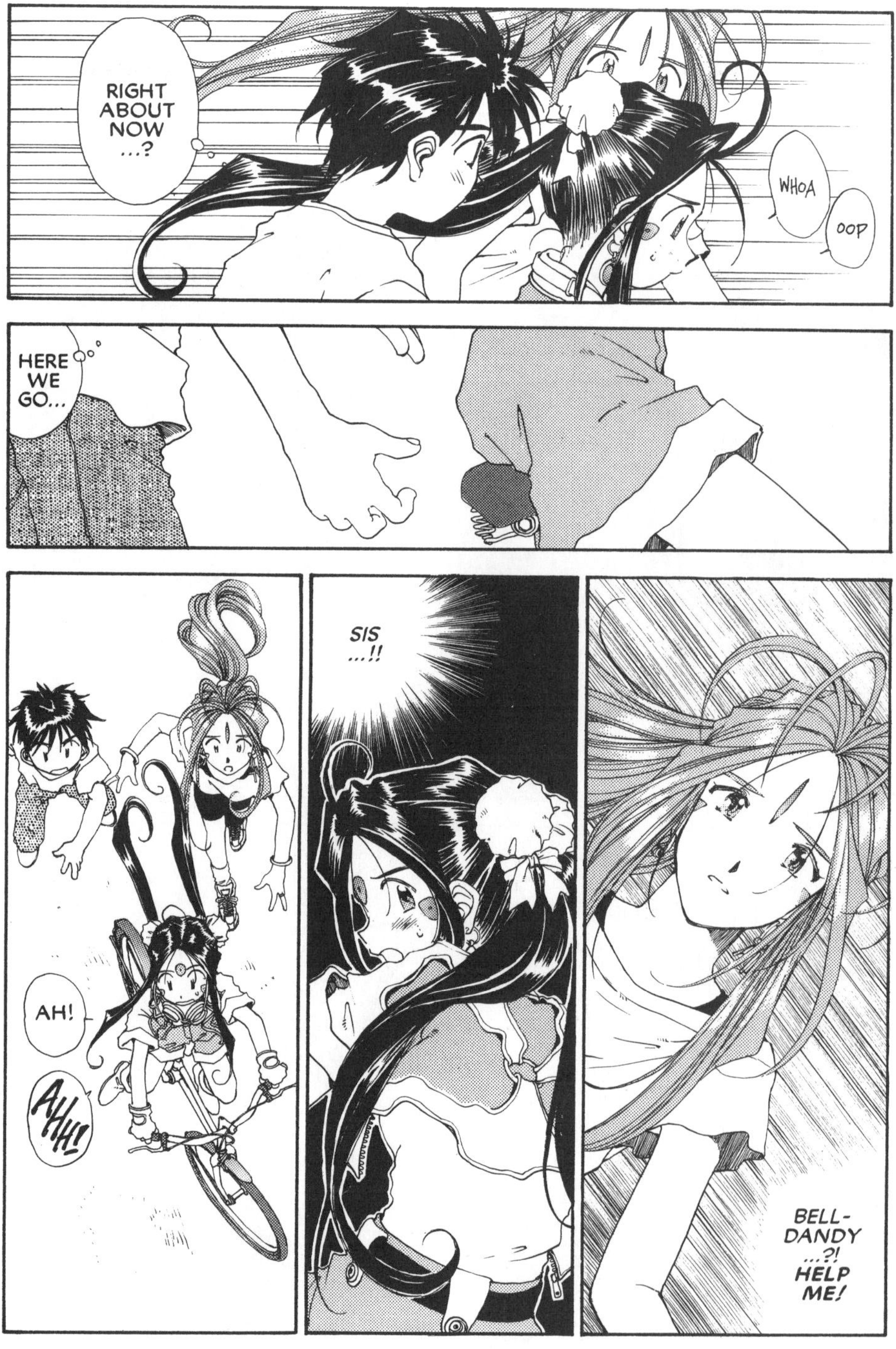
RIGHT ABOUT NOW ...?
WHOA
OOP
HERE WE GO...
AH!
AHH!
SIS ...!!
BELL-DANDY ...?! HELP ME!

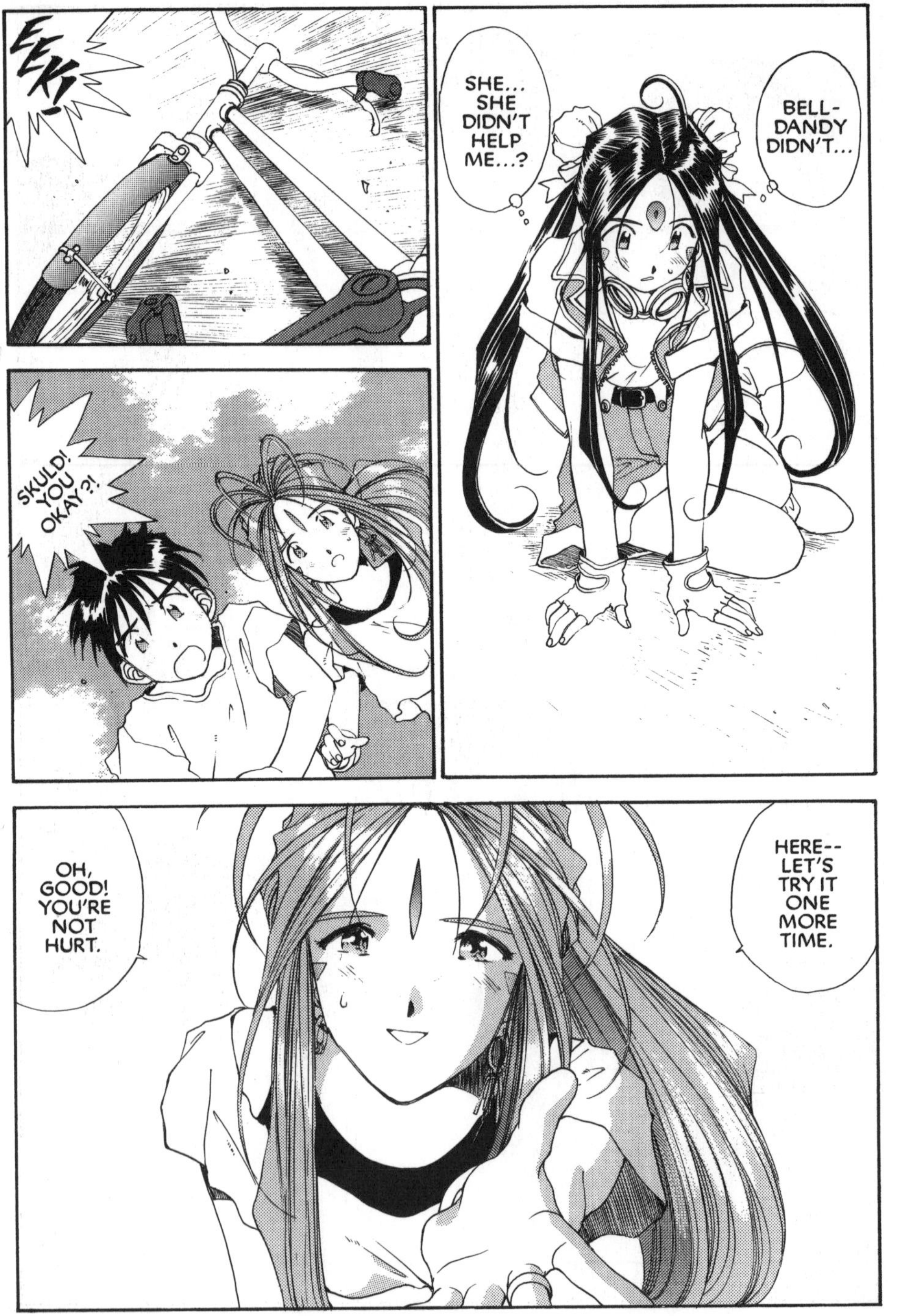
EEEK!
SKULD! YOU OKAY?!
SHE... SHE DIDN'T HELP ME...?
BELL-DANDY DIDN'T...
OH, GOOD! YOU'RE NOT HURT.
HERE--LET'S TRY IT ONE MORE TIME.

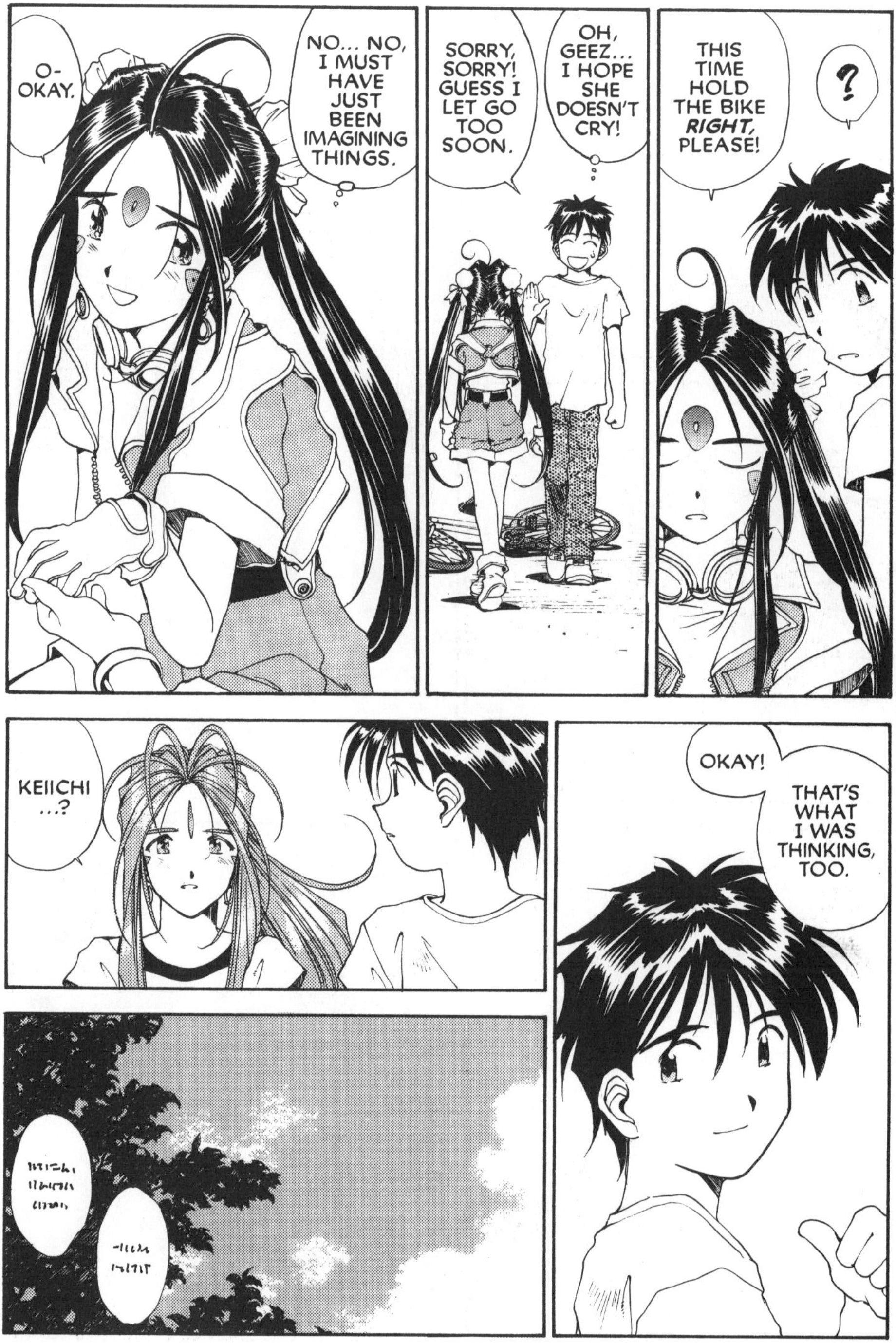
O-OKAY.
NO... NO, I MUST HAVE JUST BEEN IMAGINING THINGS.
SORRY, SORRY! GUESS I LET GO TOO SOON.
OH, GEEZ... I HOPE SHE DOESN'T CRY!
THIS TIME HOLD THE BIKE RIGHT, PLEASE!
?
KEIICHI ...?
OKAY!
THAT'S WHAT I WAS THINKING, TOO.

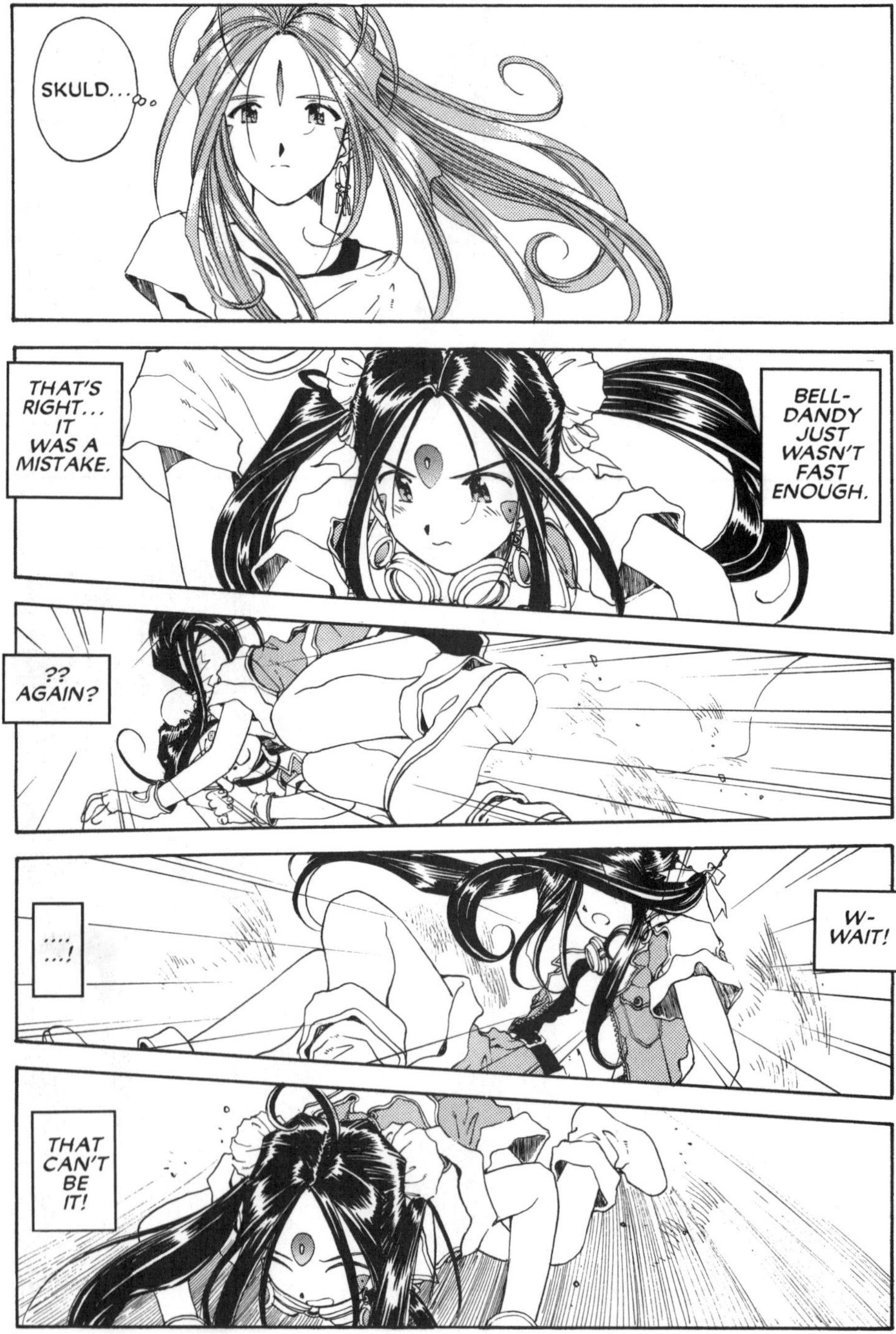
SKULD...
THAT'S RIGHT... IT WAS A MISTAKE.
BELL-DANDY JUST WASN'T FAST ENOUGH.
?? AGAIN?
....
...!
W-WAIT!
THAT CAN'T BE IT!

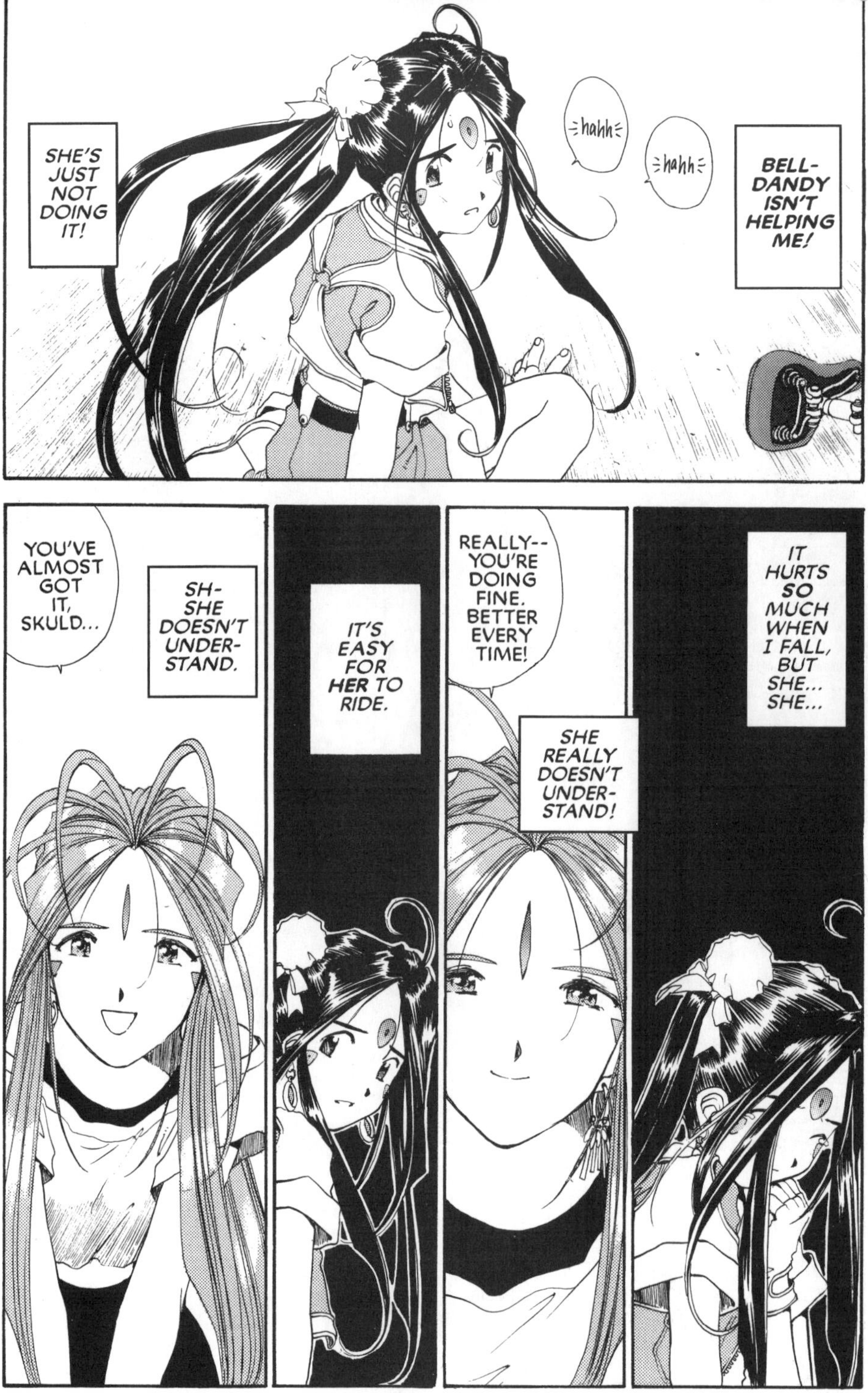
SHE'S JUST NOT DOING IT!
hahh
hahh
BELL-DANDY ISN'T HELPING ME!
YOU'VE ALMOST GOT IT, SKULD...
SH-SHE DOESN'T UNDER-STAND.
IT'S EASY FOR HER TO RIDE.
REALLY--YOU'RE DOING FINE. BETTER EVERY TIME!
SHE REALLY DOESN'T UNDER-STAND!
IT HURTS SO MUCH WHEN I FALL, BUT SHE... SHE...

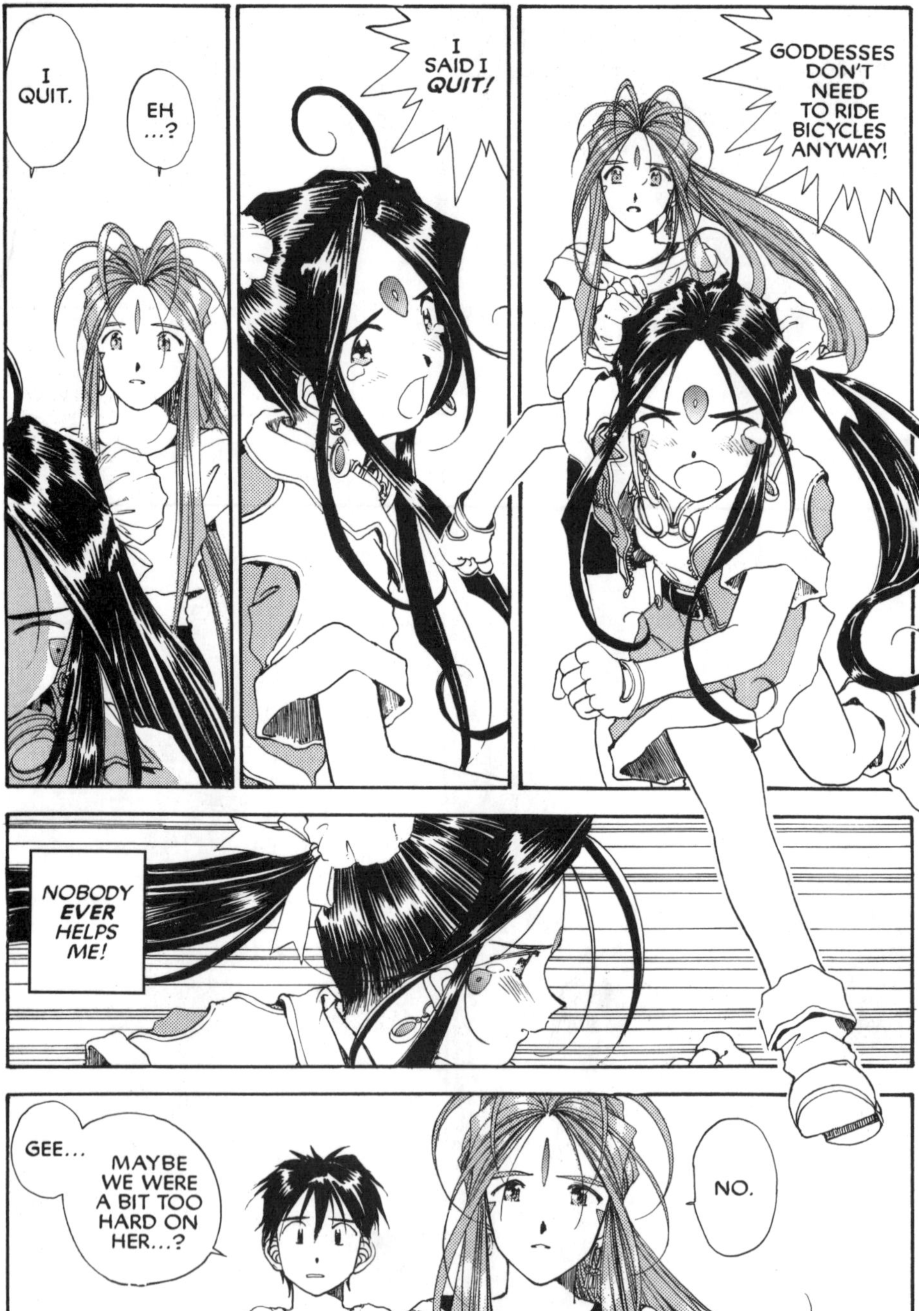
I QUIT.
EH ...?
I SAID I QUIT!
GODDESSES DON'T NEED TO RIDE BICYCLES ANYWAY!
NOBODY EVER HELPS ME!
GEE... MAYBE WE WERE A BIT TOO HARD ON HER...?
NO.

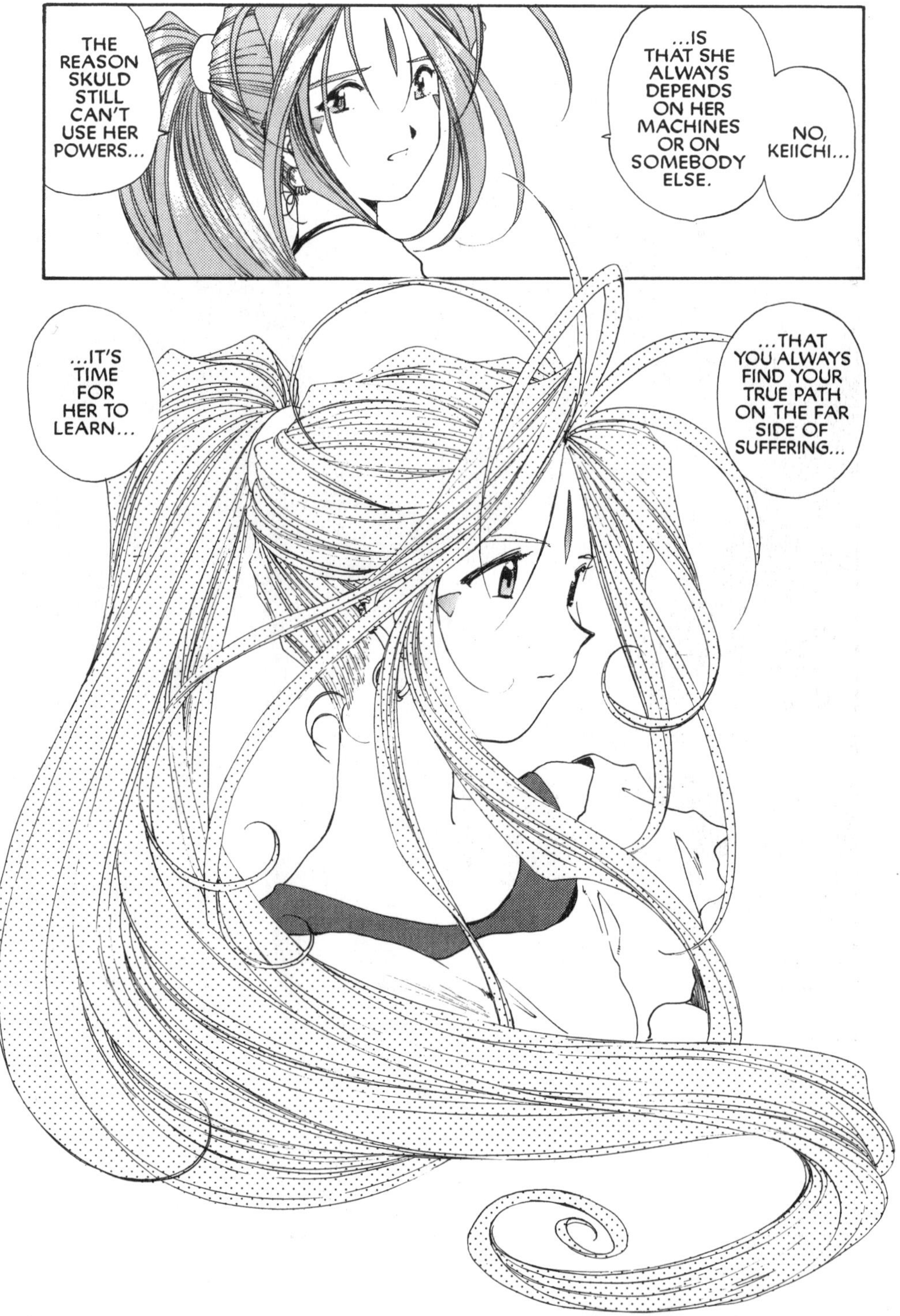
THE REASON SKULD STILL CAN'T USE HER POWERS...
...IS THAT SHE ALWAYS DEPENDS ON HER MACHINES OR ON SOMEBODY ELSE.
NO, KEIICHI...
...IT'S TIME FOR HER TO LEARN...
...THAT YOU ALWAYS FIND YOUR TRUE PATH ON THE FAR SIDE OF SUFFERING...

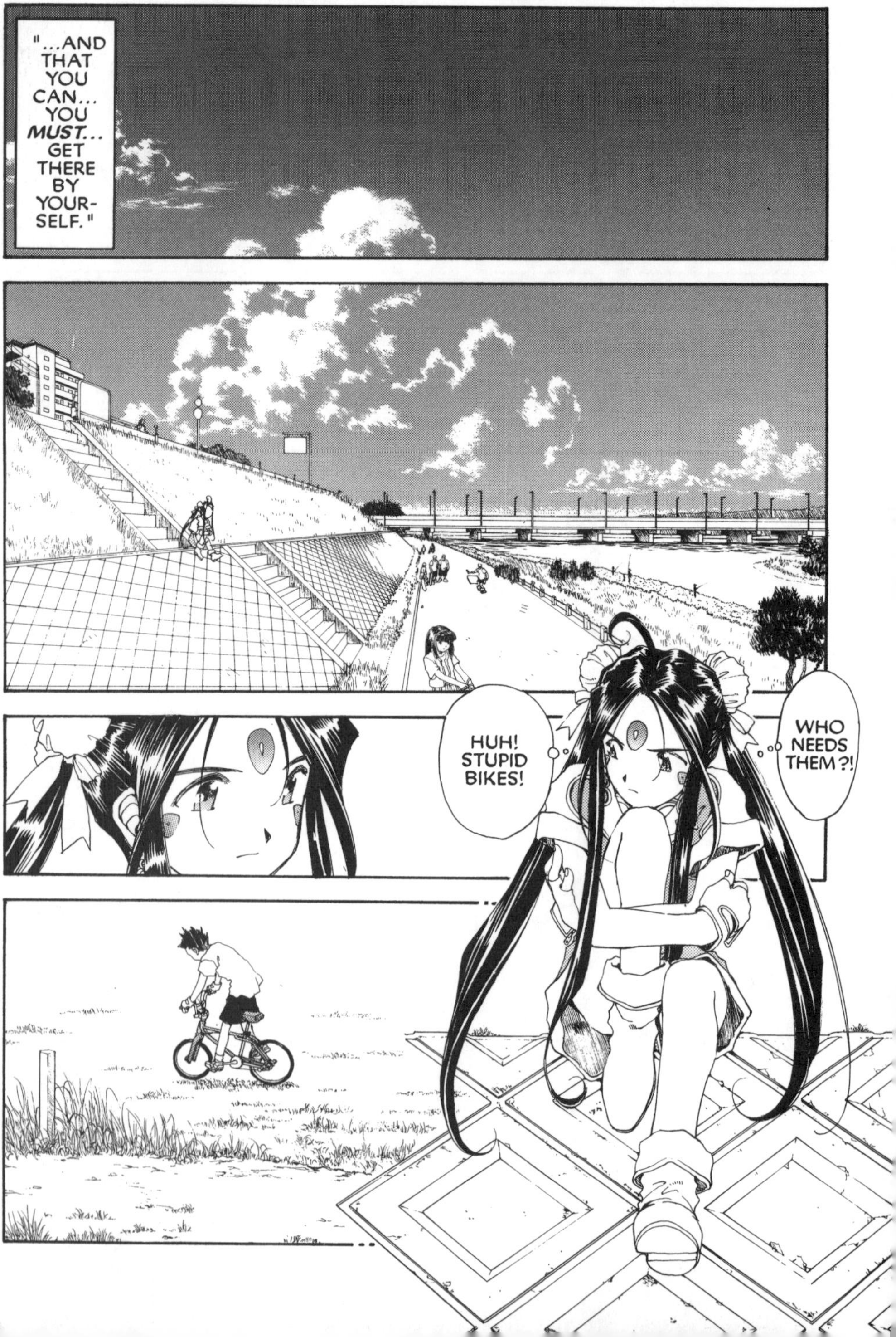
"...AND THAT YOU CAN... YOU MUST... GET THERE BY YOURSELF."
HUH! STUPID BIKES!
WHO NEEDS THEM?!

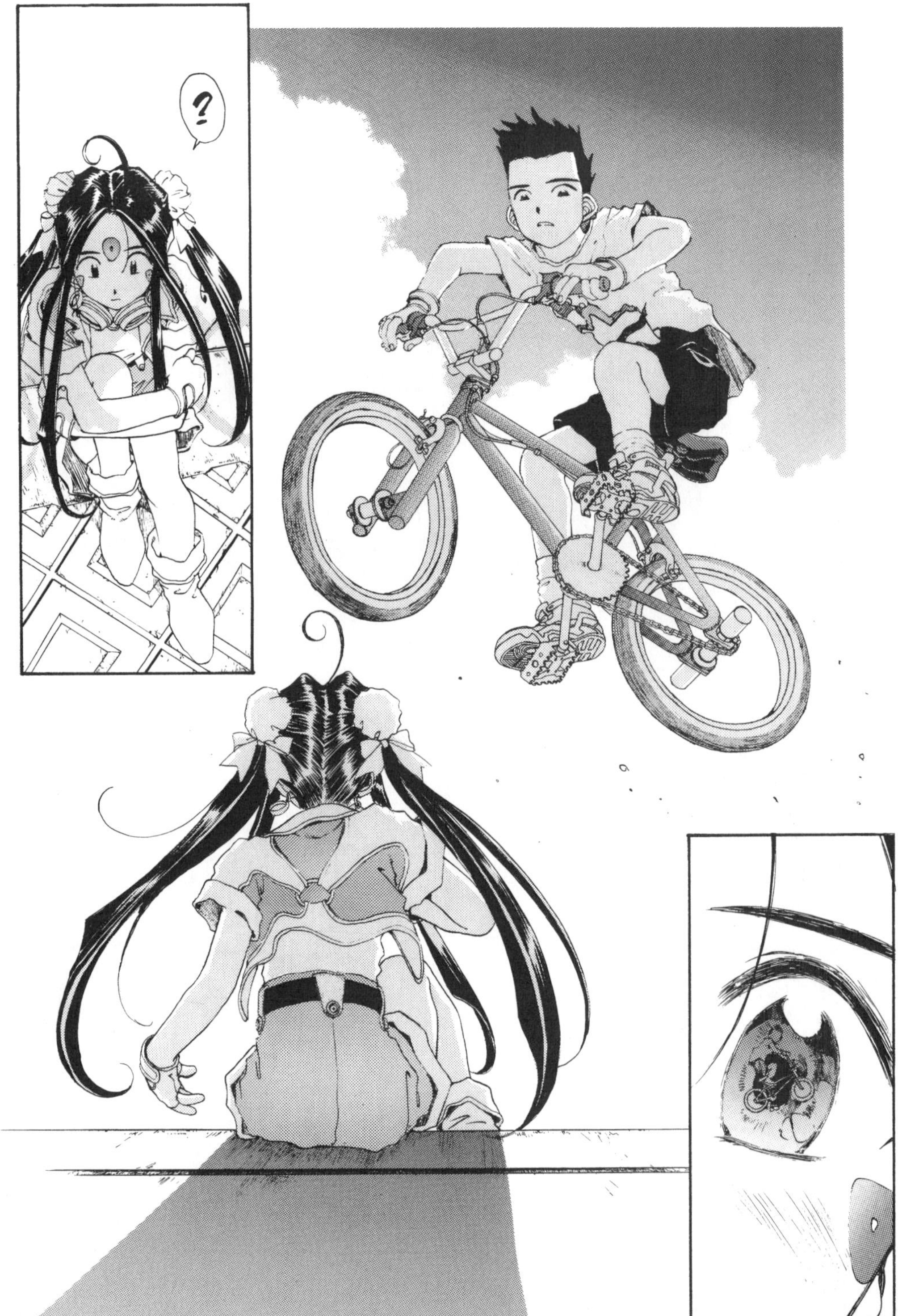
?

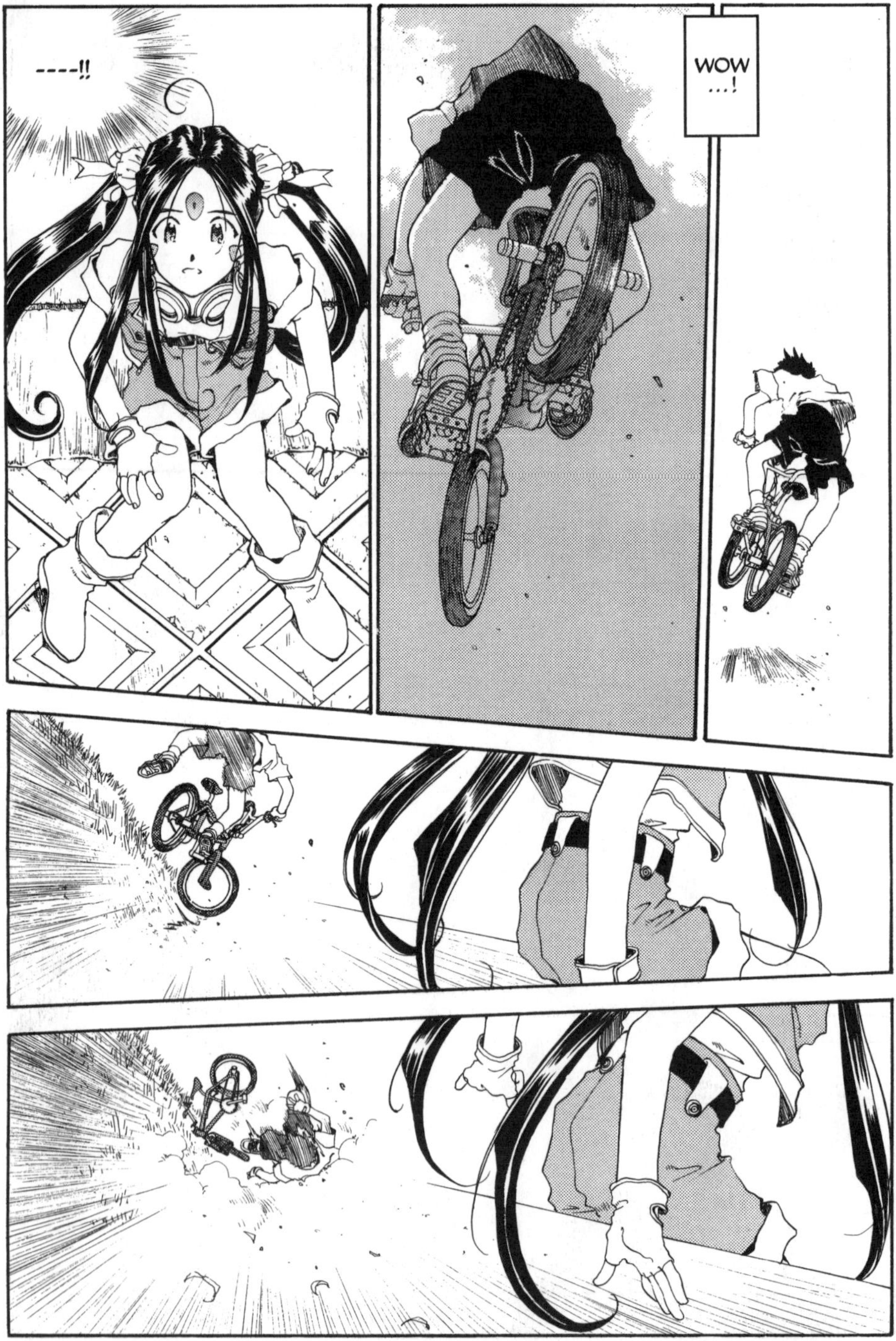
----!!
WOW
...!

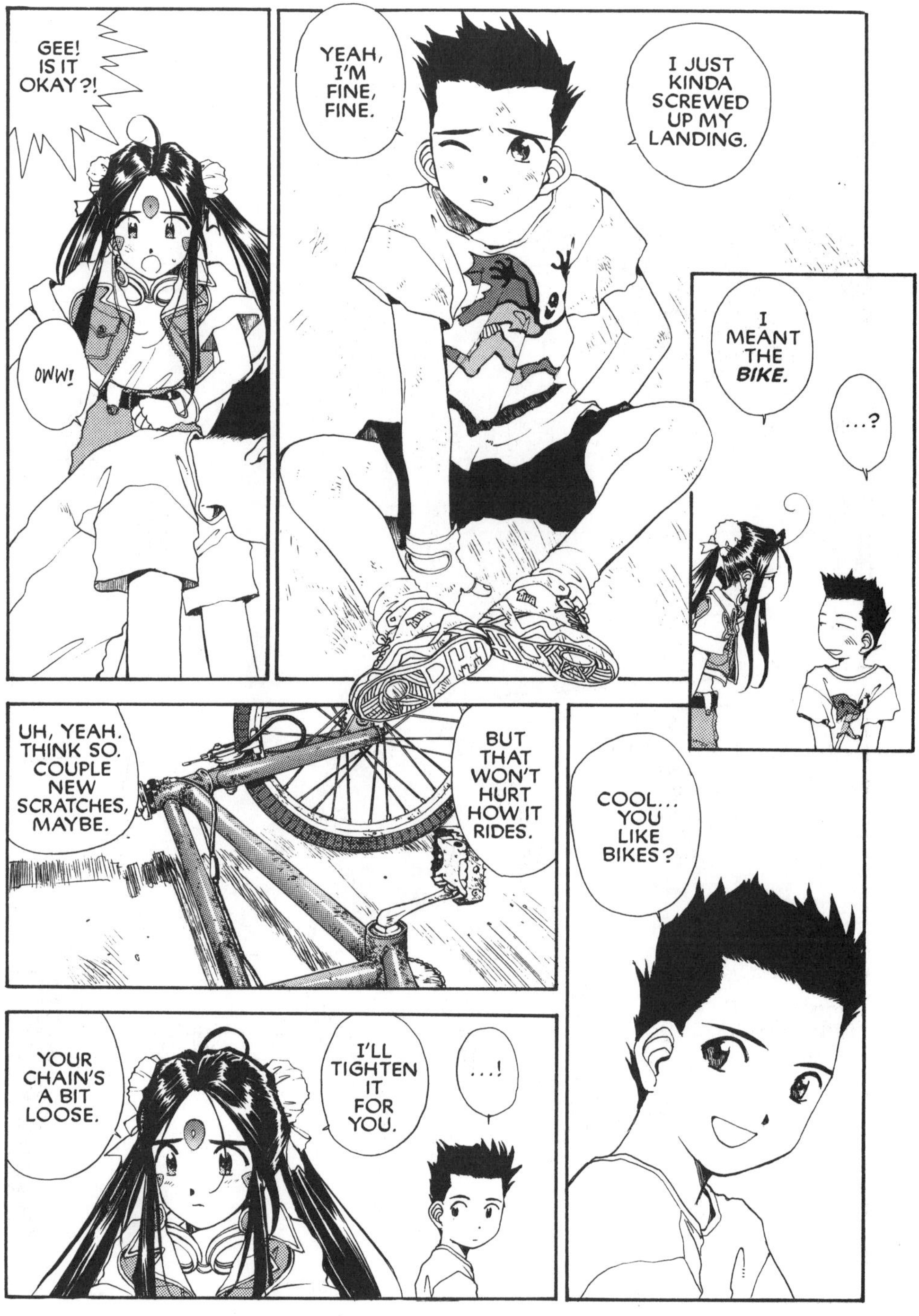
GEE! IS IT OKAY?!
OWW!
YEAH, I'M FINE, FINE.
I JUST KINDA SCREWED UP MY LANDING.
I MEANT THE ***BIKE.***
...?
UH, YEAH. THINK SO. COUPLE NEW SCRATCHES, MAYBE.
BUT THAT WON'T HURT HOW IT RIDES.
YOUR CHAIN'S A BIT LOOSE.
I'LL TIGHTEN IT FOR YOU.
...!
COOL... YOU LIKE BIKES?

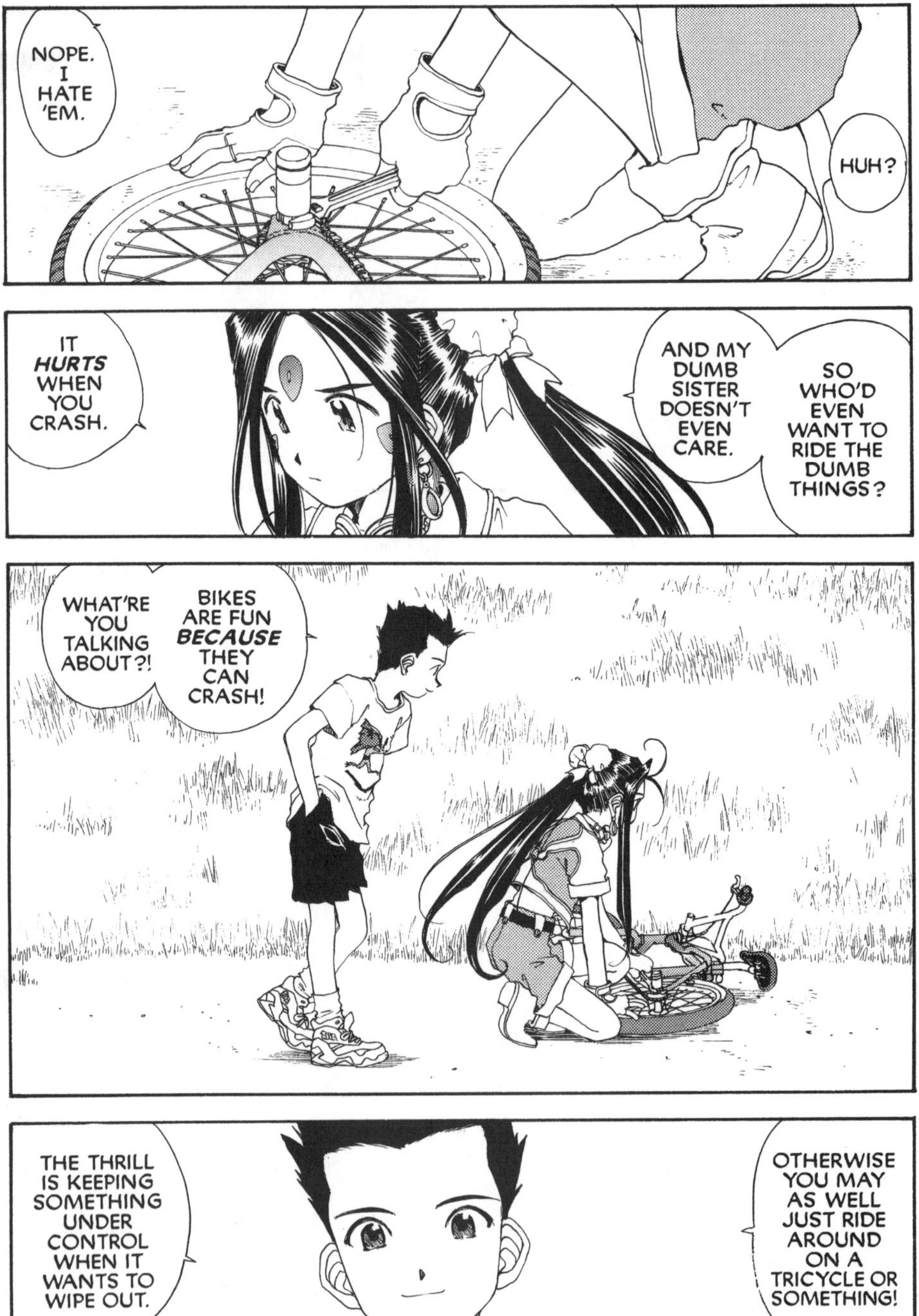
NOPE. I HATE 'EM.
HUH?
IT *HURTS* WHEN YOU CRASH.
AND MY DUMB SISTER DOESN'T EVEN CARE.
SO WHO'D EVEN WANT TO RIDE THE DUMB THINGS?
WHAT'RE YOU TALKING ABOUT?!
BIKES ARE FUN *BECAUSE* THEY CAN CRASH!
THE THRILL IS KEEPING SOMETHING UNDER CONTROL WHEN IT WANTS TO WIPE OUT.
OTHERWISE YOU MAY AS WELL JUST RIDE AROUND ON A TRICYCLE OR SOMETHING!

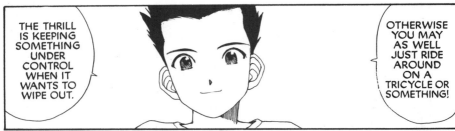

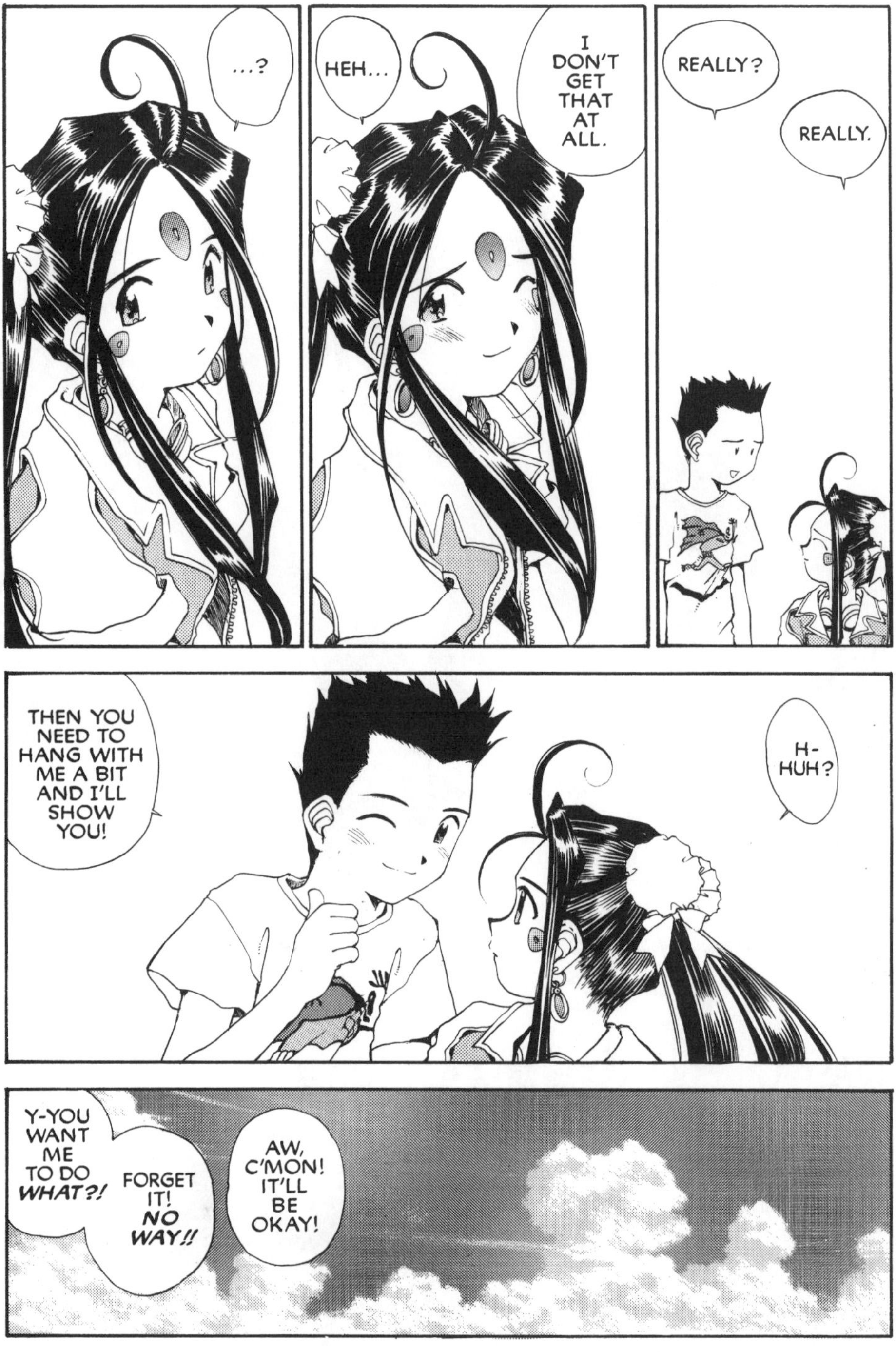
...?
HEH...
I DON'T GET THAT AT ALL.
REALLY?
REALLY.
THEN YOU NEED TO HANG WITH ME A BIT AND I'LL SHOW YOU!
H-HUH?
Y-YOU WANT ME TO DO *WHAT?!*
FORGET IT! *NO WAY!!*
AW, C'MON! IT'LL BE OKAY!

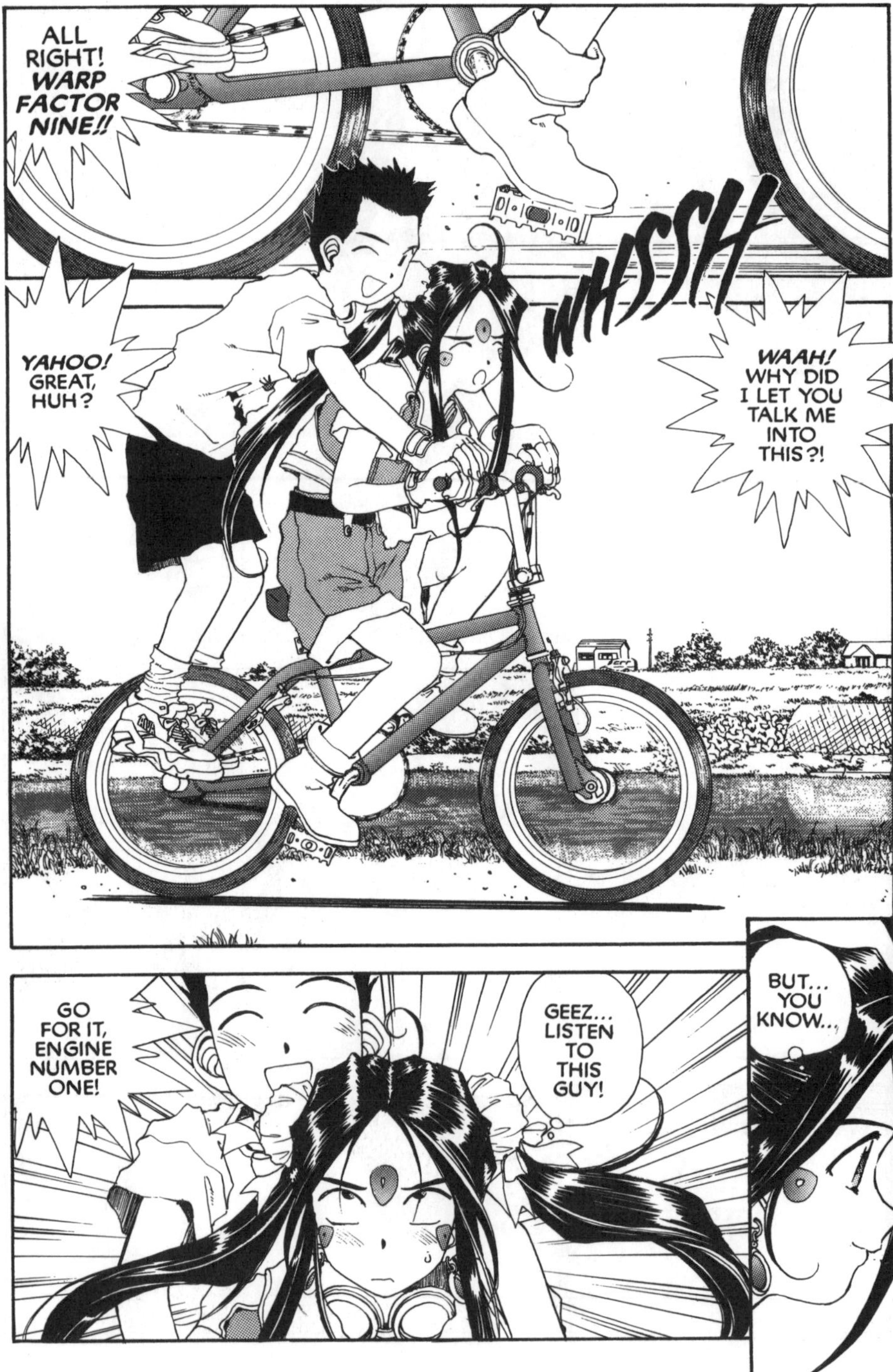
ALL RIGHT! WARP FACTOR NINE!!
YAHOO! GREAT, HUH?
WHSSH
WAAH! WHY DID I LET YOU TALK ME INTO THIS?!
GO FOR IT, ENGINE NUMBER ONE!
GEEZ... LISTEN TO THIS GUY!
BUT... YOU KNOW...

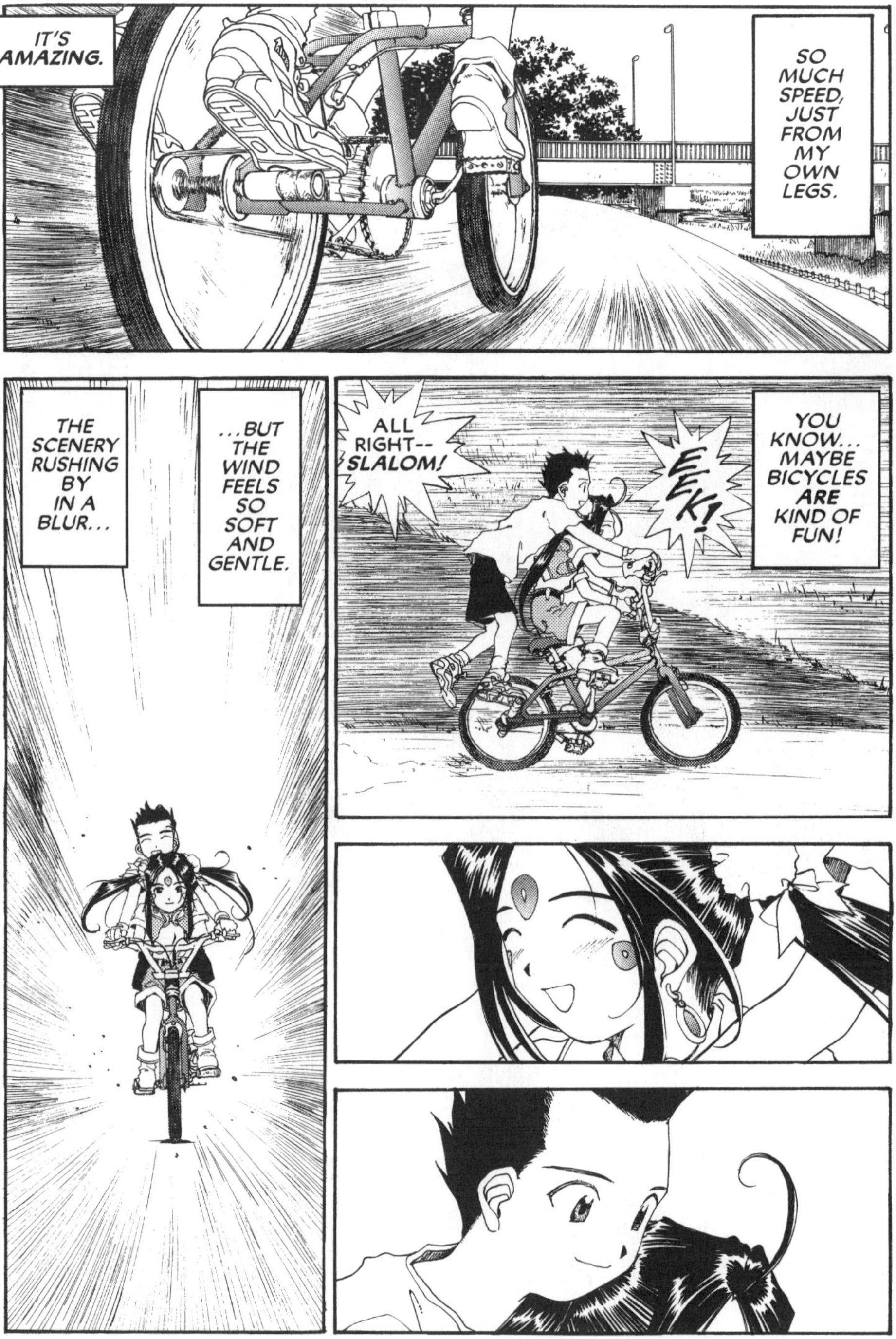
IT'S AMAZING.
SO MUCH SPEED, JUST FROM MY OWN LEGS.
THE SCENERY RUSHING BY IN A BLUR...
...BUT THE WIND FEELS SO SOFT AND GENTLE.
ALL RIGHT-- SLALOM!
EEK!
YOU KNOW... MAYBE BICYCLES ARE KIND OF FUN!

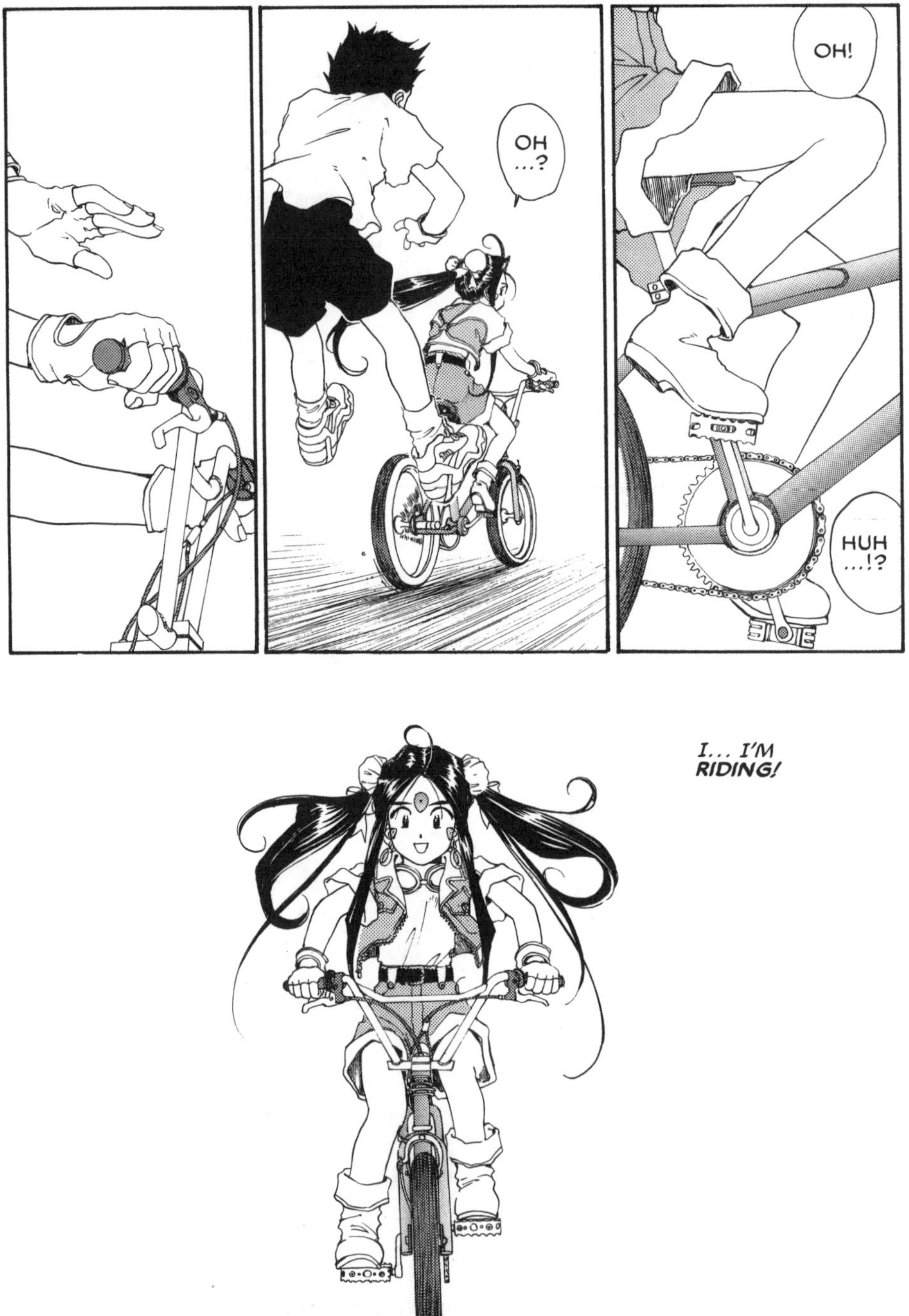
OH
...?
OH!
HUH
...!?
I... I'M
RIDING!

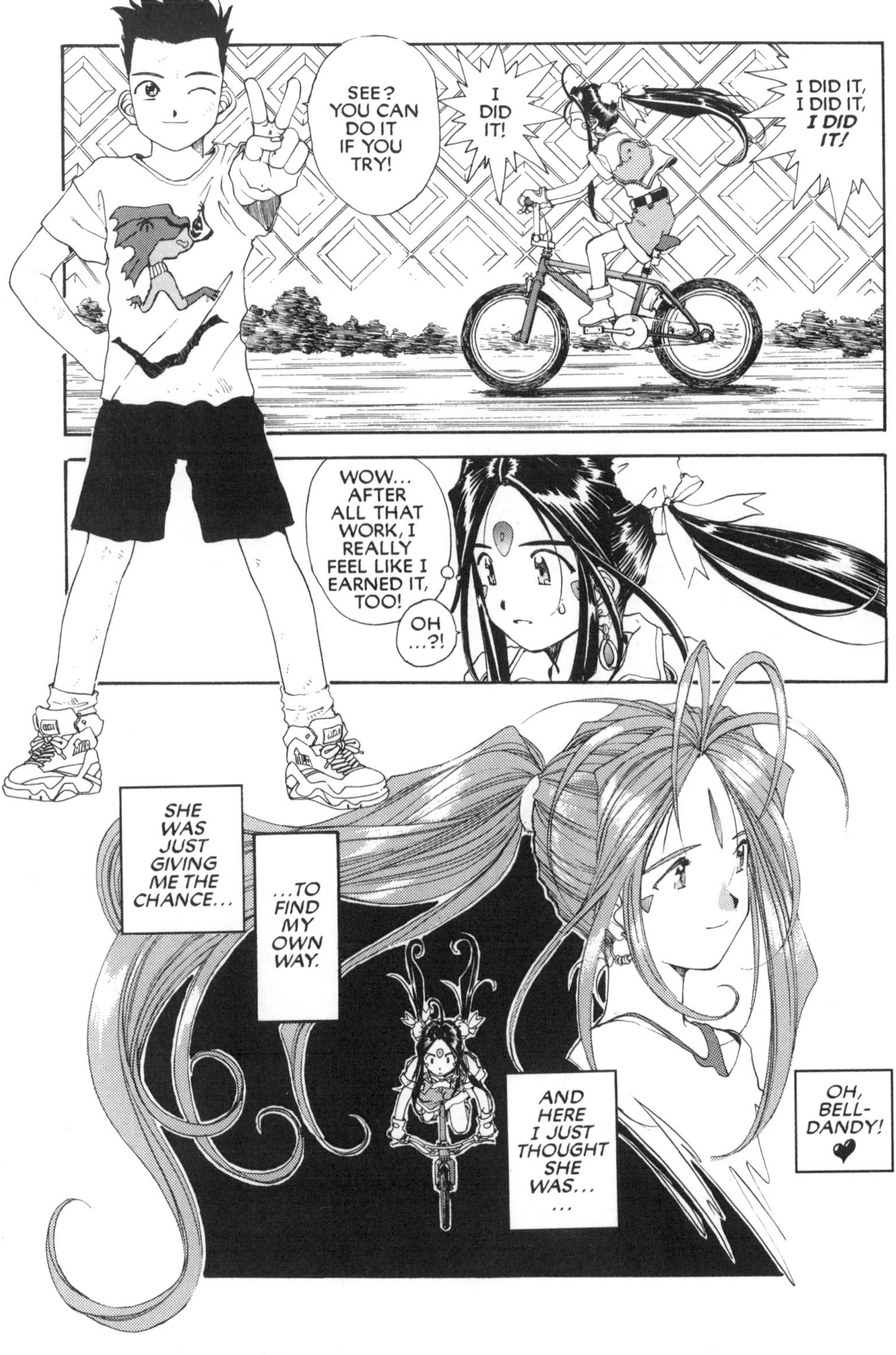
SEE? YOU CAN DO IT IF YOU TRY!
I DID IT!
I DID IT, I DID IT, *I DID IT!*
WOW... AFTER ALL THAT WORK, I REALLY FEEL LIKE I EARNED IT, TOO!
OH ...?!
SHE WAS JUST GIVING ME THE CHANCE...
...TO FIND MY OWN WAY.
AND HERE I JUST THOUGHT SHE WAS... ...
OH, BELL-DANDY! ♥

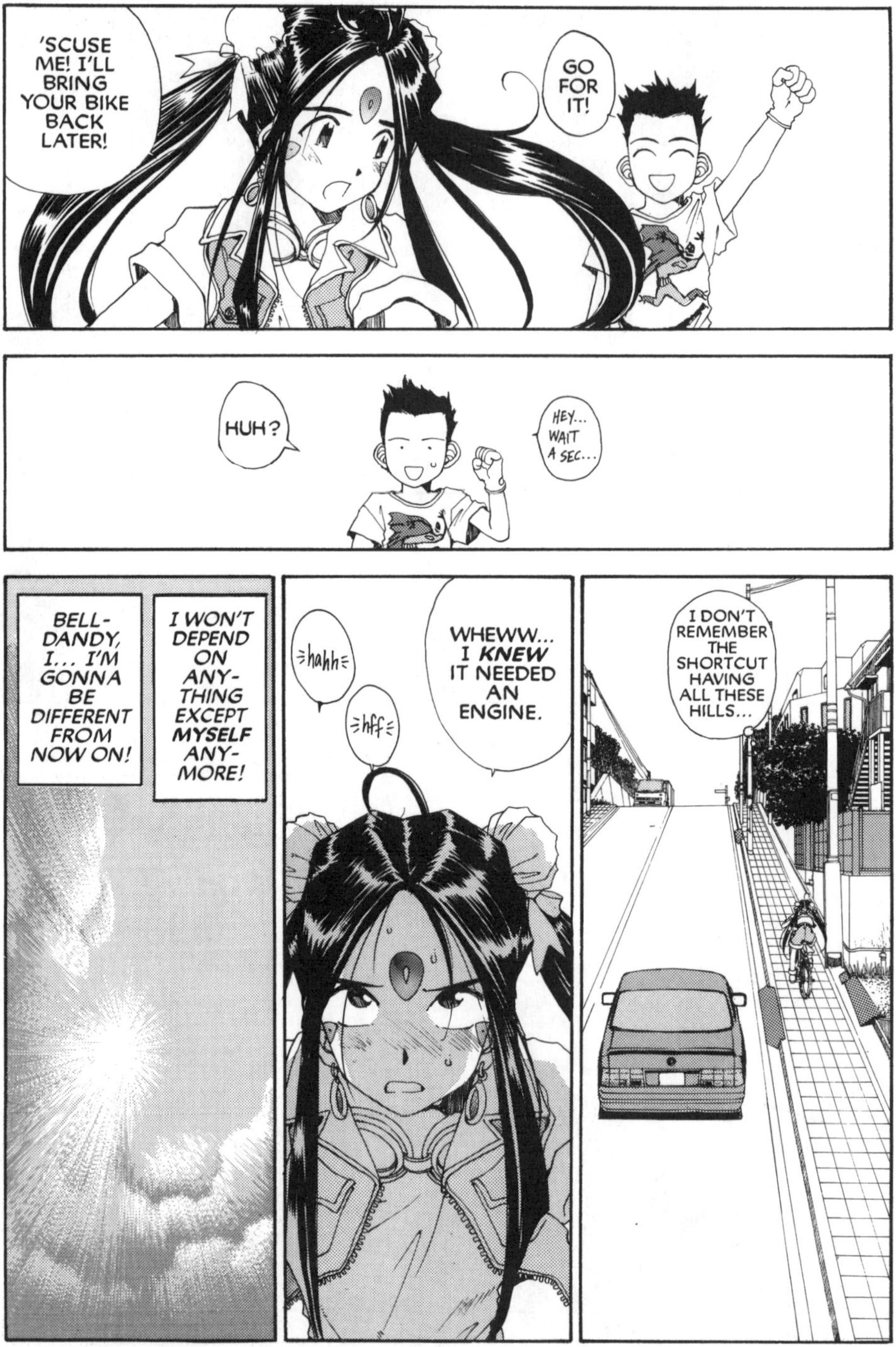
'SCUSE ME! I'LL BRING YOUR BIKE BACK LATER!
GO FOR IT!
HUH?
HEY... WAIT A SEC...
BELL-DANDY, I... I'M GONNA BE DIFFERENT FROM NOW ON!
I WON'T DEPEND ON ANY-THING EXCEPT MYSELF ANY-MORE!
hahh
hff
WHEWW... I KNEW IT NEEDED AN ENGINE.
I DON'T REMEMBER THE SHORTCUT HAVING ALL THESE HILLS...

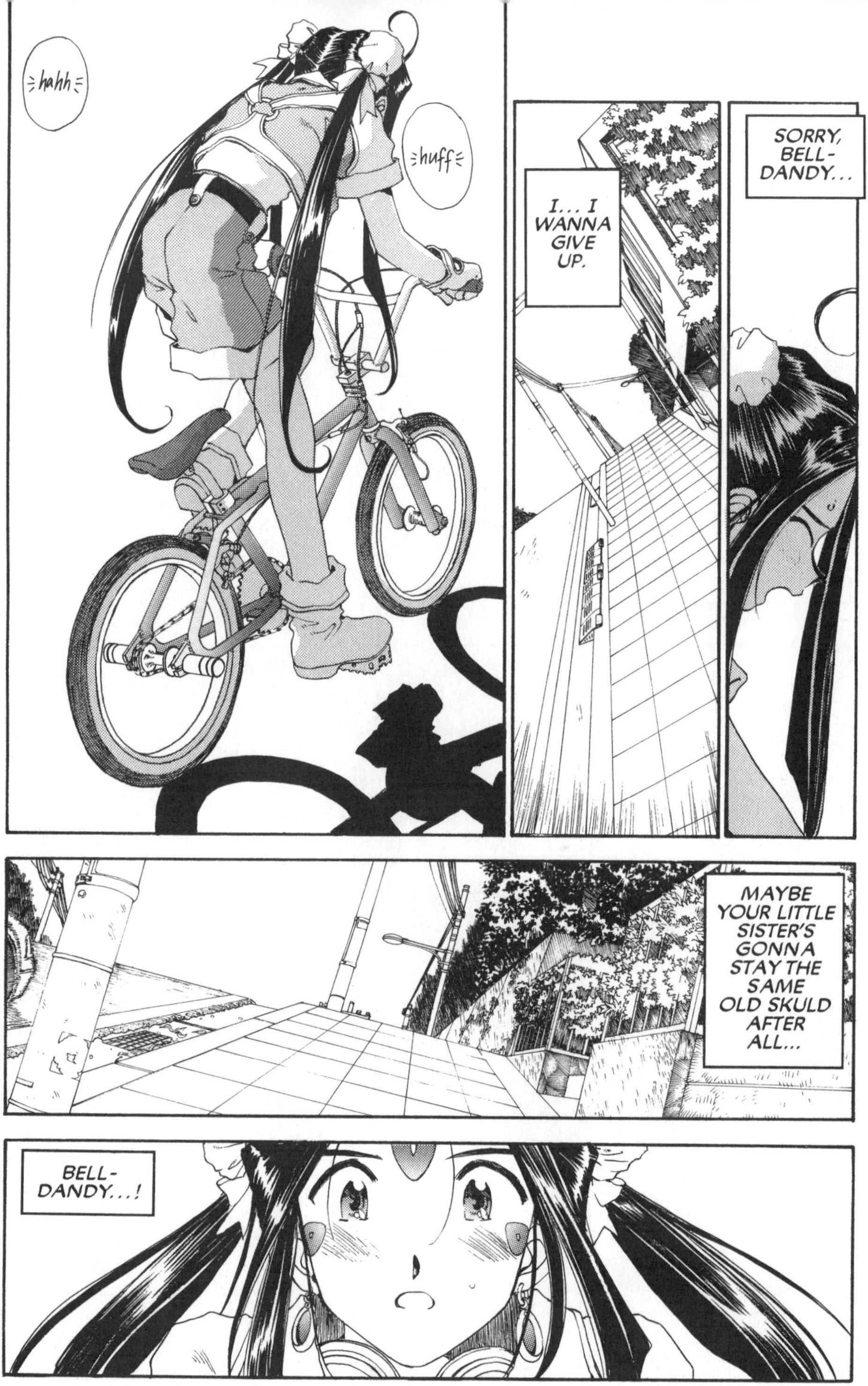
hahh
huff
I... I WANNA GIVE UP.
SORRY, BELL-DANDY...
MAYBE YOUR LITTLE SISTER'S GONNA STAY THE SAME OLD SKULD AFTER ALL...
BELL-DANDY...!

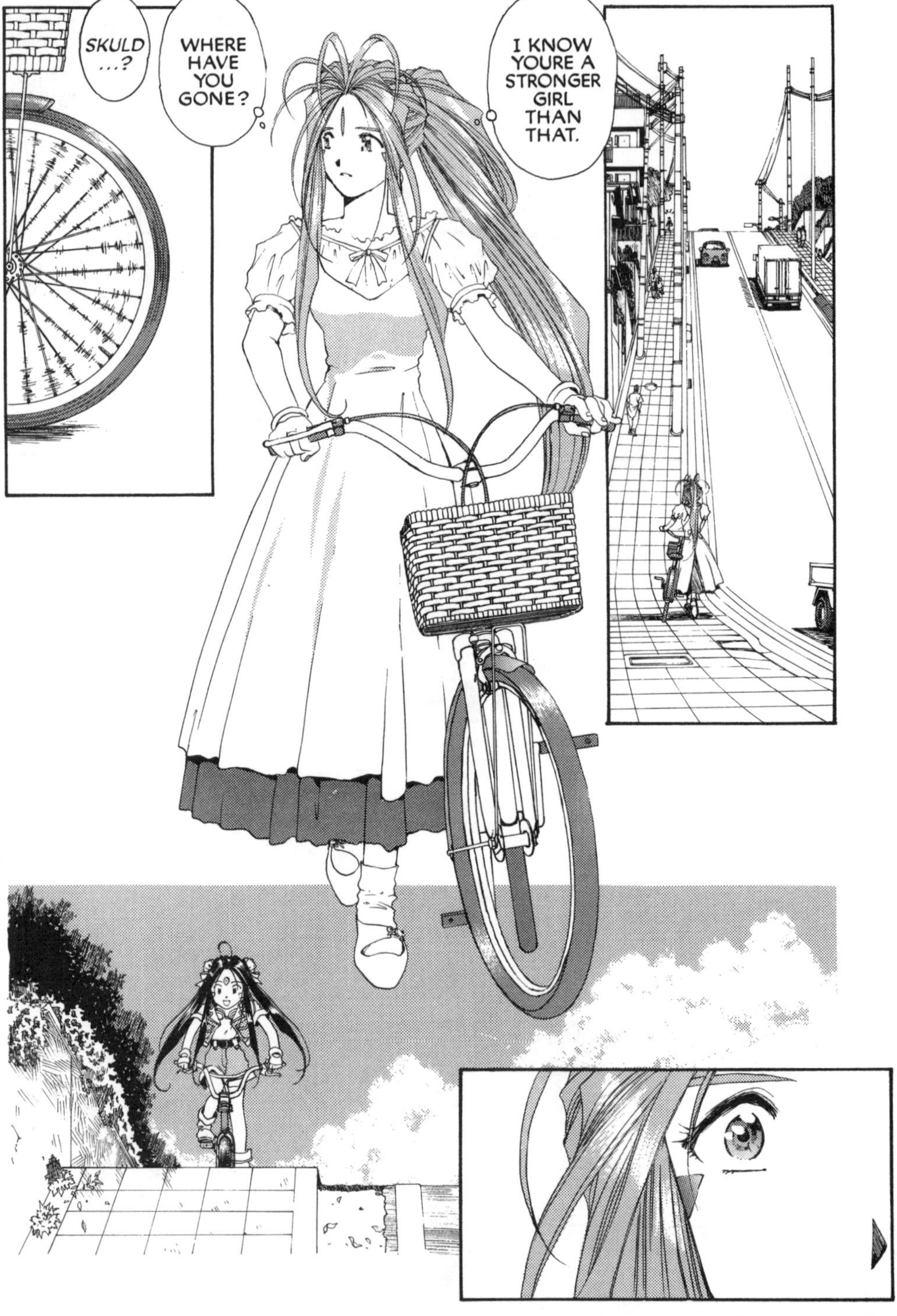

SKULD ...?
WHERE HAVE YOU GONE?
I KNOW YOURE A STRONGER GIRL THAN THAT.

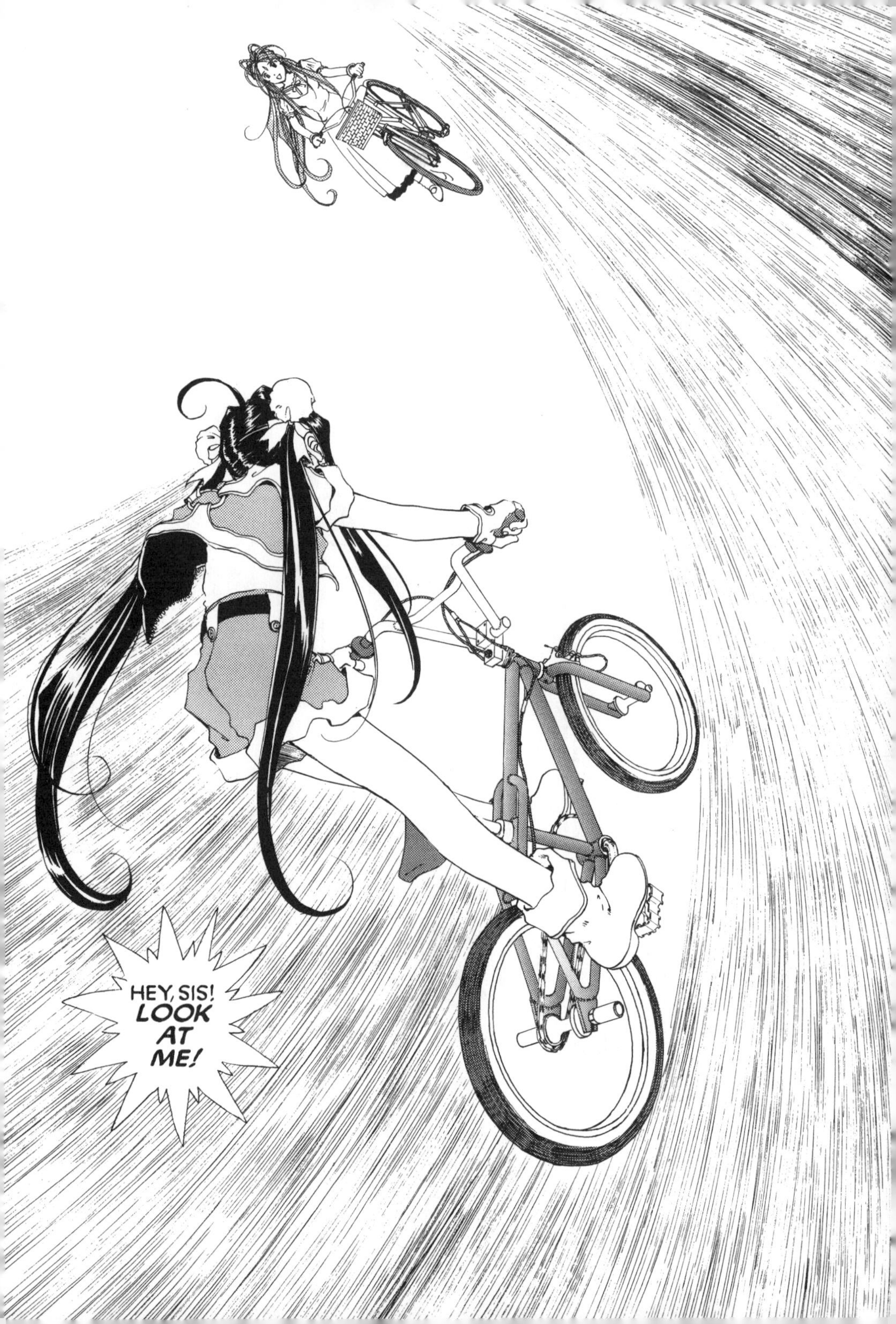
HEY, SIS! LOOK AT ME!

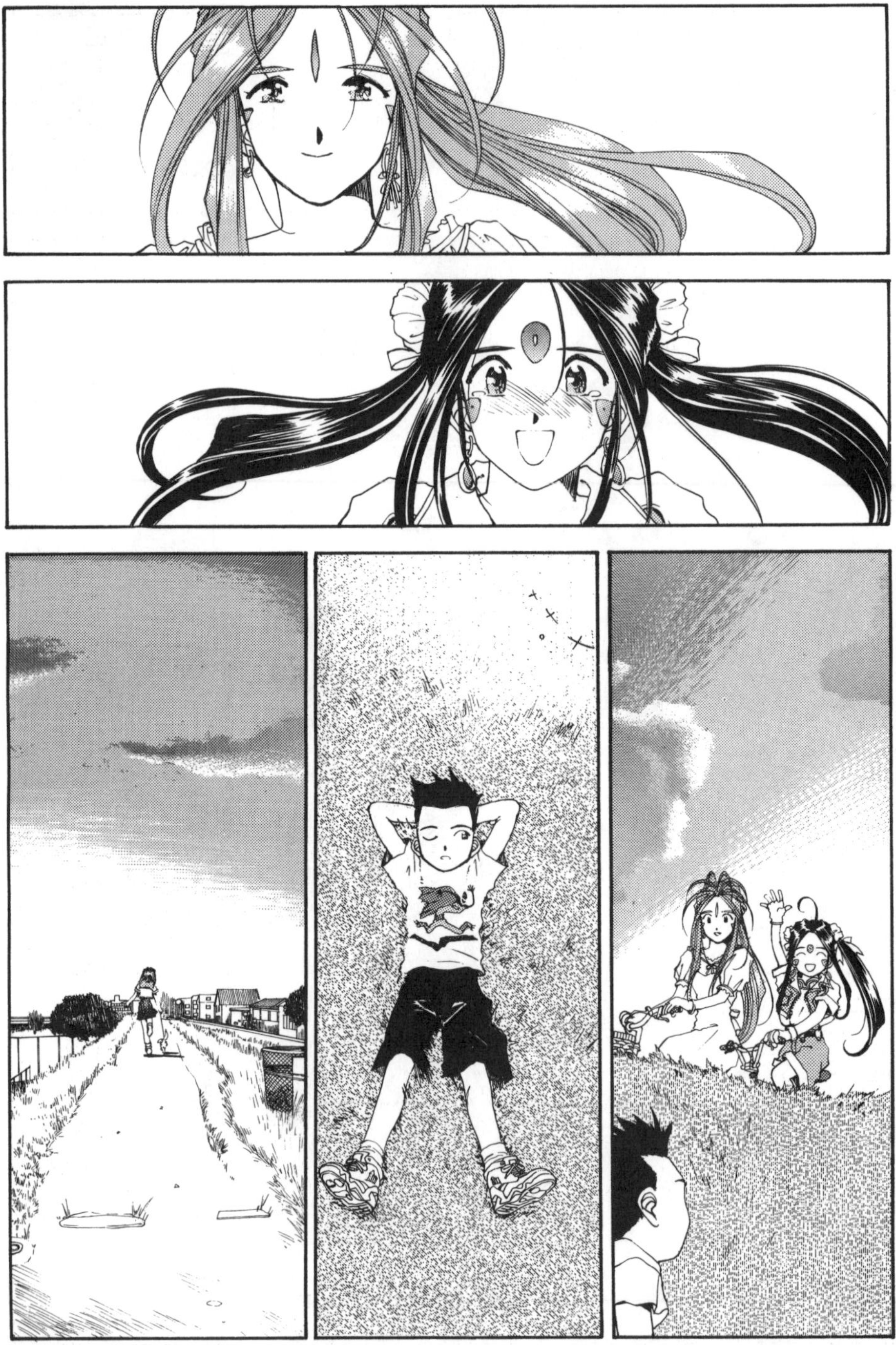

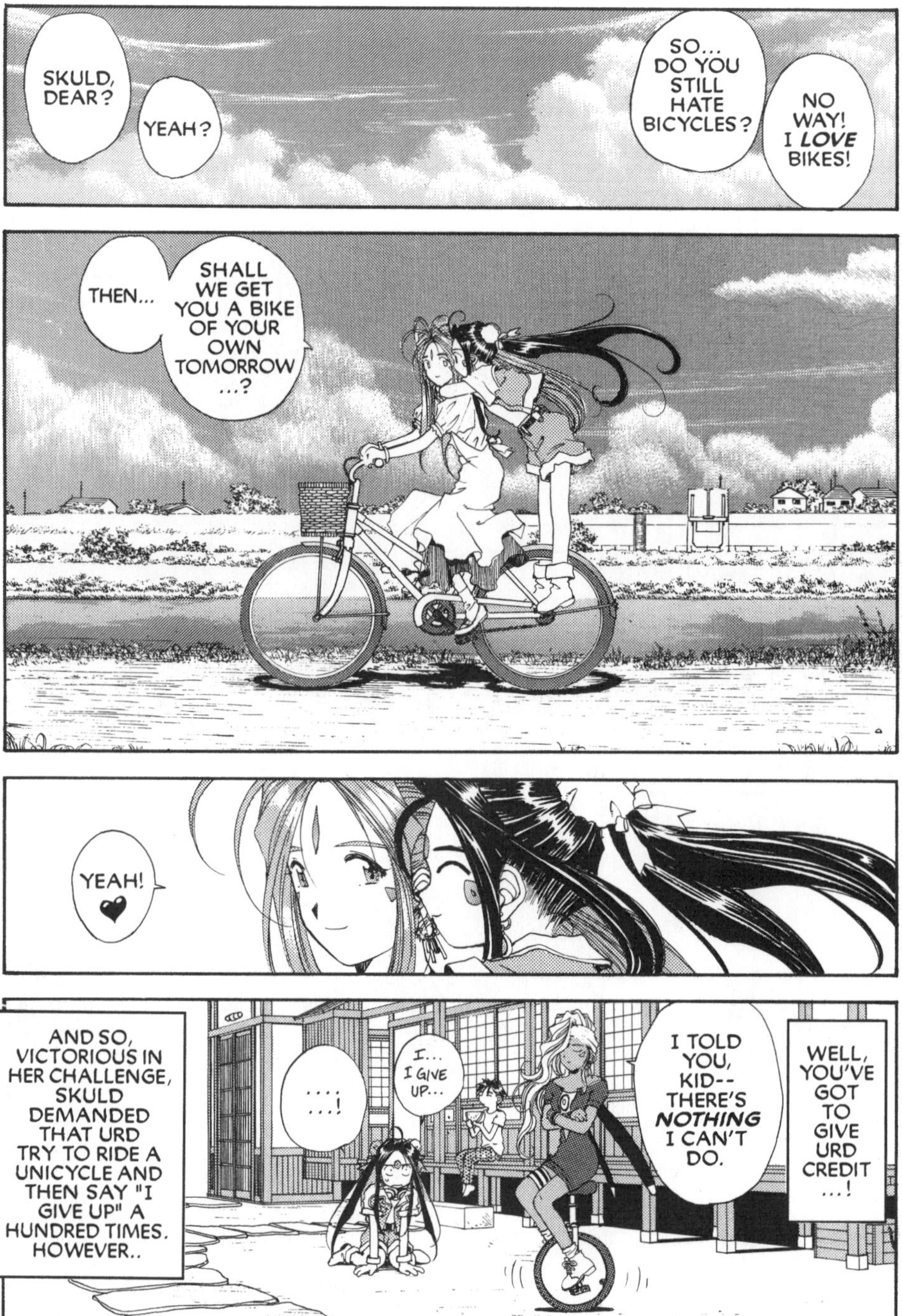
SKULD, DEAR?
YEAH?
SO... DO YOU STILL HATE BICYCLES?
NO WAY! I *LOVE* BIKES!
THEN...
SHALL WE GET YOU A BIKE OF YOUR OWN TOMORROW ...?
YEAH! ❤
AND SO, VICTORIOUS IN HER CHALLENGE, SKULD DEMANDED THAT URD TRY TO RIDE A UNICYCLE AND THEN SAY "I GIVE UP" A HUNDRED TIMES. HOWEVER..
...; ...!
I... I GIVE UP...
I TOLD YOU, KID-- THERE'S ***NOTHING*** I CAN'T DO.
WELL, YOU'VE GOT TO GIVE URD CREDIT ...!

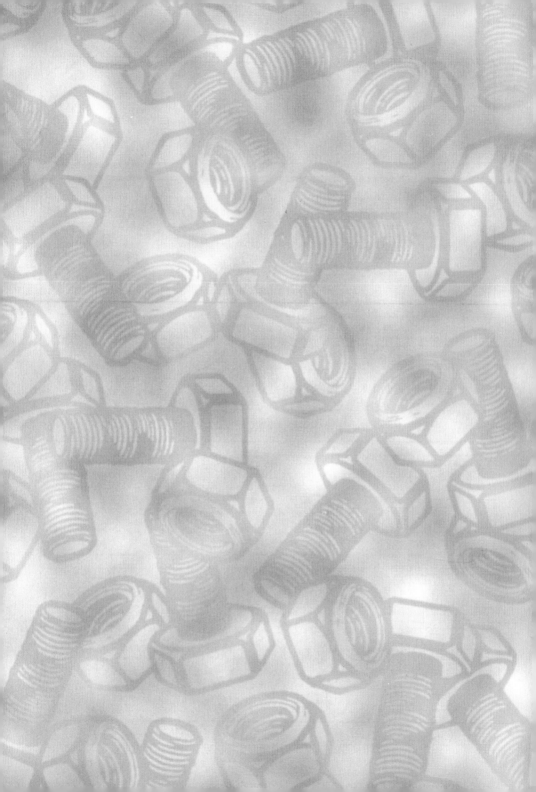

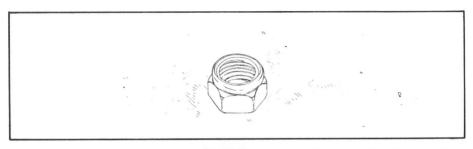

THAT'S RIGHT. IN THAT POSITION, COMPILE THE PROGRAM-ALGORITHM...

FOCUS NOT ON THE OBJECT, BUT *INSIDE.*

CONCENTRATE YOUR CONSCIOUS-NESS.

THE ALGORITHM IS JUST A GUIDE.

WHAT SPRINGS UP FROM *WITHIN...*

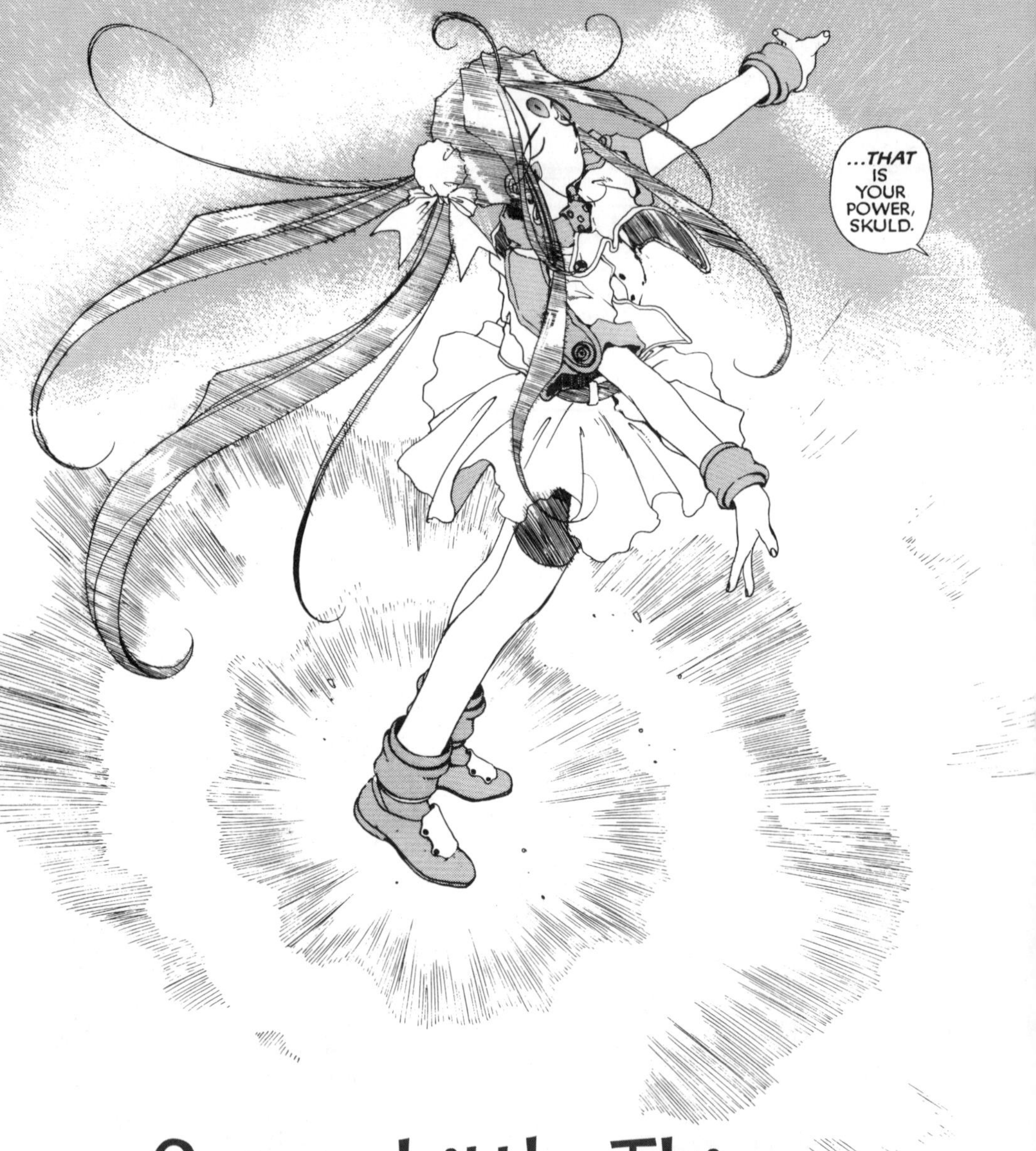
...THAT IS YOUR POWER, SKULD.

Crazy Little Thing Called Love

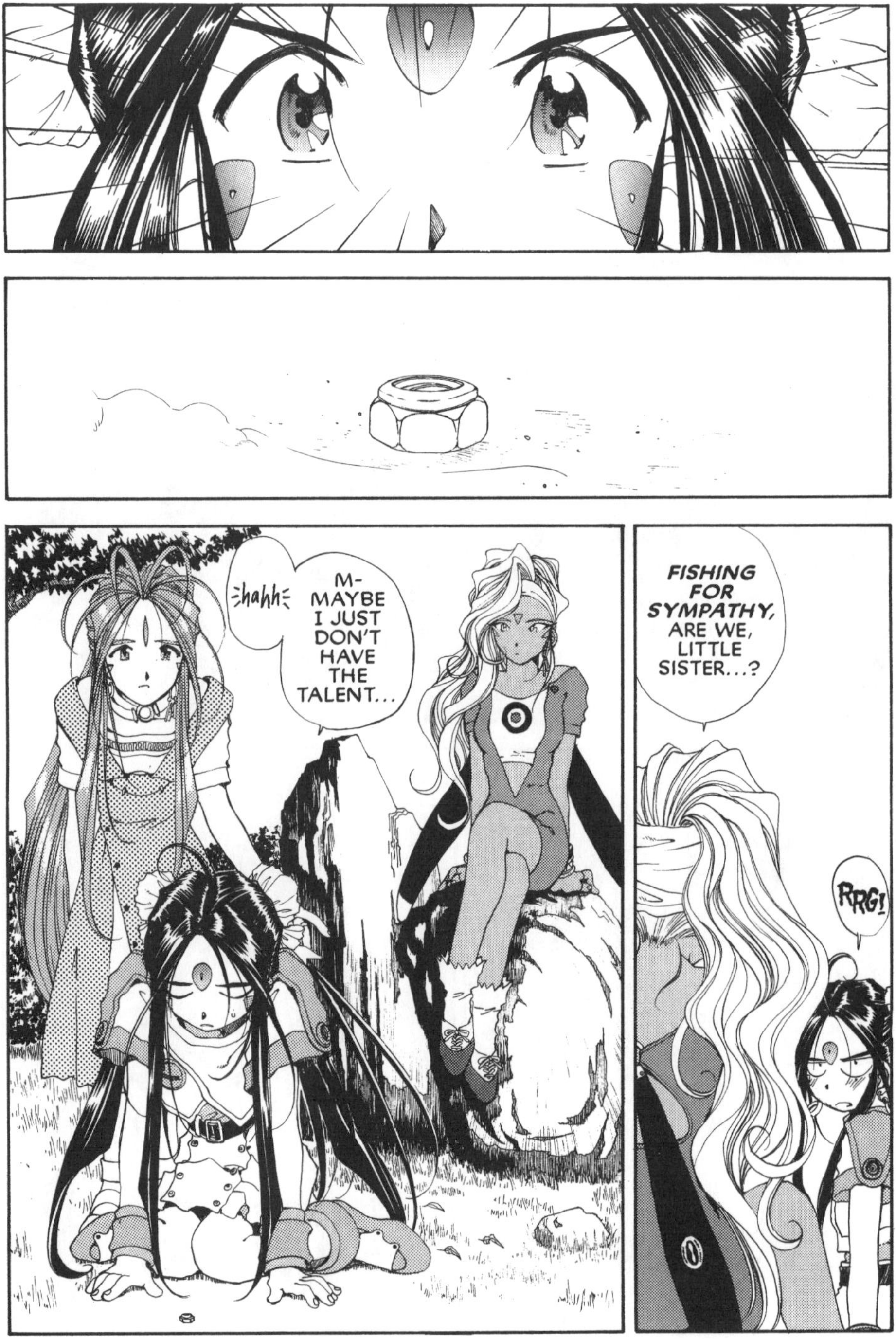
hahh
M-MAYBE I JUST DON'T HAVE THE TALENT...
FISHING FOR SYMPATHY, ARE WE, LITTLE SISTER...?
RRG!

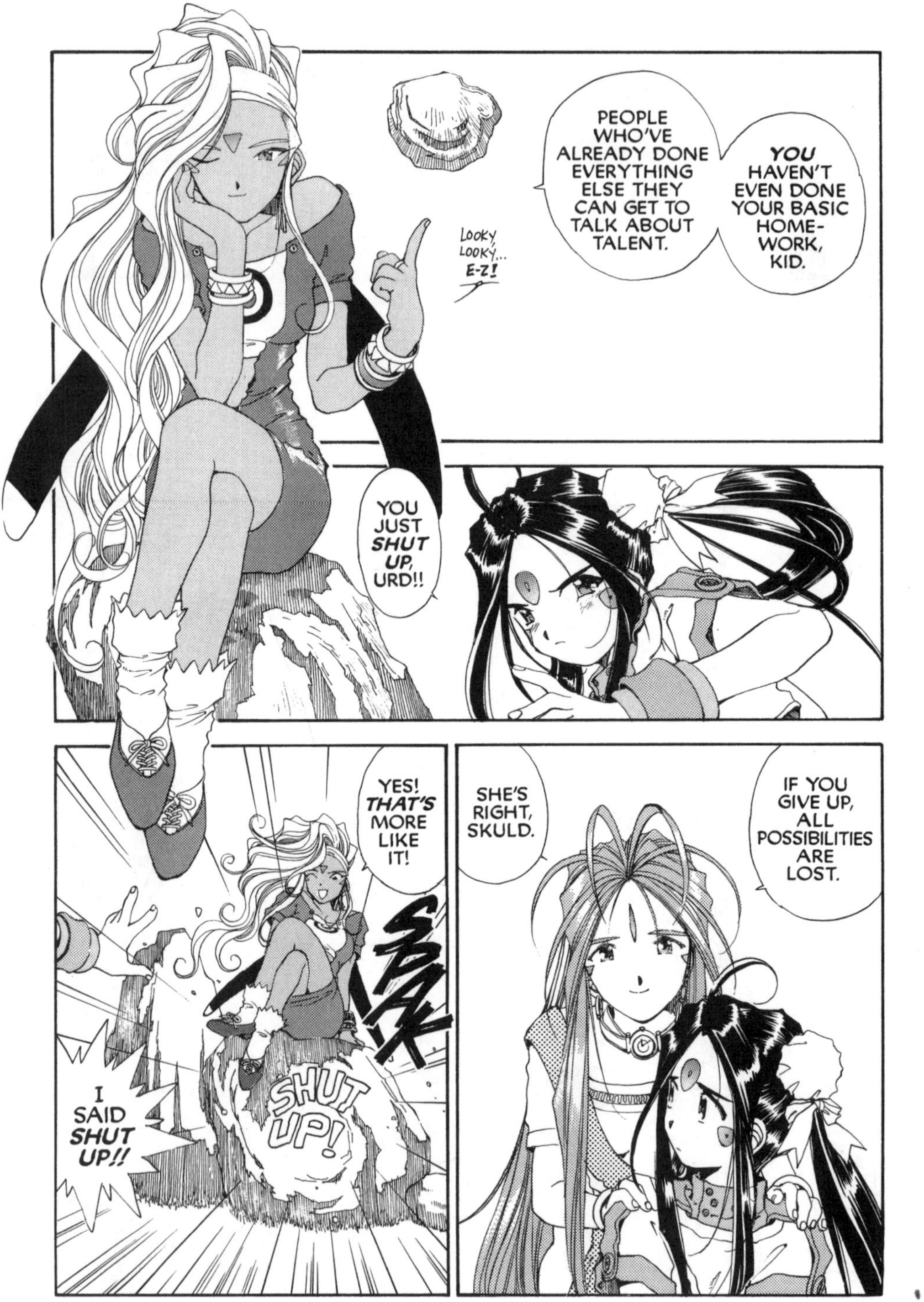
LOOKY, LOOKY... E-Z!
PEOPLE WHO'VE ALREADY DONE EVERYTHING ELSE THEY CAN GET TO TALK ABOUT TALENT.
YOU HAVEN'T EVEN DONE YOUR BASIC HOME-WORK, KID.
YOU JUST SHUT UP, URD!!
YES! THAT'S MORE LIKE IT!
SMAK
SHUT UP!
I SAID SHUT UP!!
SHE'S RIGHT, SKULD.
IF YOU GIVE UP, ALL POSSIBILITIES ARE LOST.

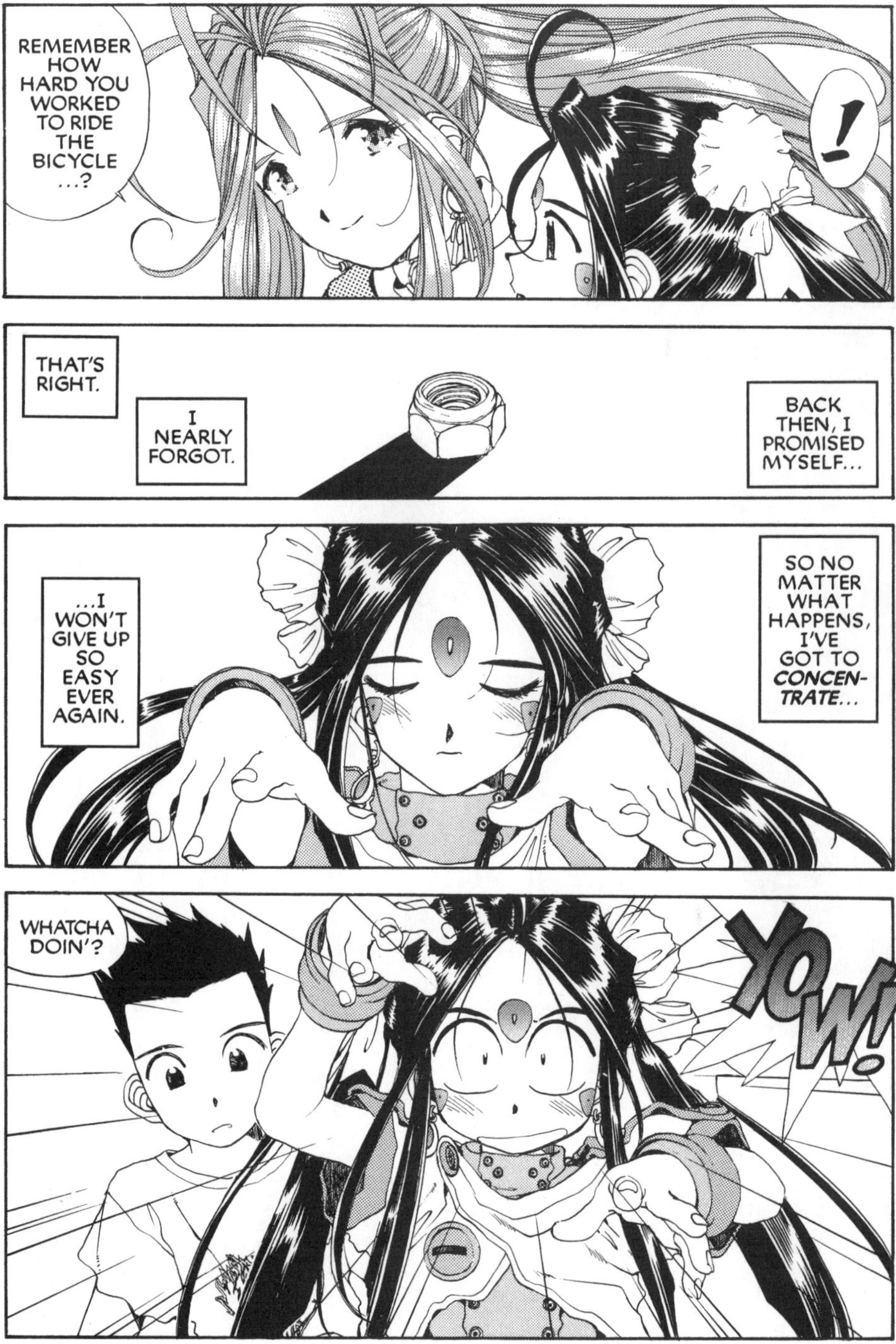
REMEMBER HOW HARD YOU WORKED TO RIDE THE BICYCLE ...?
!
THAT'S RIGHT.
I NEARLY FORGOT.
BACK THEN, I PROMISED MYSELF...
...I WON'T GIVE UP SO EASY EVER AGAIN.
SO NO MATTER WHAT HAPPENS, I'VE GOT TO *CONCENTRATE*...
WHATCHA DOIN'?
YOW!

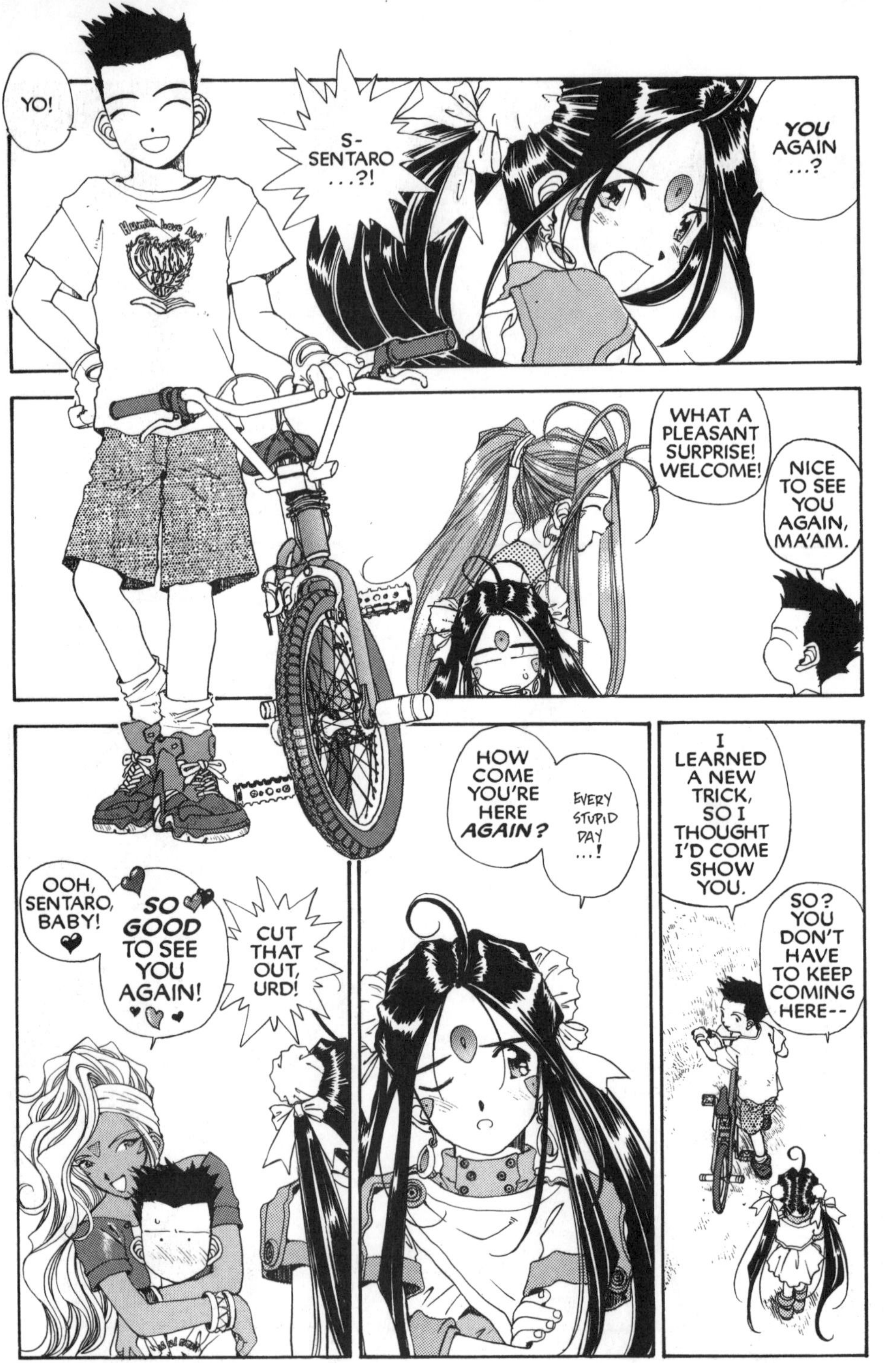
YO!
S-SENTARO ...?!
YOU AGAIN ...?
WHAT A PLEASANT SURPRISE! WELCOME!
NICE TO SEE YOU AGAIN, MA'AM.
OOH, SENTARO, BABY! SO GOOD TO SEE YOU AGAIN!
CUT THAT OUT, URD!
HOW COME YOU'RE HERE AGAIN?
EVERY STUPID DAY ...!
I LEARNED A NEW TRICK, SO I THOUGHT I'D COME SHOW YOU.
SO? YOU DON'T HAVE TO KEEP COMING HERE--

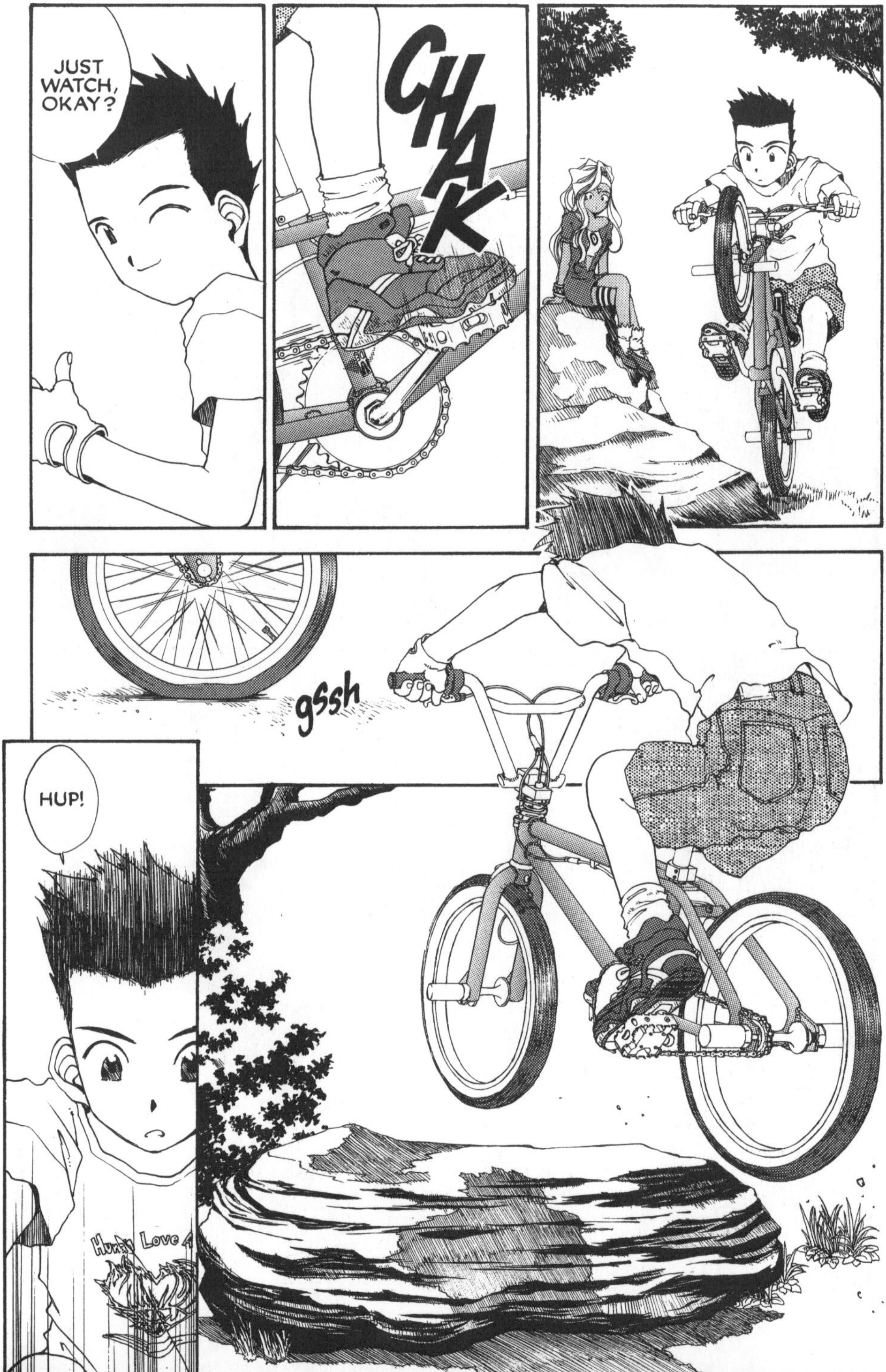
JUST WATCH, OKAY?
CHAK
gssh
HUP!
Hunny Love

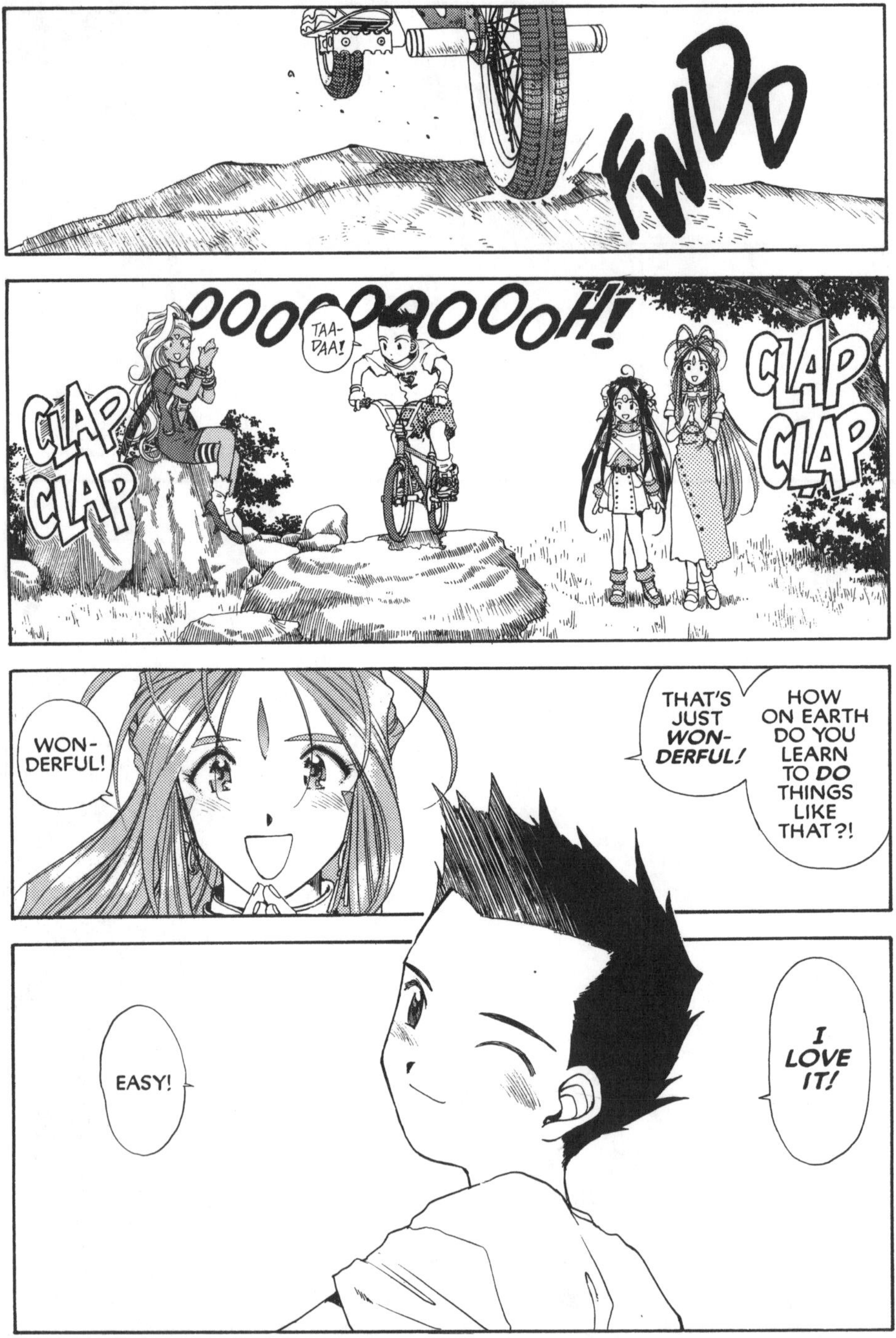
FWDD
OOOOOOOOOOOH!
CLAP CLAP
TAA-DAA!
CLAP CLAP
WON-DERFUL!
THAT'S JUST *WON-DERFUL!*
HOW ON EARTH DO YOU LEARN TO *DO* THINGS LIKE THAT?!
EASY!
I LOVE IT!

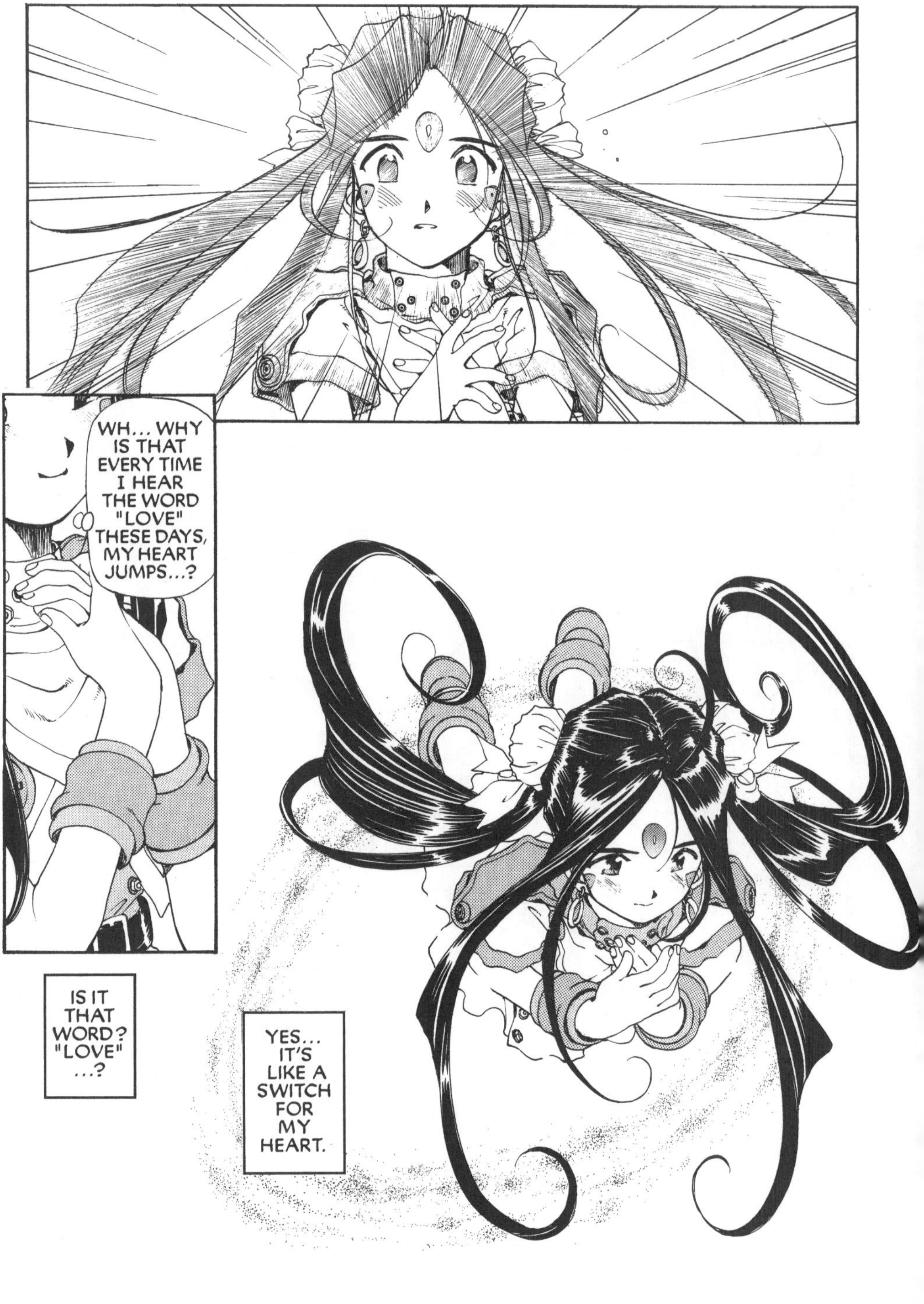

WH... WHY IS THAT EVERY TIME I HEAR THE WORD "LOVE" THESE DAYS, MY HEART JUMPS...?
IS IT THAT WORD? "LOVE" ...?
YES... IT'S LIKE A SWITCH FOR MY HEART.

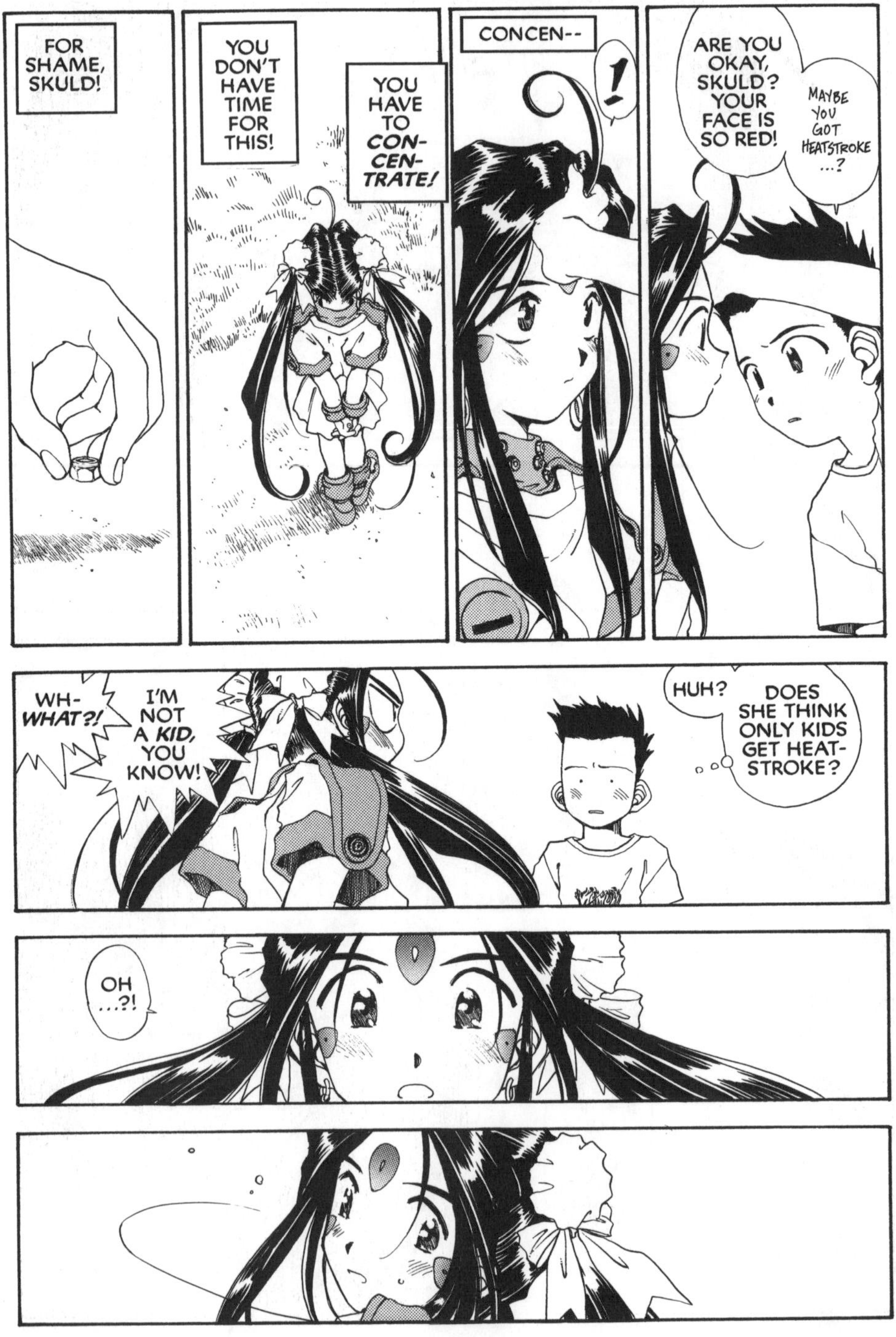
FOR SHAME, SKULD!
YOU DON'T HAVE TIME FOR THIS!
YOU HAVE TO CON-CEN-TRATE!
CONCEN--
!
ARE YOU OKAY, SKULD? YOUR FACE IS SO RED!
MAYBE YOU GOT HEATSTROKE ...?
WH- WHAT?!
I'M NOT A KID, YOU KNOW!
HUH?
DOES SHE THINK ONLY KIDS GET HEAT-STROKE?
OH ...?!

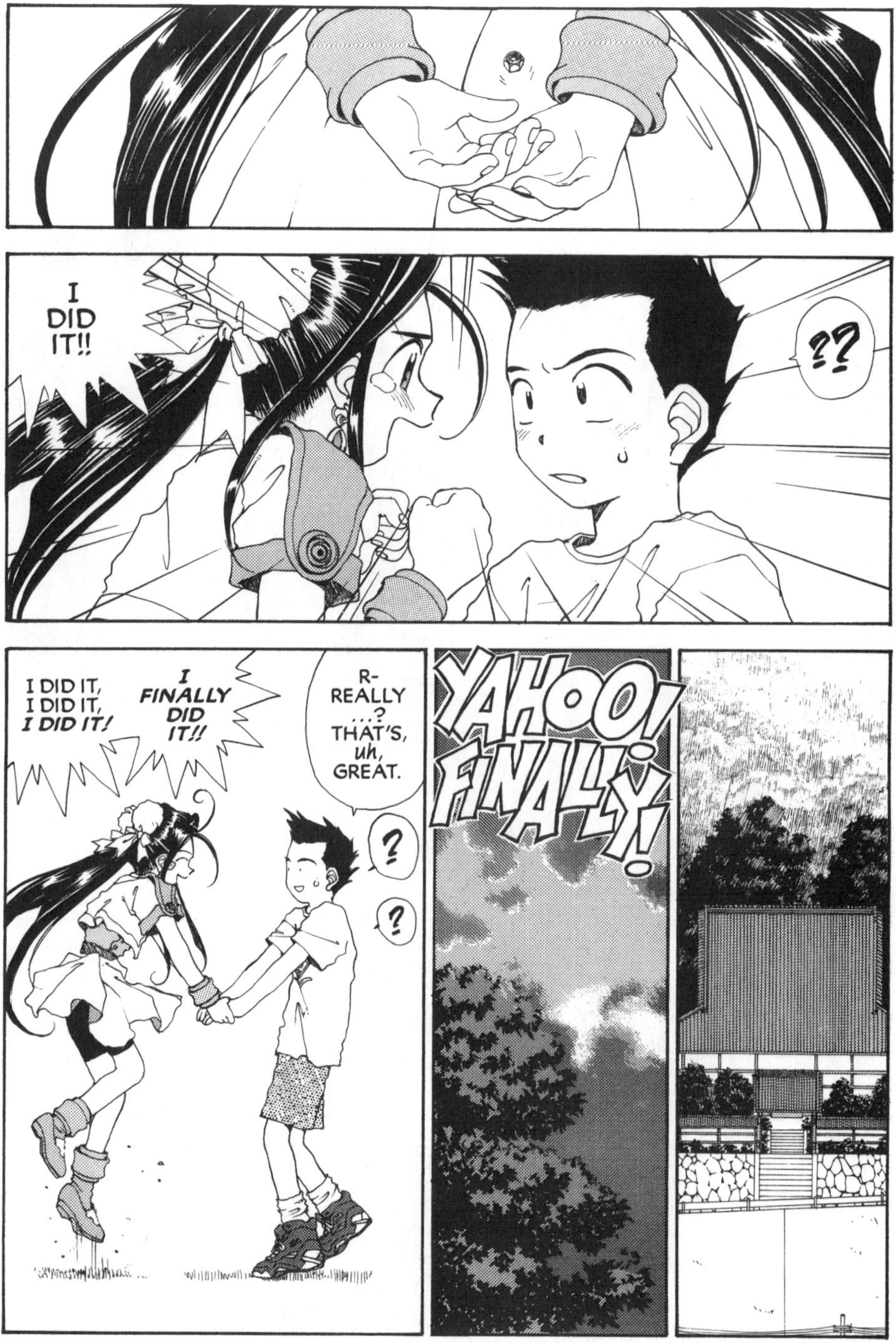
I DID IT!!
??
I DID IT, I DID IT, *I DID IT!*
I FINALLY DID IT!!
R- REALLY ...? THAT'S, *uh*, GREAT.
?
?
YAHOO! FINALLY!

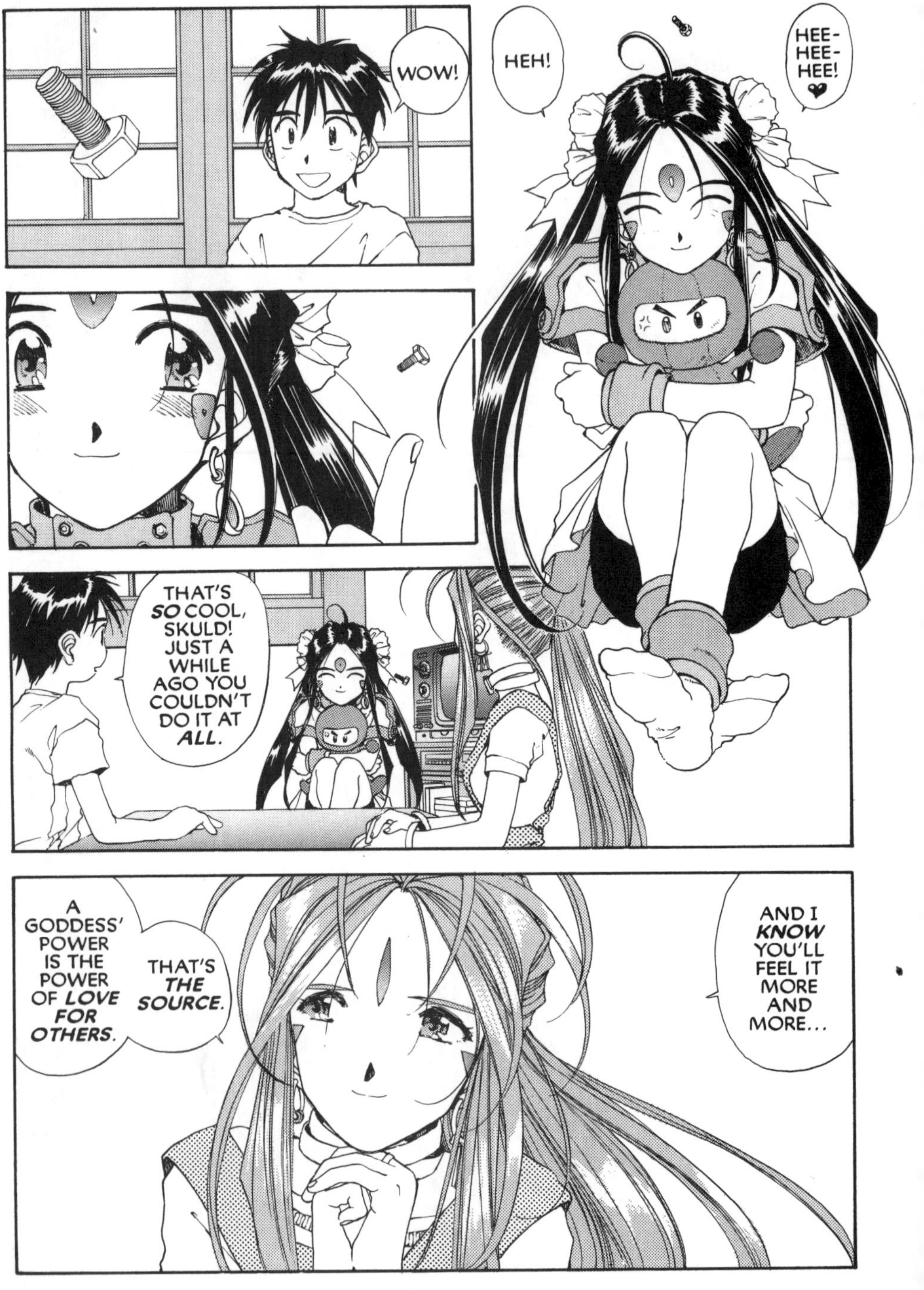
WOW!
HEH!
HEE-HEE-HEE! ❤
THAT'S *SO* COOL, SKULD! JUST A WHILE AGO YOU COULDN'T DO IT AT *ALL*.
A GODDESS' POWER IS THE POWER OF *LOVE FOR OTHERS*.
THAT'S *THE SOURCE*.
AND I *KNOW* YOU'LL FEEL IT MORE AND MORE...

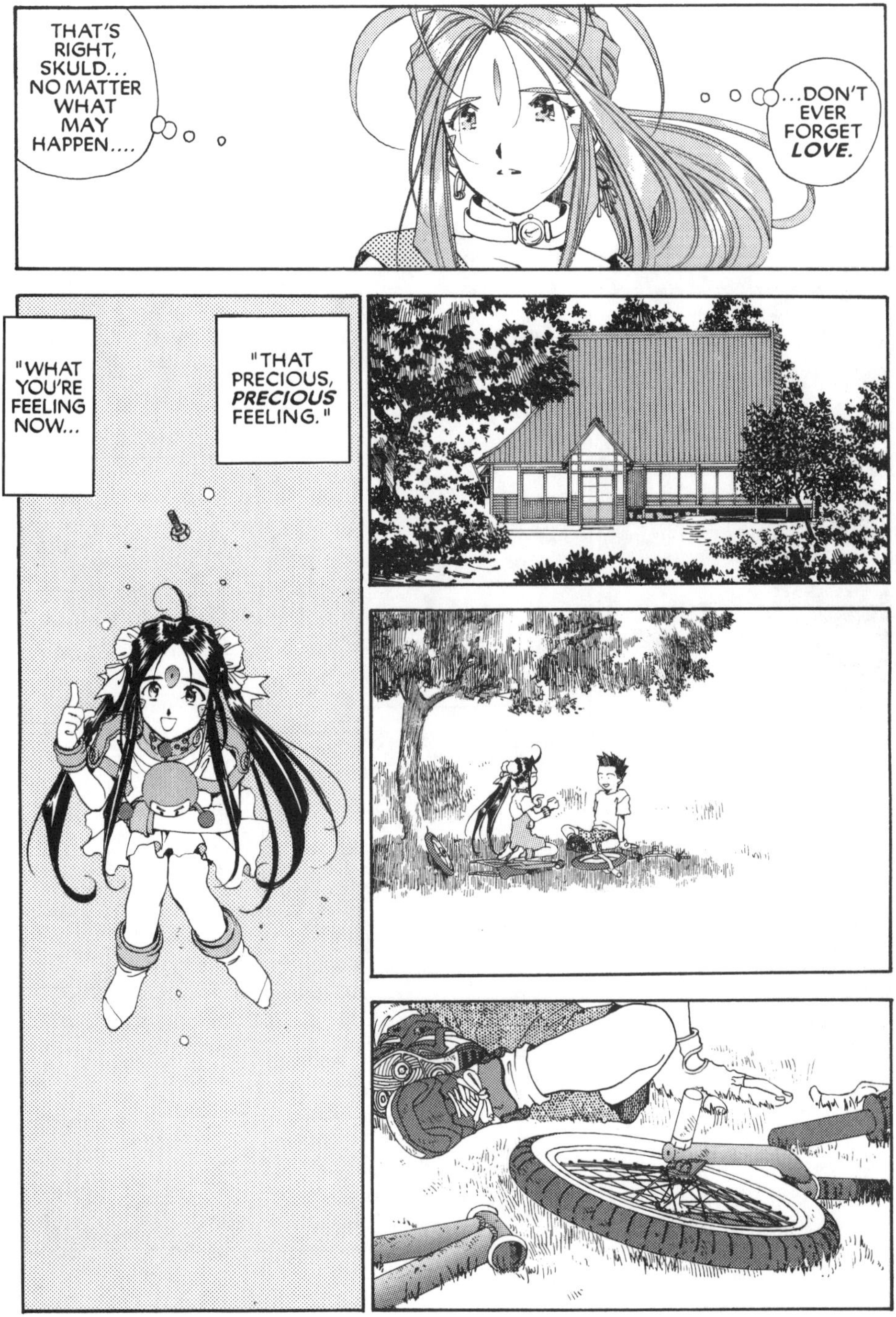
THAT'S RIGHT, SKULD... NO MATTER WHAT MAY HAPPEN....
...DON'T EVER FORGET LOVE.
"WHAT YOU'RE FEELING NOW...
"THAT PRECIOUS, PRECIOUS FEELING."

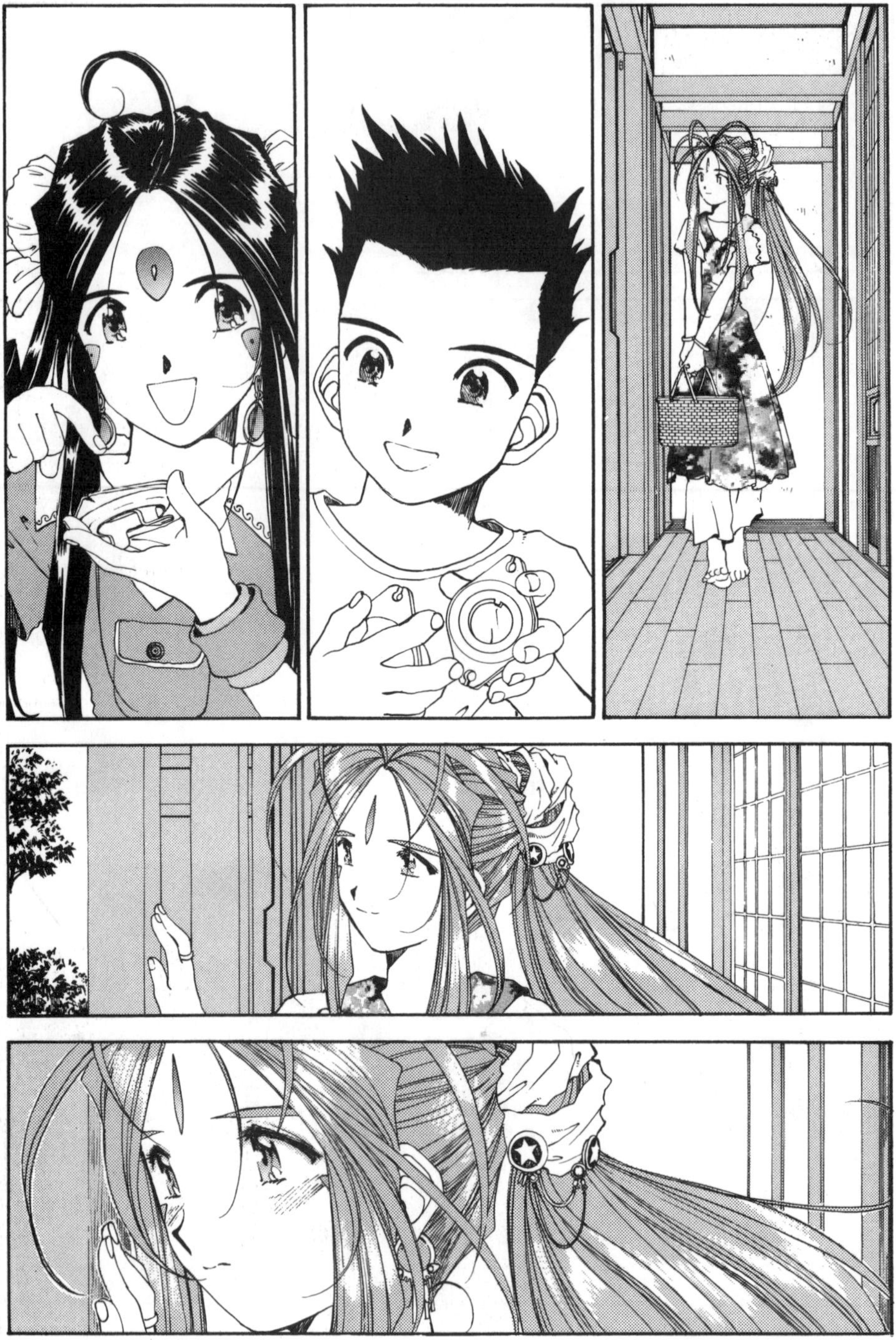

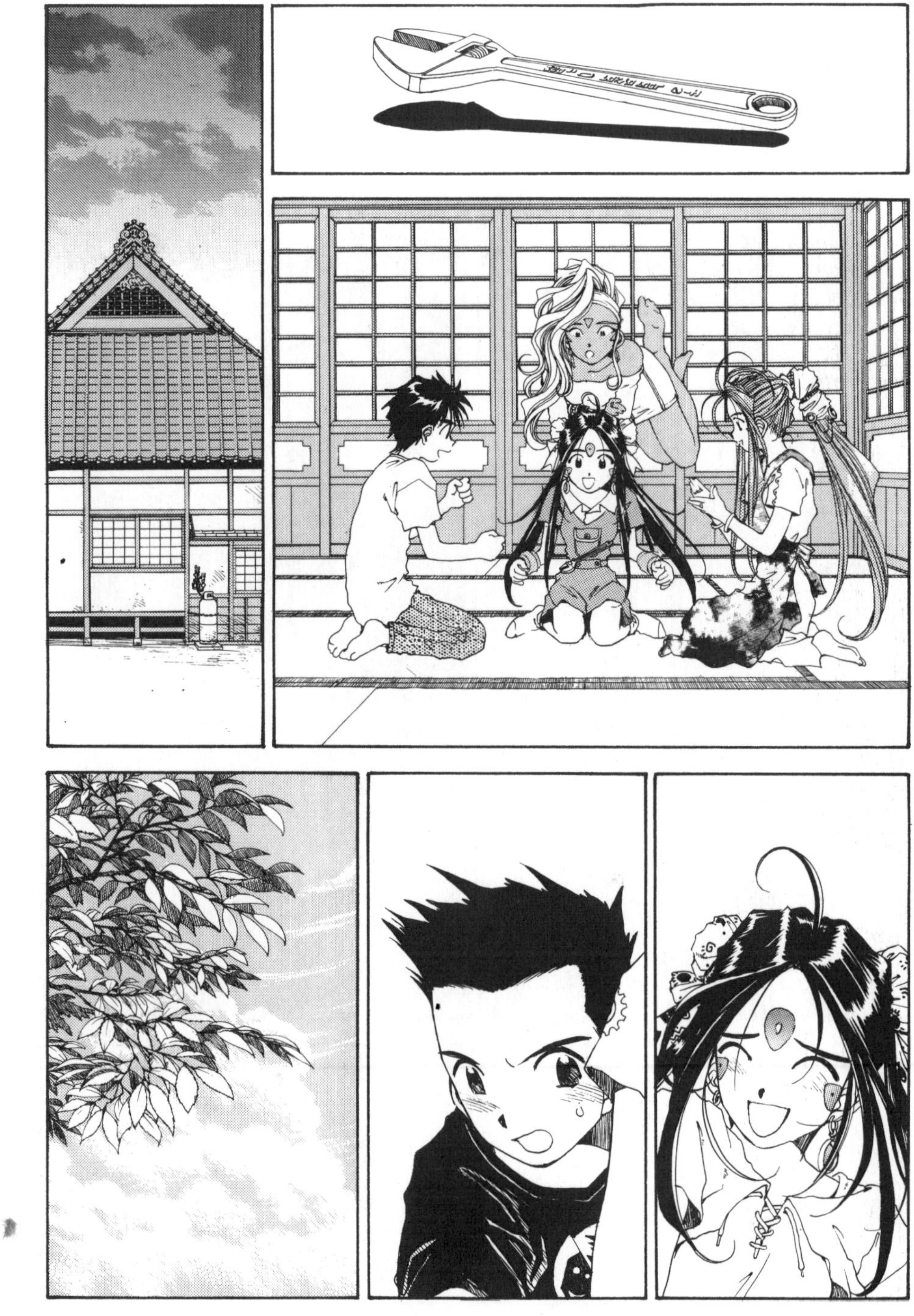

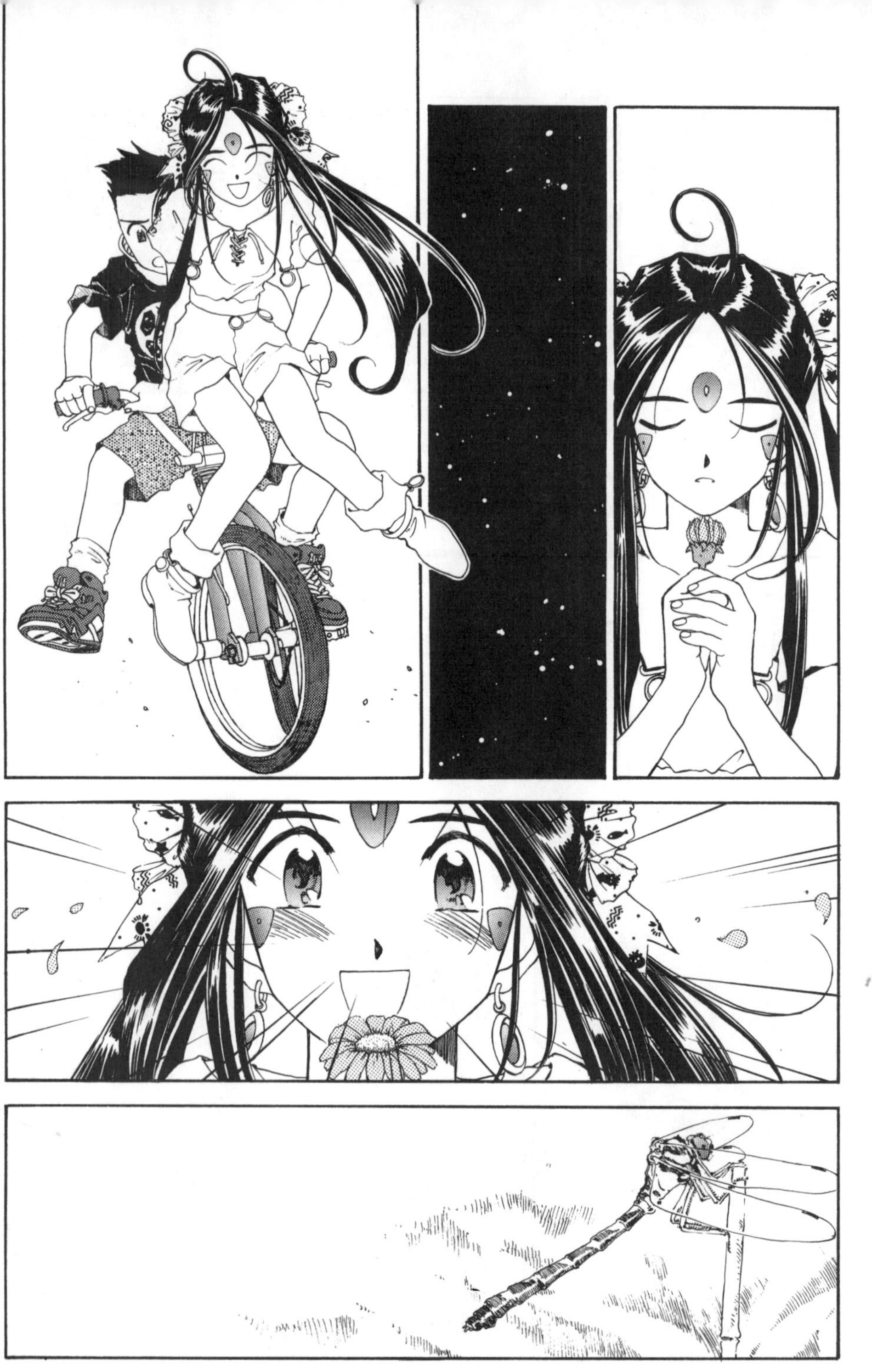

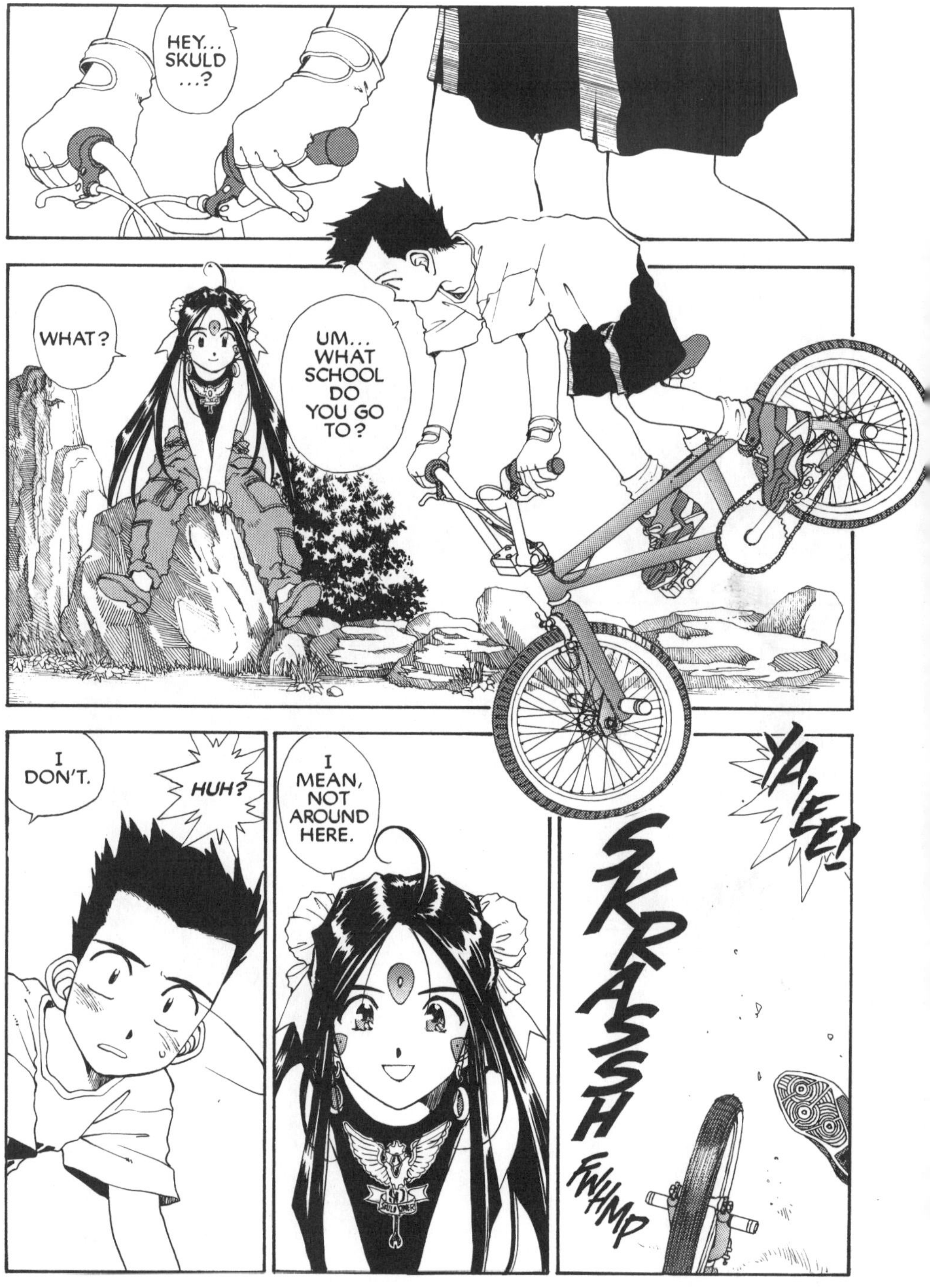
HEY... SKULD ...?
WHAT?
UM... WHAT SCHOOL DO YOU GO TO?
I DON'T.
HUH?
I MEAN, NOT AROUND HERE.
YAIEEE!
SKRASSH
FWHMP

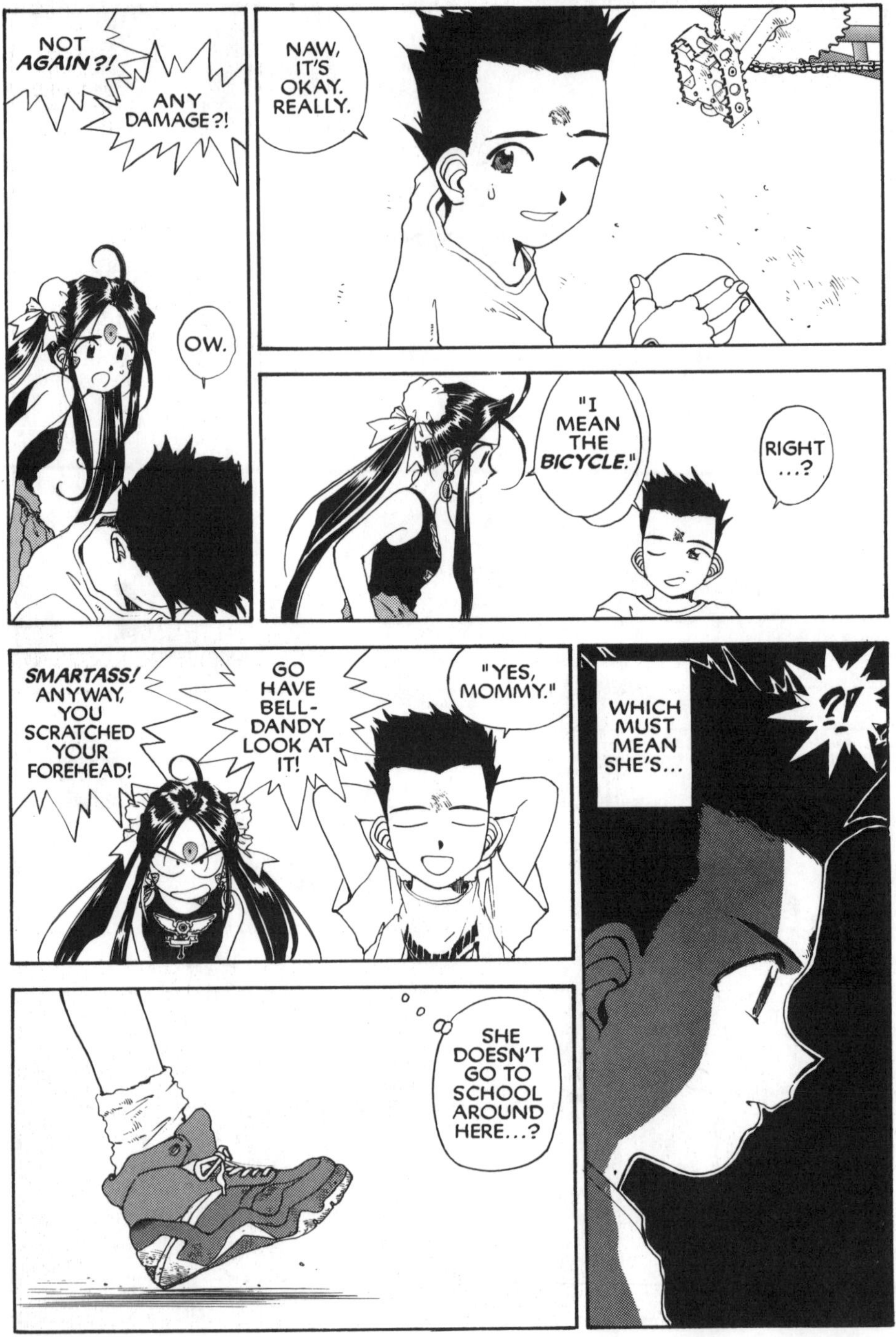
NOT AGAIN?!
ANY DAMAGE?!
OW.
NAW, IT'S OKAY. REALLY.
"I MEAN THE BICYCLE."
RIGHT ...?
SMARTASS! ANYWAY, YOU SCRATCHED YOUR FOREHEAD!
GO HAVE BELL-DANDY LOOK AT IT!
"YES, MOMMY."
SHE DOESN'T GO TO SCHOOL AROUND HERE...?
WHICH MUST MEAN SHE'S...
?!

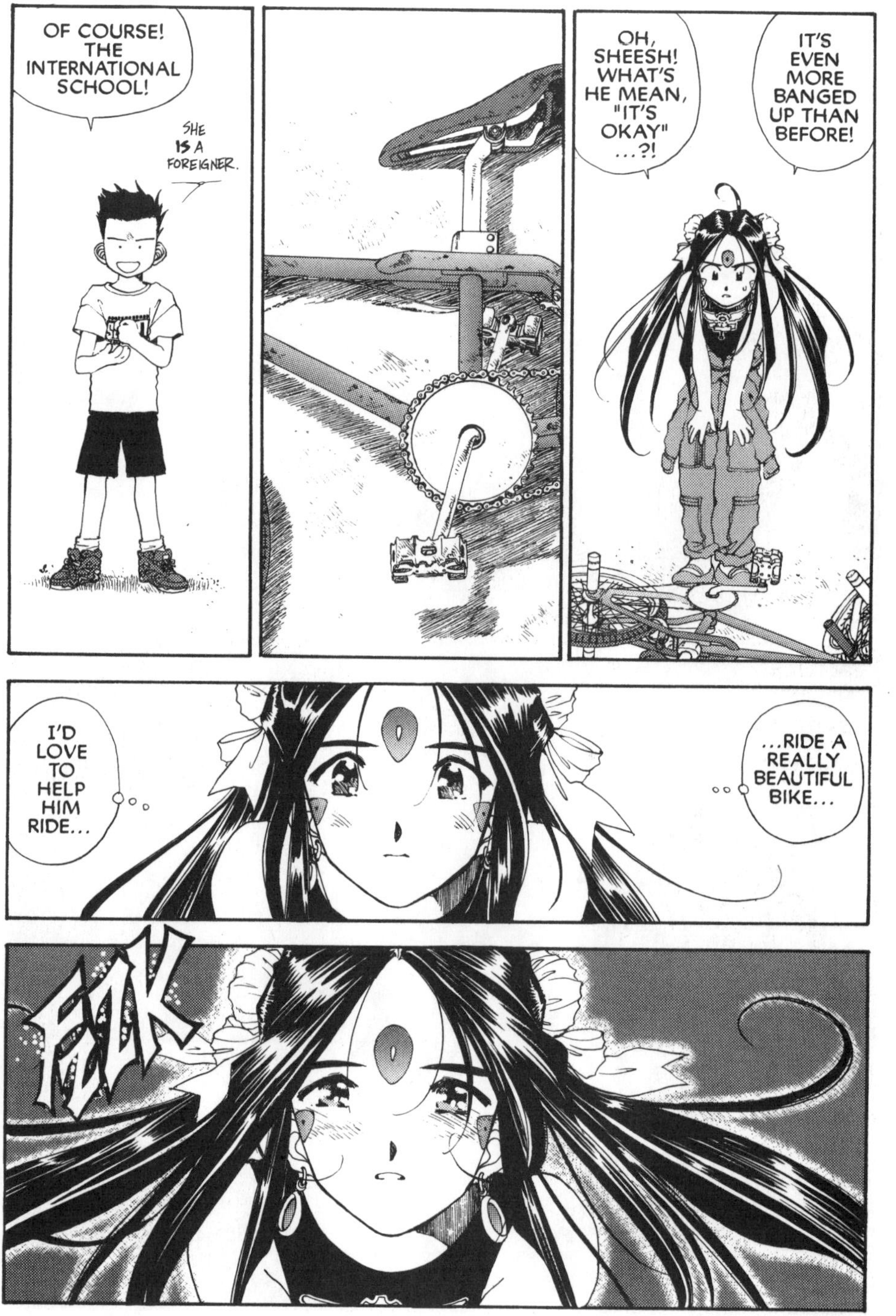
OF COURSE! THE INTERNATIONAL SCHOOL!
SHE IS A FOREIGNER.
OH, SHEESH! WHAT'S HE MEAN, "IT'S OKAY" ...?!
IT'S EVEN MORE BANGED UP THAN BEFORE!
I'D LOVE TO HELP HIM RIDE...
...RIDE A REALLY BEAUTIFUL BIKE...
FZK

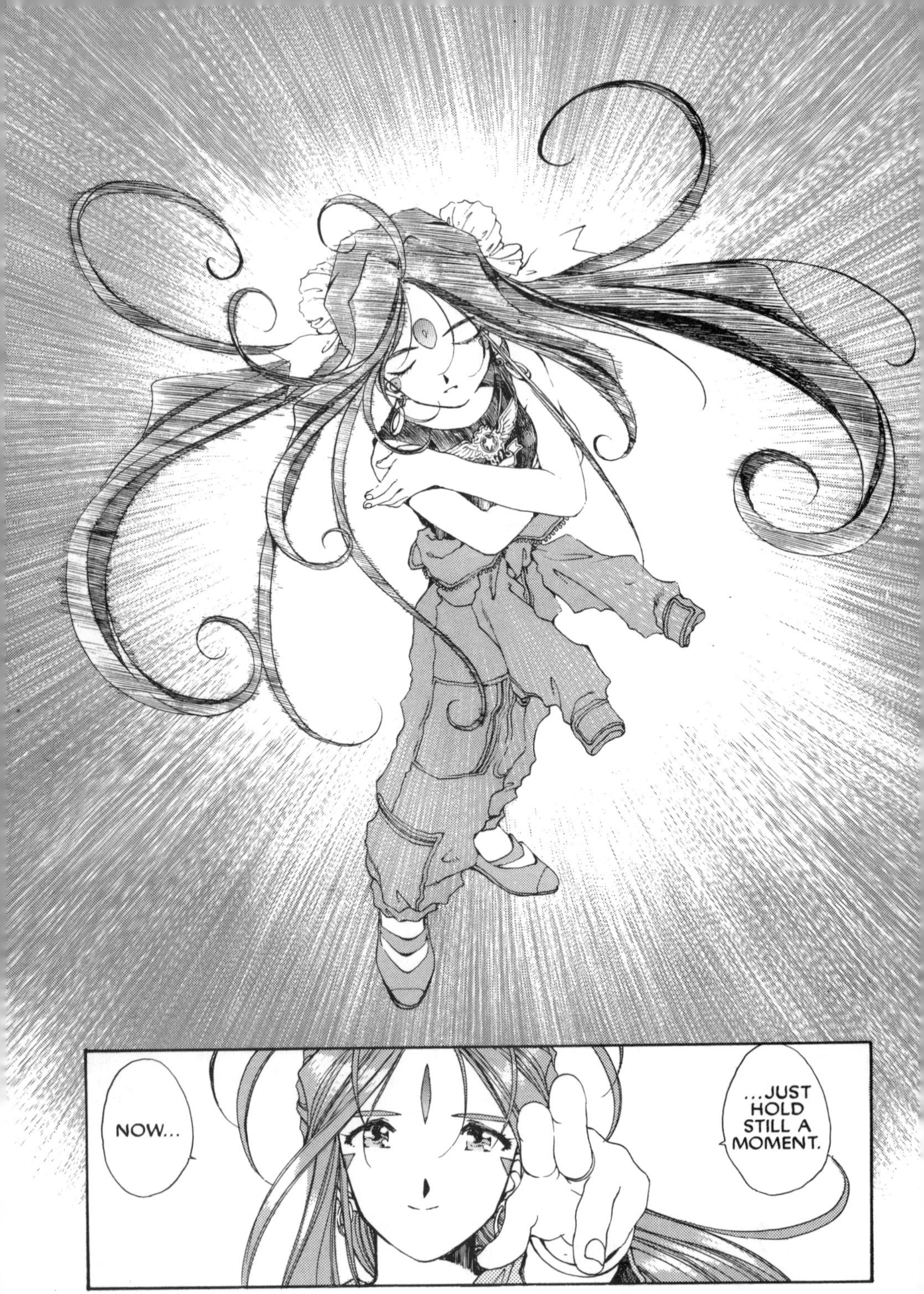
NOW...
...JUST HOLD STILL A MOMENT.

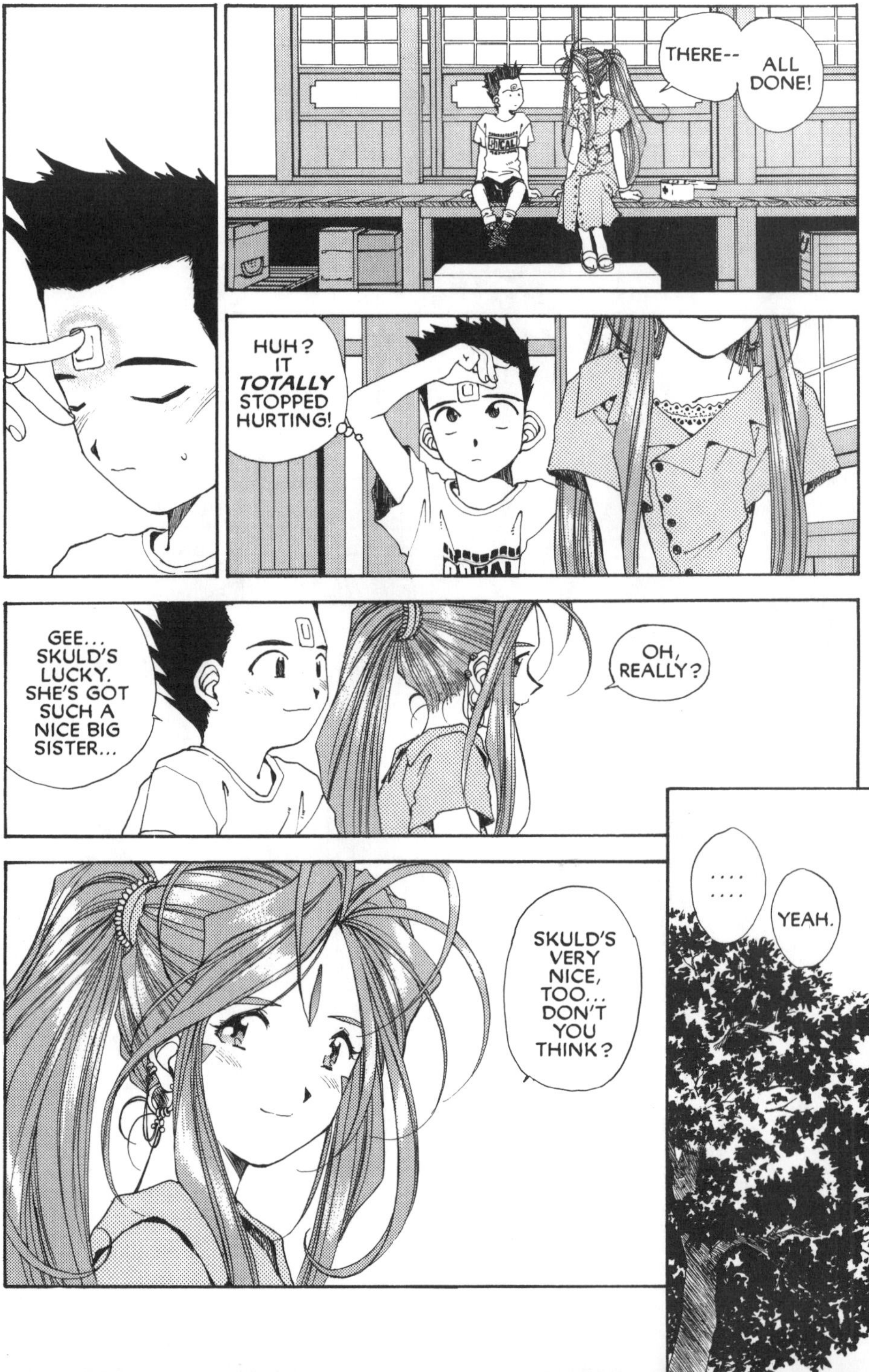
THERE-- ALL DONE!
HUH? IT *TOTALLY* STOPPED HURTING!
GEE... SKULD'S LUCKY. SHE'S GOT SUCH A NICE BIG SISTER...
OH, REALLY?
SKULD'S VERY NICE, TOO... DON'T YOU THINK?
....
....
YEAH.

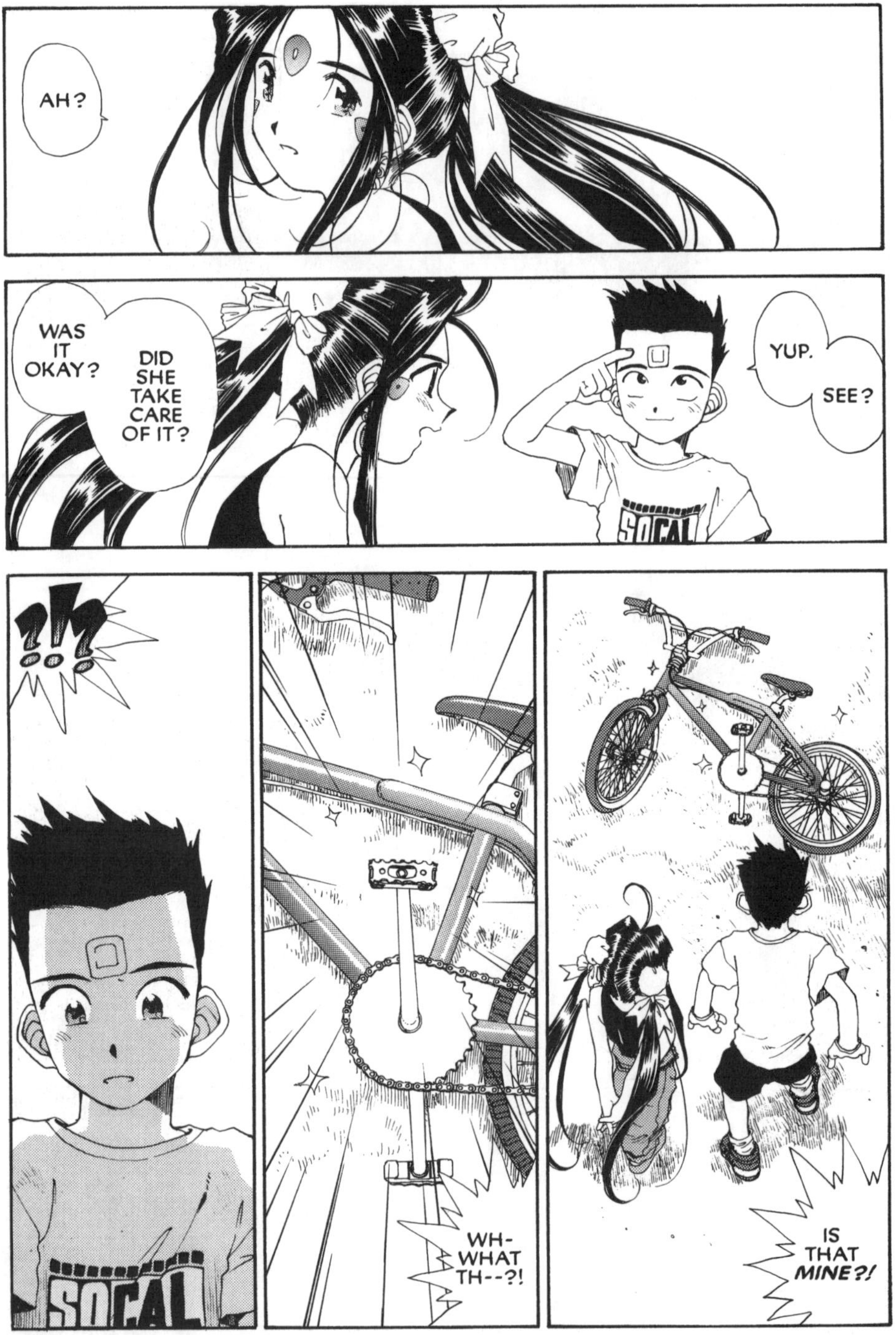
AH?
WAS IT OKAY?
DID SHE TAKE CARE OF IT?
YUP.
SEE?
SOCAL
?!!
SOCAL
WH- WHAT TH--?!
IS THAT *MINE?!*

SURE IS. ♥

DO YOU DID THAT, SKULD...?

UH... YEAH.

WHY, SKULD? WHY'D YOU GO AND DO *THAT?!*

HUH?! B-BUT...

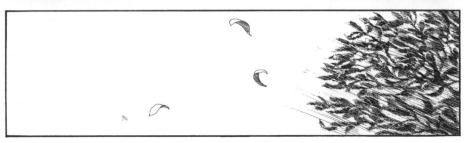

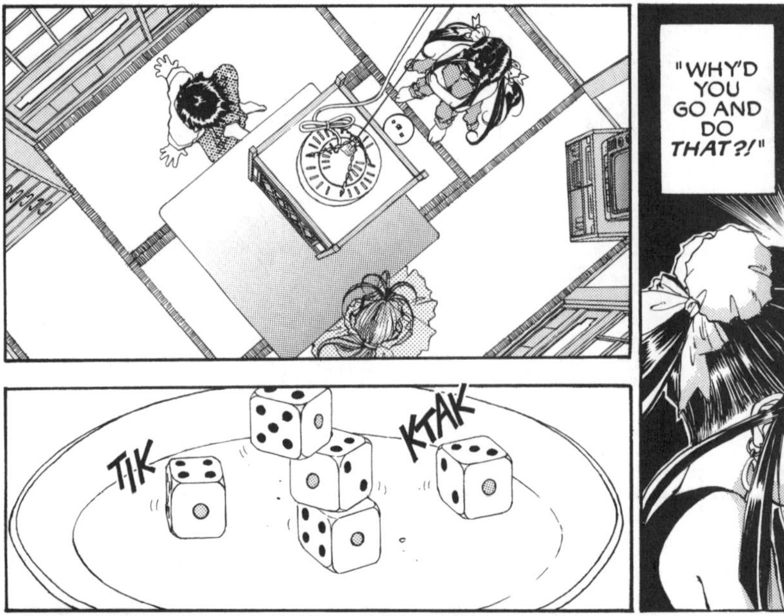
TIK
KTAK
"WHY'D YOU GO AND DO *THAT?!*"

▲SPECIAL TRAINING TO CONTROL HER POWER--SHE HAS TO LINE UP ALL THE NUMBERS ON THE DICE.

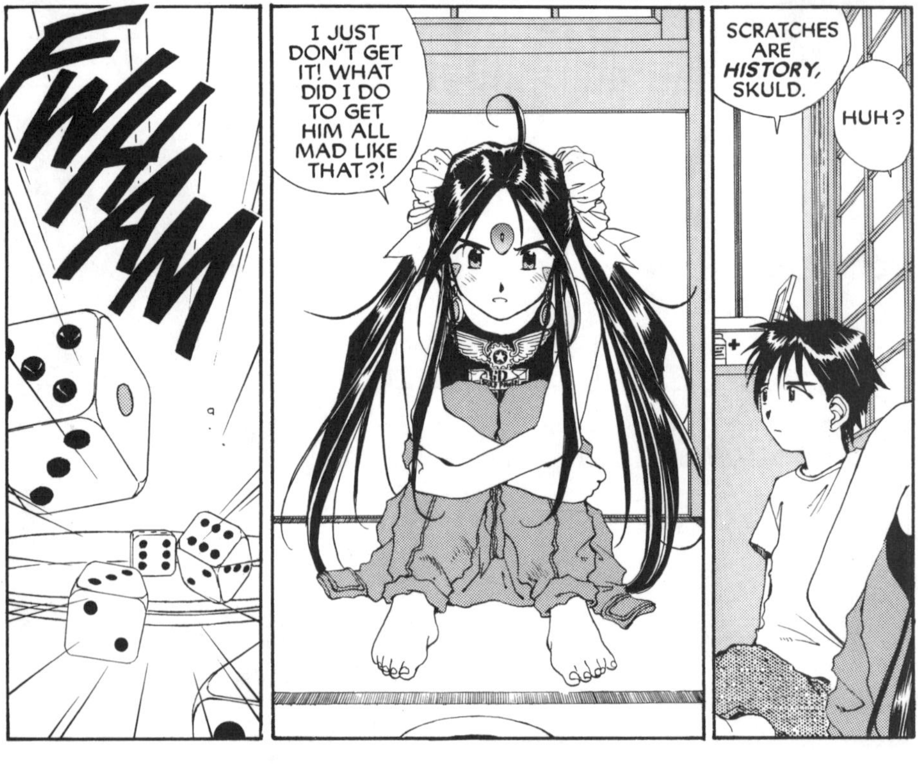
FWHAM
I JUST DON'T GET IT! WHAT DID I DO TO GET HIM ALL MAD LIKE THAT?!
SCRATCHES ARE *HISTORY*, SKULD.
HUH?

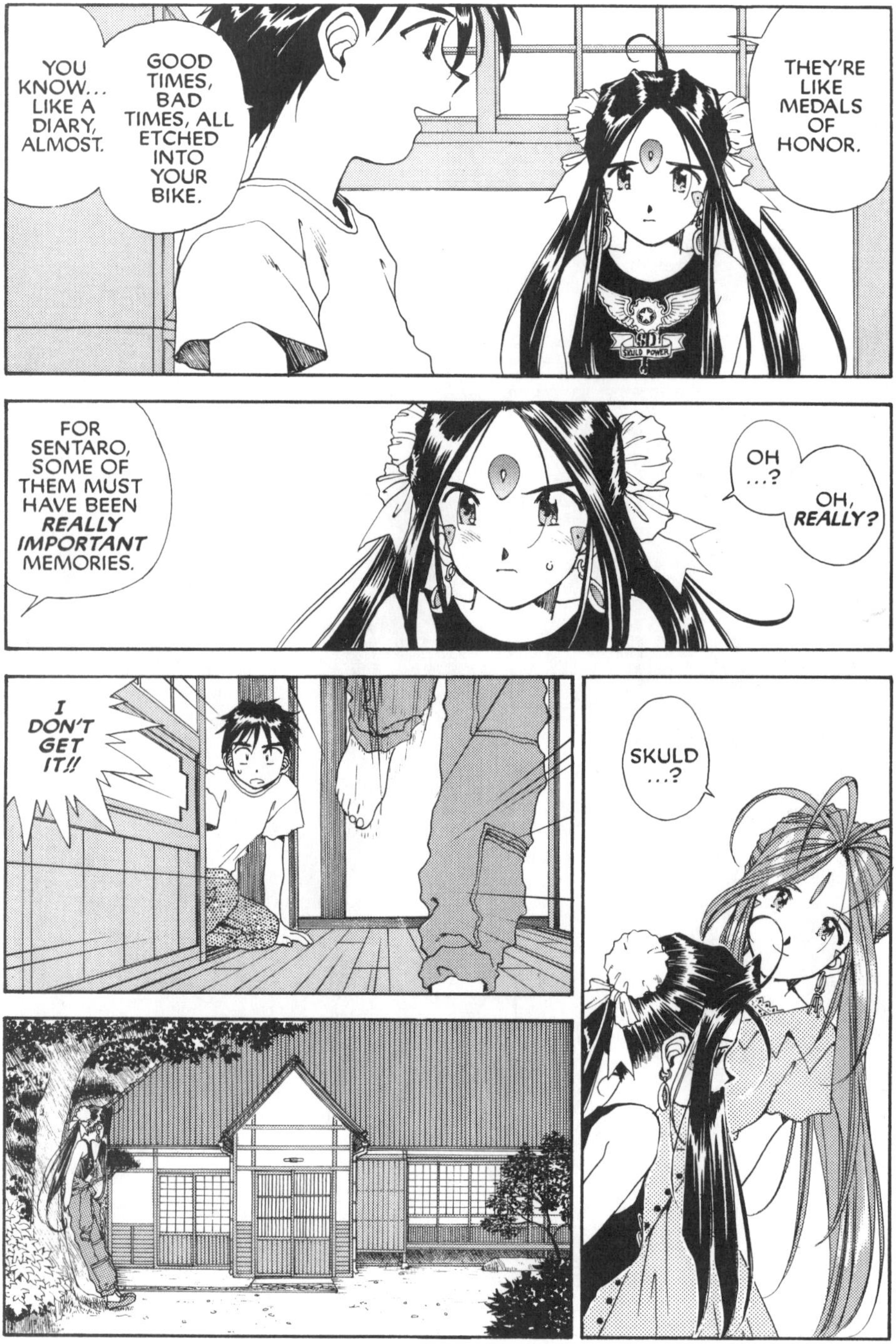
YOU KNOW... LIKE A DIARY, ALMOST.
GOOD TIMES, BAD TIMES, ALL ETCHED INTO YOUR BIKE.
THEY'RE LIKE MEDALS OF HONOR.
SKULD POWER
FOR SENTARO, SOME OF THEM MUST HAVE BEEN *REALLY IMPORTANT* MEMORIES.
OH ...?
OH, *REALLY?*
I DON'T GET IT!!
SKULD ...?

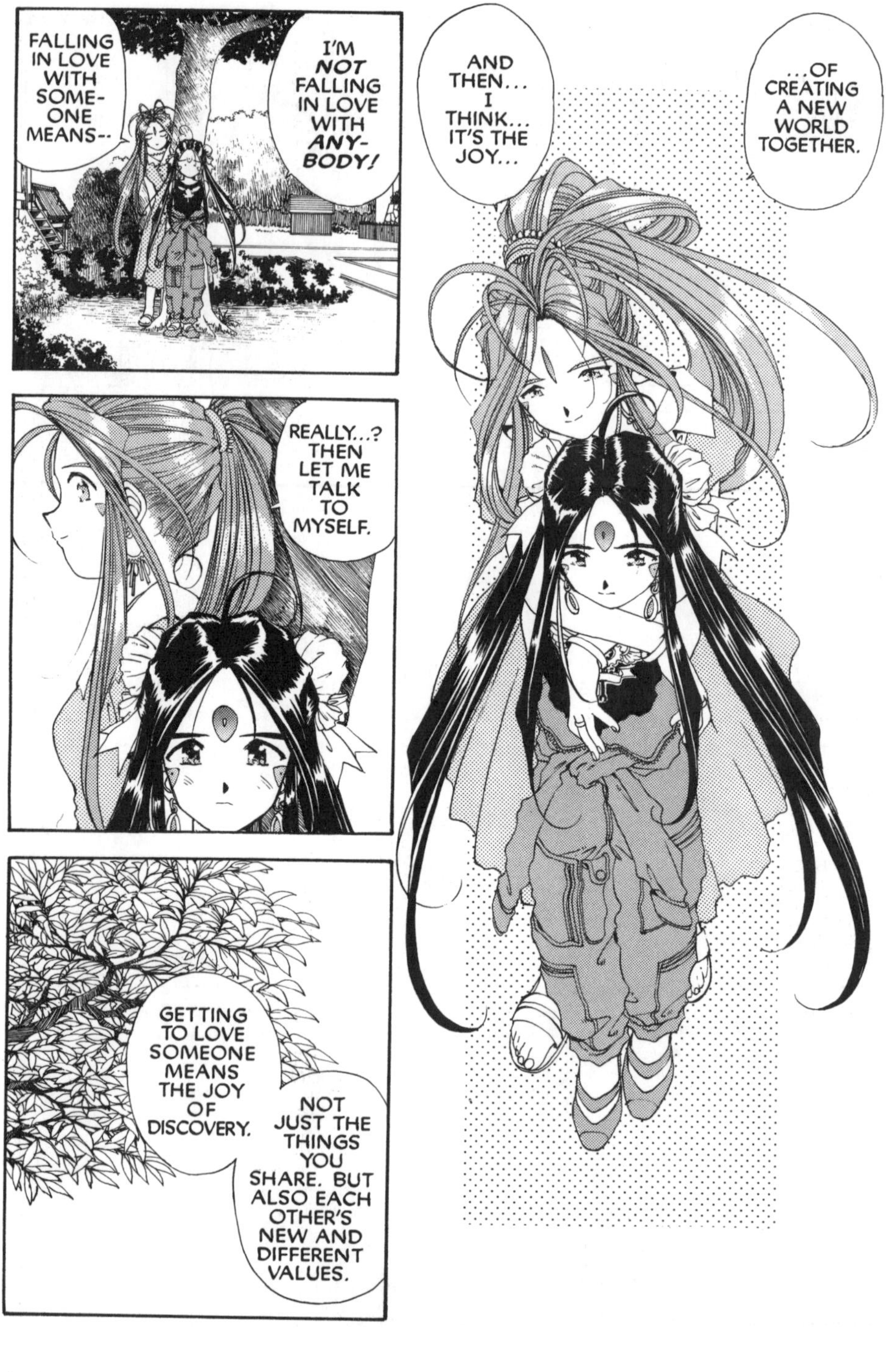
FALLING IN LOVE WITH SOME-ONE MEANS--
I'M NOT FALLING IN LOVE WITH ANY-BODY!
REALLY...? THEN LET ME TALK TO MYSELF.
GETTING TO LOVE SOMEONE MEANS THE JOY OF DISCOVERY.
NOT JUST THE THINGS YOU SHARE. BUT ALSO EACH OTHER'S NEW AND DIFFERENT VALUES.
AND THEN... I THINK... IT'S THE JOY...
...OF CREATING A NEW WORLD TOGETHER.

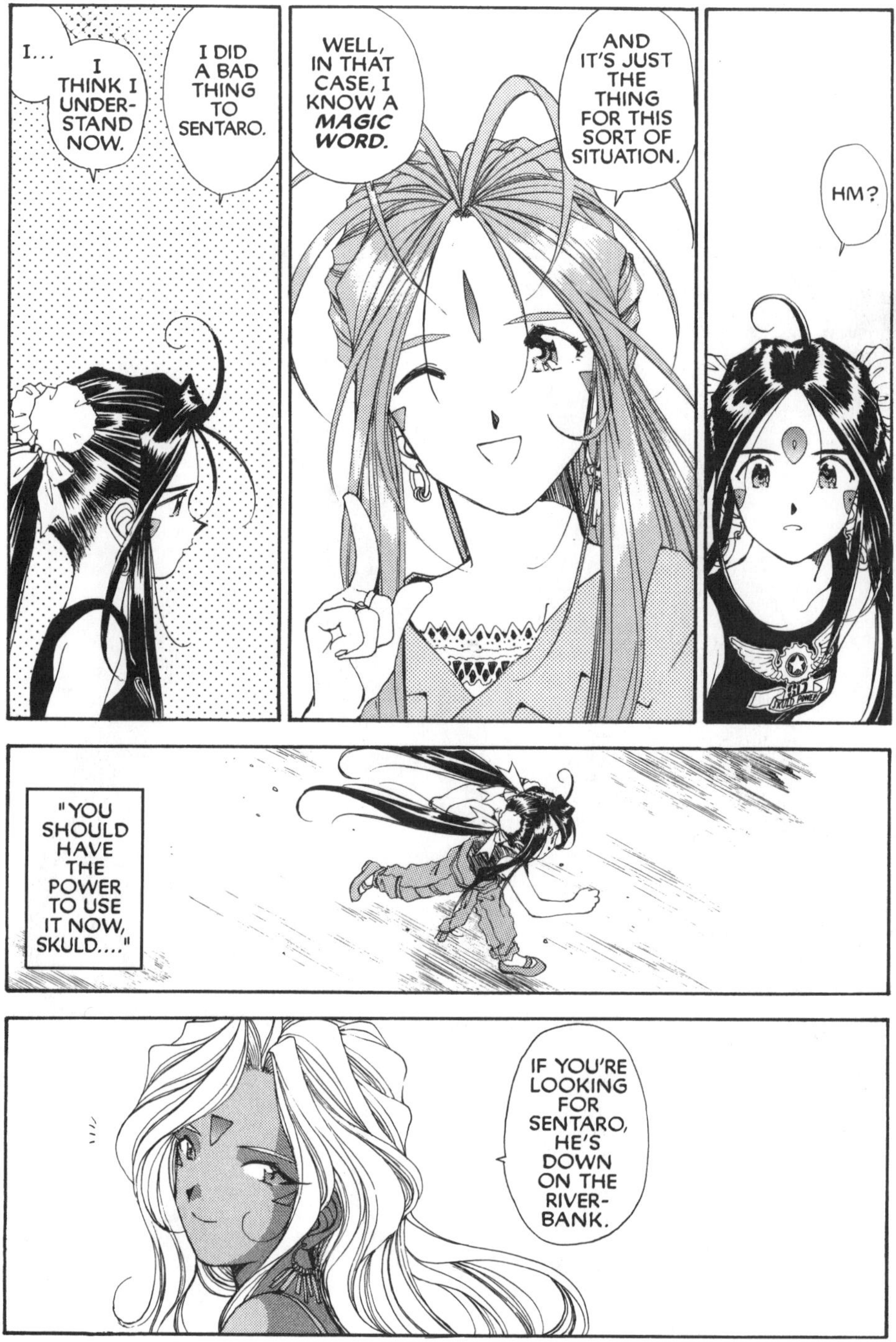
I...
I THINK I UNDERSTAND NOW.
I DID A BAD THING TO SENTARO.
WELL, IN THAT CASE, I KNOW A *MAGIC WORD.*
AND IT'S JUST THE THING FOR THIS SORT OF SITUATION.
HM?
"YOU SHOULD HAVE THE POWER TO USE IT NOW, SKULD...."
IF YOU'RE LOOKING FOR SENTARO, HE'S DOWN ON THE RIVERBANK.

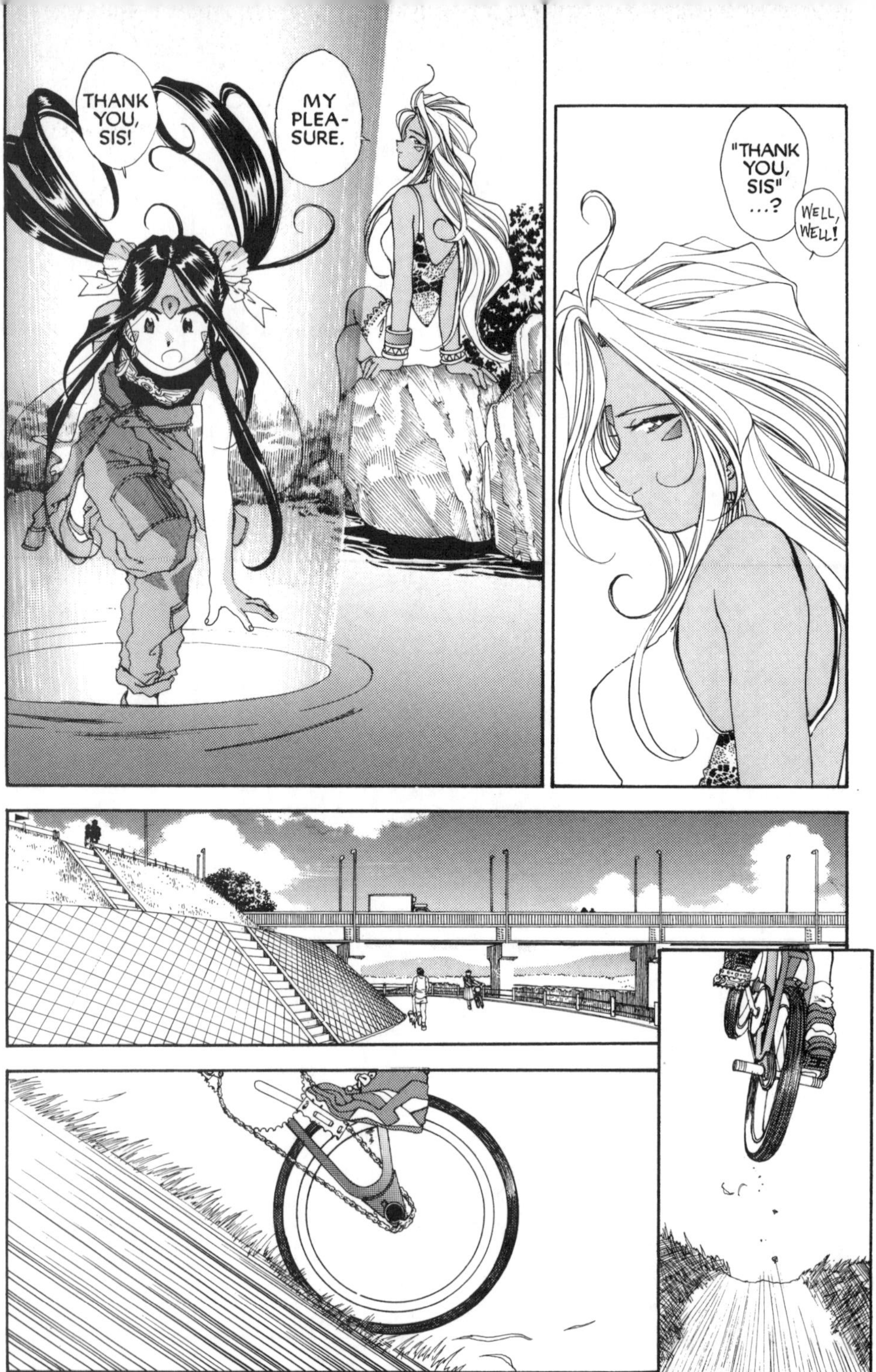
THANK YOU, SIS!
MY PLEASURE.
"THANK YOU, SIS" ...?
WELL, WELL!

…!

SHAKK

WHNCH

GURK!

!!

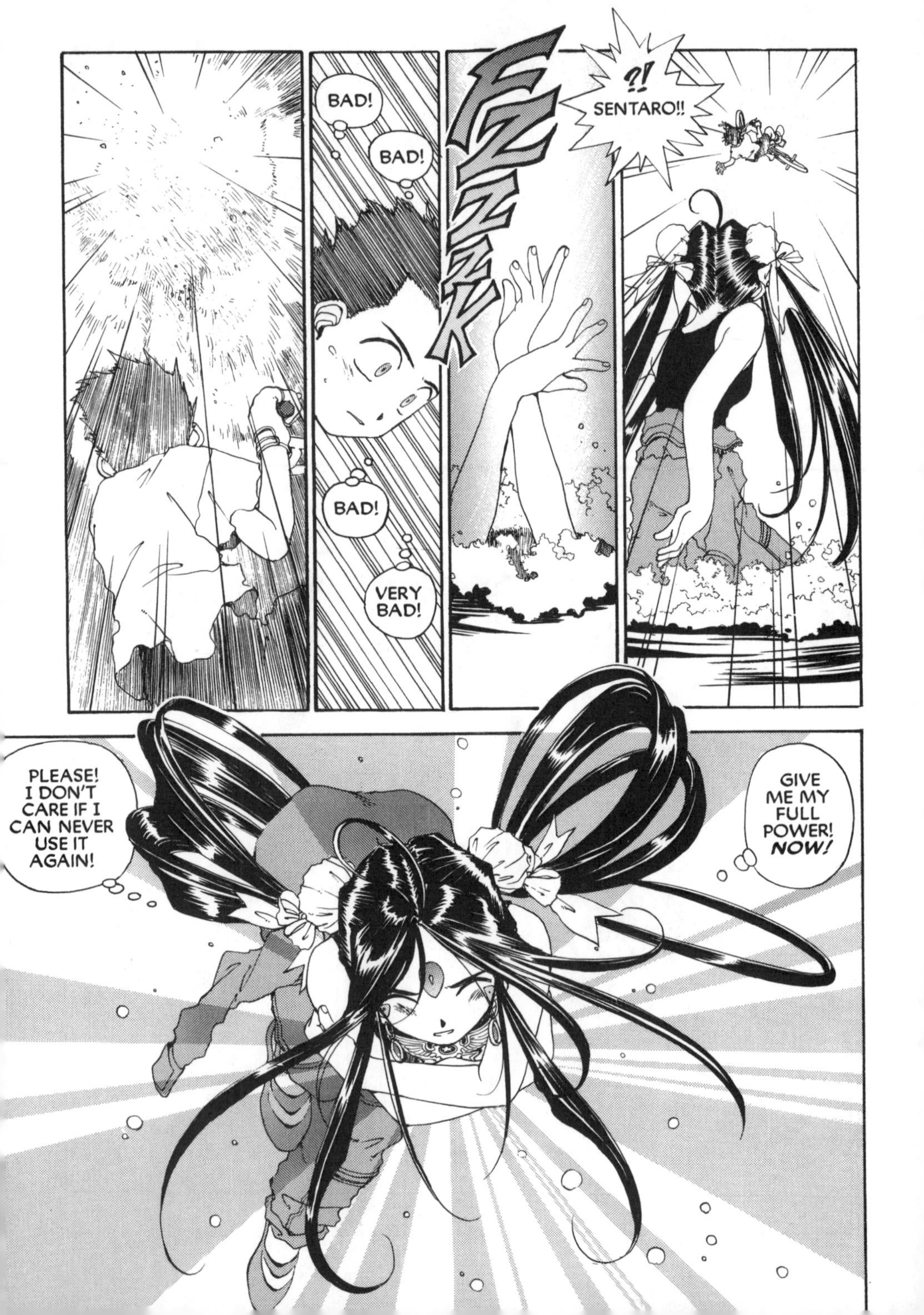
BAD!
BAD!
BAD!
VERY BAD!
FZZZZK
?! SENTARO!!
PLEASE! I DON'T CARE IF I CAN NEVER USE IT AGAIN!
GIVE ME MY FULL POWER! NOW!

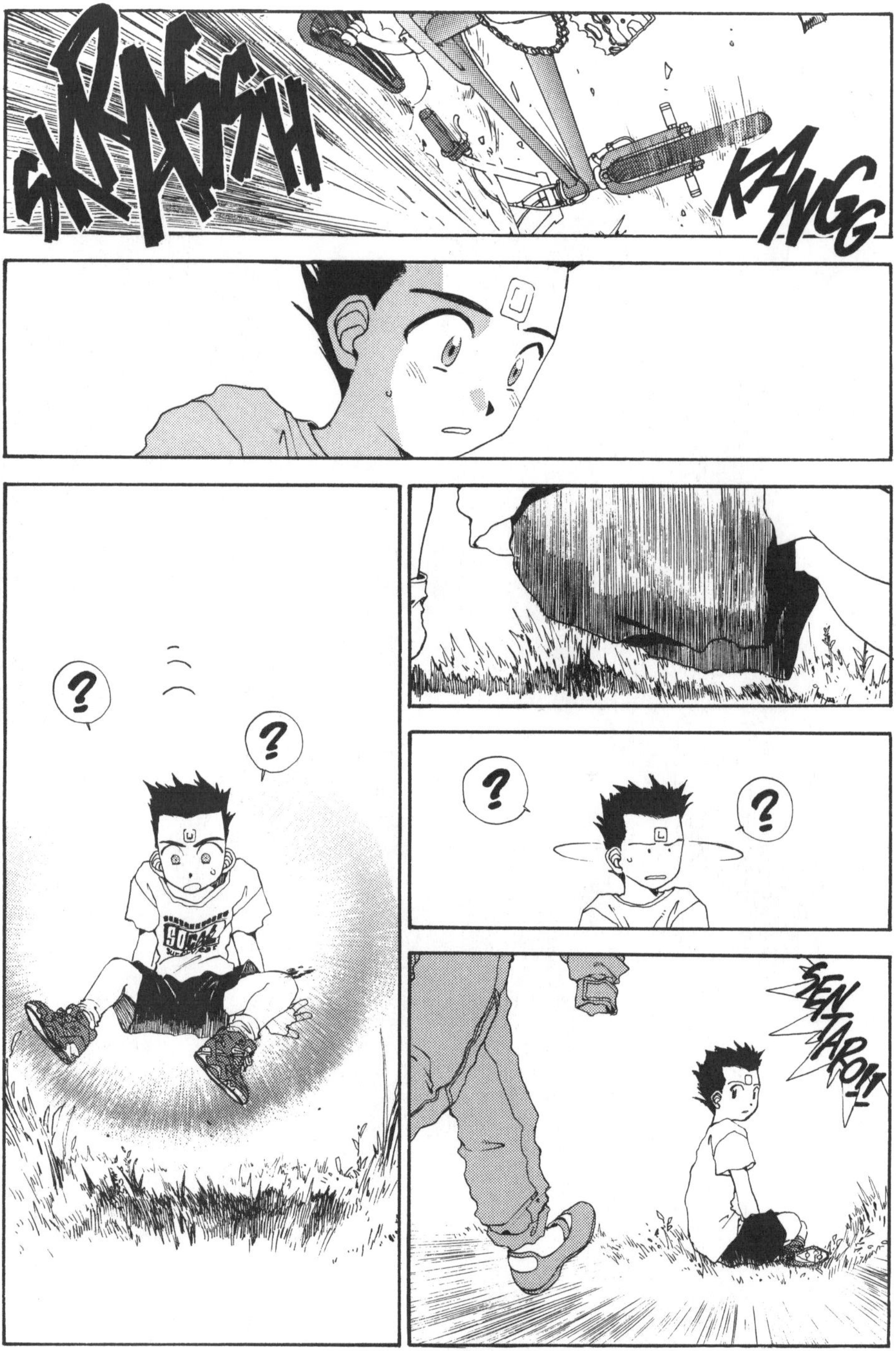
SKRASSH
KANGG
?
?
?
?
SENTARO!!

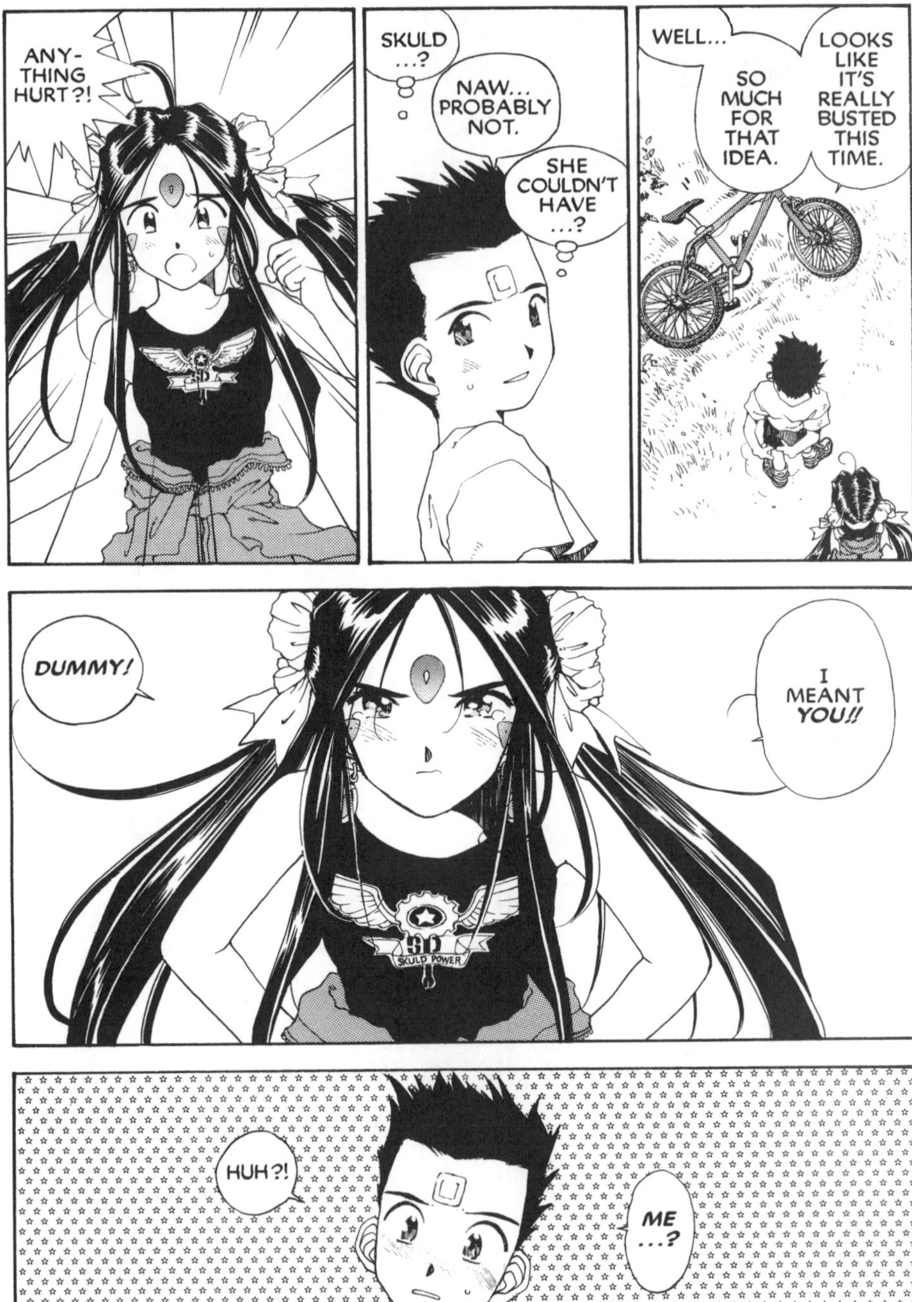
ANY-THING HURT?!
SKULD ...?
NAW... PROBABLY NOT.
SHE COULDN'T HAVE ...?
WELL...
LOOKS LIKE IT'S REALLY BUSTED THIS TIME.
SO MUCH FOR THAT IDEA.
DUMMY!
I MEANT *YOU!!*
SKULD POWER
HUH?!
ME ...?

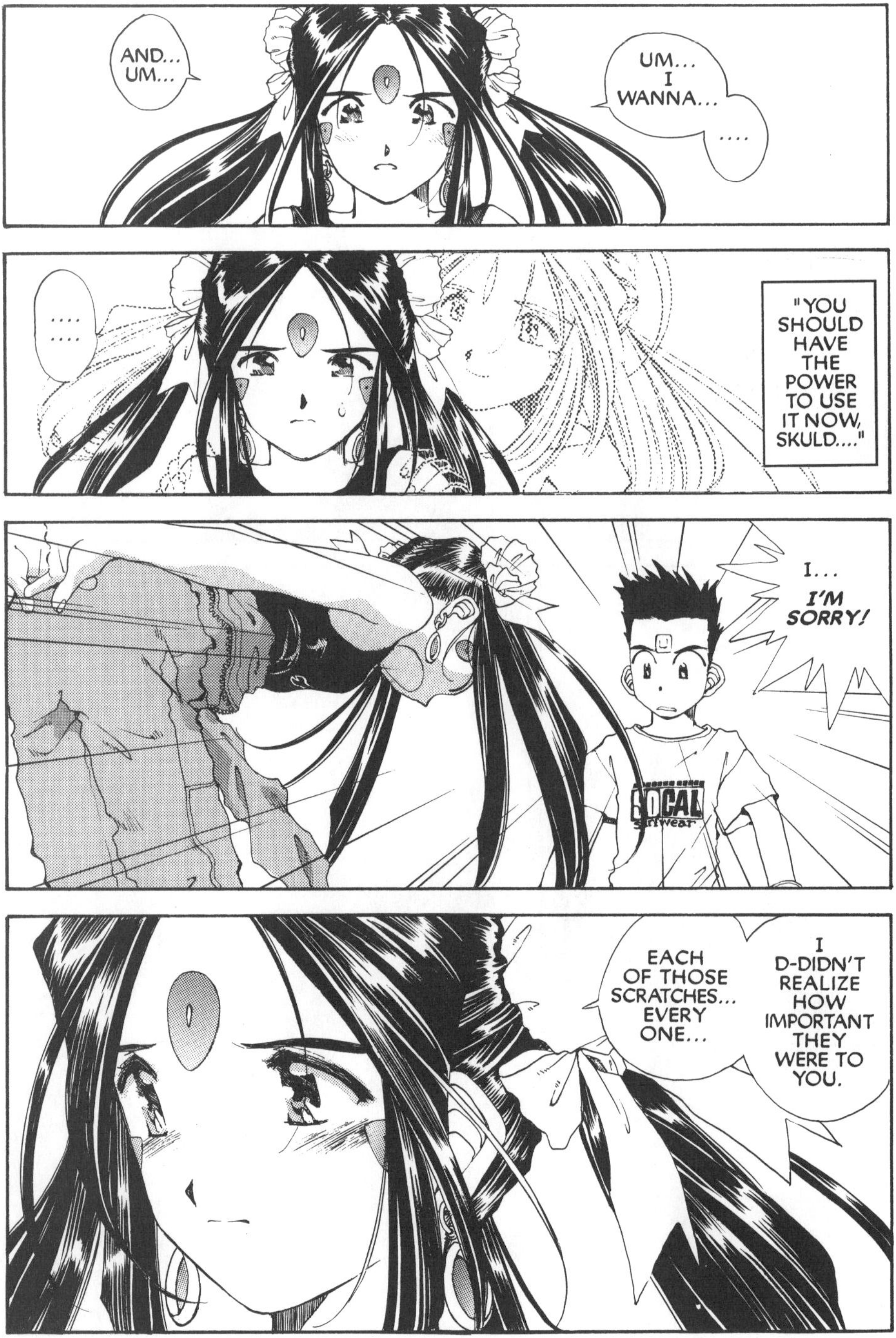
AND... UM...
UM... I WANNA...
....
....
....
"YOU SHOULD HAVE THE POWER TO USE IT NOW, SKULD...."
I... *I'M SORRY!*
SOCAL surfwear
EACH OF THOSE SCRATCHES... EVERY ONE...
I D-DIDN'T REALIZE HOW IMPORTANT THEY WERE TO YOU.

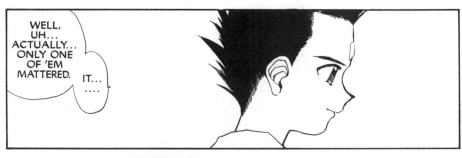

WELL, UH... ACTUALLY... ONLY ONE OF 'EM MATTERED. IT... ....

OH...? BUT THAT ONE WAS REALLY IMPORTANT, RIGHT?

AW, HEY, FORGET IT.

ANYWAY, YOU FIXED MY BIKE FOR ME, AND NOW JUST LOOK AT IT!

REALLY SCREWED UP, DIDN'T I?

SENTARO...? THAT REALLY IMPORTANT SCRATCH?

YOU WANNA KNOW WHY?

UM... YEAH.

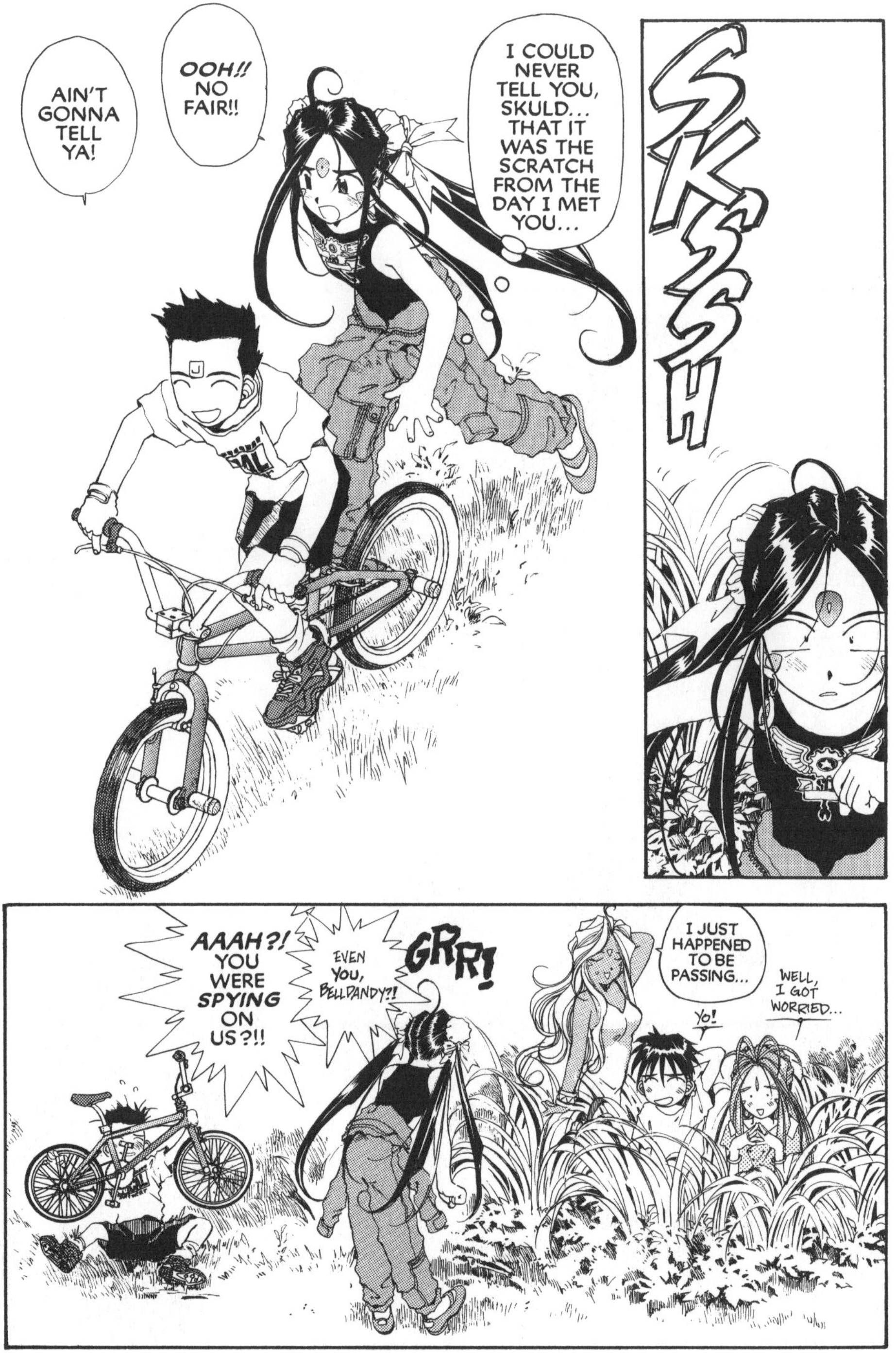
AIN'T GONNA TELL YA!
OOH!! NO FAIR!!
I COULD NEVER TELL YOU, SKULD... THAT IT WAS THE SCRATCH FROM THE DAY I MET YOU...
SKSSH
AAAH?! YOU WERE SPYING ON US?!!
EVEN YOU, BELLDANDY?!
GRR!
I JUST HAPPENED TO BE PASSING...
YO!
WELL, I GOT WORRIED...

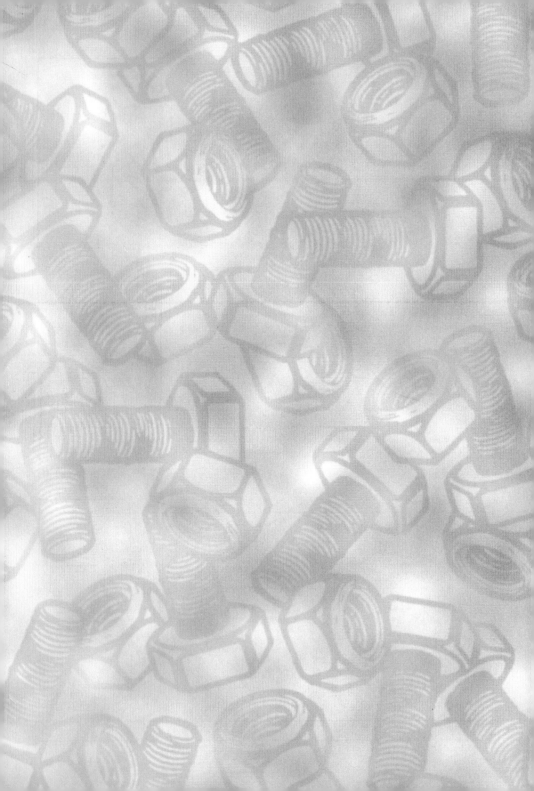

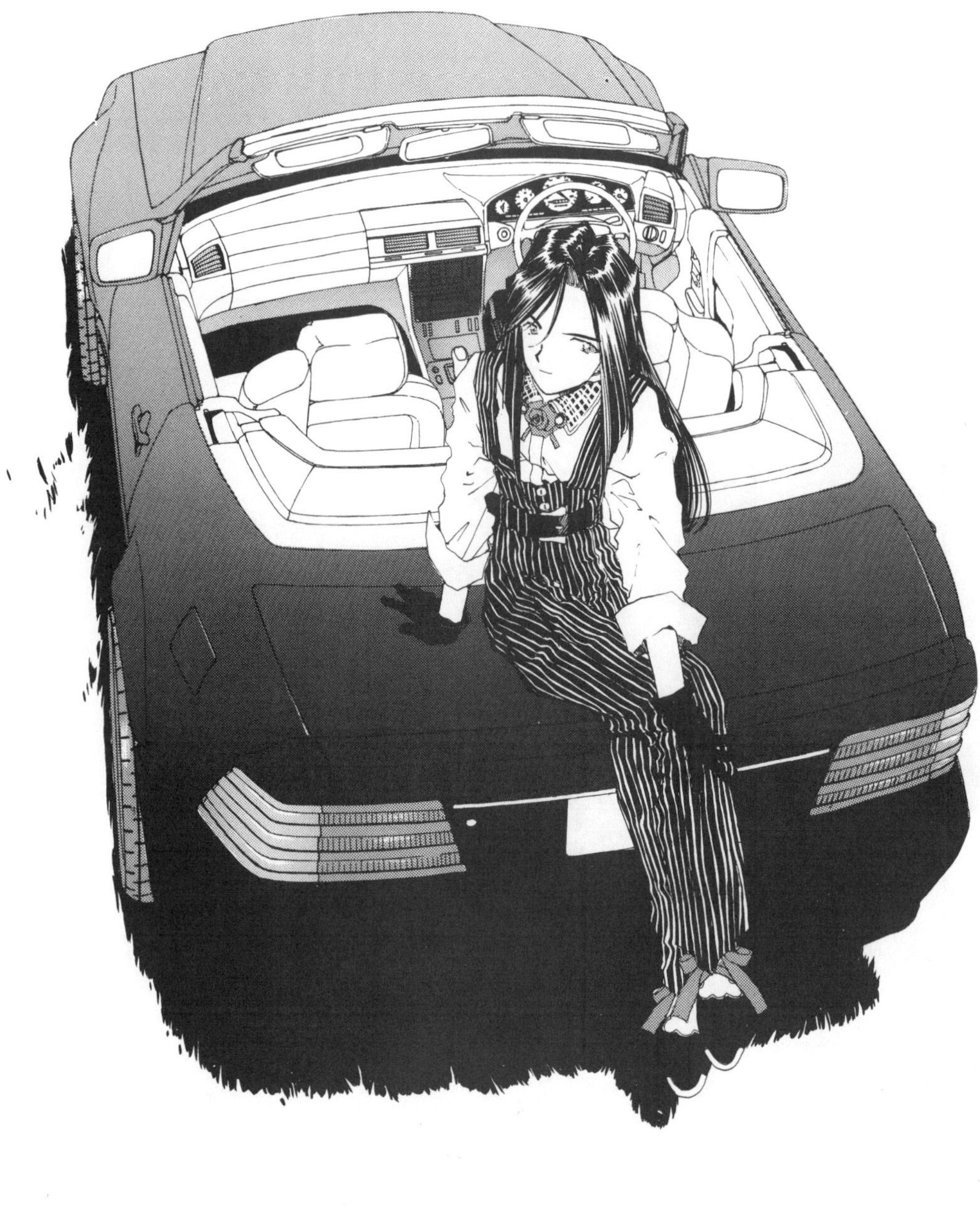

The Queen and the Goddess

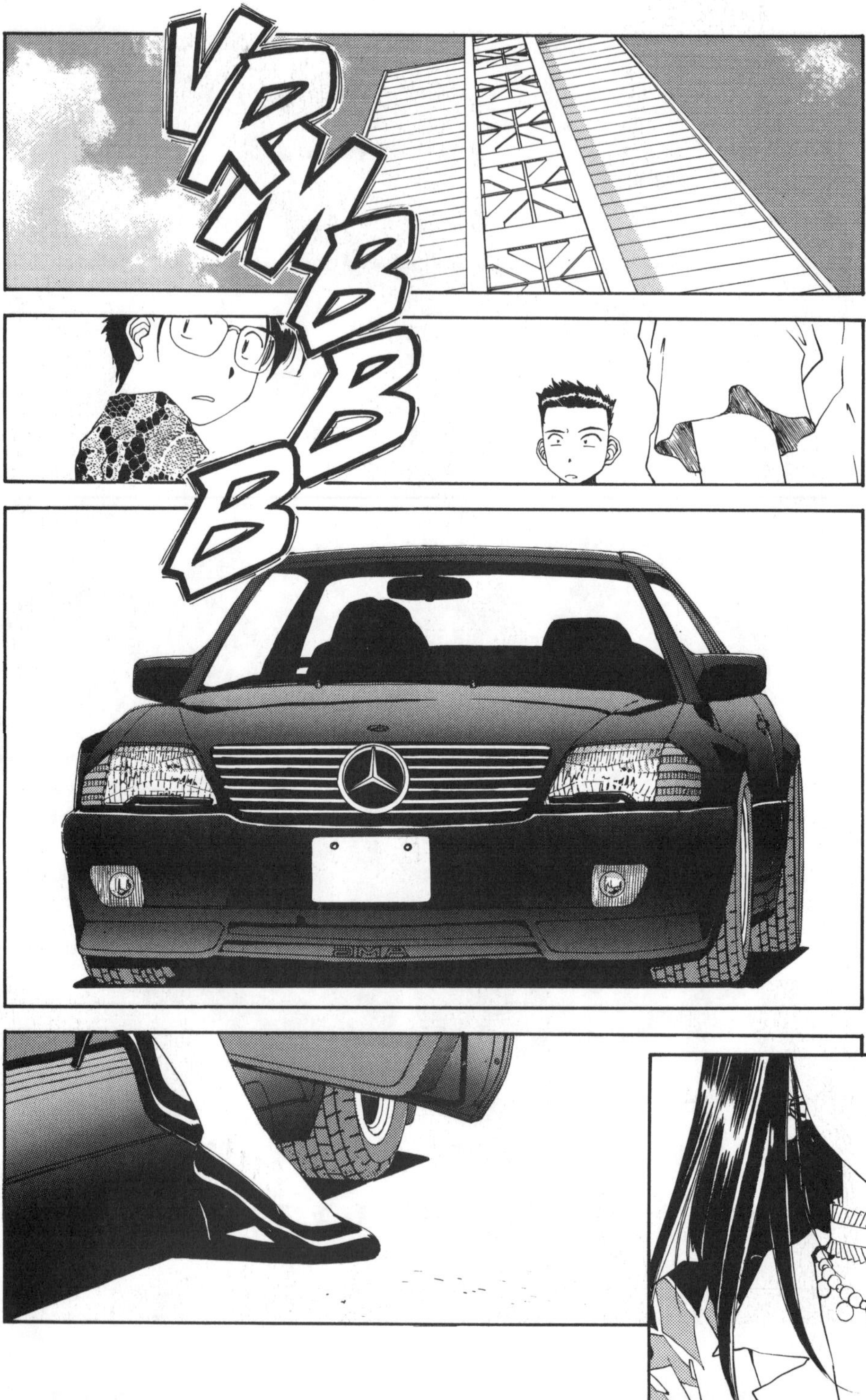
VRMBBB

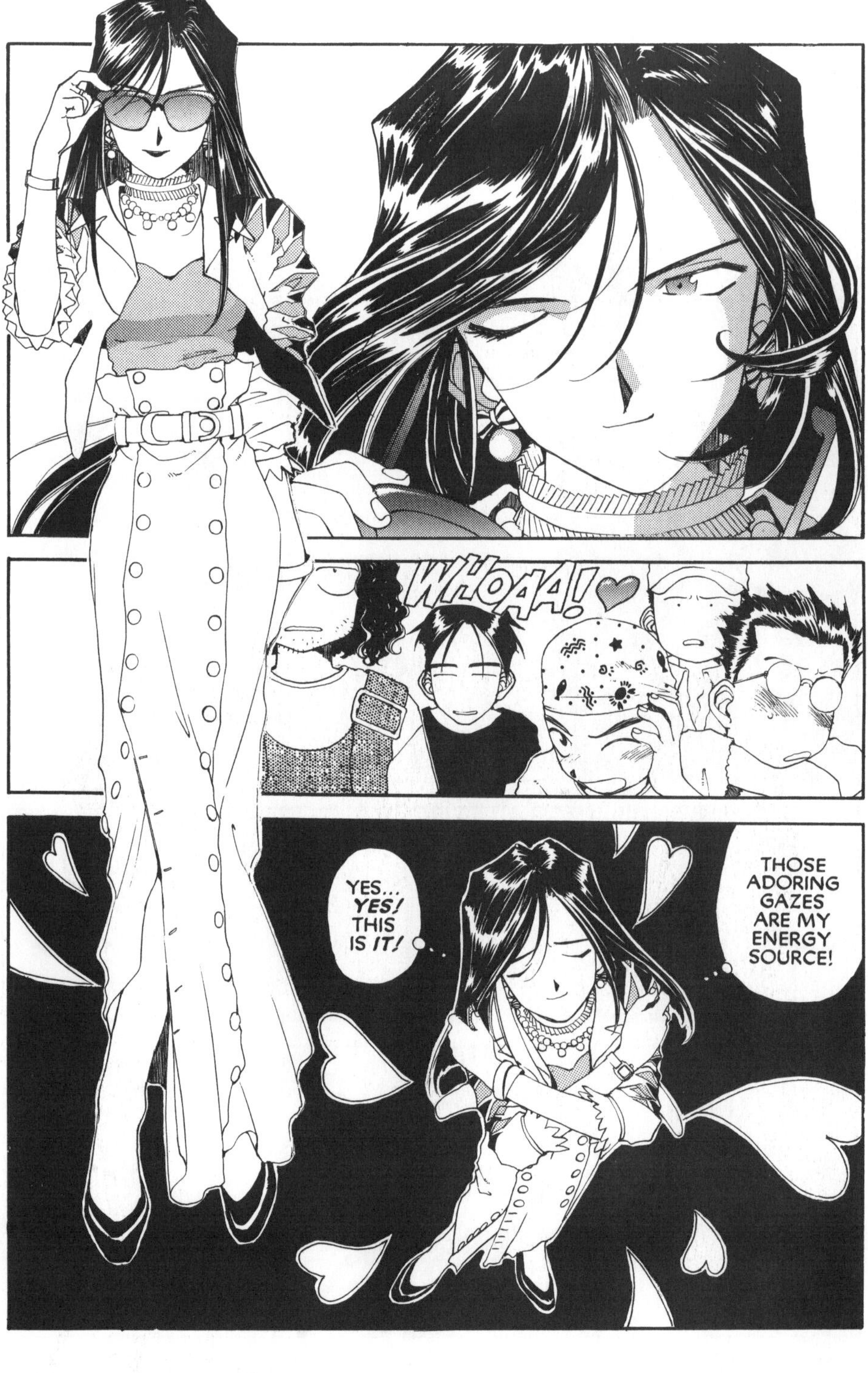
WHOAA!
YES... YES! THIS IS IT!
THOSE ADORING GAZES ARE MY ENERGY SOURCE!

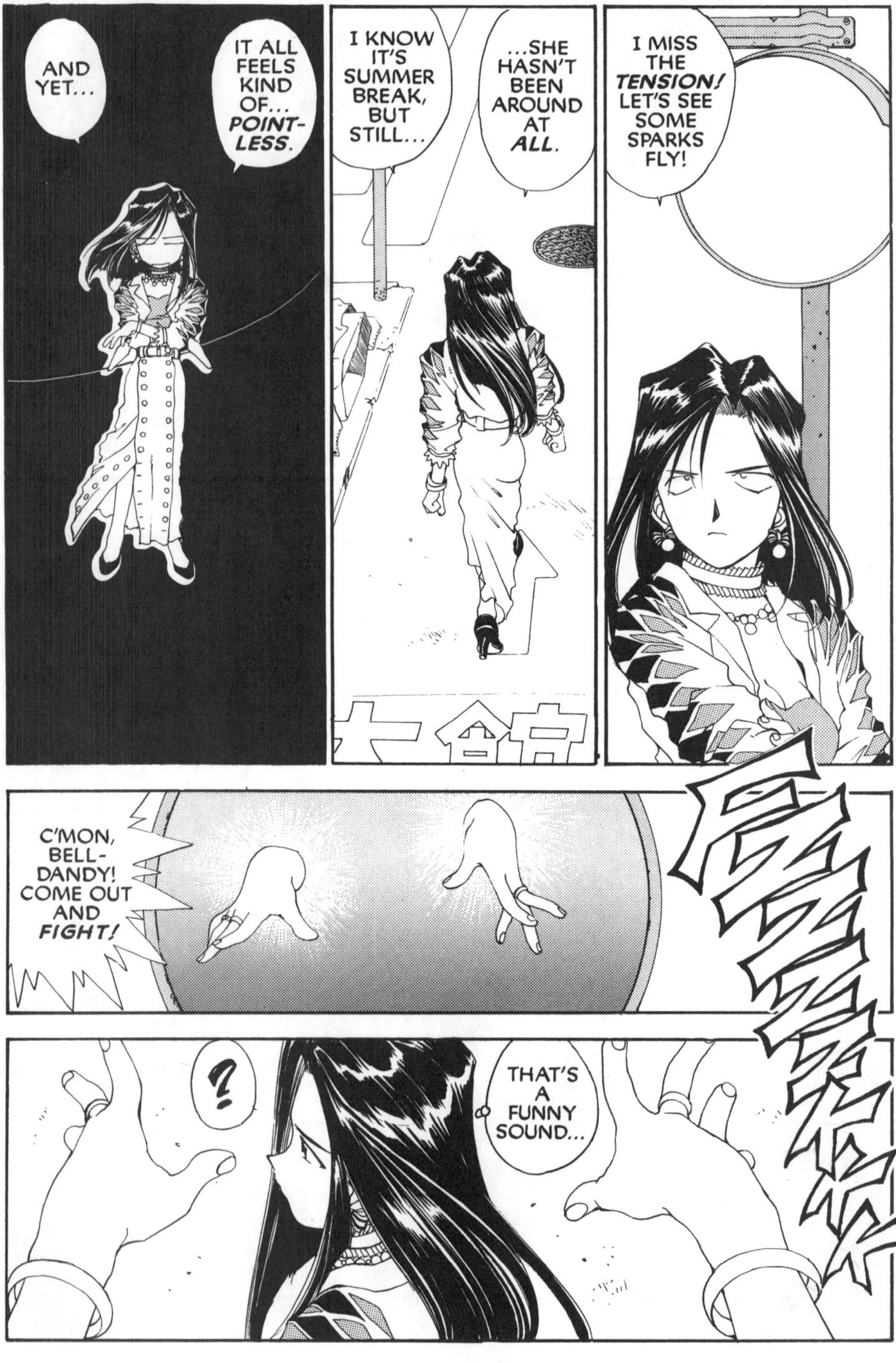
AND YET...
IT ALL FEELS KIND OF... POINTLESS.
I KNOW IT'S SUMMER BREAK, BUT STILL...
...SHE HASN'T BEEN AROUND AT ALL.
I MISS THE TENSION! LET'S SEE SOME SPARKS FLY!
C'MON, BELL-DANDY! COME OUT AND FIGHT!
?
THAT'S A FUNNY SOUND...

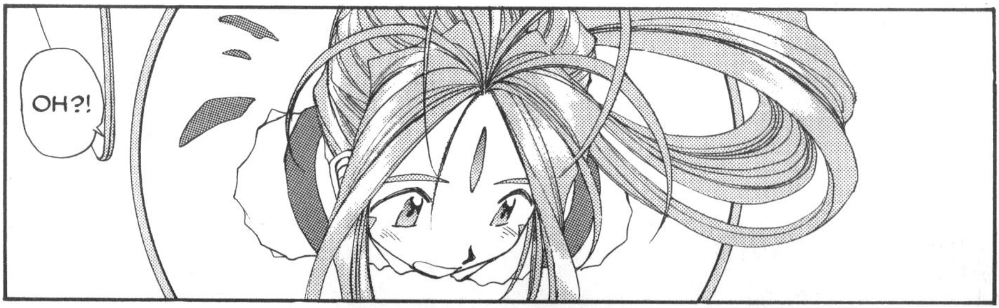
OH?!

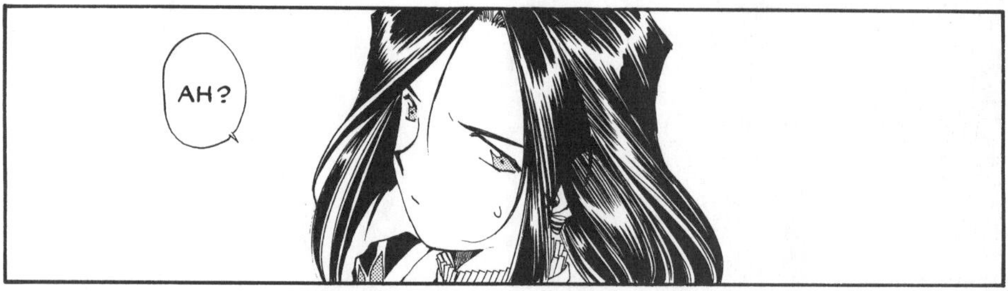
AH?

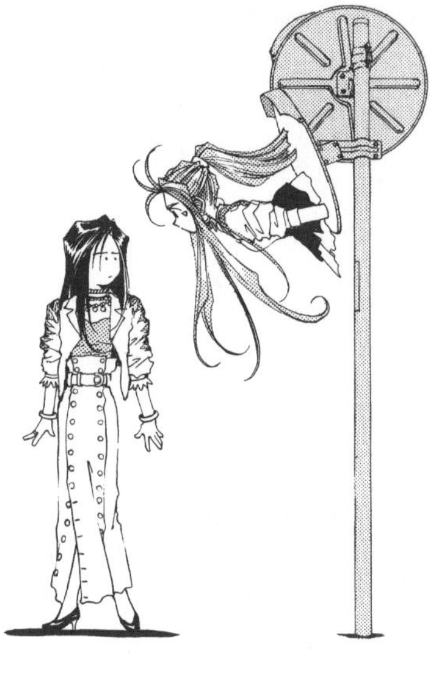

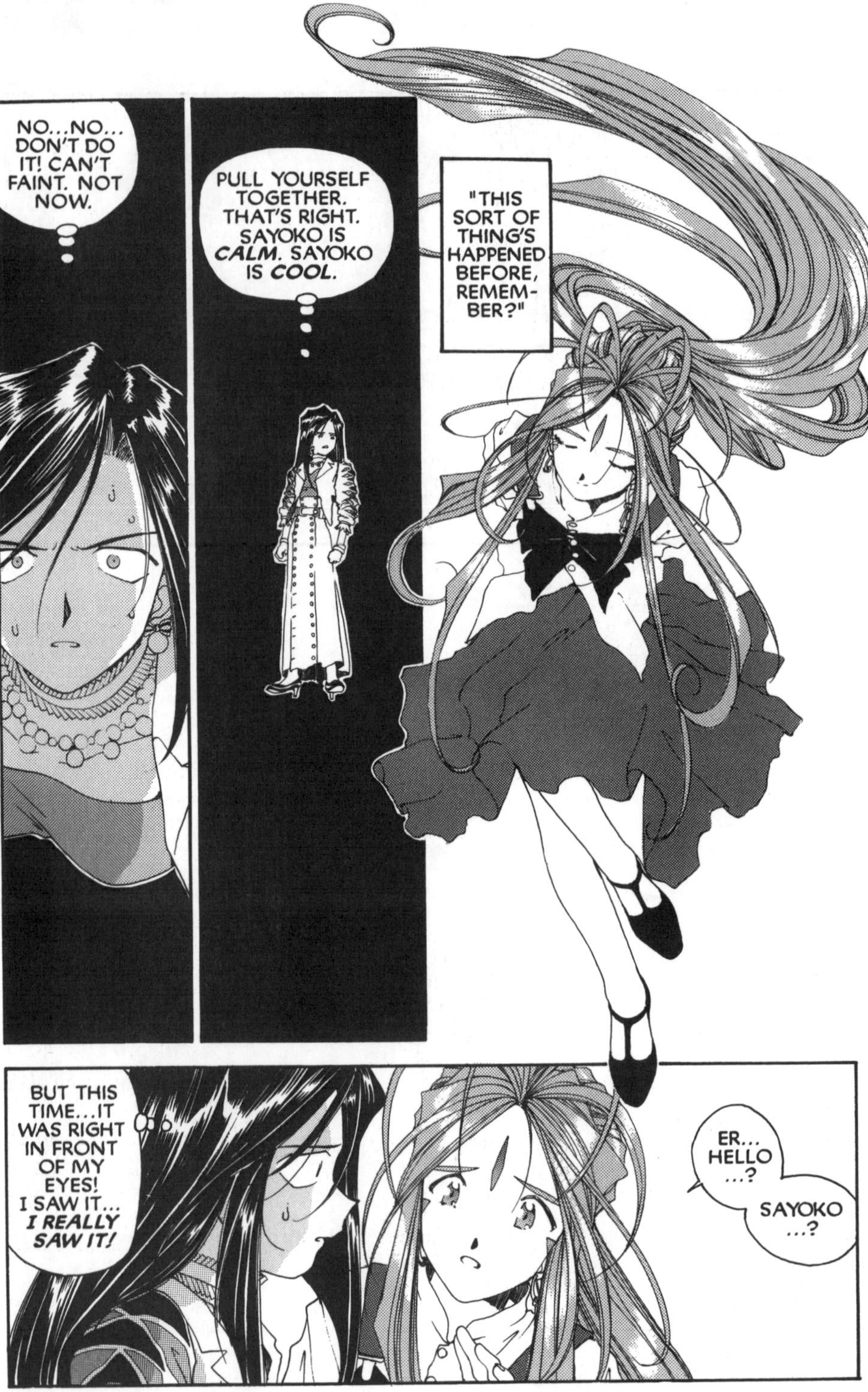
NO...NO... DON'T DO IT! CAN'T FAINT. NOT NOW.
PULL YOURSELF TOGETHER. THAT'S RIGHT. SAYOKO IS *CALM*. SAYOKO IS *COOL*.
"THIS SORT OF THING'S HAPPENED BEFORE, REMEMBER?"
BUT THIS TIME...IT WAS RIGHT IN FRONT OF MY EYES! I SAW IT... *I REALLY SAW IT!*
ER... HELLO ...?
SAYOKO ...?

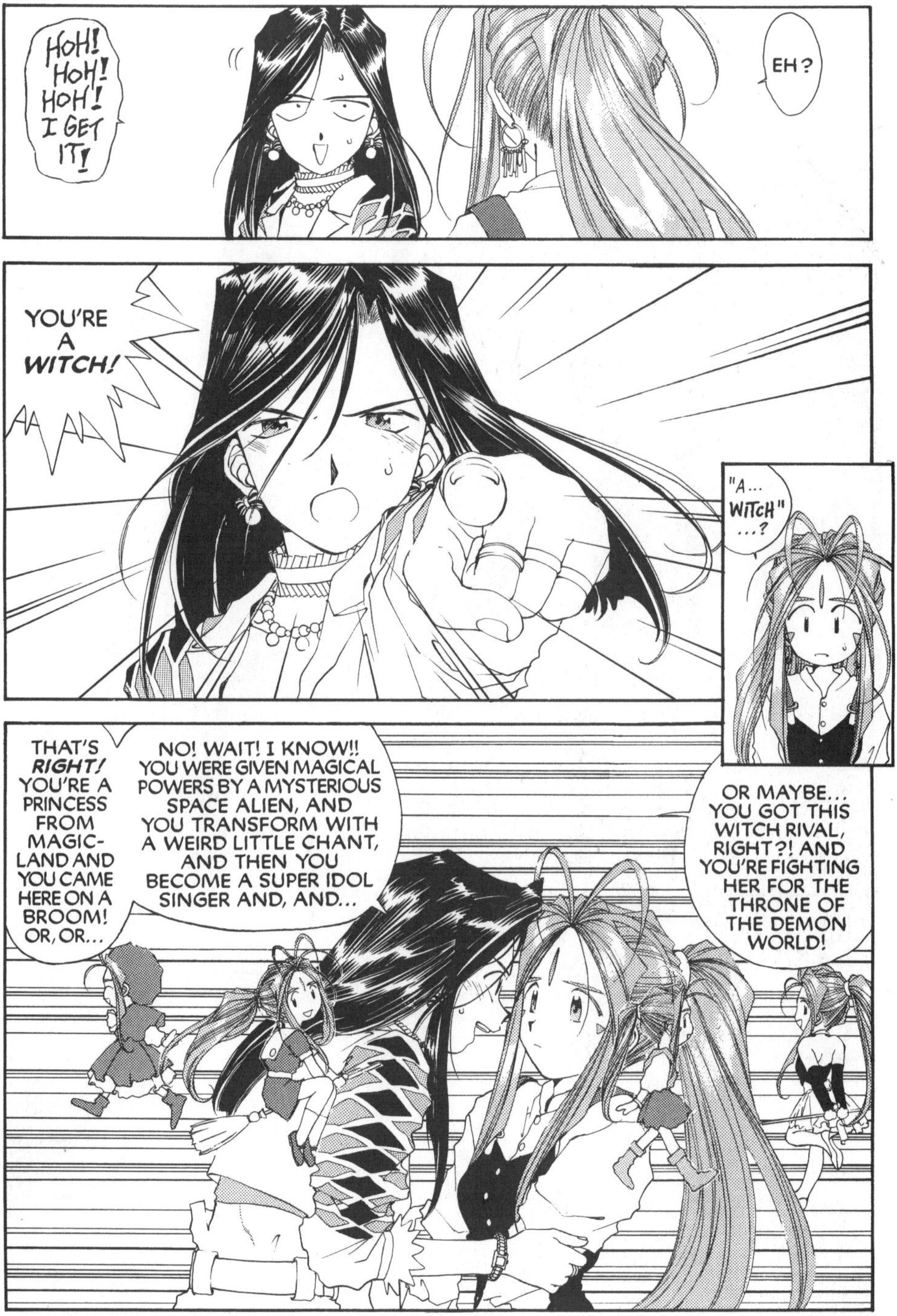
HOH! HOH! HOH! I GET IT!
EH?
YOU'RE A WITCH!
"A... WITCH" ...?
THAT'S RIGHT! YOU'RE A PRINCESS FROM MAGIC-LAND AND YOU CAME HERE ON A BROOM! OR, OR...
NO! WAIT! I KNOW!! YOU WERE GIVEN MAGICAL POWERS BY A MYSTERIOUS SPACE ALIEN, AND YOU TRANSFORM WITH A WEIRD LITTLE CHANT, AND THEN YOU BECOME A SUPER IDOL SINGER AND, AND...
OR MAYBE... YOU GOT THIS WITCH RIVAL, RIGHT?! AND YOU'RE FIGHTING HER FOR THE THRONE OF THE DEMON WORLD!

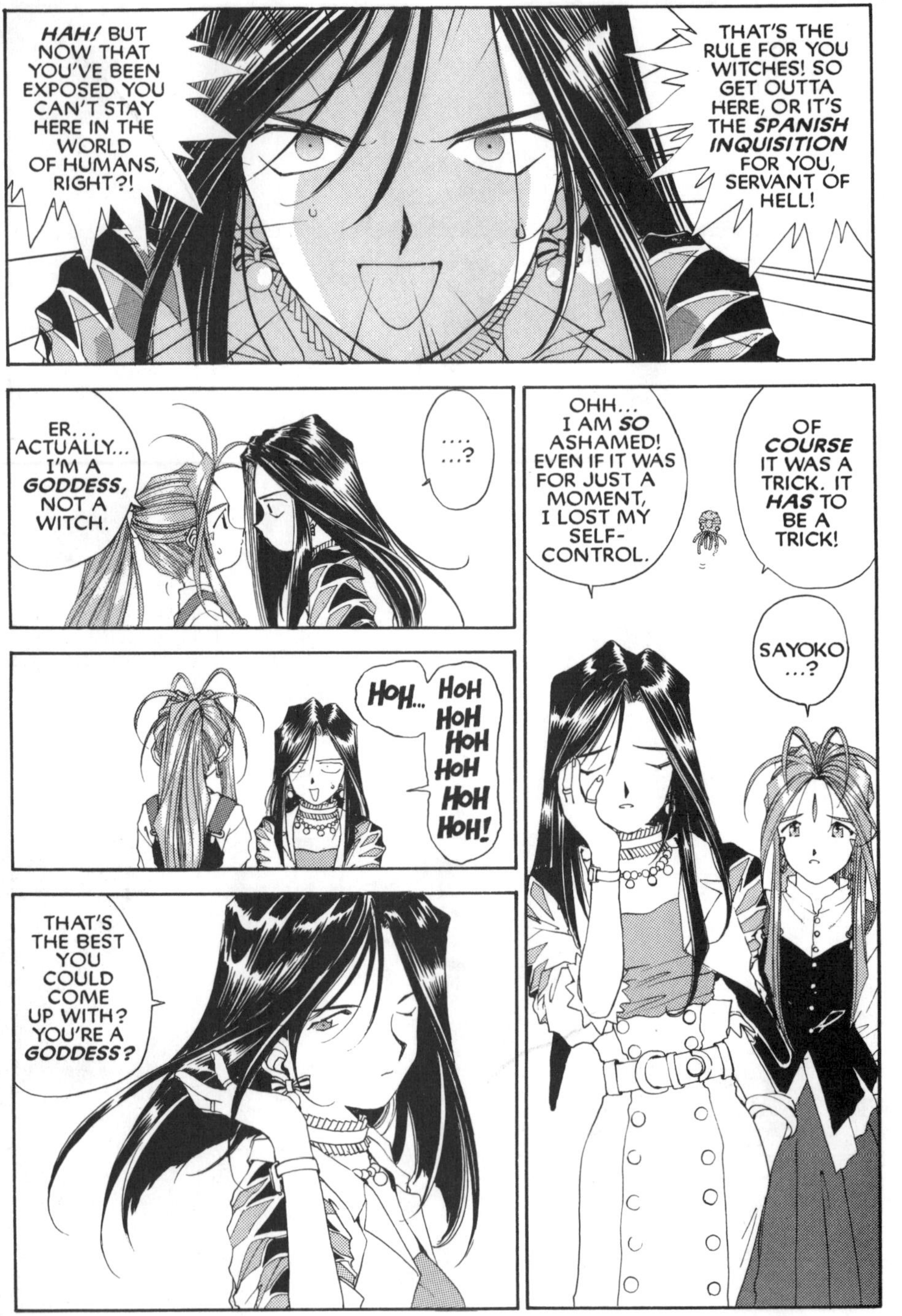
HAH! BUT NOW THAT YOU'VE BEEN EXPOSED YOU CAN'T STAY HERE IN THE WORLD OF HUMANS, RIGHT?!
THAT'S THE RULE FOR YOU WITCHES! SO GET OUTTA HERE, OR IT'S THE SPANISH INQUISITION FOR YOU, SERVANT OF HELL!
ER... ACTUALLY... I'M A GODDESS, NOT A WITCH.
...., ...?
HOH... HOH HOH HOH HOH HOH HOH!
THAT'S THE BEST YOU COULD COME UP WITH? YOU'RE A GODDESS?
OHH... I AM SO ASHAMED! EVEN IF IT WAS FOR JUST A MOMENT, I LOST MY SELF-CONTROL.
OF COURSE IT WAS A TRICK. IT HAS TO BE A TRICK!
SAYOKO ...?

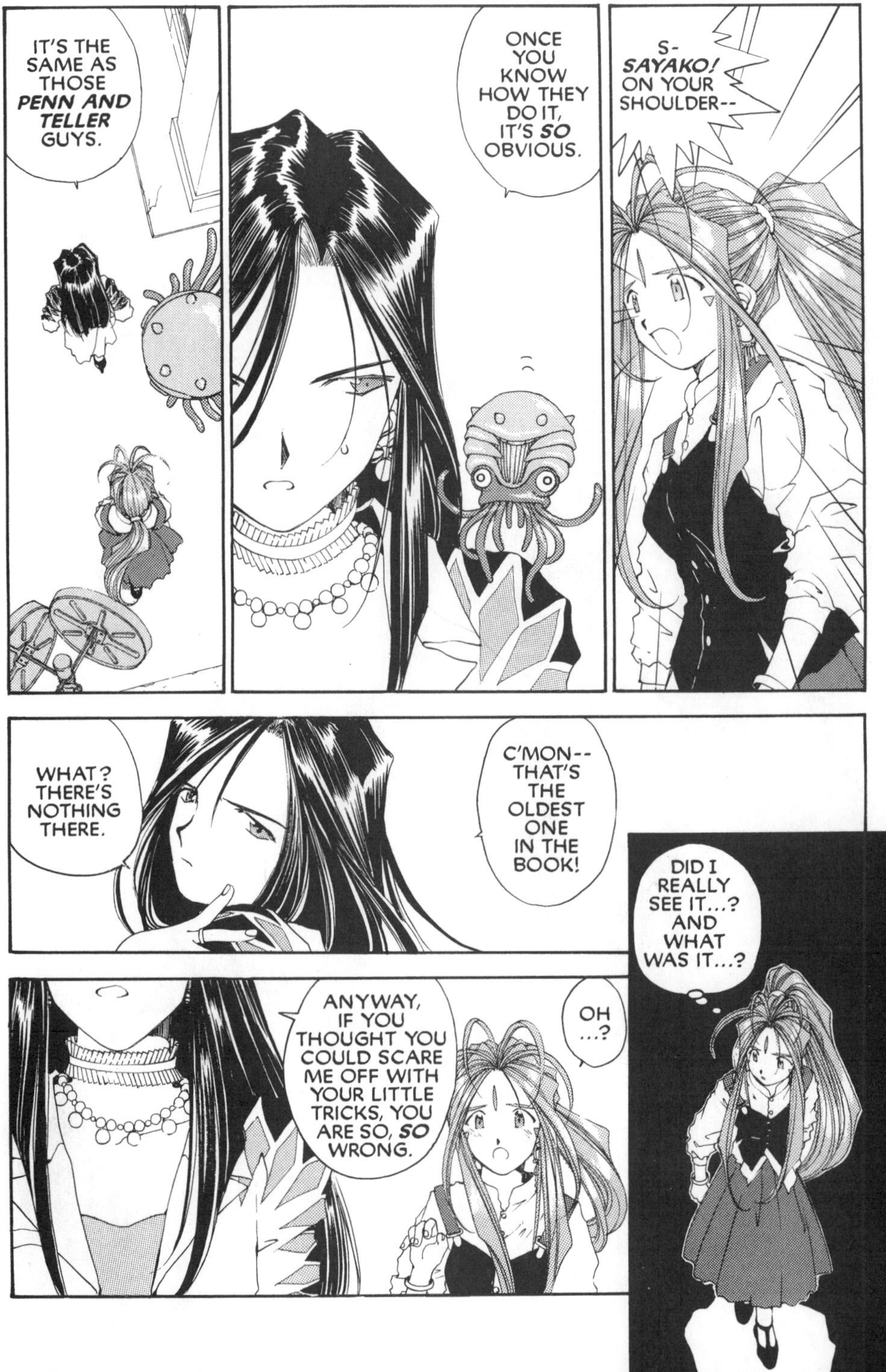
IT'S THE SAME AS THOSE PENN AND TELLER GUYS.
ONCE YOU KNOW HOW THEY DO IT, IT'S SO OBVIOUS.
S- SAYAKO! ON YOUR SHOULDER--
WHAT? THERE'S NOTHING THERE.
C'MON-- THAT'S THE OLDEST ONE IN THE BOOK!
DID I REALLY SEE IT...? AND WHAT WAS IT...?
ANYWAY, IF YOU THOUGHT YOU COULD SCARE ME OFF WITH YOUR LITTLE TRICKS, YOU ARE SO, SO WRONG.
OH ...?

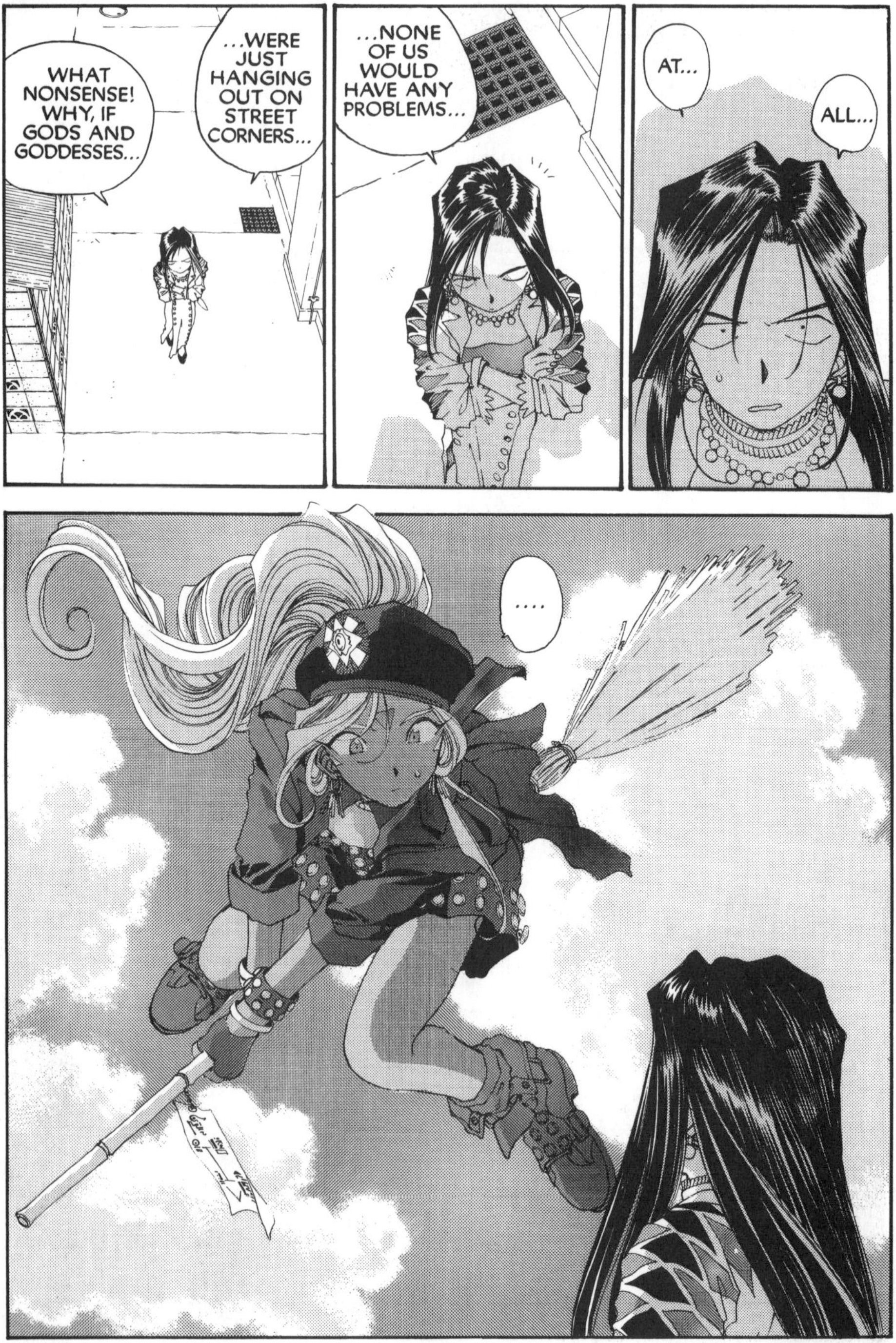
WHAT NONSENSE! WHY, IF GODS AND GODDESSES...
...WERE JUST HANGING OUT ON STREET CORNERS...
...NONE OF US WOULD HAVE ANY PROBLEMS...
AT...
ALL...
....

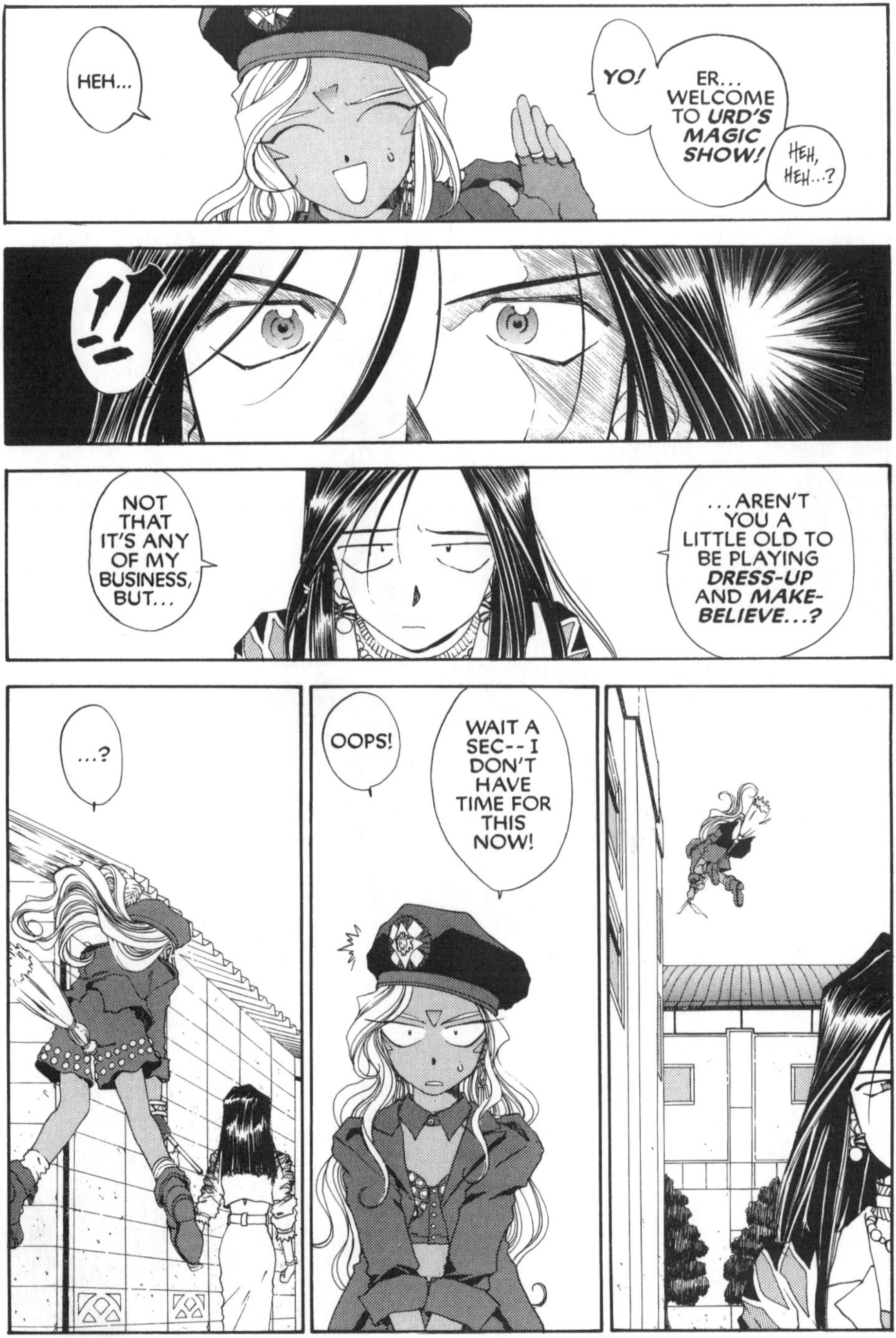
HEH...
YO!
ER... WELCOME TO URD'S MAGIC SHOW!
HEH, HEH...?
!
NOT THAT IT'S ANY OF MY BUSINESS, BUT...
...AREN'T YOU A LITTLE OLD TO BE PLAYING DRESS-UP AND MAKE-BELIEVE...?
...?
OOPS!
WAIT A SEC-- I DON'T HAVE TIME FOR THIS NOW!

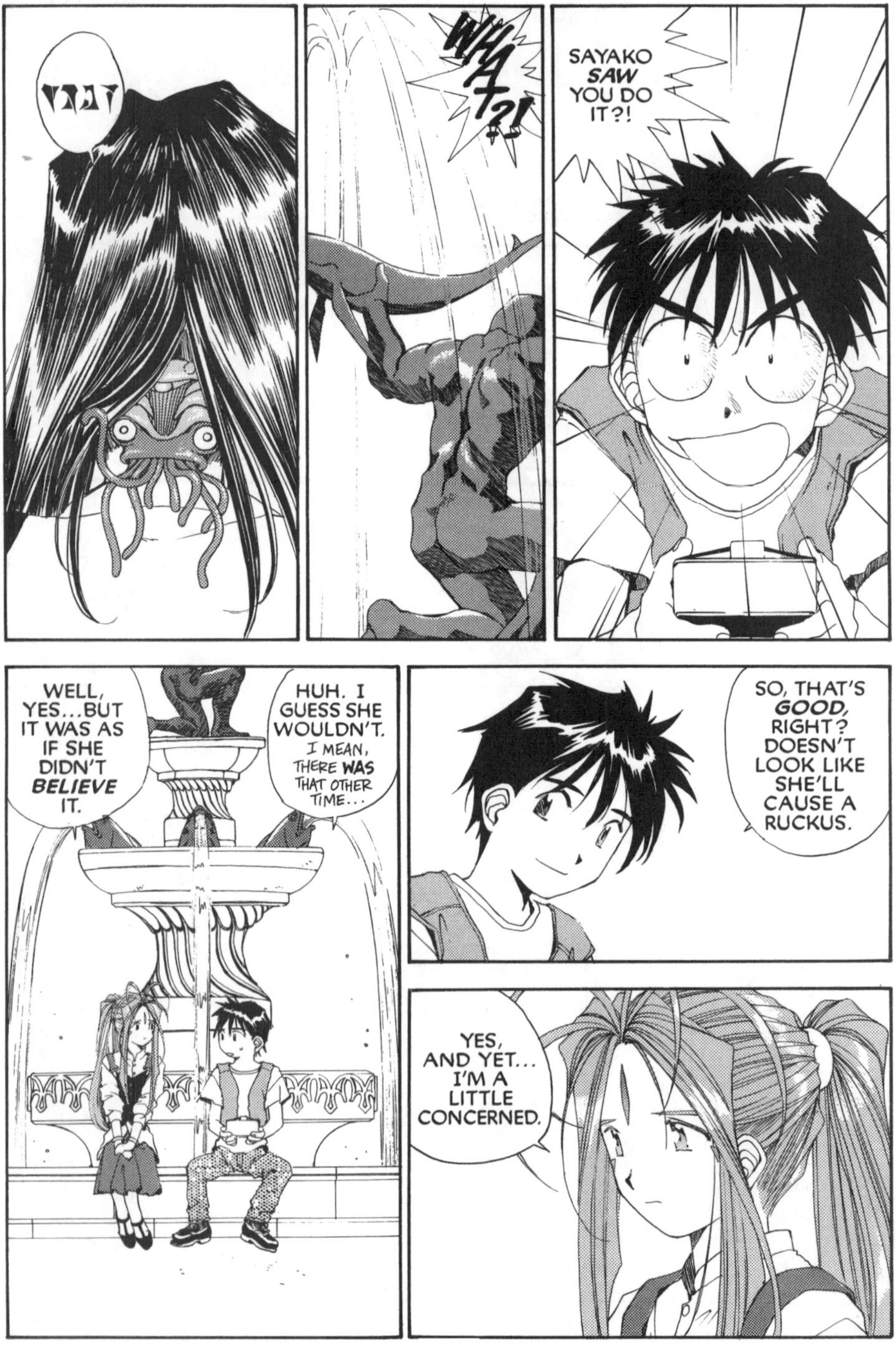
WHAT?!
SAYAKO SAW YOU DO IT?!
WELL, YES...BUT IT WAS AS IF SHE DIDN'T BELIEVE IT.
HUH. I GUESS SHE WOULDN'T. I MEAN, THERE WAS THAT OTHER TIME...
SO, THAT'S GOOD, RIGHT? DOESN'T LOOK LIKE SHE'LL CAUSE A RUCKUS.
YES, AND YET... I'M A LITTLE CONCERNED.

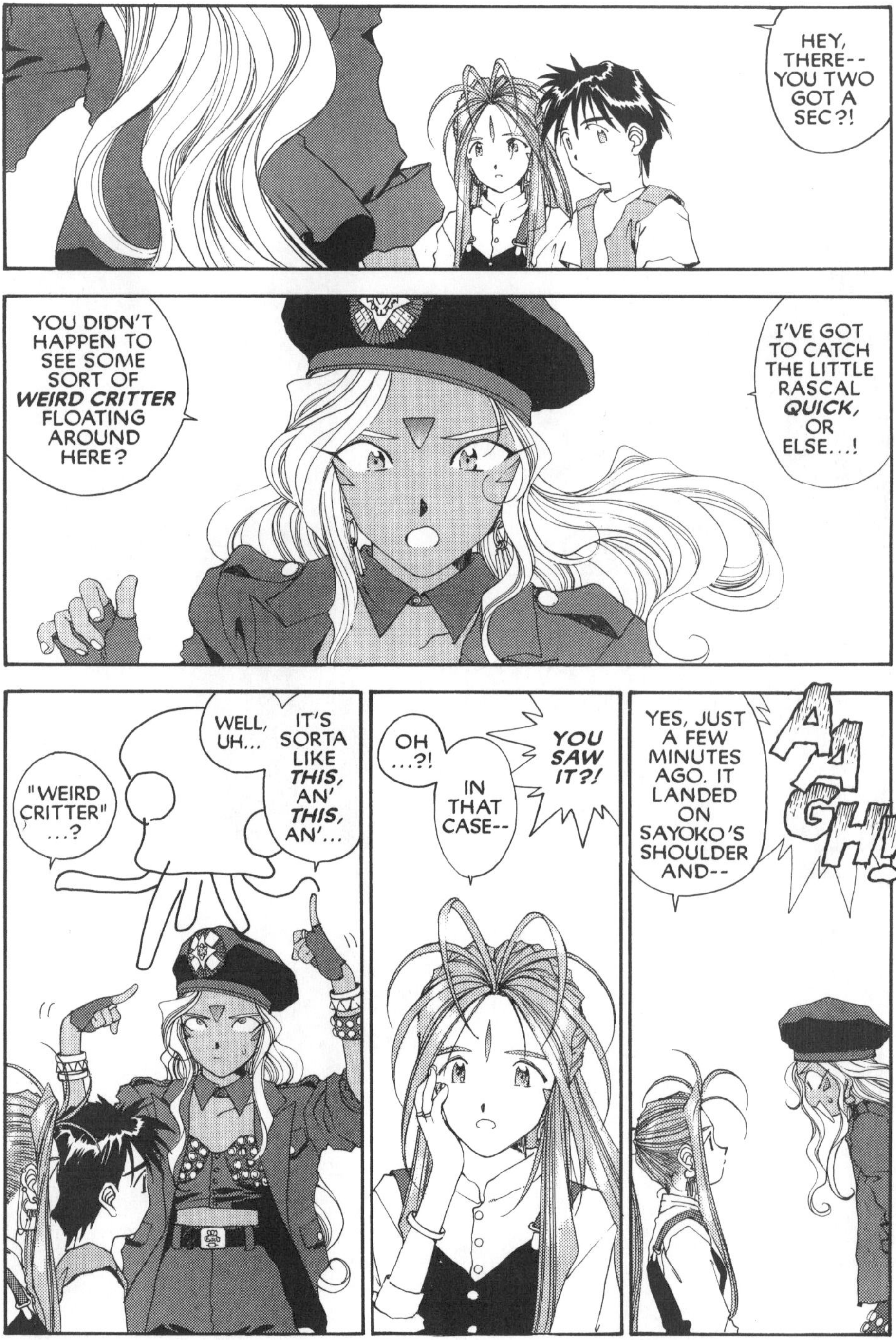
HEY, THERE-- YOU TWO GOT A SEC?!
YOU DIDN'T HAPPEN TO SEE SOME SORT OF **WEIRD CRITTER** FLOATING AROUND HERE?
I'VE GOT TO CATCH THE LITTLE RASCAL **QUICK,** OR ELSE...!
"WEIRD CRITTER" ...?
WELL, UH...
IT'S SORTA LIKE **THIS,** AN' **THIS,** AN'...
OH ...?!
IN THAT CASE--
YOU SAW IT?!
YES, JUST A FEW MINUTES AGO. IT LANDED ON SAYOKO'S SHOULDER AND--
AAGH!

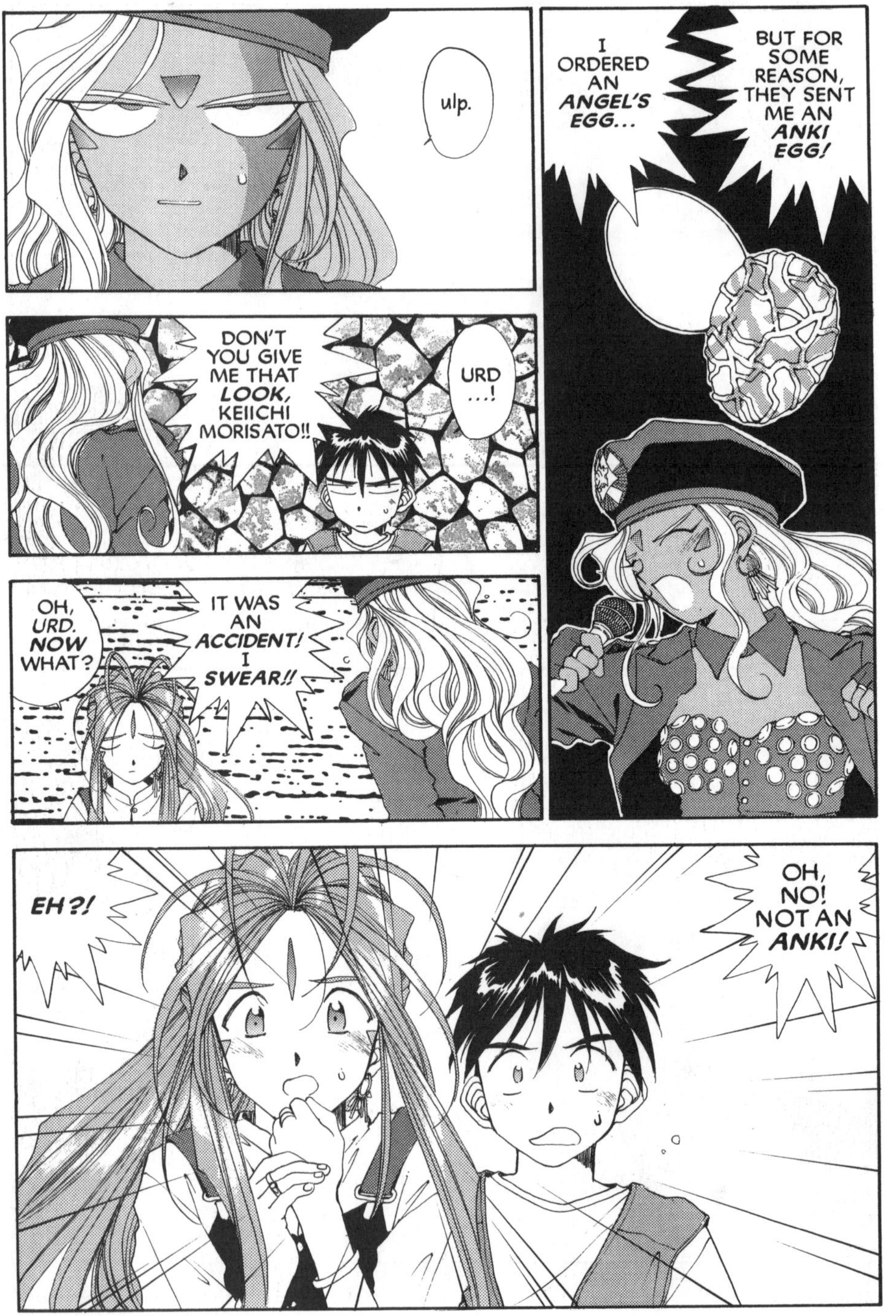
ulp.
DON'T YOU GIVE ME THAT *LOOK*, KEIICHI MORISATO!!
URD ...!
OH, *URD*. *NOW* WHAT?
IT WAS AN *ACCIDENT!* I *SWEAR!!*
I ORDERED AN *ANGEL'S EGG...*
BUT FOR SOME REASON, THEY SENT ME AN *ANKI EGG!*
EH?!
OH, NO! NOT AN *ANKI!*

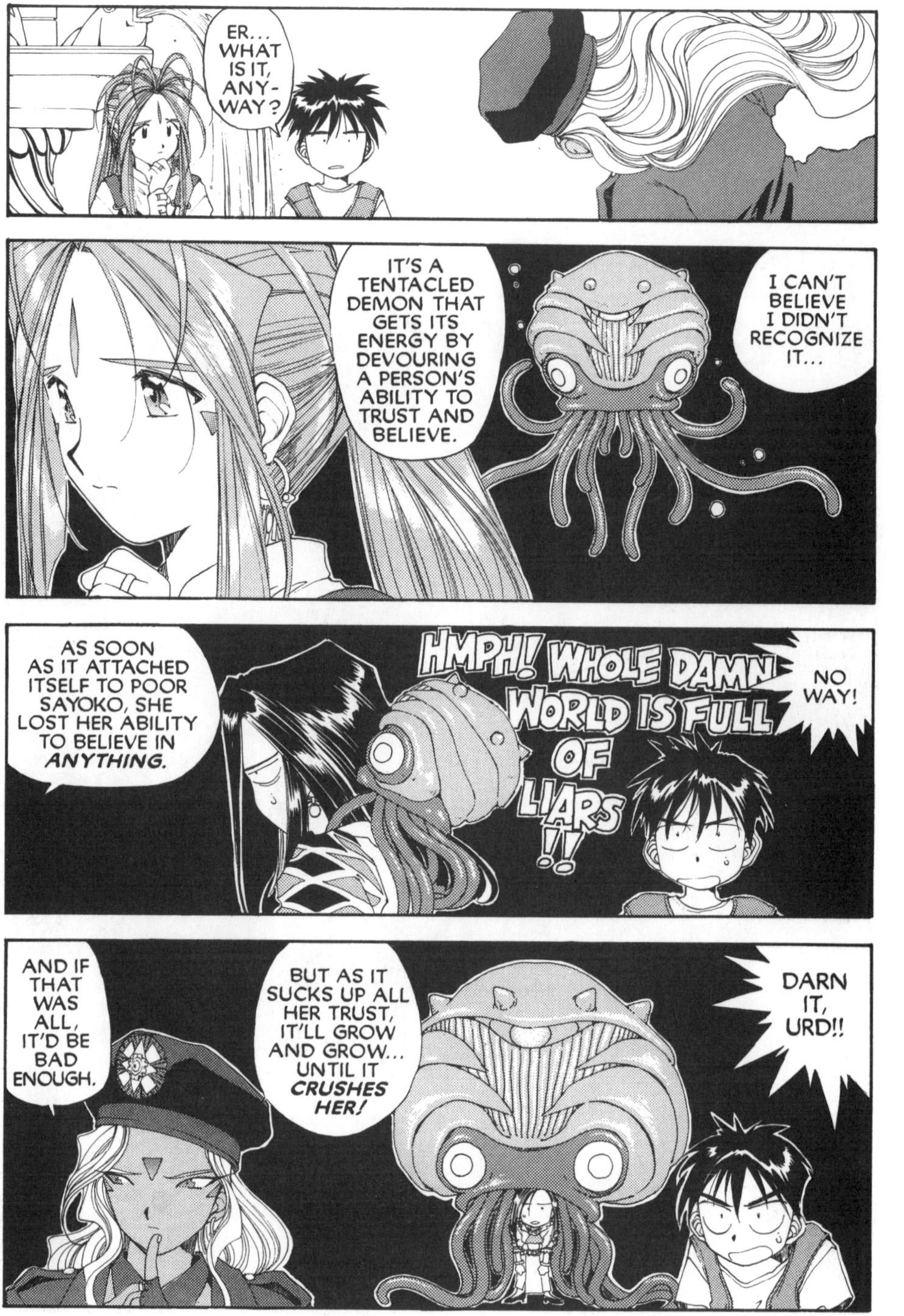
ER... WHAT IS IT, ANY-WAY?
IT'S A TENTACLED DEMON THAT GETS ITS ENERGY BY DEVOURING A PERSON'S ABILITY TO TRUST AND BELIEVE.
I CAN'T BELIEVE I DIDN'T RECOGNIZE IT...
AS SOON AS IT ATTACHED ITSELF TO POOR SAYOKO, SHE LOST HER ABILITY TO BELIEVE IN *ANYTHING.*
HMPH! WHOLE DAMN WORLD IS FULL OF LIARS!!
NO WAY!
AND IF THAT WAS ALL, IT'D BE BAD ENOUGH.
BUT AS IT SUCKS UP ALL HER TRUST, IT'LL GROW AND GROW... UNTIL IT *CRUSHES HER!*
DARN IT, URD!!

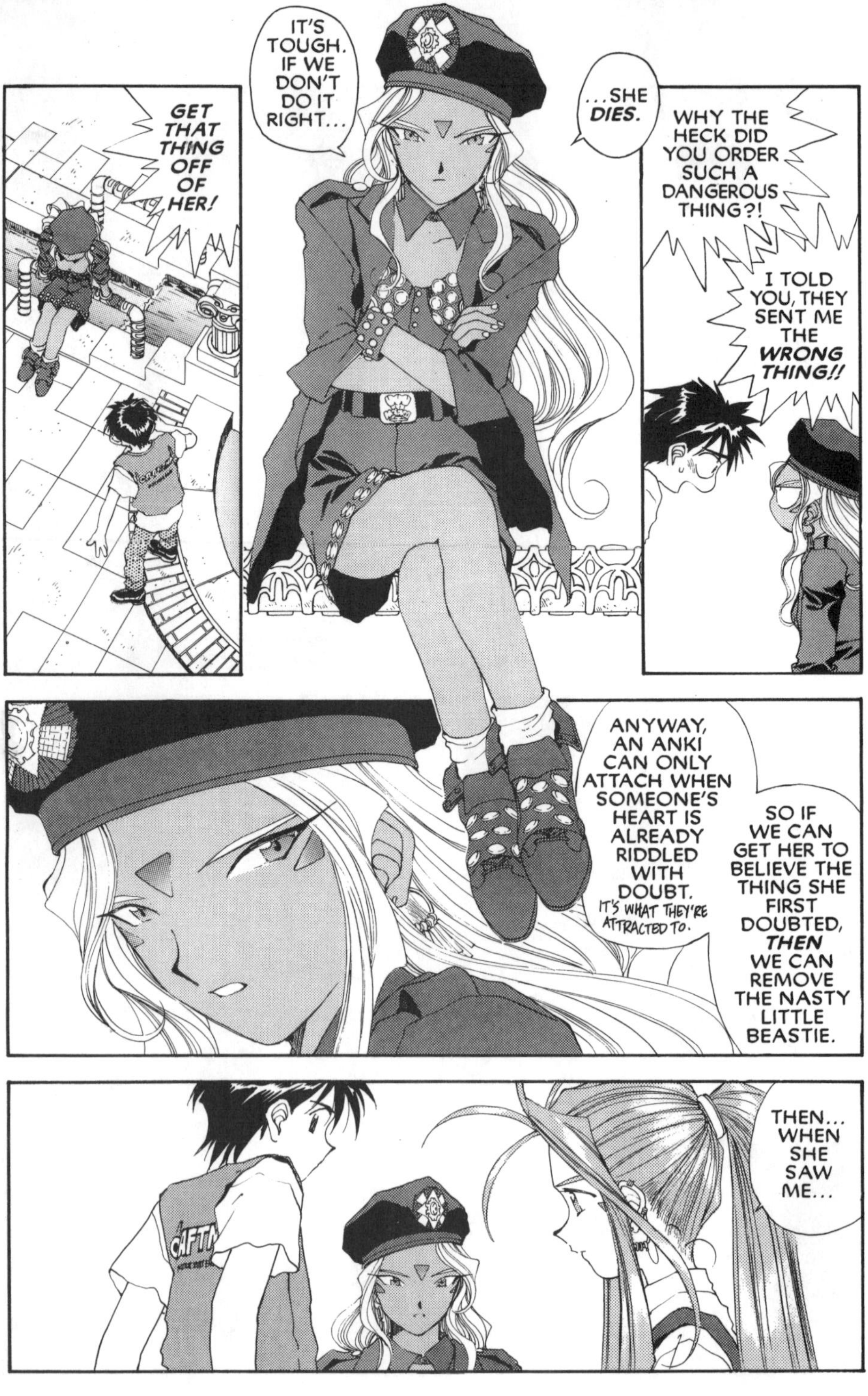
GET THAT THING OFF OF HER!
IT'S TOUGH. IF WE DON'T DO IT RIGHT...
...SHE DIES.
WHY THE HECK DID YOU ORDER SUCH A DANGEROUS THING?!
I TOLD YOU, THEY SENT ME THE WRONG THING!!
ANYWAY, AN ANKI CAN ONLY ATTACH WHEN SOMEONE'S HEART IS ALREADY RIDDLED WITH DOUBT.
IT'S WHAT THEY'RE ATTRACTED TO.
SO IF WE CAN GET HER TO BELIEVE THE THING SHE FIRST DOUBTED, THEN WE CAN REMOVE THE NASTY LITTLE BEASTIE.
THEN... WHEN SHE SAW ME...

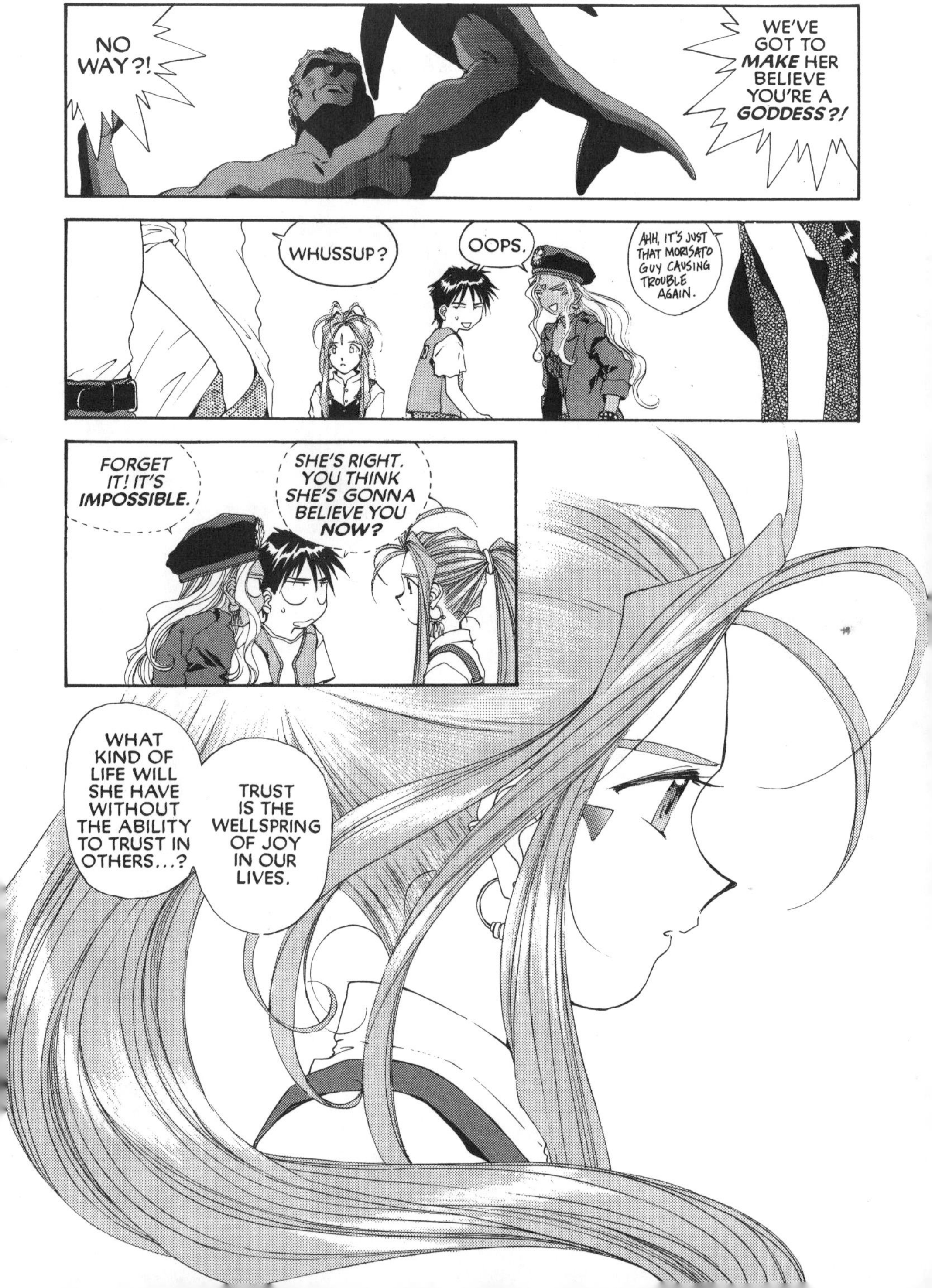
NO WAY?!
WE'VE GOT TO MAKE HER BELIEVE YOU'RE A GODDESS?!
WHUSSUP?
OOPS.
AHH, IT'S JUST THAT MORISATO GUY CAUSING TROUBLE AGAIN.
FORGET IT! IT'S IMPOSSIBLE.
SHE'S RIGHT. YOU THINK SHE'S GONNA BELIEVE YOU NOW?
WHAT KIND OF LIFE WILL SHE HAVE WITHOUT THE ABILITY TO TRUST IN OTHERS...?
TRUST IS THE WELLSPRING OF JOY IN OUR LIVES.

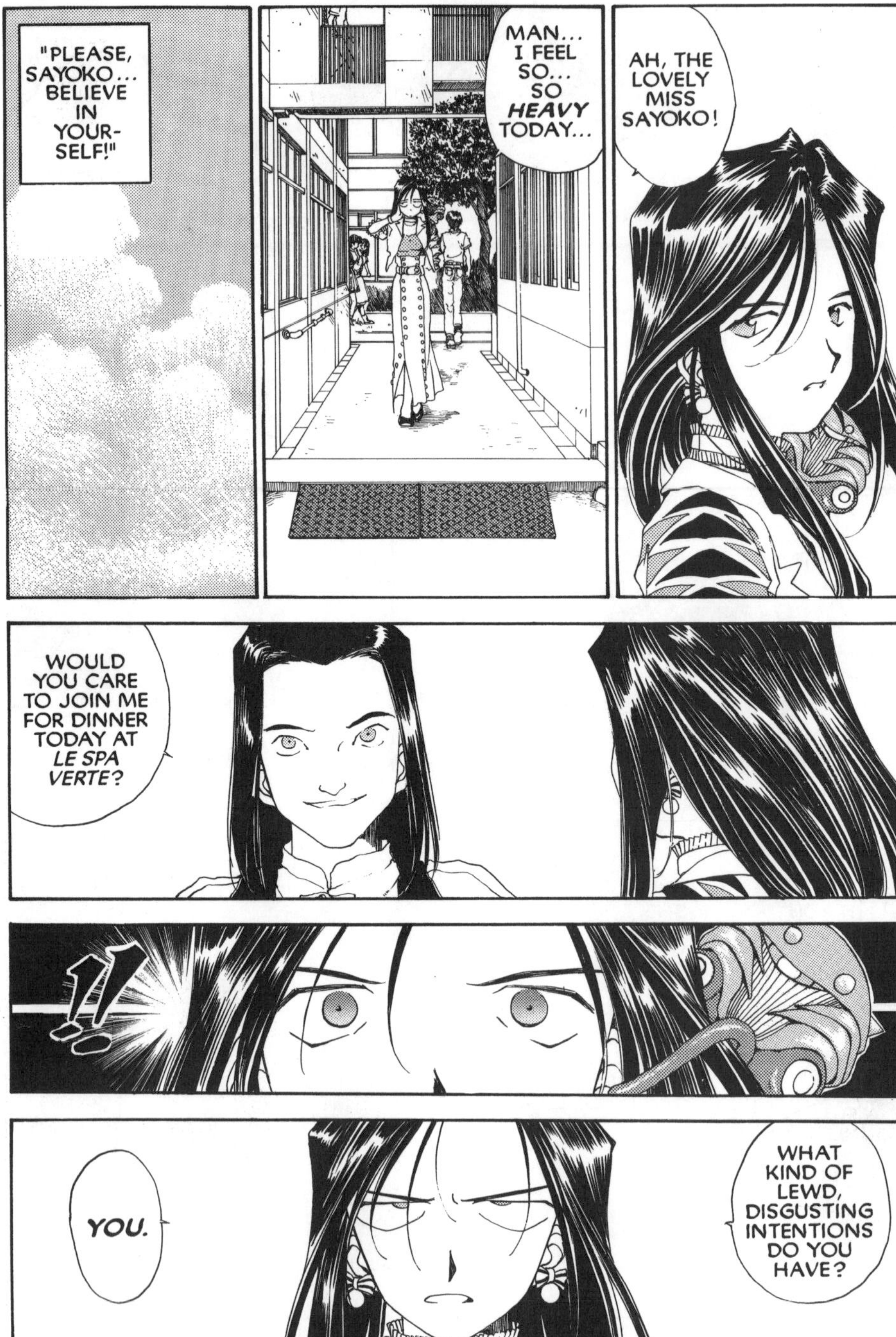
"PLEASE, SAYOKO... BELIEVE IN YOURSELF!"
MAN... I FEEL SO... SO *HEAVY* TODAY...
AH, THE LOVELY MISS SAYOKO!
WOULD YOU CARE TO JOIN ME FOR DINNER TODAY AT *LE SPA VERTE*?
!!
YOU.
WHAT KIND OF LEWD, DISGUSTING INTENTIONS DO YOU HAVE?

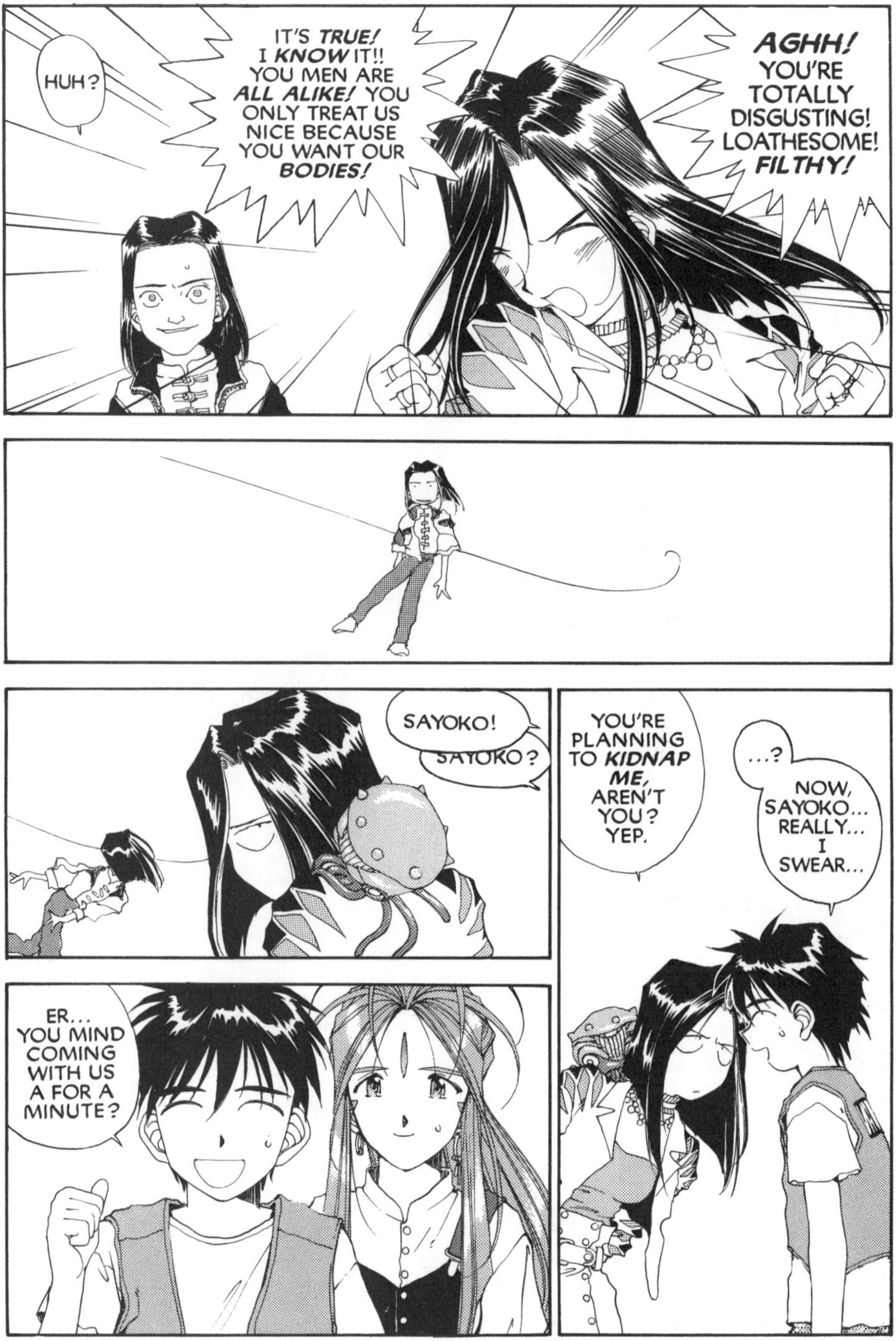

HUH?
IT'S TRUE! I KNOW IT!! YOU MEN ARE ALL ALIKE! YOU ONLY TREAT US NICE BECAUSE YOU WANT OUR BODIES!
AGHH! YOU'RE TOTALLY DISGUSTING! LOATHESOME! FILTHY!
SAYOKO!
SAYOKO?
ER... YOU MIND COMING WITH US A FOR A MINUTE?
YOU'RE PLANNING TO KIDNAP ME, AREN'T YOU? YEP.
...?
NOW, SAYOKO... REALLY... I SWEAR...

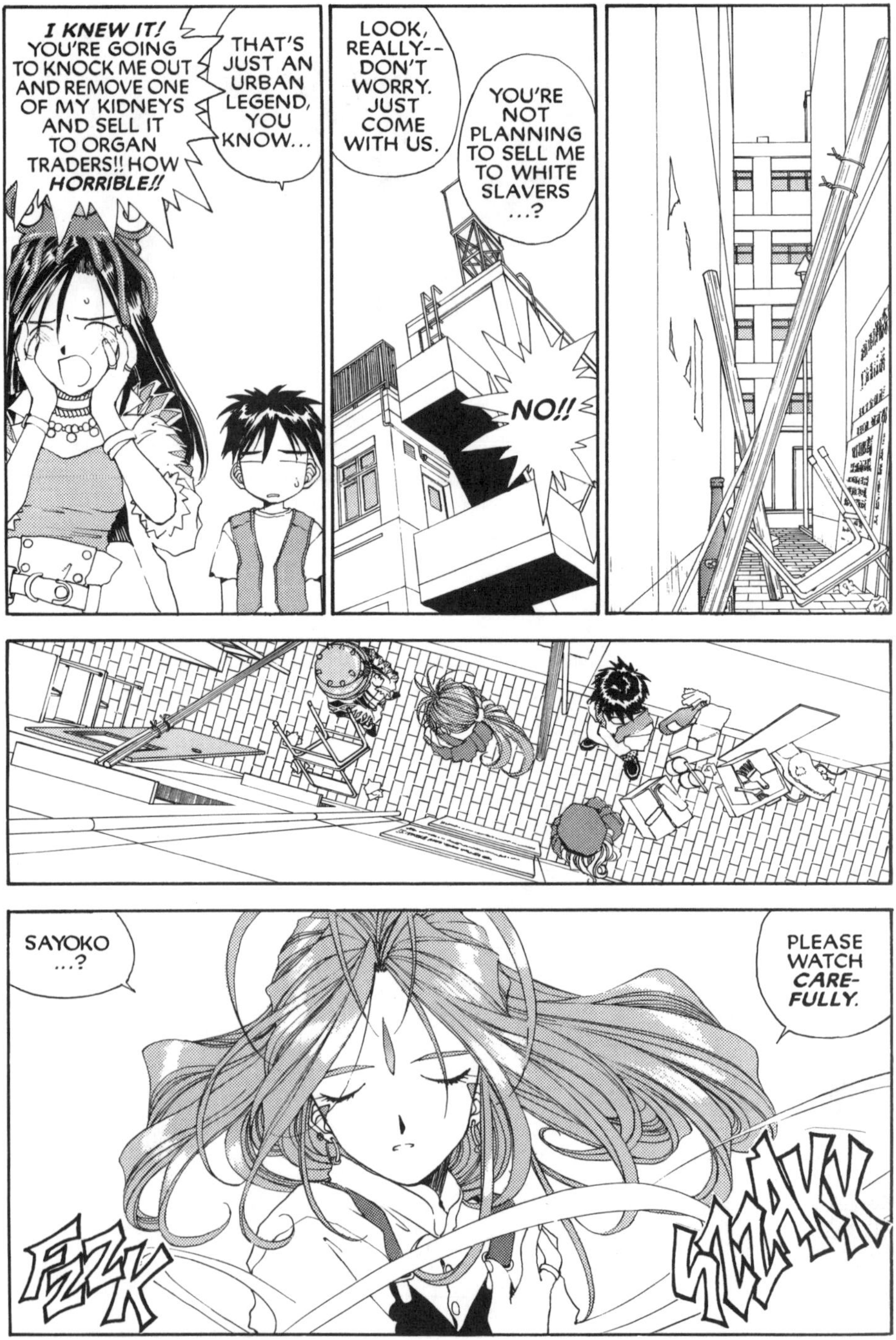
I KNEW IT! YOU'RE GOING TO KNOCK ME OUT AND REMOVE ONE OF MY KIDNEYS AND SELL IT TO ORGAN TRADERS!! HOW *HORRIBLE!!*
THAT'S JUST AN URBAN LEGEND, YOU KNOW...
LOOK, REALLY-- DON'T WORRY. JUST COME WITH US.
YOU'RE NOT PLANNING TO SELL ME TO WHITE SLAVERS ...?
NO!!
SAYOKO ...?
PLEASE WATCH *CARE-FULLY.*

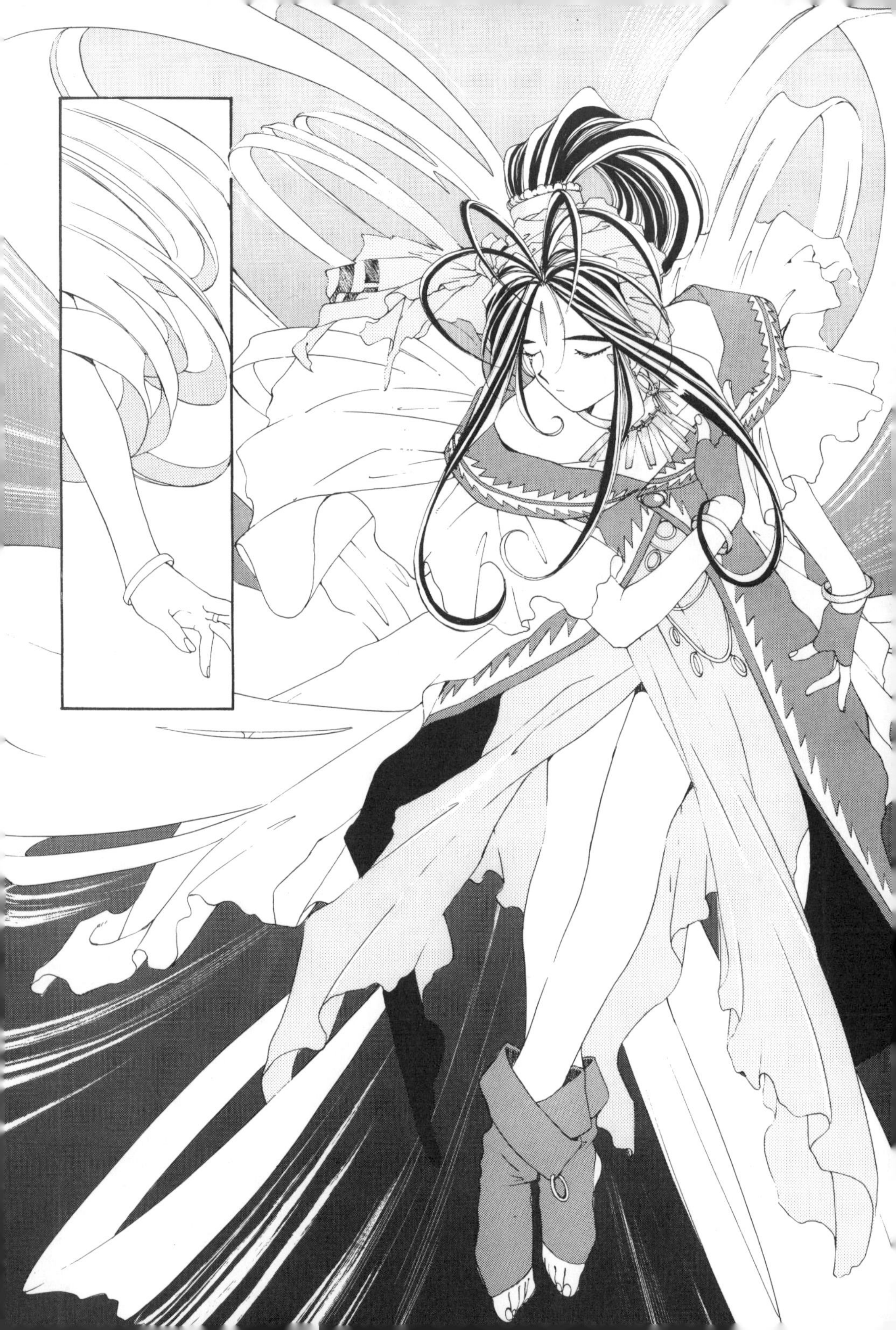

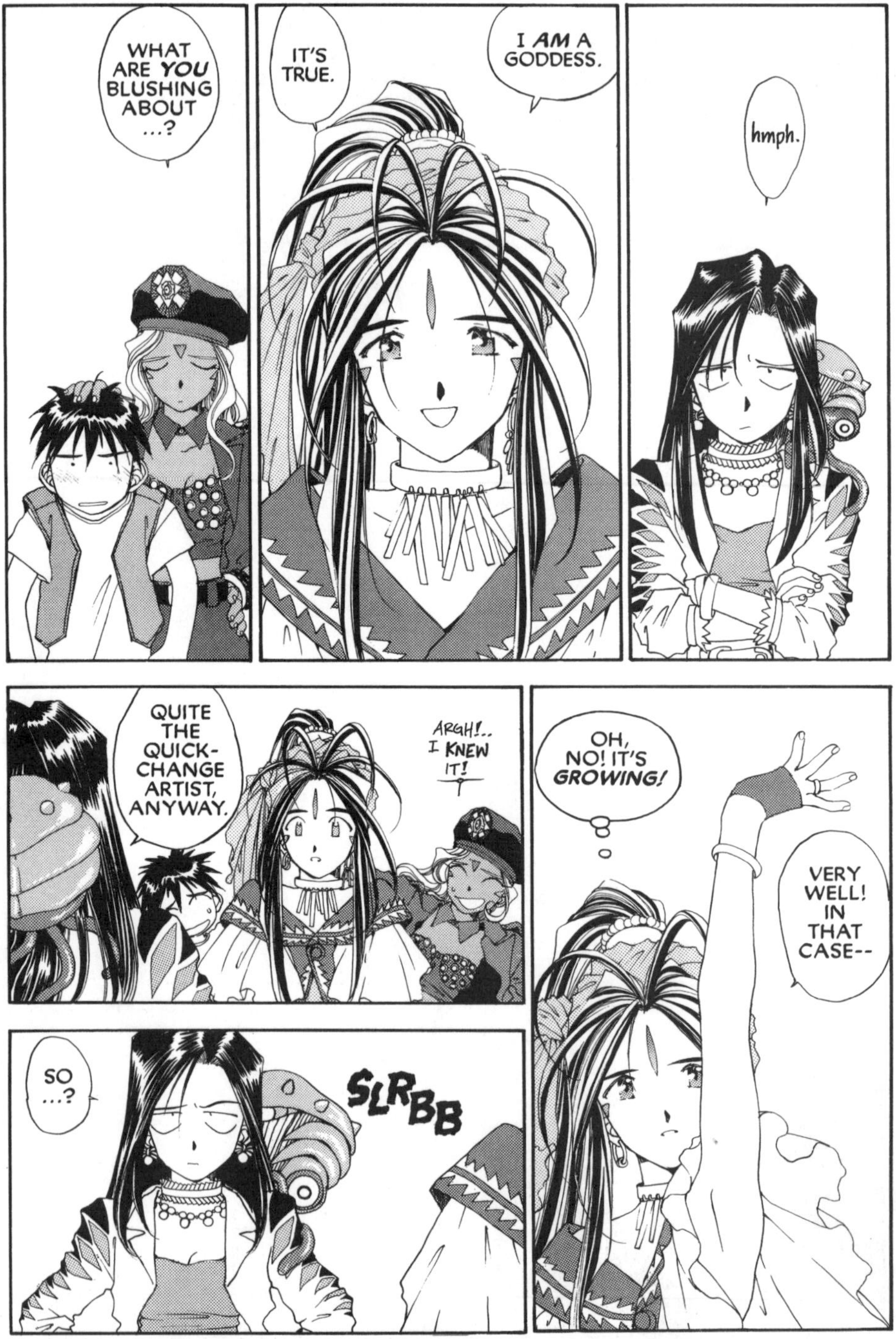
WHAT ARE YOU BLUSHING ABOUT ...?
IT'S TRUE.
I AM A GODDESS.
hmph.
QUITE THE QUICK-CHANGE ARTIST, ANYWAY.
ARGH!.. I KNEW IT!
SO ...?
SLRBB
OH, NO! IT'S GROWING!
VERY WELL! IN THAT CASE--

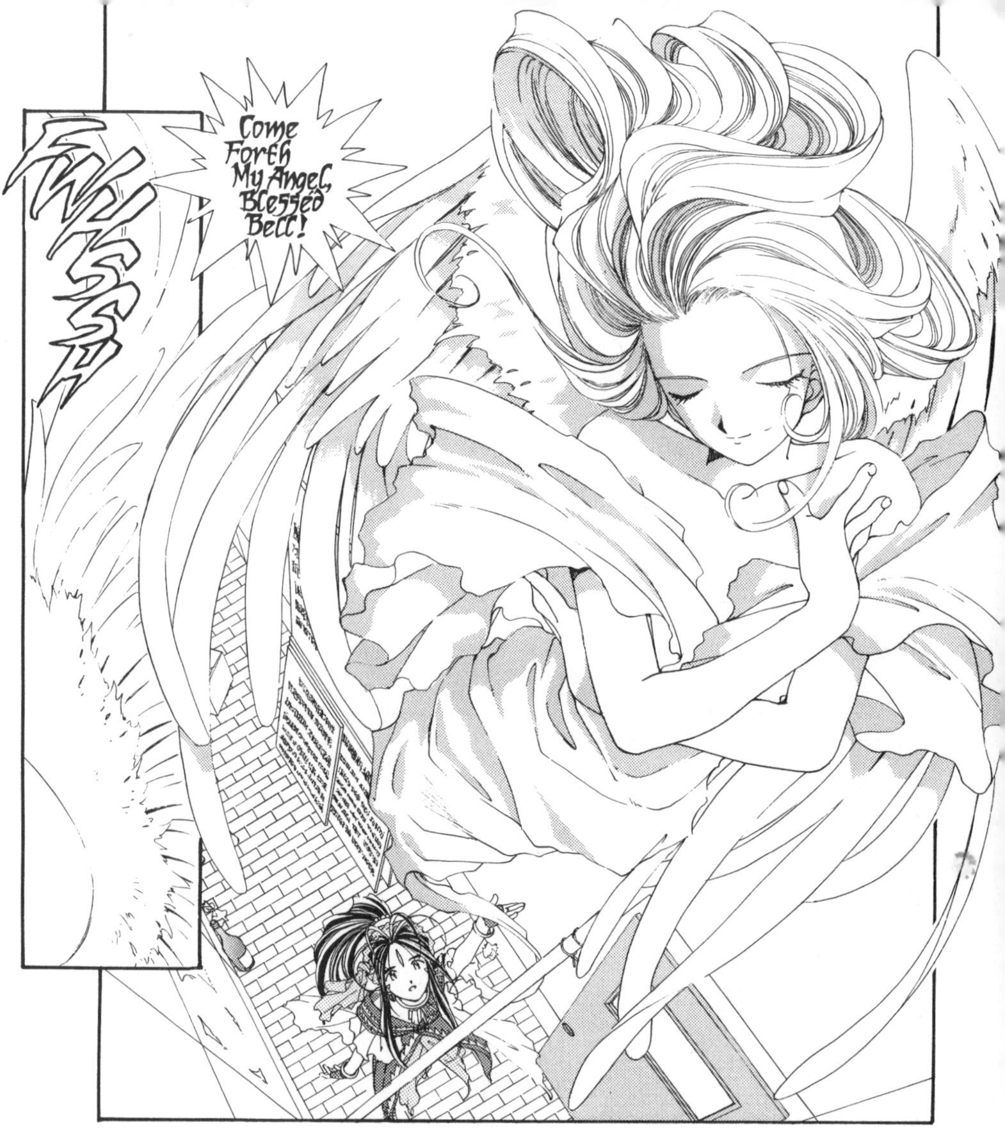
FWUSSH
Come Forth My Angel, Blessed Bell!

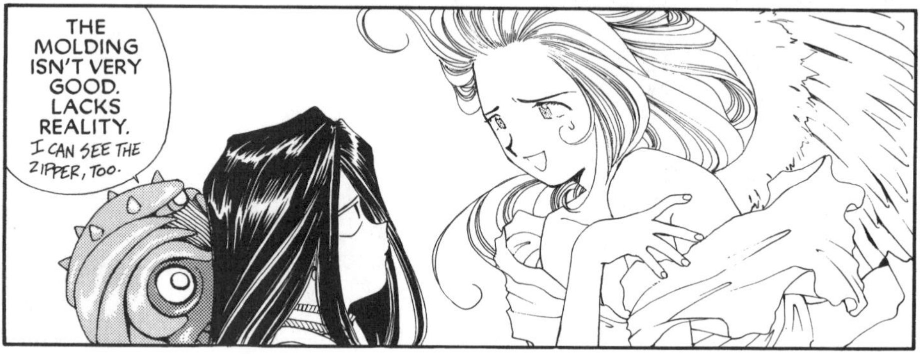
THE MOLDING ISN'T VERY GOOD. LACKS REALITY. I CAN SEE THE ZIPPER, TOO.

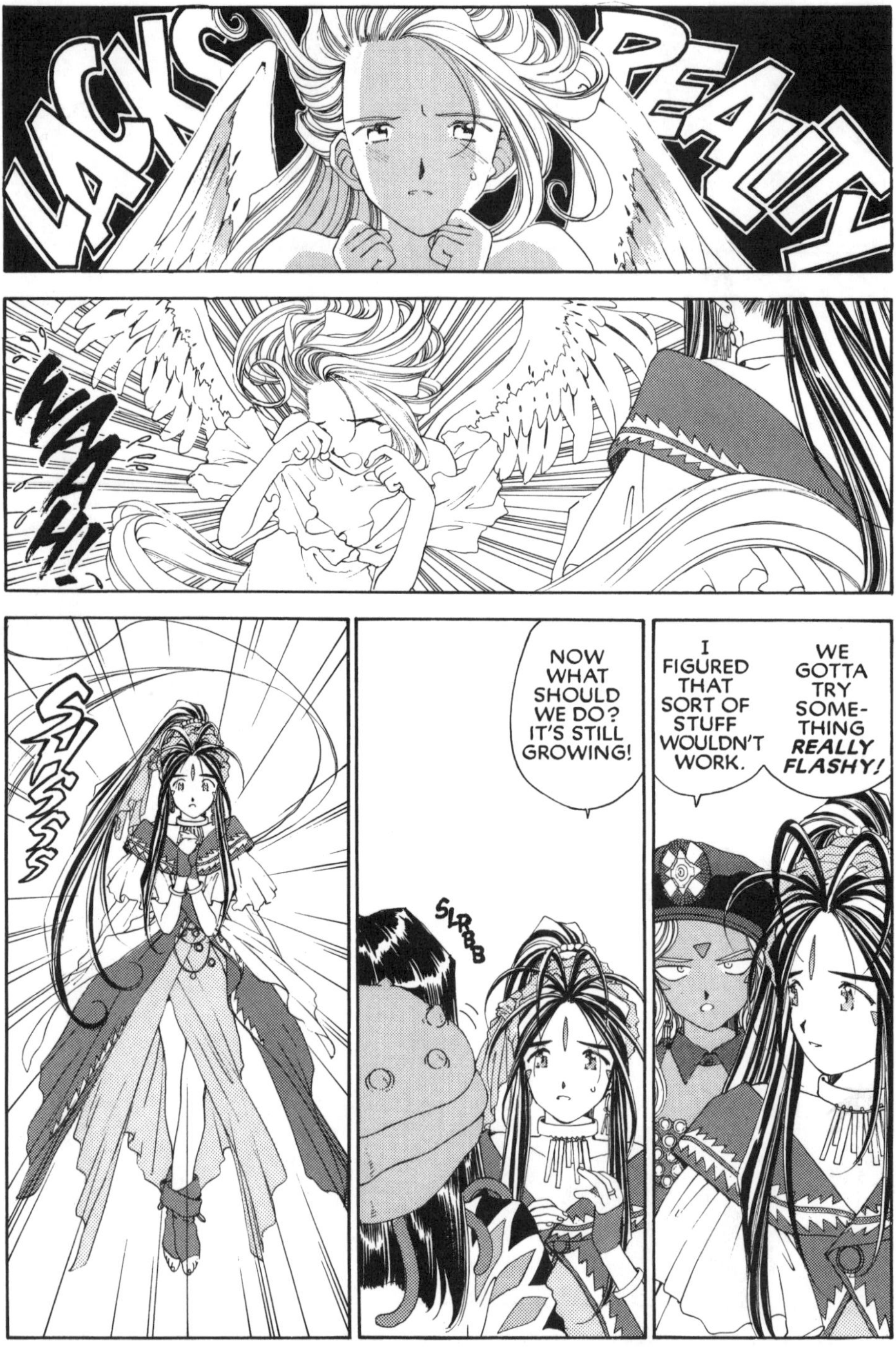
LACKS REALITY
WAAAH!
SHHSSSS
NOW WHAT SHOULD WE DO? IT'S STILL GROWING!
SLRBBB
I FIGURED THAT SORT OF STUFF WOULDN'T WORK.
WE GOTTA TRY SOME-THING *REALLY FLASHY!*

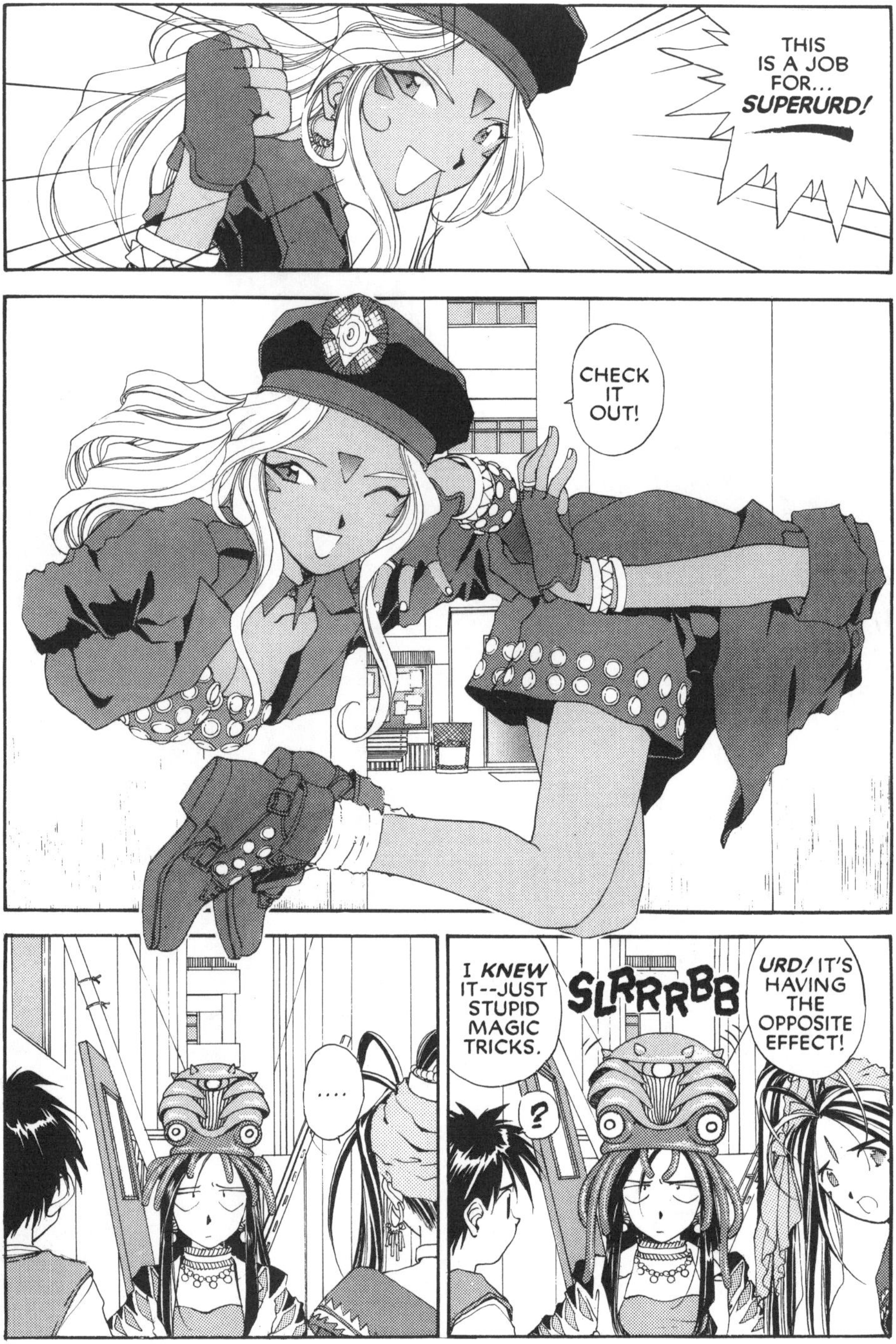
THIS IS A JOB FOR... SUPERURD!
CHECK IT OUT!
....
I KNEW IT--JUST STUPID MAGIC TRICKS.
SLRRRRBB
URD! IT'S HAVING THE OPPOSITE EFFECT!
?

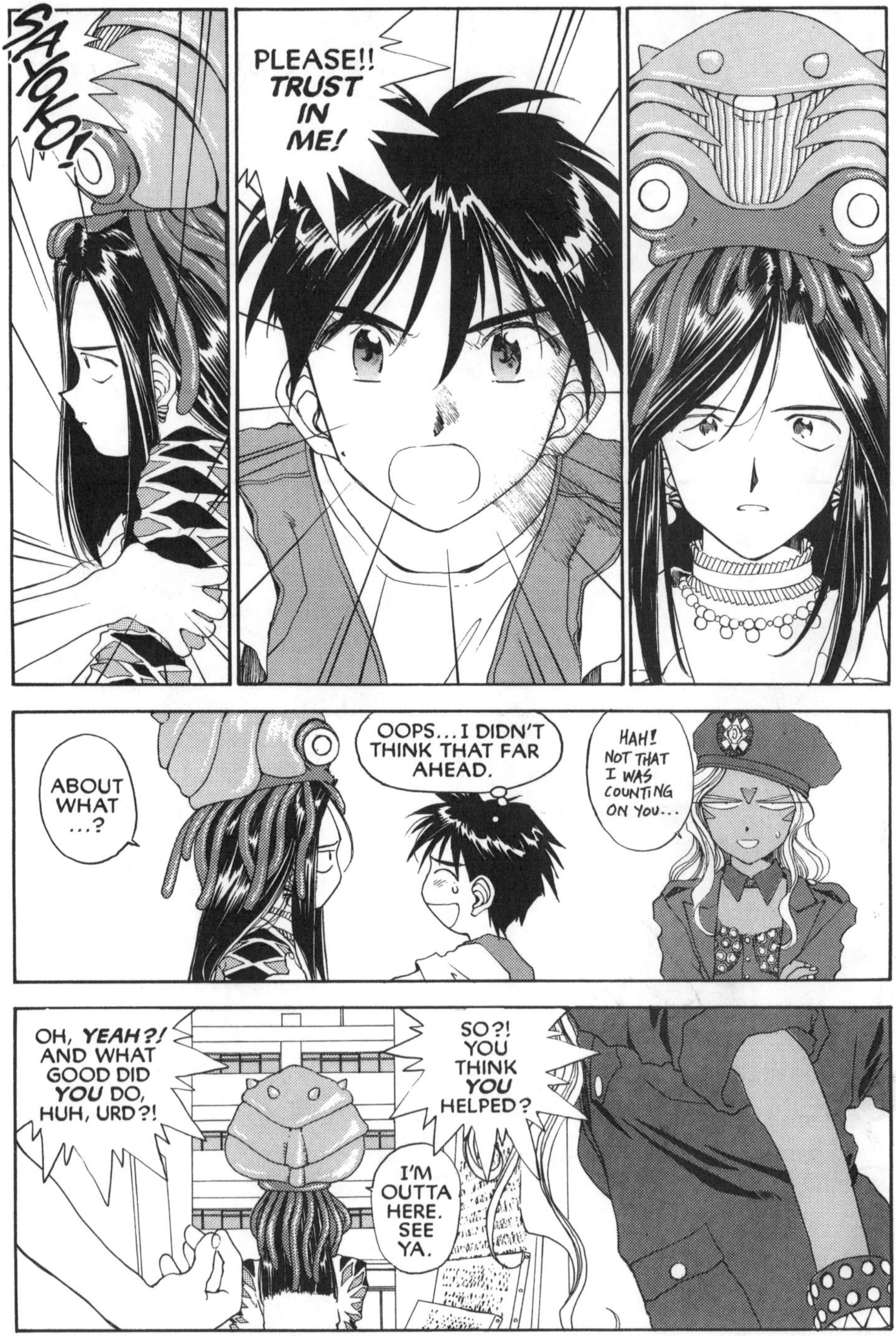
SAYOKO!
PLEASE!! TRUST IN ME!
ABOUT WHAT ...?
OOPS... I DIDN'T THINK THAT FAR AHEAD.
HAH! NOT THAT I WAS COUNTING ON YOU...
OH, YEAH?! AND WHAT GOOD DID YOU DO, HUH, URD?!
SO?! YOU THINK YOU HELPED?
I'M OUTTA HERE. SEE YA.

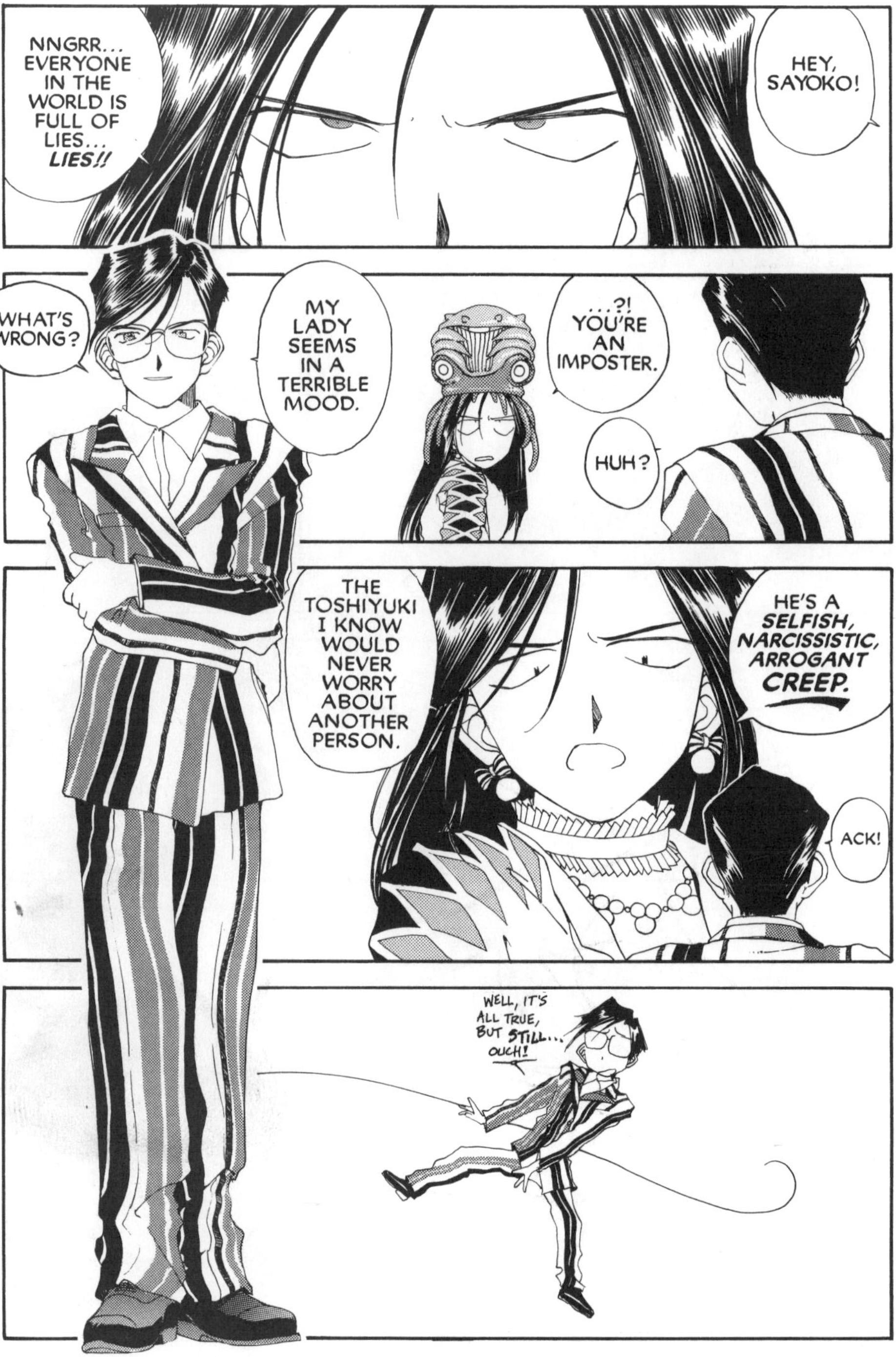
NNGRR... EVERYONE IN THE WORLD IS FULL OF LIES... LIES!!
HEY, SAYOKO!
WHAT'S WRONG?
MY LADY SEEMS IN A TERRIBLE MOOD.
...?! YOU'RE AN IMPOSTER.
HUH?
THE TOSHIYUKI I KNOW WOULD NEVER WORRY ABOUT ANOTHER PERSON.
HE'S A SELFISH, NARCISSISTIC, ARROGANT CREEP.
ACK!
WELL, IT'S ALL TRUE, BUT STILL... OUCH!

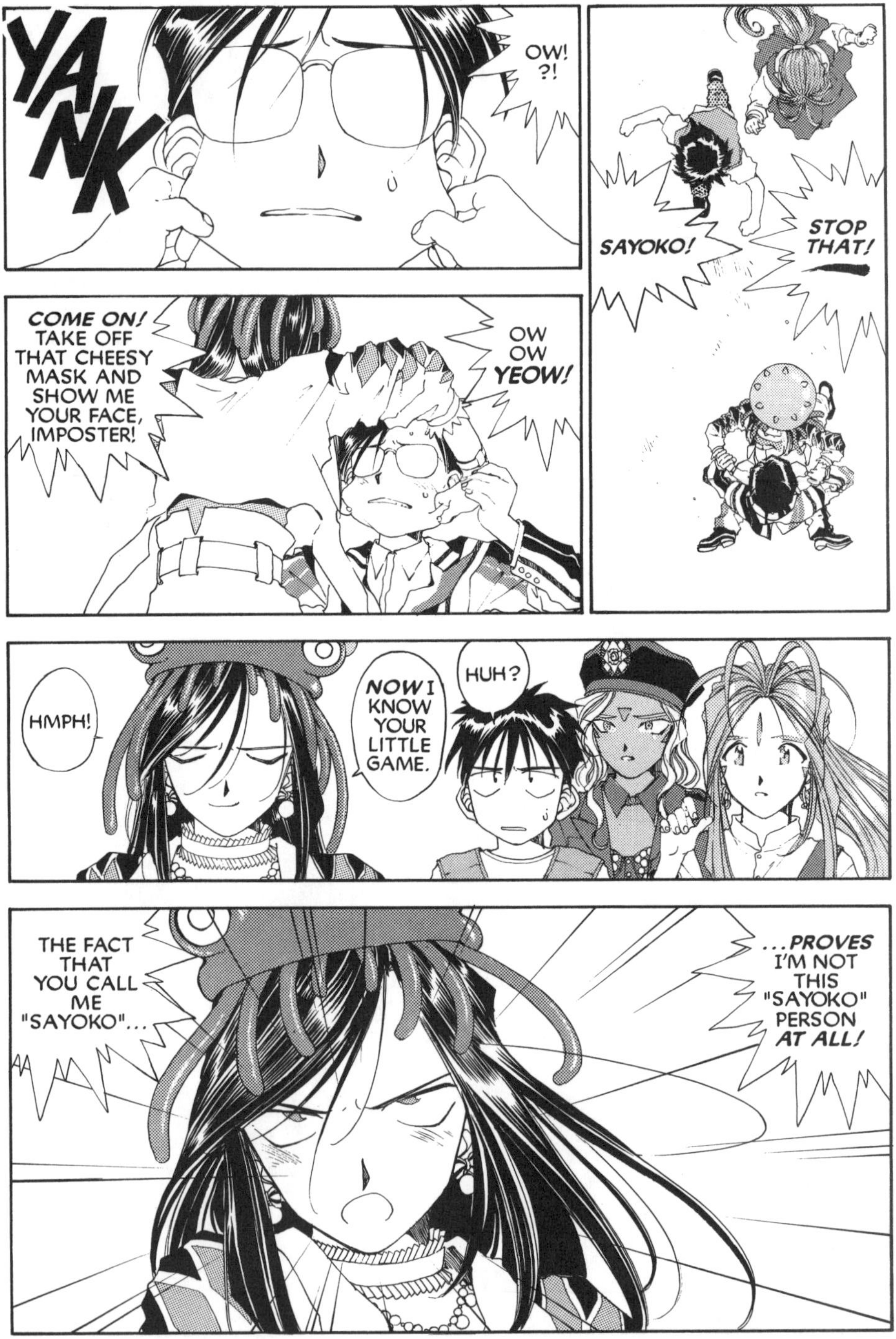
YANK
OW! ?!
COME ON! TAKE OFF THAT CHEESY MASK AND SHOW ME YOUR FACE, IMPOSTER!
OW OW YEOW!
SAYOKO!
STOP THAT!
HMPH!
NOW I KNOW YOUR LITTLE GAME.
HUH?
THE FACT THAT YOU CALL ME "SAYOKO"...
...PROVES I'M NOT THIS "SAYOKO" PERSON AT ALL!

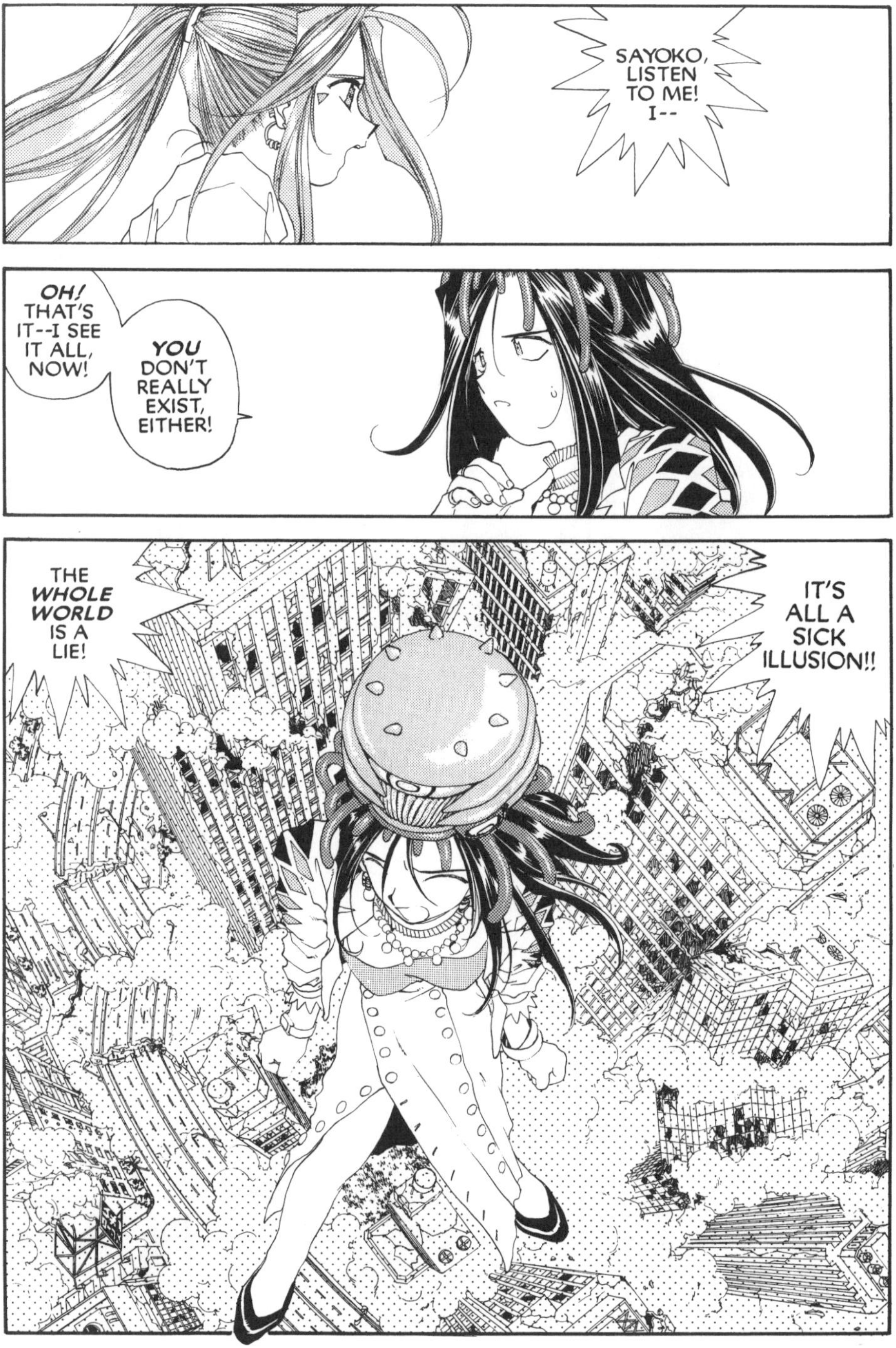
SAYOKO, LISTEN TO ME! I--
OH! THAT'S IT--I SEE IT ALL, NOW!
YOU DON'T REALLY EXIST, EITHER!
THE *WHOLE WORLD* IS A LIE!
IT'S ALL A SICK ILLUSION!!

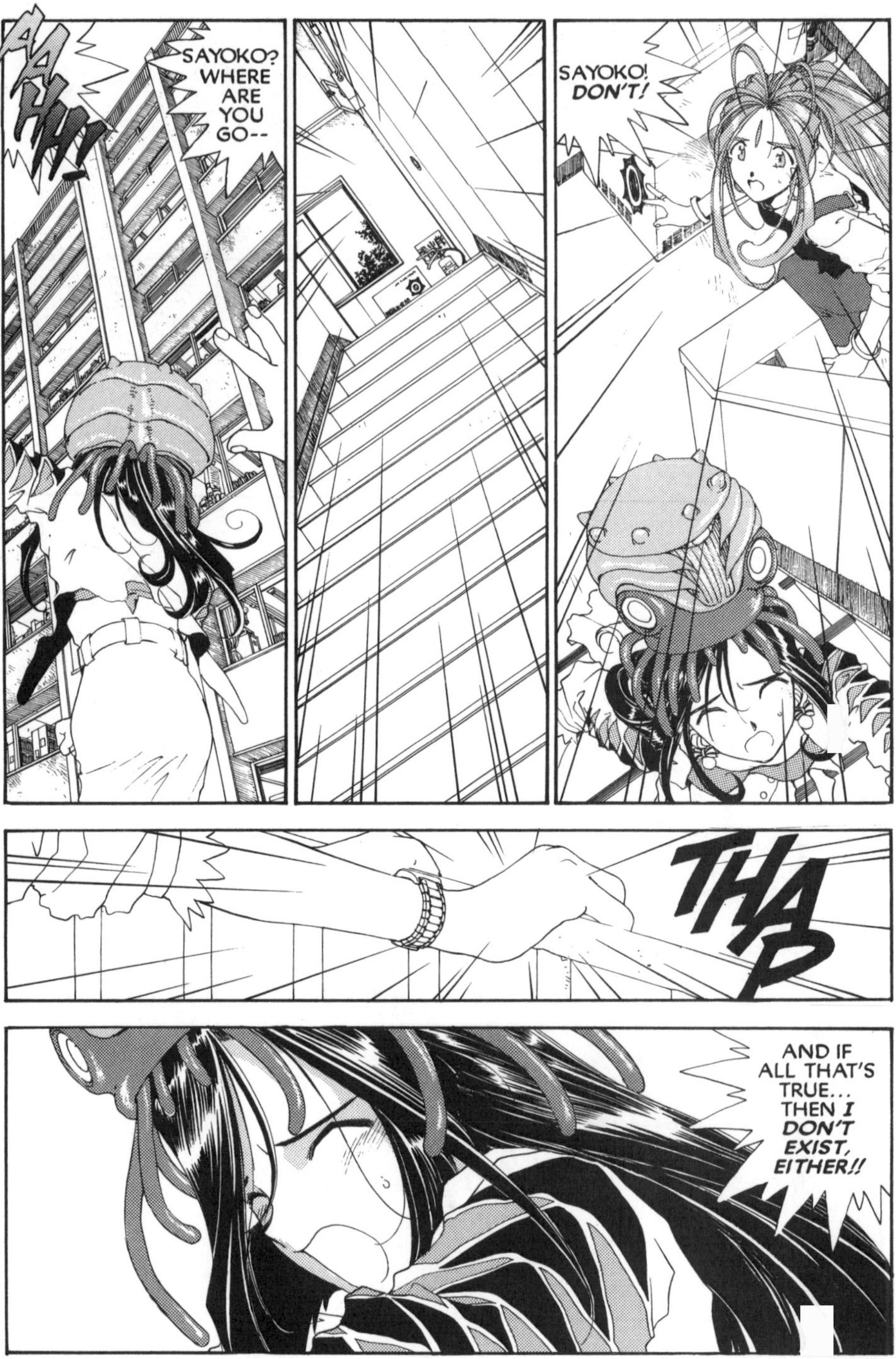
AAHH!
SAYOKO? WHERE ARE YOU GO--
SAYOKO! DON'T!
THAP
AND IF ALL THAT'S TRUE... THEN I DON'T EXIST, EITHER!!

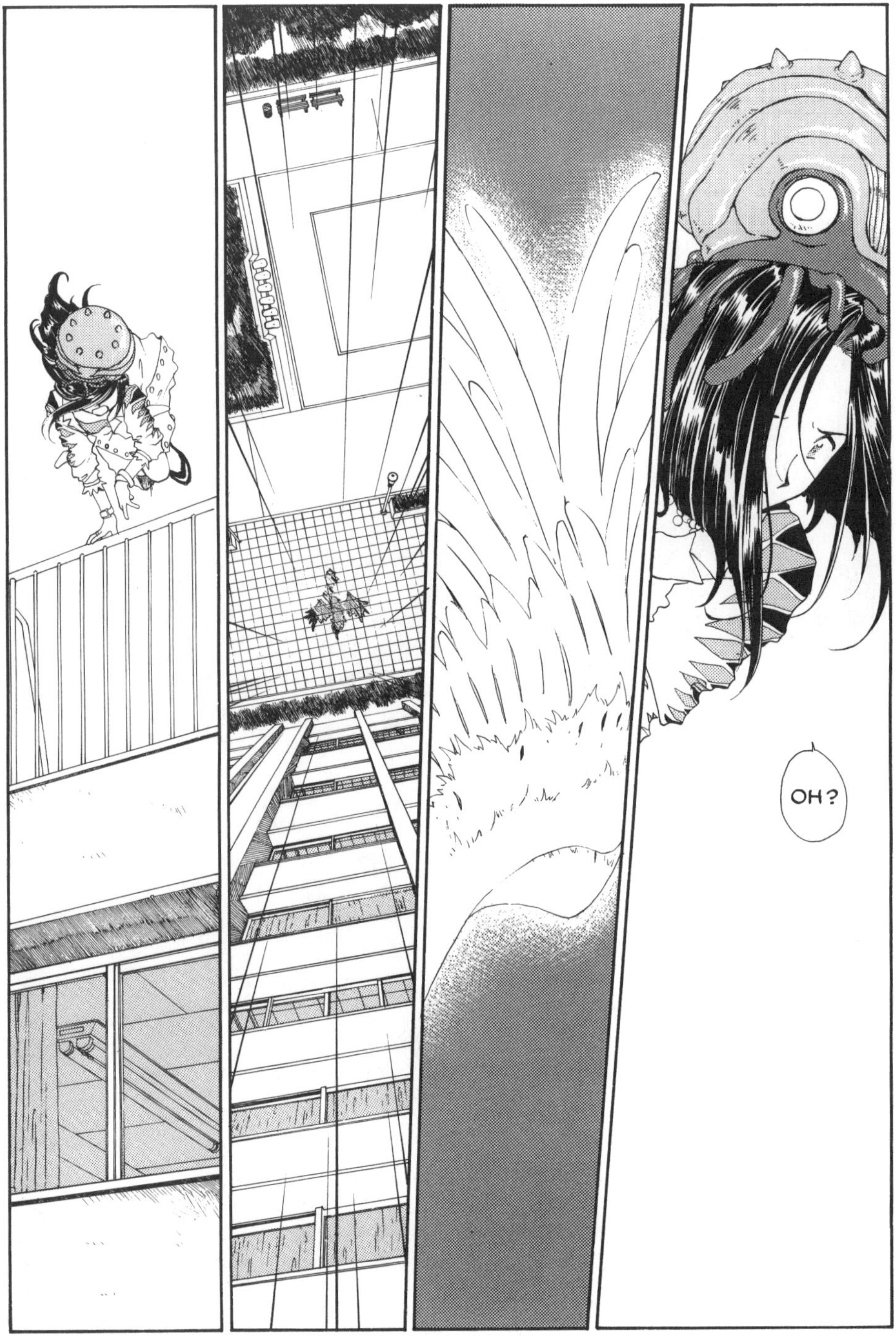
OH?

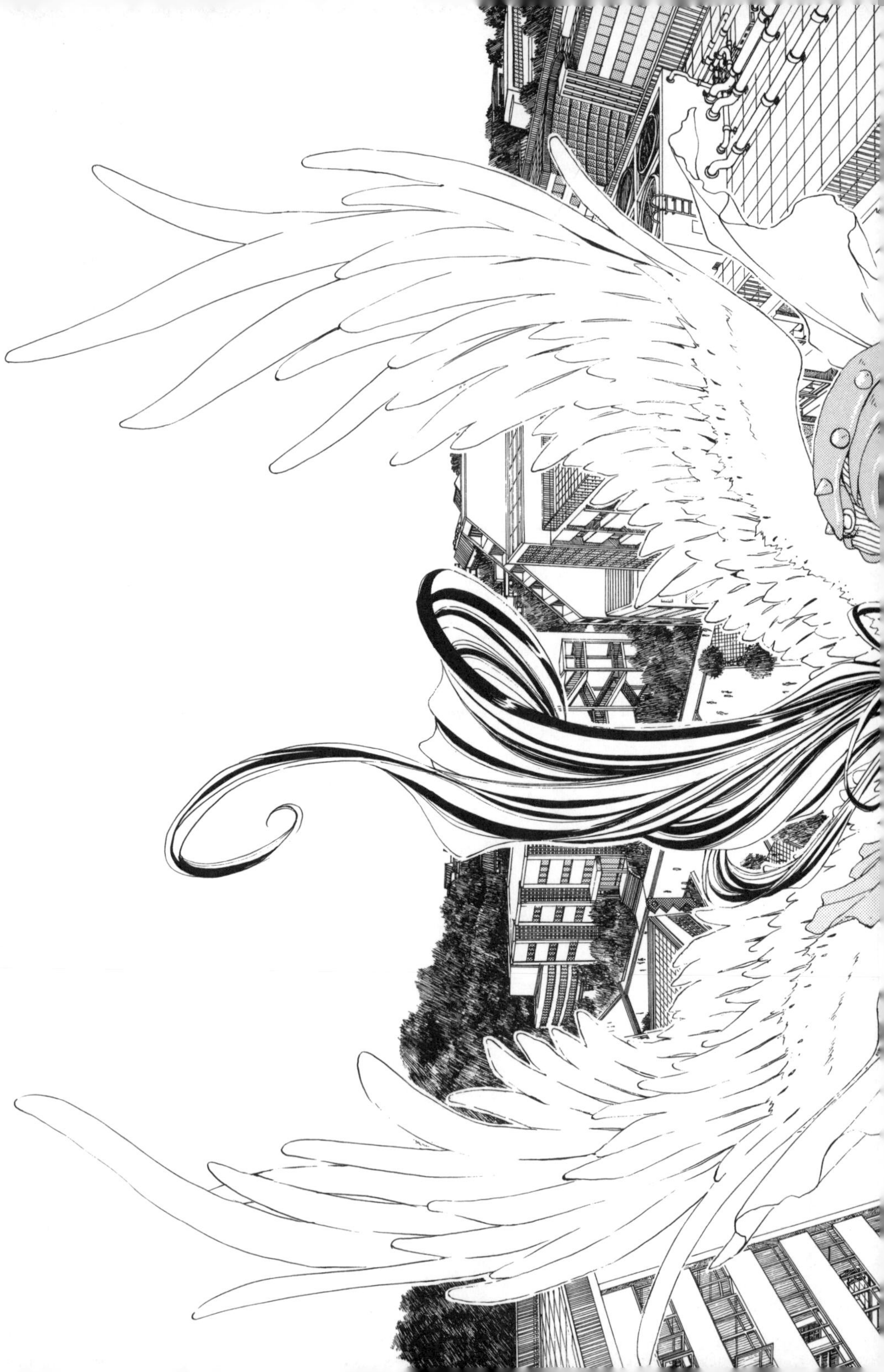

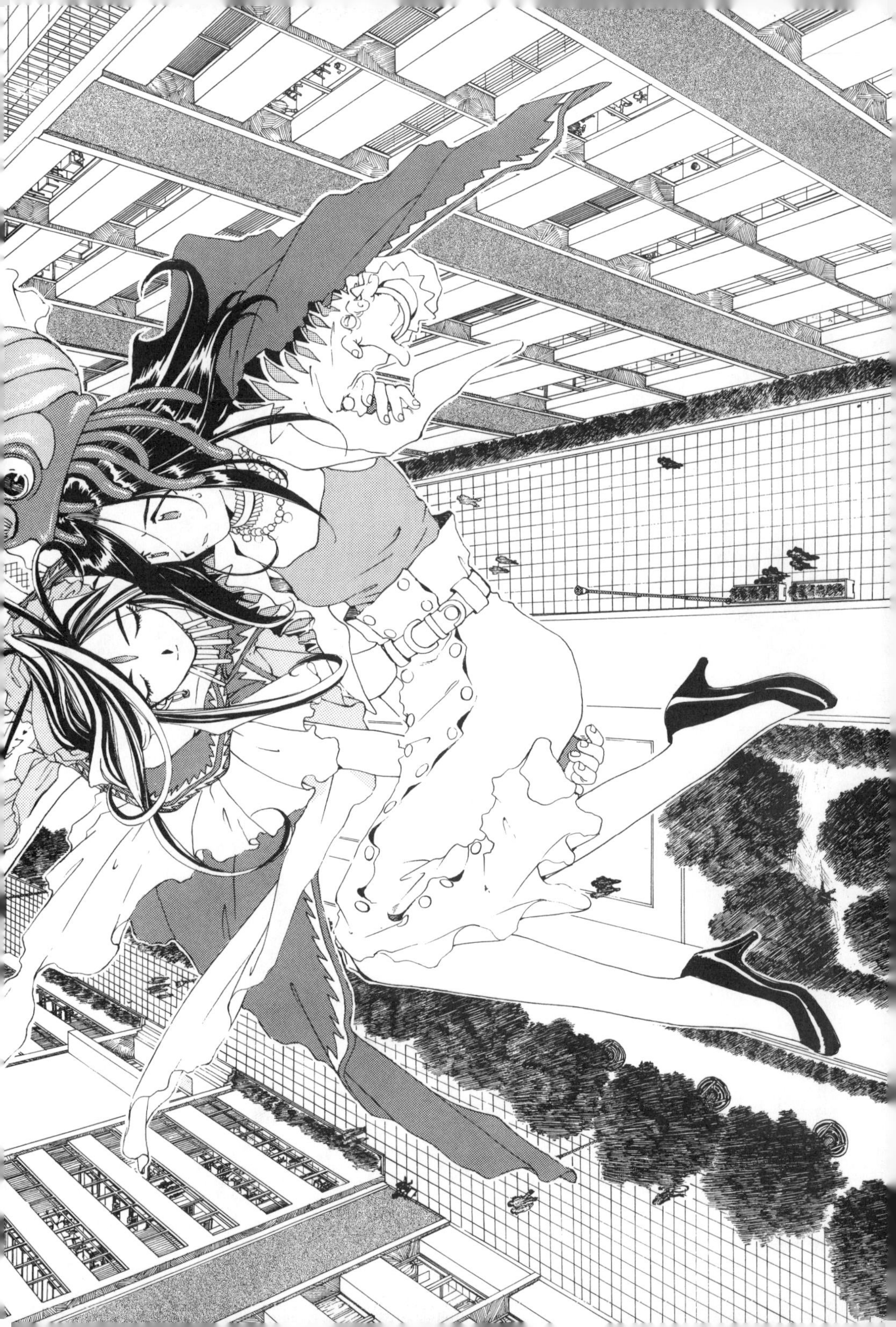

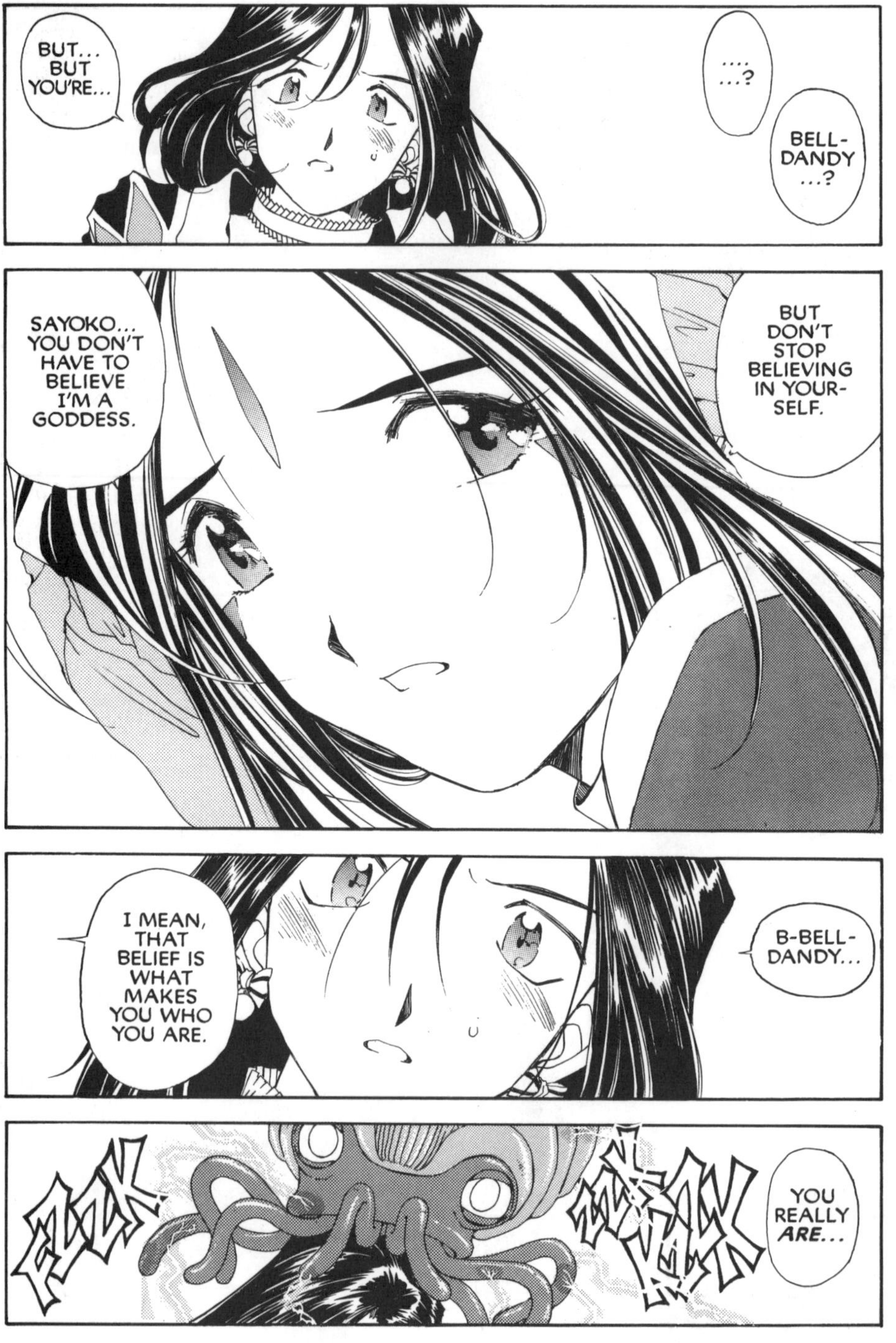
BUT... BUT YOU'RE...
....?
BELL-DANDY ...?
SAYOKO... YOU DON'T HAVE TO BELIEVE I'M A GODDESS.
BUT DON'T STOP BELIEVING IN YOUR-SELF.
I MEAN, THAT BELIEF IS WHAT MAKES YOU WHO YOU ARE.
B-BELL-DANDY...
YOU REALLY *ARE*...

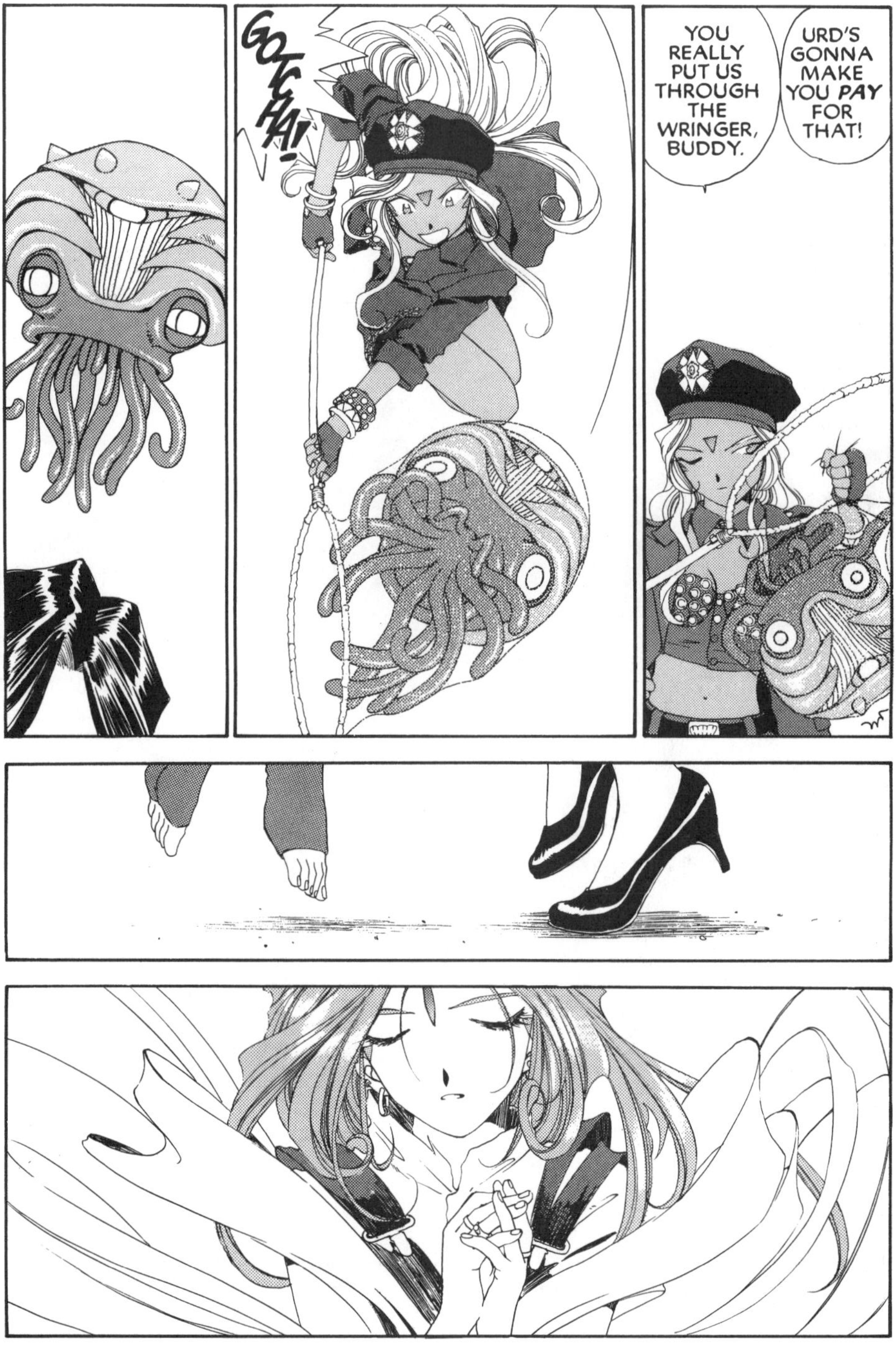
GOTCHA!!
YOU REALLY PUT US THROUGH THE WRINGER, BUDDY.
URD'S GONNA MAKE YOU PAY FOR THAT!

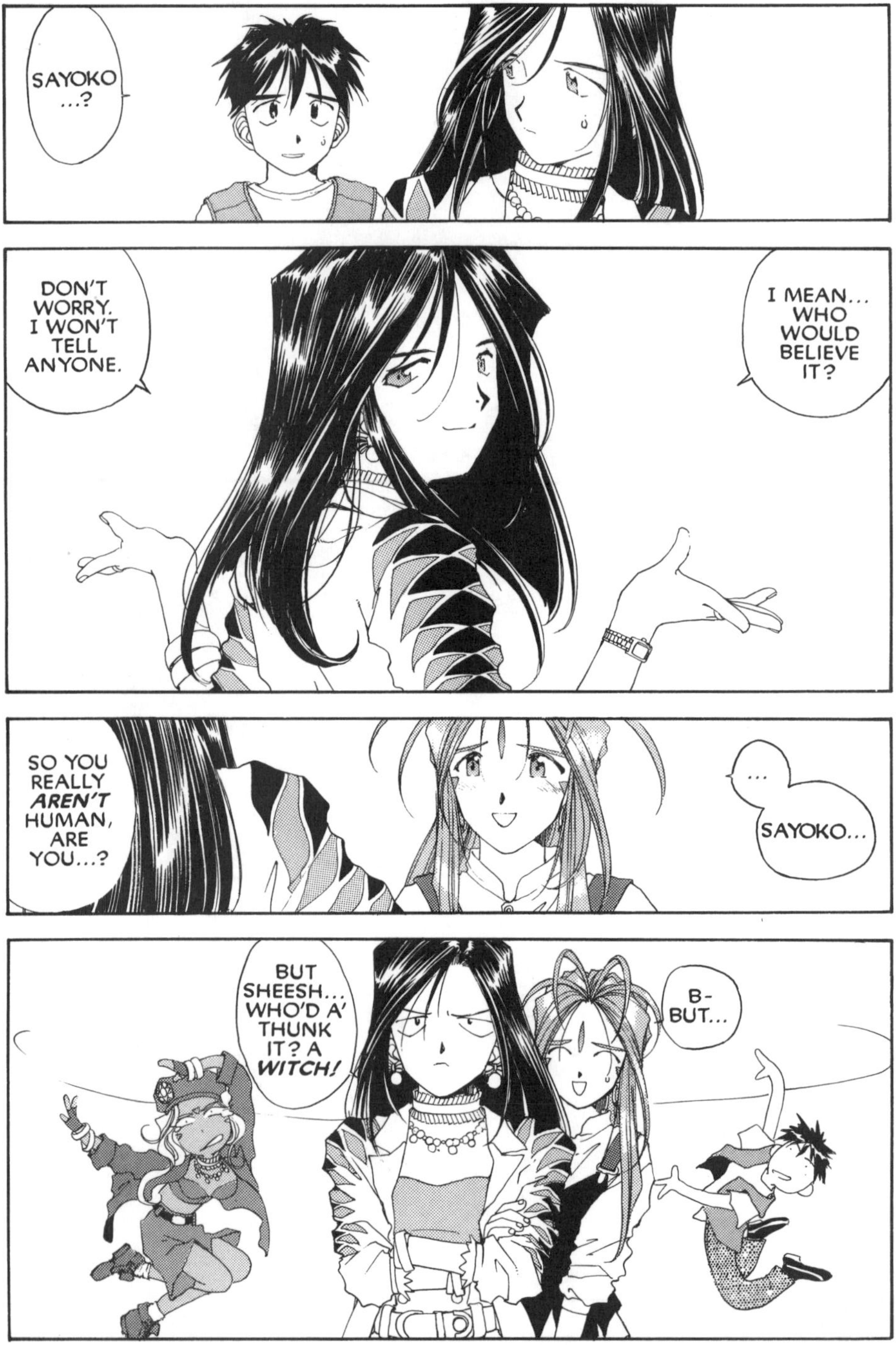
SAYOKO ...?
DON'T WORRY. I WON'T TELL ANYONE.
I MEAN... WHO WOULD BELIEVE IT?
SO YOU REALLY ***AREN'T*** HUMAN, ARE YOU...?
... SAYOKO...
BUT SHEESH... WHO'D A' THUNK IT? A ***WITCH!***
B- BUT...

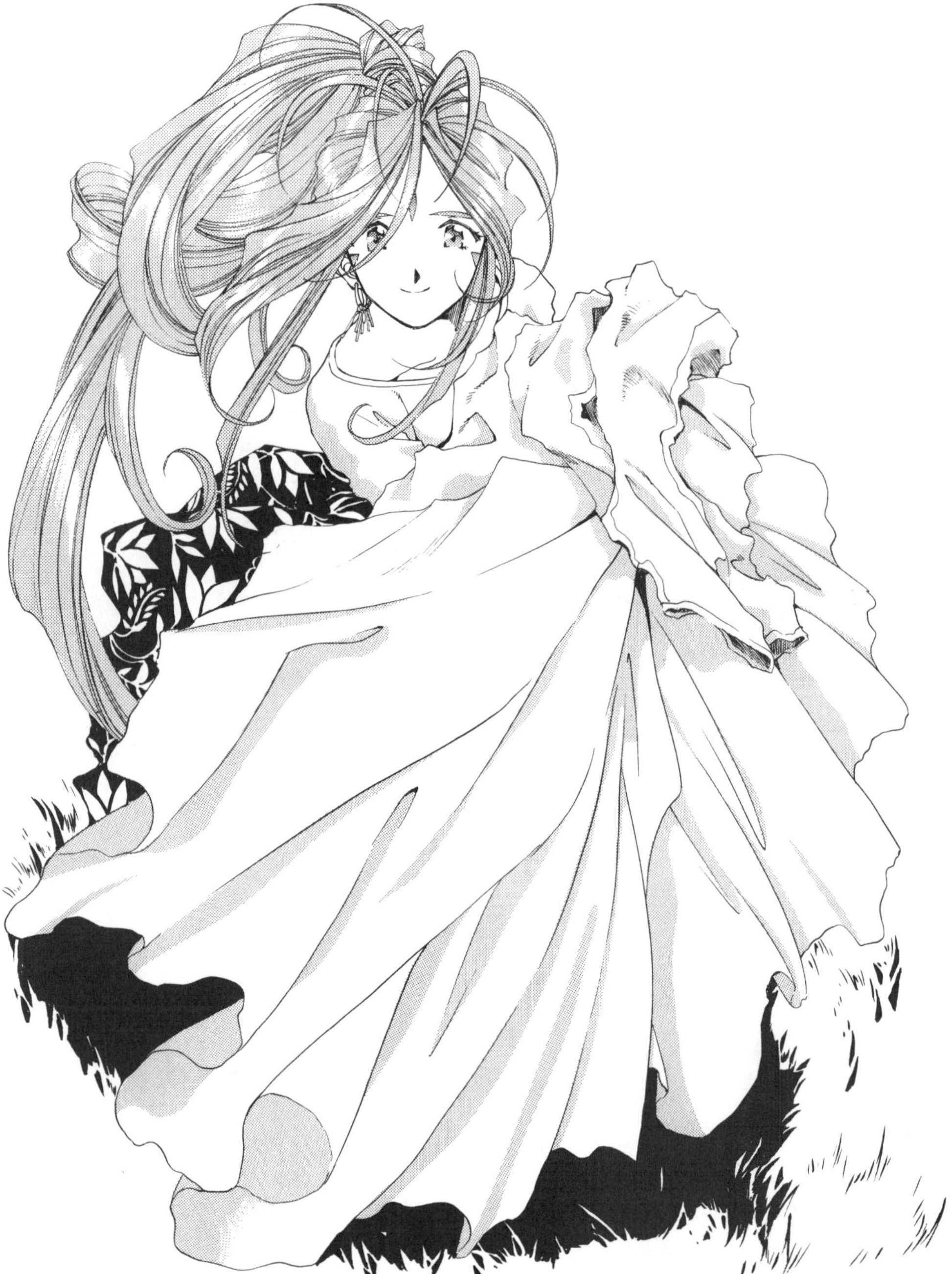

Hail to the Chief

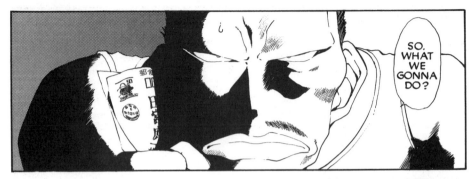

SO, WHAT WE GONNA DO?

DUNNO.

THIS IS BAD. *VERY* BAD.

WHY WOULD SHE COME BACK *NOW*?

AFTER ALL THIS TIME ...?

SIGN: MOTOR CLUB

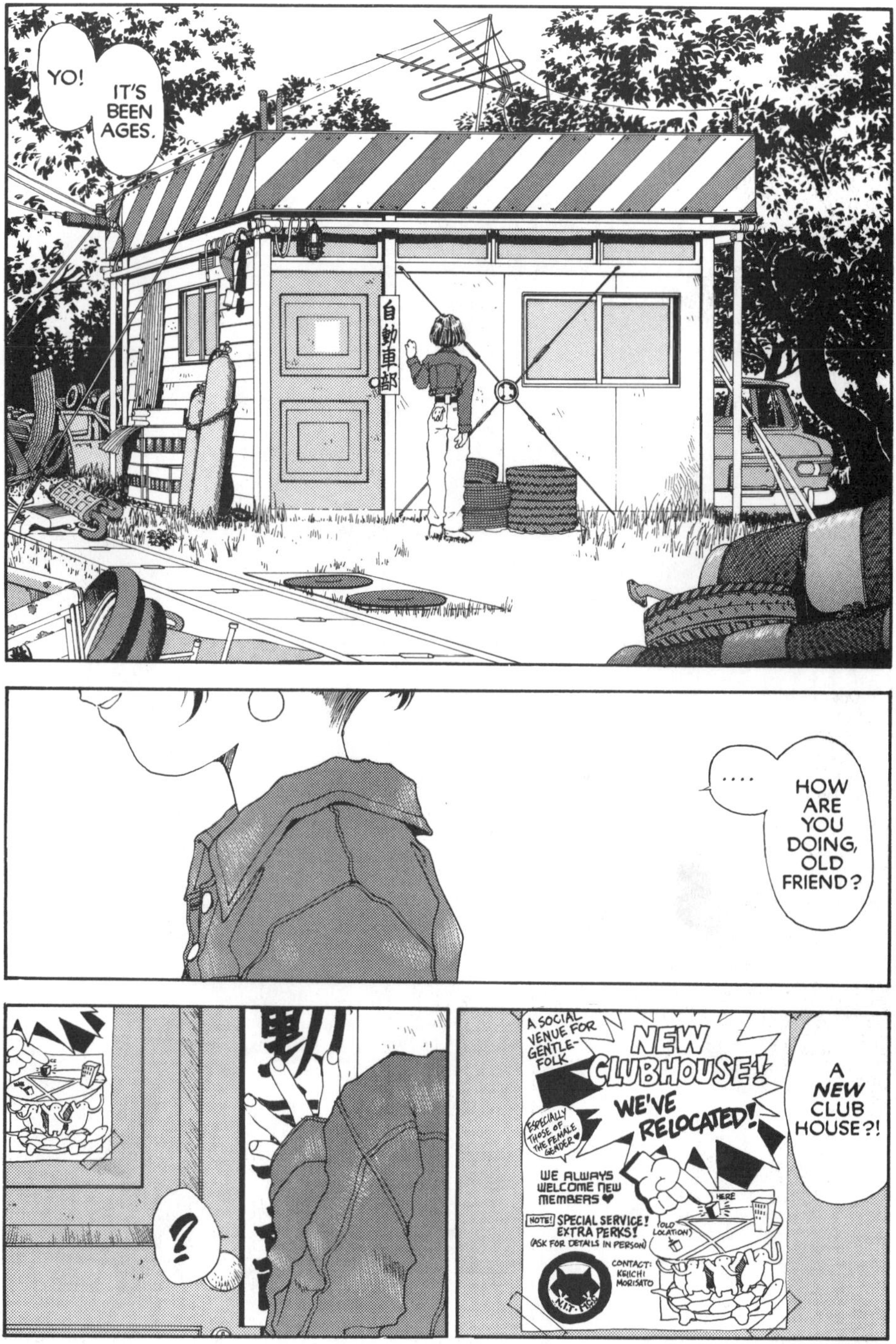
YO!
IT'S BEEN AGES.
自動車部
....
HOW ARE YOU DOING, OLD FRIEND?
?
A SOCIAL VENUE FOR GENTLE-FOLK
NEW CLUBHOUSE!
WE'VE RELOCATED!
ESPECIALLY THOSE OF THE FEMALE GENDER♥
WE ALWAYS WELCOME NEW MEMBERS♥
HERE
NOTE! SPECIAL SERVICE! EXTRA PERKS! (ASK FOR DETAILS IN PERSON)
OLD LOCATION
CONTACT: KEIICHI MORISATO
A NEW CLUB HOUSE?!

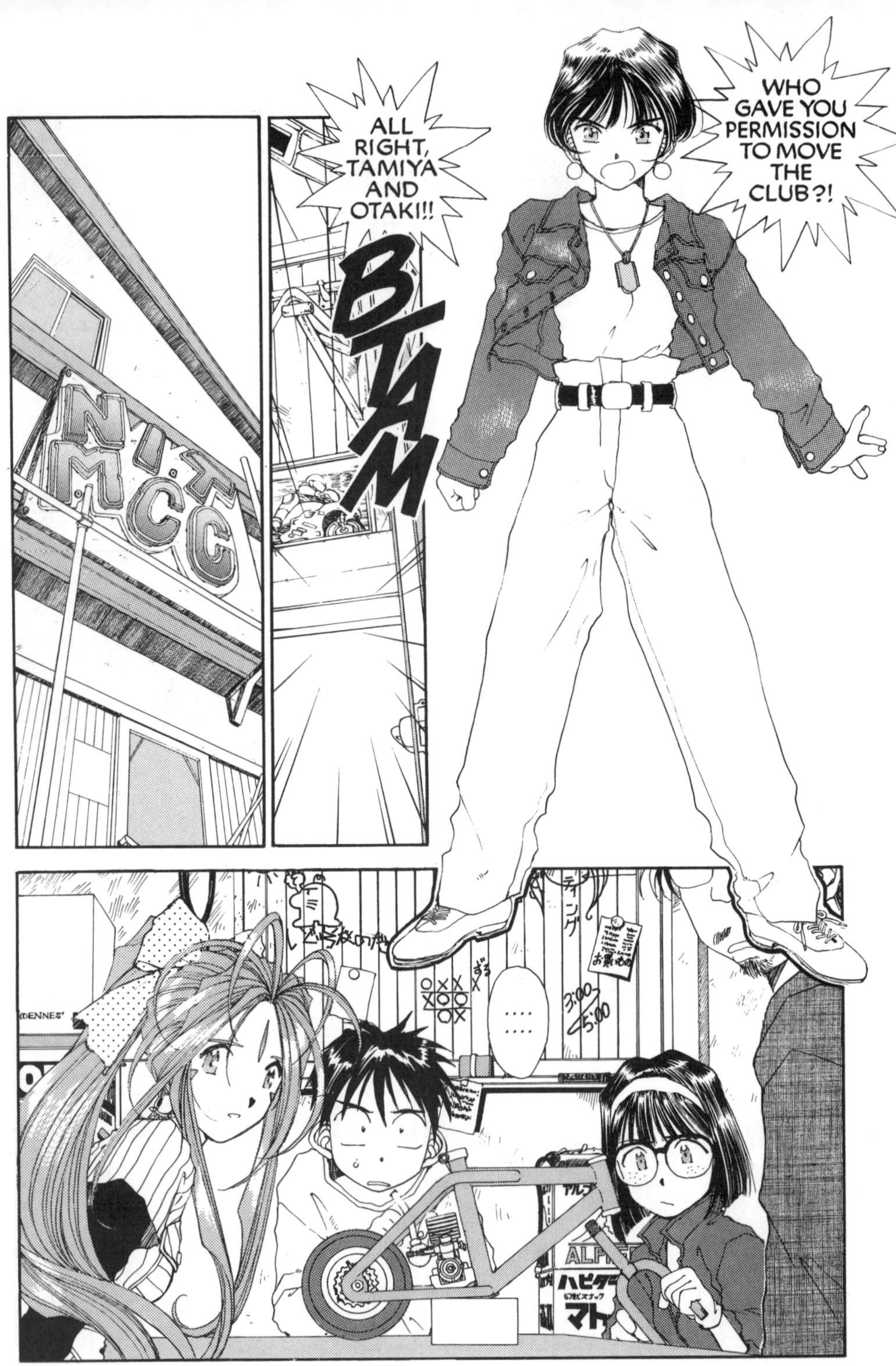

NIT
MCC
ALL RIGHT, TAMIYA AND OTAKI!!
BTAM
WHO GAVE YOU PERMISSION TO MOVE THE CLUB?!
....
....

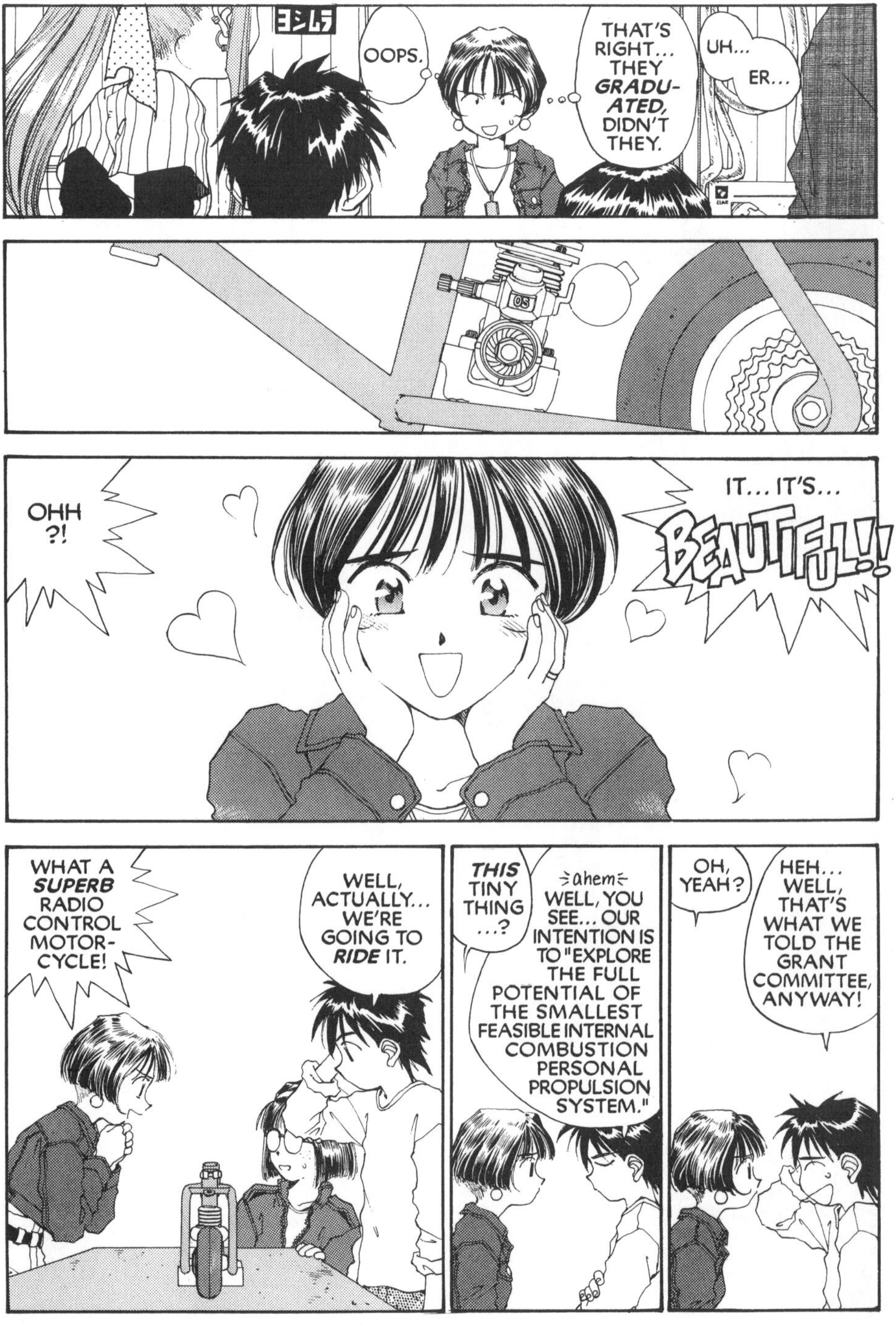
ヨシムラ
OOPS.
THAT'S RIGHT... THEY GRADU-ATED, DIDN'T THEY.
UH... ER...
OHH ?!
IT... IT'S...
BEAUTIFUL!!
WHAT A SUPERB RADIO CONTROL MOTOR-CYCLE!
WELL, ACTUALLY... WE'RE GOING TO RIDE IT.
THIS TINY THING ...?
ahem
WELL, YOU SEE... OUR INTENTION IS TO "EXPLORE THE FULL POTENTIAL OF THE SMALLEST FEASIBLE INTERNAL COMBUSTION PERSONAL PROPULSION SYSTEM."
OH, YEAH?
HEH... WELL, THAT'S WHAT WE TOLD THE GRANT COMMITTEE, ANYWAY!

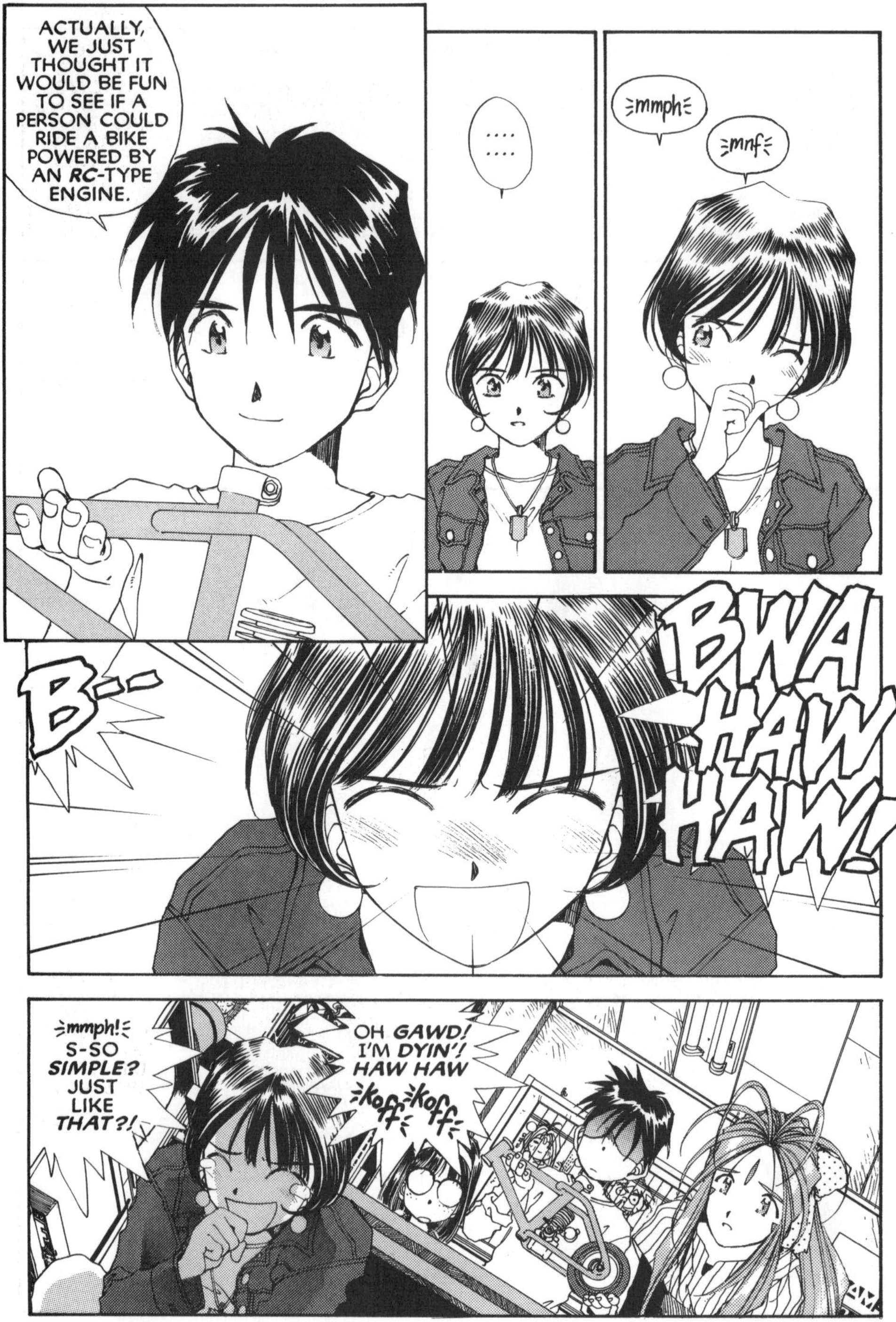

ACTUALLY, WE JUST THOUGHT IT WOULD BE FUN TO SEE IF A PERSON COULD RIDE A BIKE POWERED BY AN *RC*-TYPE ENGINE.
....
mmph
mnf
BWA HAW HAW!
B--
OH *GAWD!* I'M *DYIN'!* HAW HAW
koff koff
mmph! S-SO *SIMPLE?* JUST LIKE *THAT?!*

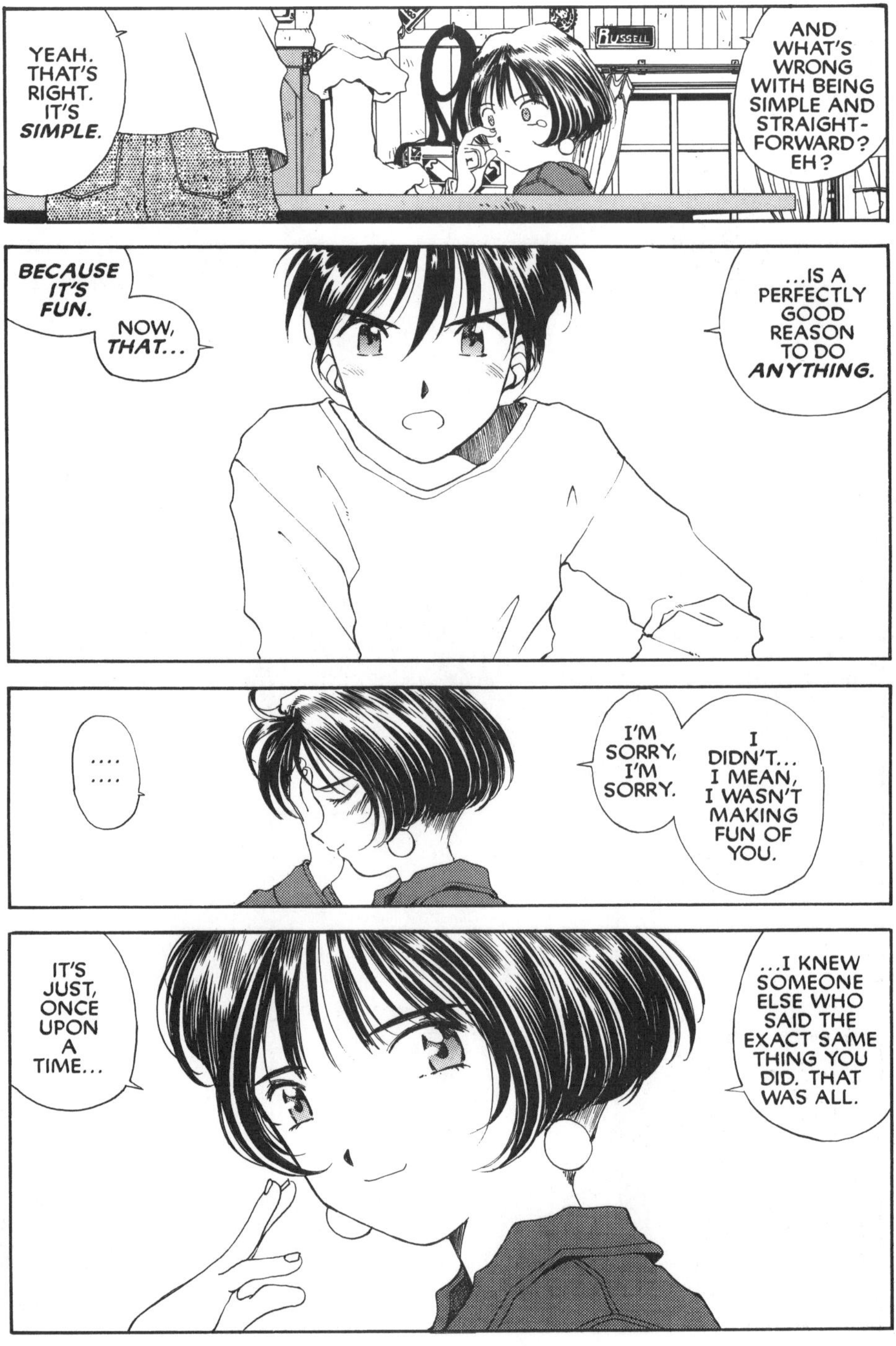
YEAH. THAT'S RIGHT. IT'S *SIMPLE*.
AND WHAT'S WRONG WITH BEING SIMPLE AND STRAIGHT-FORWARD? EH?
RUSSELL
BECAUSE IT'S FUN.
NOW, *THAT...*
...IS A PERFECTLY GOOD REASON TO DO *ANYTHING.*
....
....
I'M SORRY, I'M SORRY.
I DIDN'T... I MEAN, I WASN'T MAKING FUN OF YOU.
IT'S JUST, ONCE UPON A TIME...
...I KNEW SOMEONE ELSE WHO SAID THE EXACT SAME THING YOU DID. THAT WAS ALL.

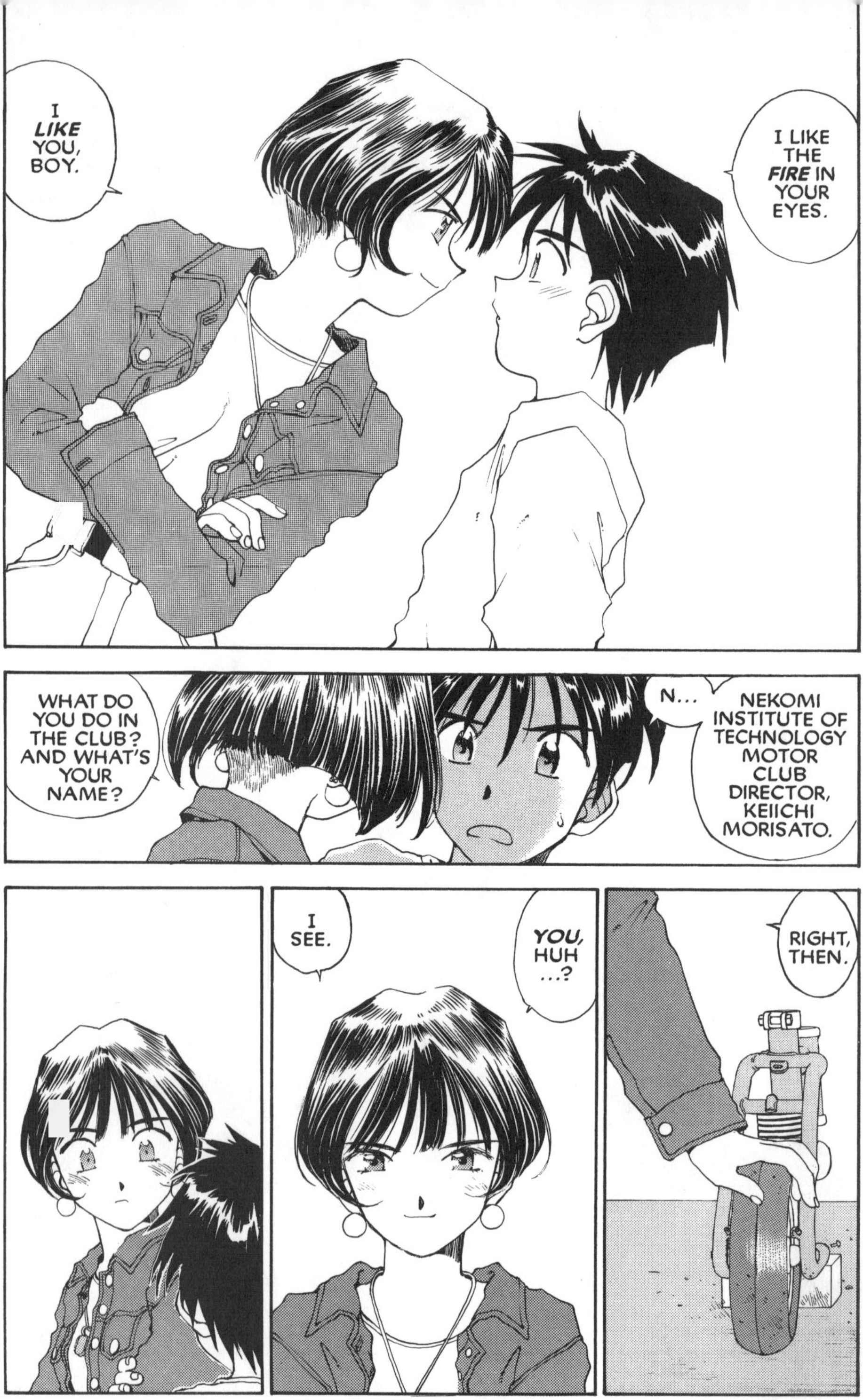
I LIKE YOU, BOY.
I LIKE THE FIRE IN YOUR EYES.
WHAT DO YOU DO IN THE CLUB? AND WHAT'S YOUR NAME?
N...
NEKOMI INSTITUTE OF TECHNOLOGY MOTOR CLUB DIRECTOR, KEIICHI MORISATO.
I SEE.
YOU, HUH ...?
RIGHT, THEN.

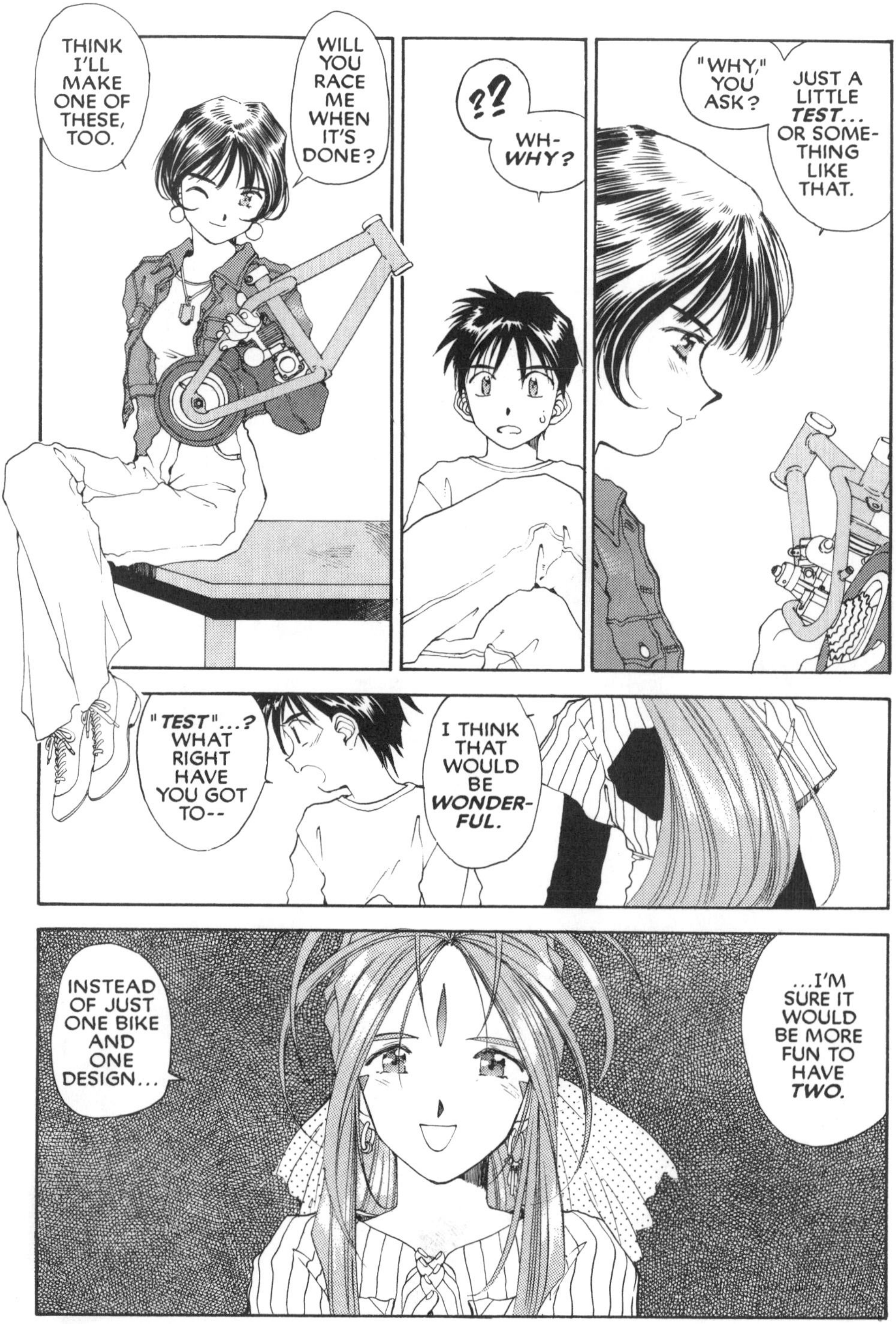
THINK I'LL MAKE ONE OF THESE, TOO.
WILL YOU RACE ME WHEN IT'S DONE?
??
WH-WHY?
"WHY," YOU ASK?
JUST A LITTLE TEST... OR SOMETHING LIKE THAT.
"TEST"...? WHAT RIGHT HAVE YOU GOT TO--
I THINK THAT WOULD BE WONDERFUL.
INSTEAD OF JUST ONE BIKE AND ONE DESIGN...
...I'M SURE IT WOULD BE MORE FUN TO HAVE TWO.

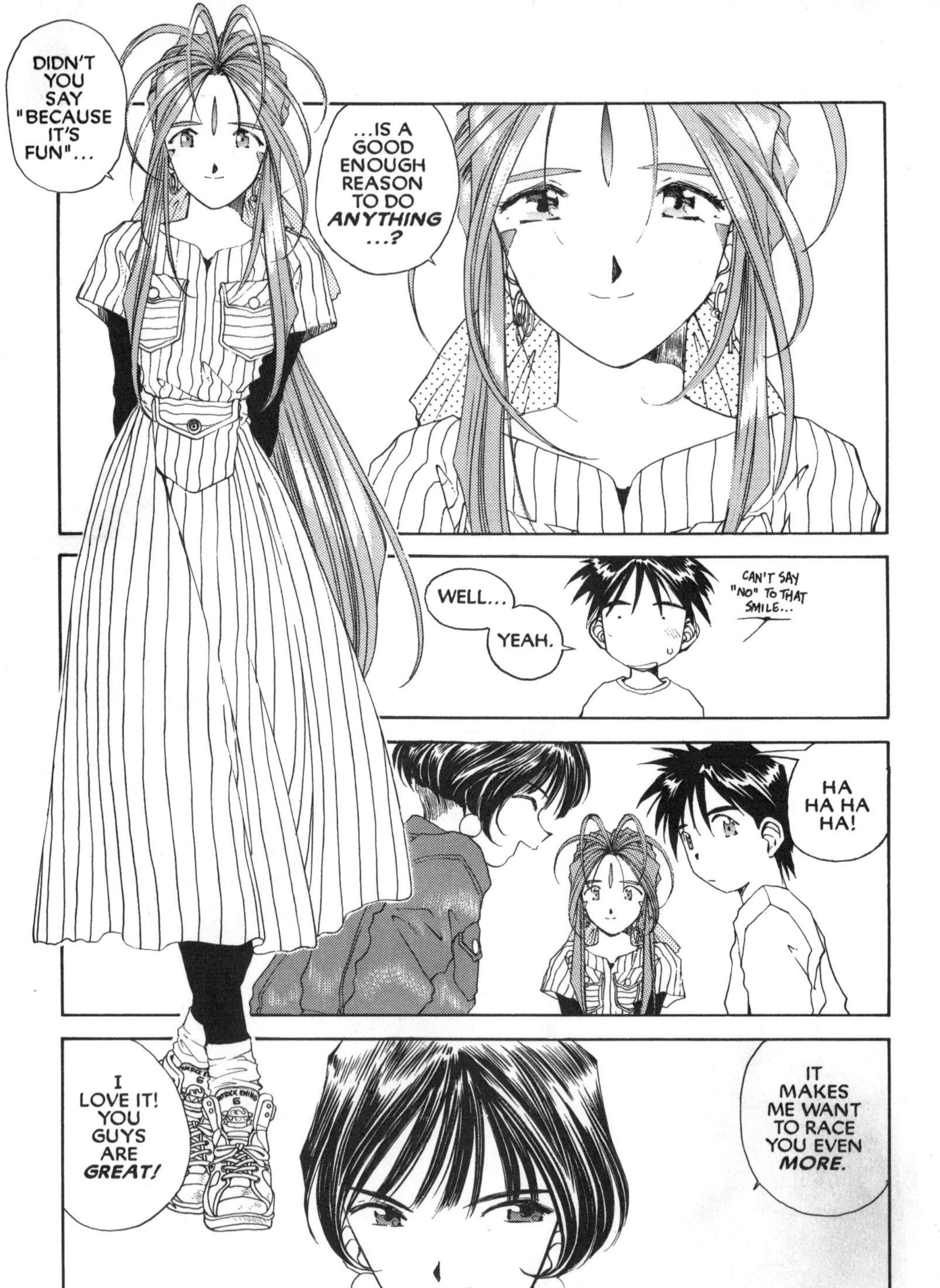
DIDN'T YOU SAY "BECAUSE IT'S FUN"...
...IS A GOOD ENOUGH REASON TO DO ANYTHING ...?
WELL...
YEAH.
CAN'T SAY "NO" TO THAT SMILE...
HA HA HA HA!
I LOVE IT! YOU GUYS ARE GREAT!
IT MAKES ME WANT TO RACE YOU EVEN MORE.

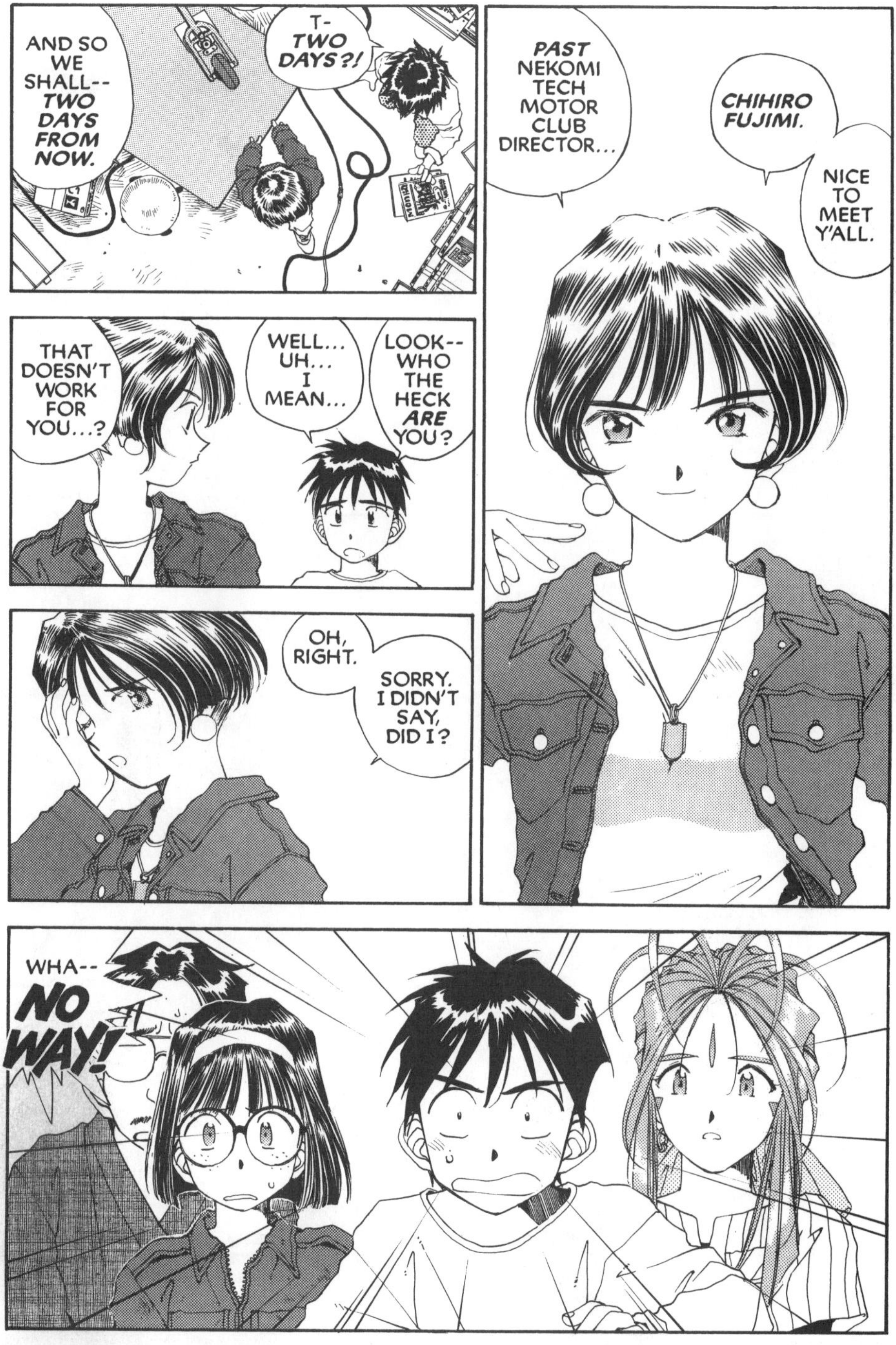
AND SO WE SHALL-- TWO DAYS FROM NOW.
T- TWO DAYS?!
THAT DOESN'T WORK FOR YOU...?
WELL... UH... I MEAN...
LOOK-- WHO THE HECK ARE YOU?
OH, RIGHT.
SORRY. I DIDN'T SAY, DID I?
PAST NEKOMI TECH MOTOR CLUB DIRECTOR...
CHIHIRO FUJIMI.
NICE TO MEET Y'ALL.
WHA--
NO WAY!

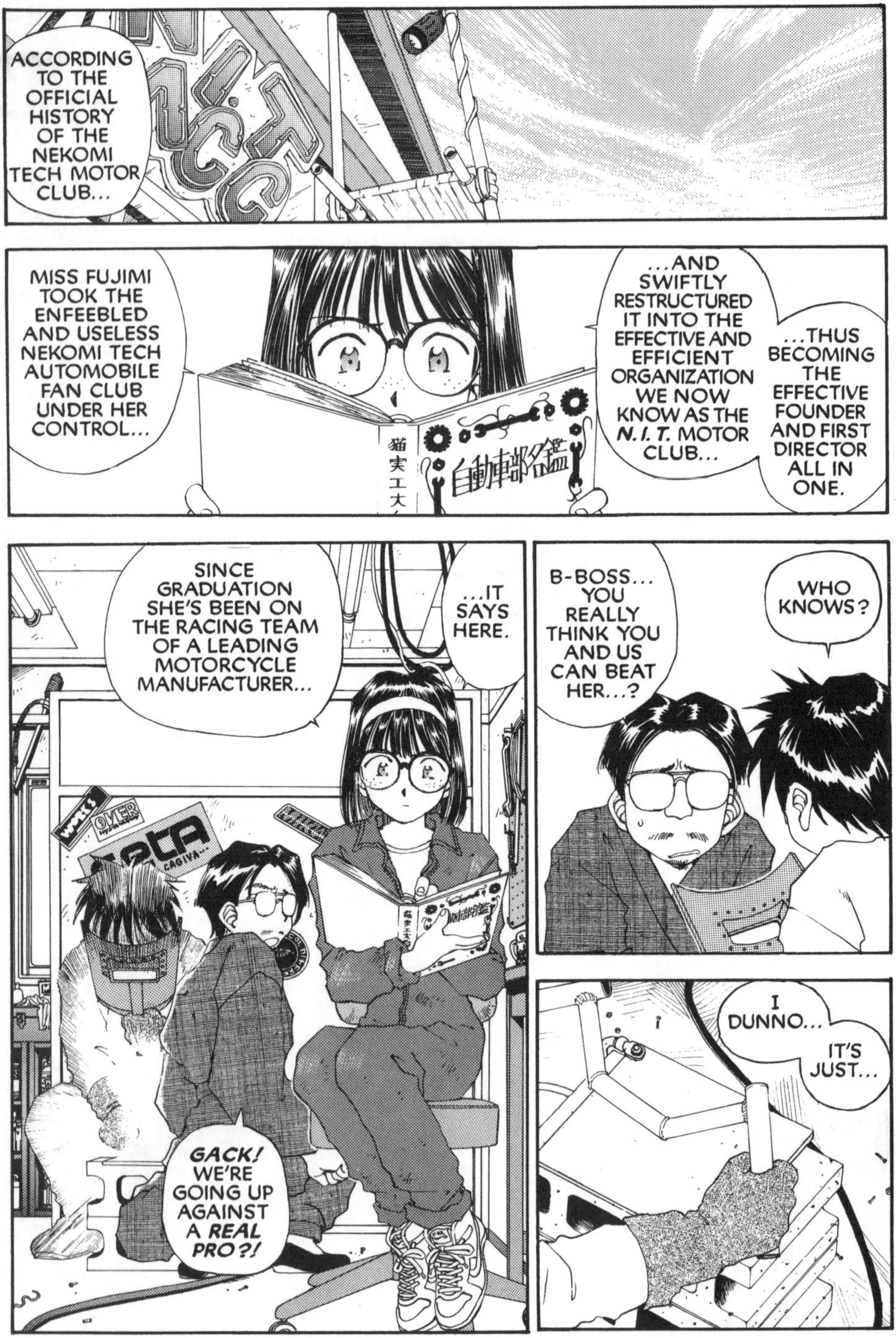
ACCORDING TO THE OFFICIAL HISTORY OF THE NEKOMI TECH MOTOR CLUB...
MISS FUJIMI TOOK THE ENFEEBLED AND USELESS NEKOMI TECH AUTOMOBILE FAN CLUB UNDER HER CONTROL...
自動車部名鑑
...AND SWIFTLY RESTRUCTURED IT INTO THE EFFECTIVE AND EFFICIENT ORGANIZATION WE NOW KNOW AS THE *N.I.T.* MOTOR CLUB...
...THUS BECOMING THE EFFECTIVE FOUNDER AND FIRST DIRECTOR ALL IN ONE.
SINCE GRADUATION SHE'S BEEN ON THE RACING TEAM OF A LEADING MOTORCYCLE MANUFACTURER...
...IT SAYS HERE.
GACK! WE'RE GOING UP AGAINST A *REAL PRO?!*
B-BOSS... YOU REALLY THINK YOU AND US CAN BEAT HER...?
WHO KNOWS?
I DUNNO... IT'S JUST...

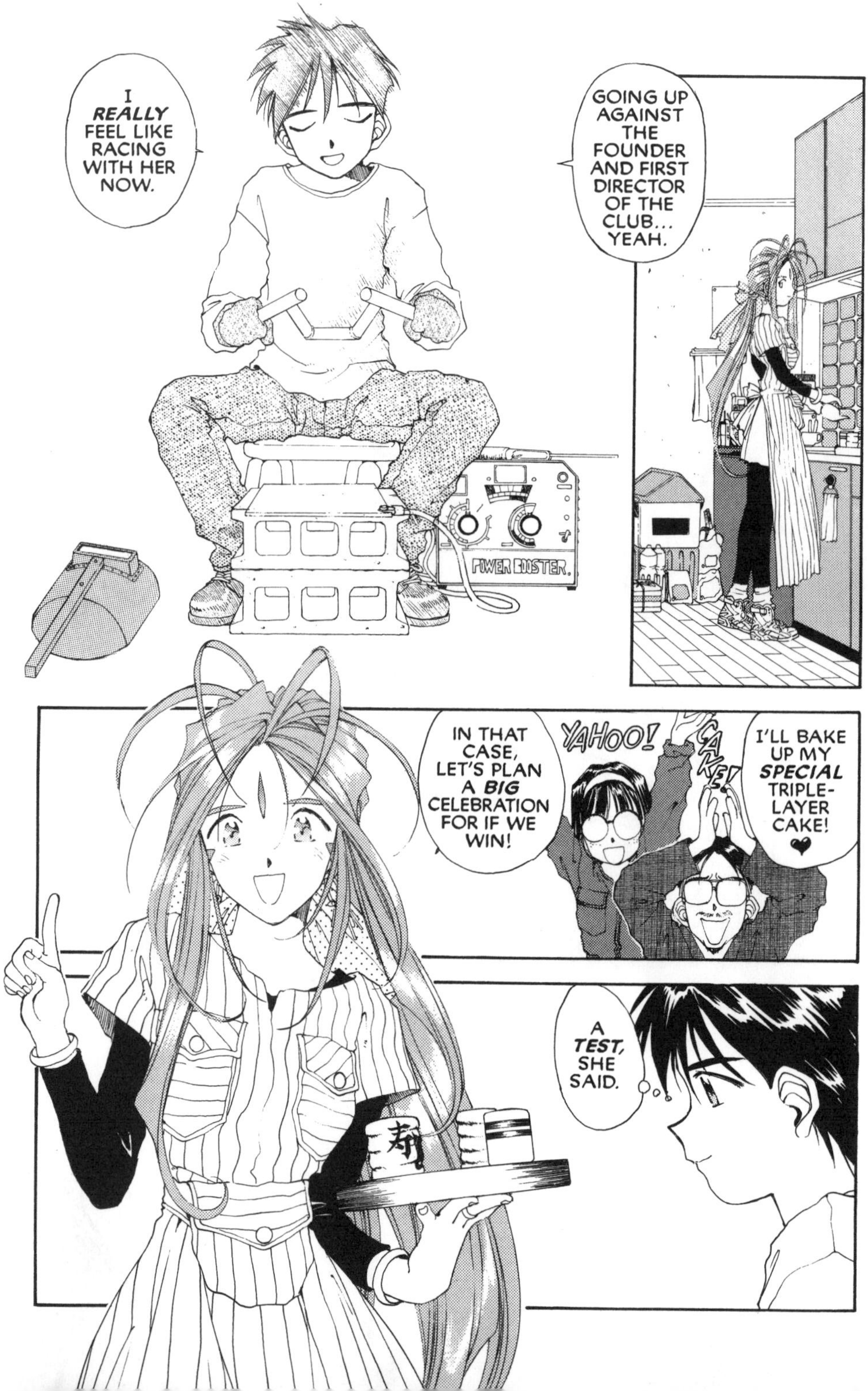
I *REALLY* FEEL LIKE RACING WITH HER NOW.
POWER BOOSTER.
GOING UP AGAINST THE FOUNDER AND FIRST DIRECTOR OF THE CLUB... YEAH.
IN THAT CASE, LET'S PLAN A *BIG* CELEBRATION FOR IF WE WIN!
YAHOO!
CAKE!
I'LL BAKE UP MY *SPECIAL* TRIPLE-LAYER CAKE! ♥
A *TEST,* SHE SAID.

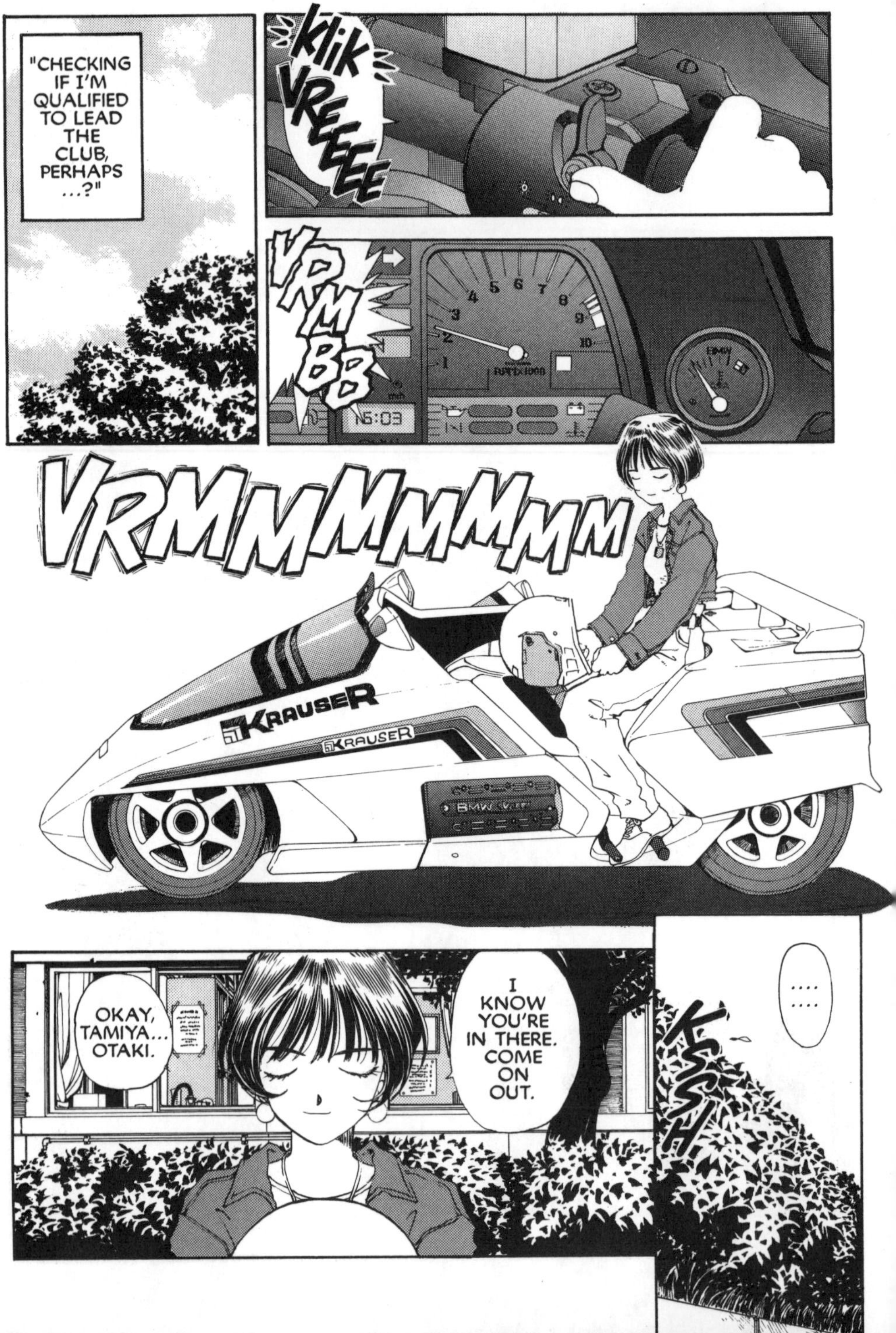
"CHECKING IF I'M QUALIFIED TO LEAD THE CLUB, PERHAPS ...?"
KLIK
VREEEEEE
VRMBB
VRMMMMMMMM
KRAUSER
KRAUSER
OKAY, TAMIYA... OTAKI.
I KNOW YOU'RE IN THERE. COME ON OUT.
....
....
KSSH

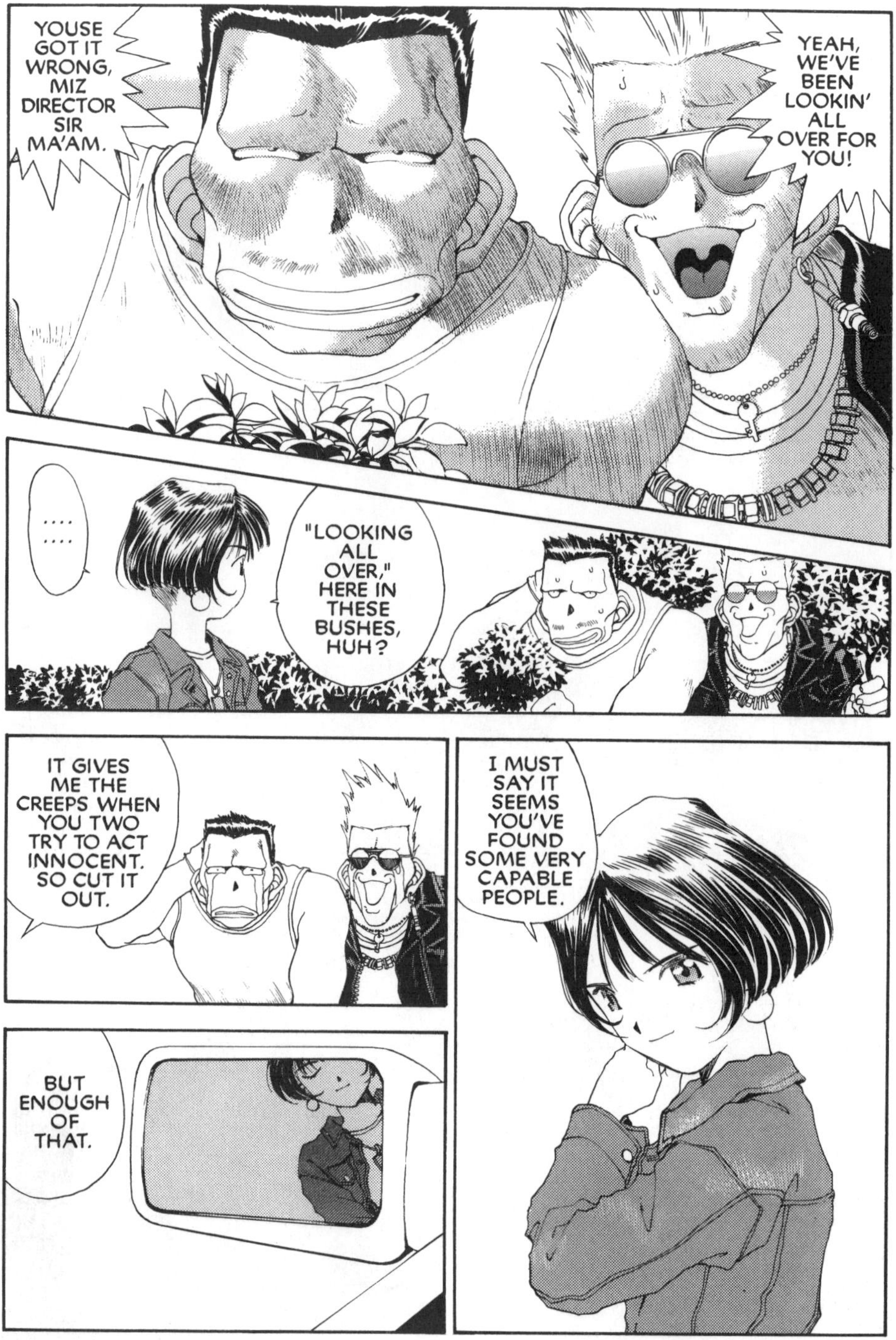
YOUSE GOT IT WRONG, MIZ DIRECTOR SIR MA'AM.
YEAH, WE'VE BEEN LOOKIN' ALL OVER FOR YOU!
....
"LOOKING ALL OVER," HERE IN THESE BUSHES, HUH?
IT GIVES ME THE CREEPS WHEN YOU TWO TRY TO ACT INNOCENT. SO CUT IT OUT.
BUT ENOUGH OF THAT.
I MUST SAY IT SEEMS YOU'VE FOUND SOME VERY CAPABLE PEOPLE.

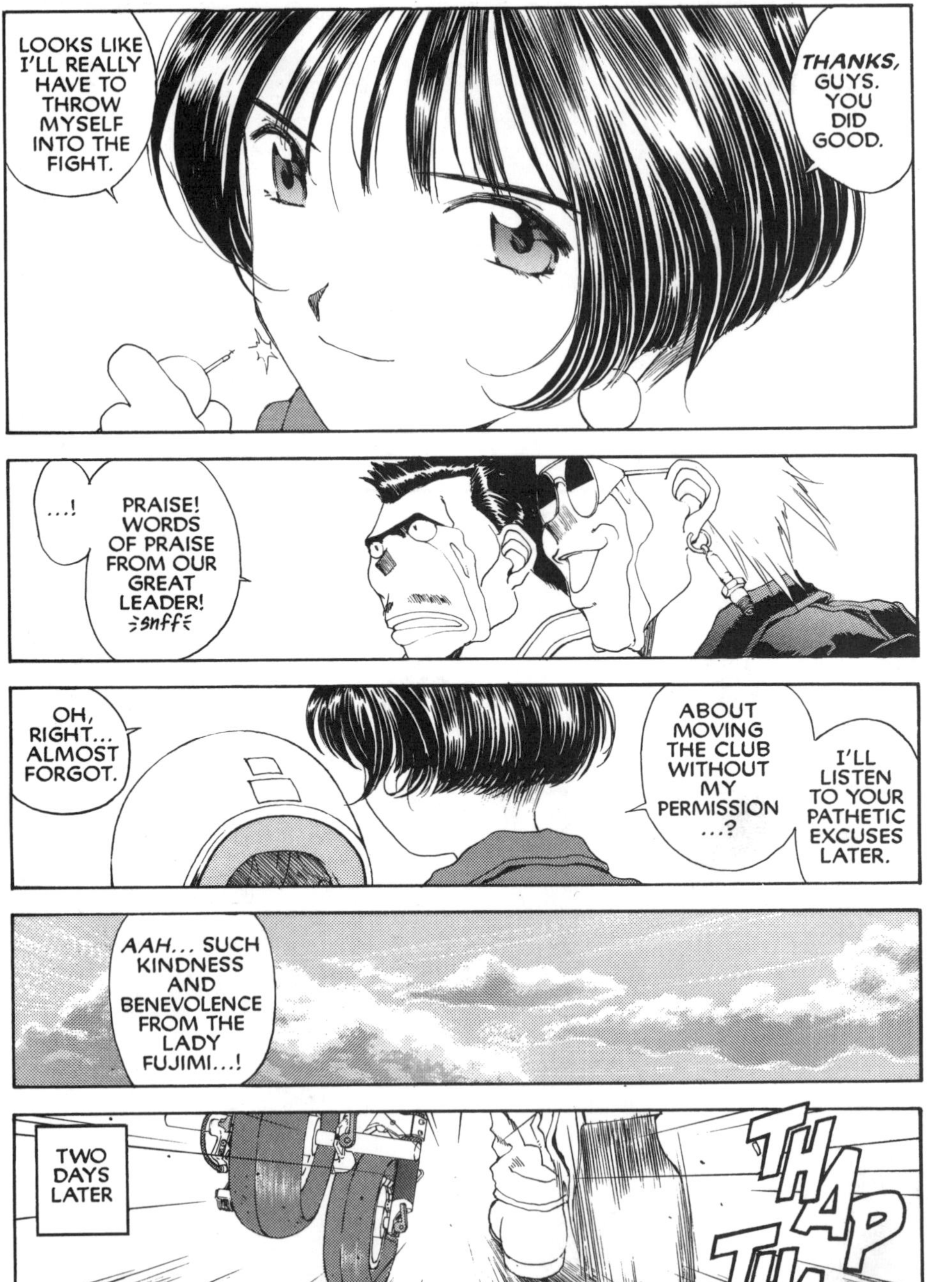
LOOKS LIKE I'LL REALLY HAVE TO THROW MYSELF INTO THE FIGHT.
THANKS, GUYS. YOU DID GOOD.
...!
PRAISE! WORDS OF PRAISE FROM OUR GREAT LEADER! snff
OH, RIGHT... ALMOST FORGOT.
ABOUT MOVING THE CLUB WITHOUT MY PERMISSION ...?
I'LL LISTEN TO YOUR PATHETIC EXCUSES LATER.
AAH... SUCH KINDNESS AND BENEVOLENCE FROM THE LADY FUJIMI...!
TWO DAYS LATER
THAP THAP

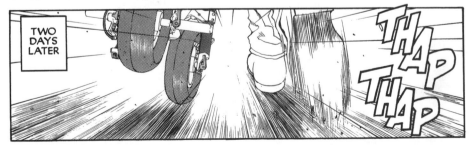

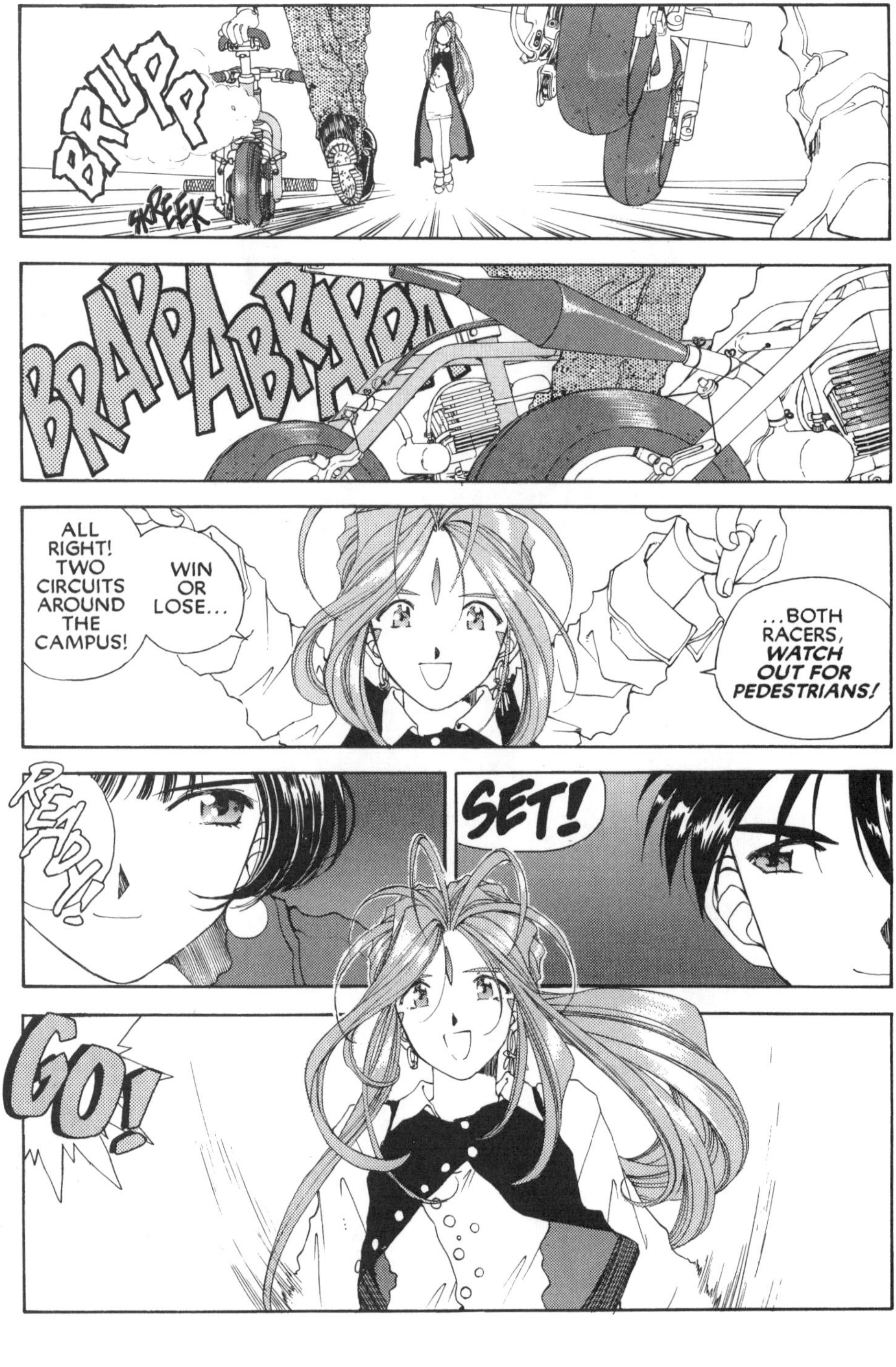
BRUPP
SKREEEK
BRAPPABRAPP
ALL RIGHT! TWO CIRCUITS AROUND THE CAMPUS!
WIN OR LOSE...
...BOTH RACERS, WATCH OUT FOR PEDESTRIANS!
READY!!
SET!
GO!

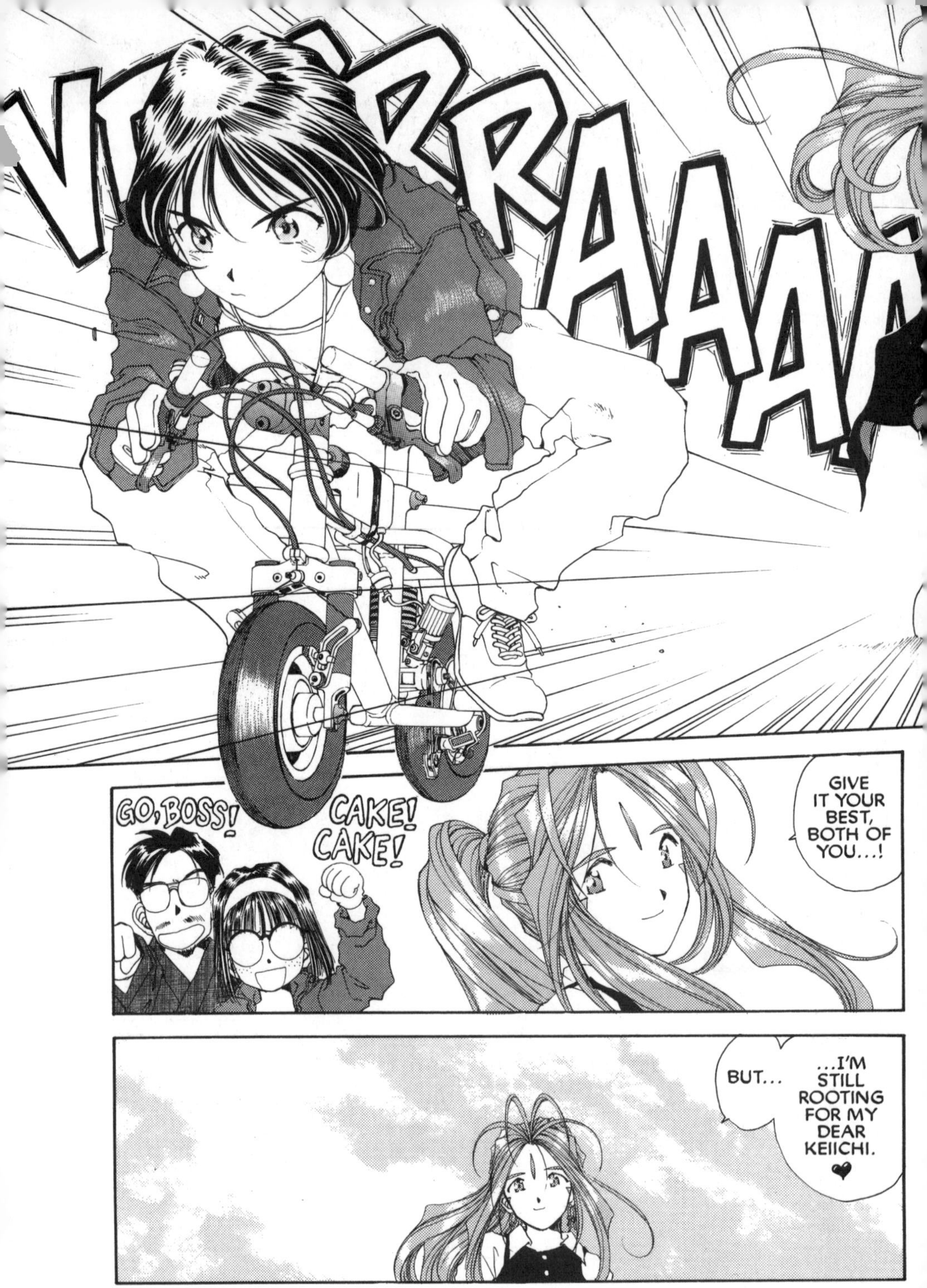
GO, BOSS!
CAKE! CAKE!
GIVE IT YOUR BEST, BOTH OF YOU...!
BUT...
...I'M STILL ROOTING FOR MY DEAR KEIICHI. ♥

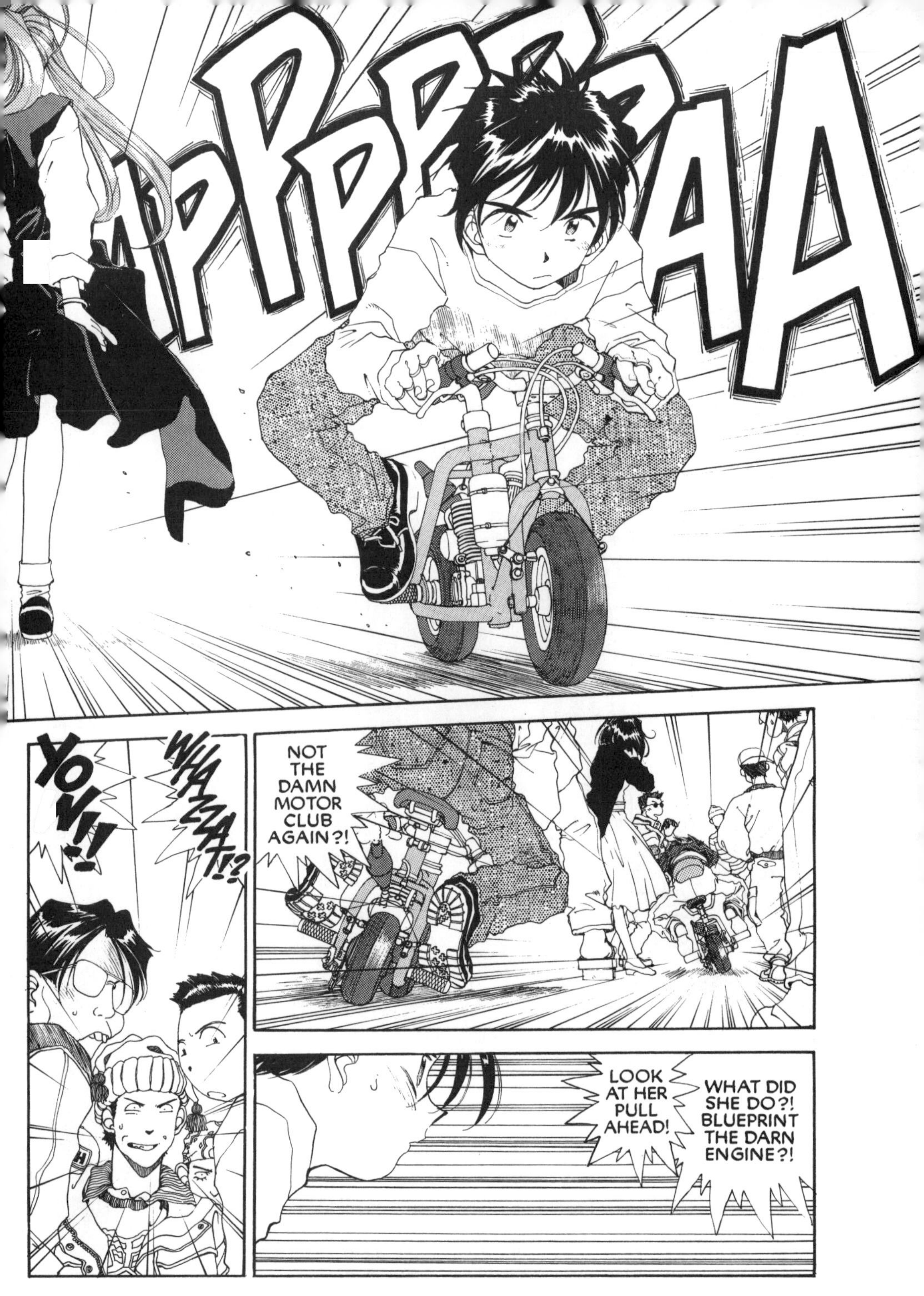
PPPPPAA
YOW!!
WHAZZAT!!?
NOT THE DAMN MOTOR CLUB AGAIN?!
LOOK AT HER PULL AHEAD!
WHAT DID SHE DO?! BLUEPRINT THE DARN ENGINE?!

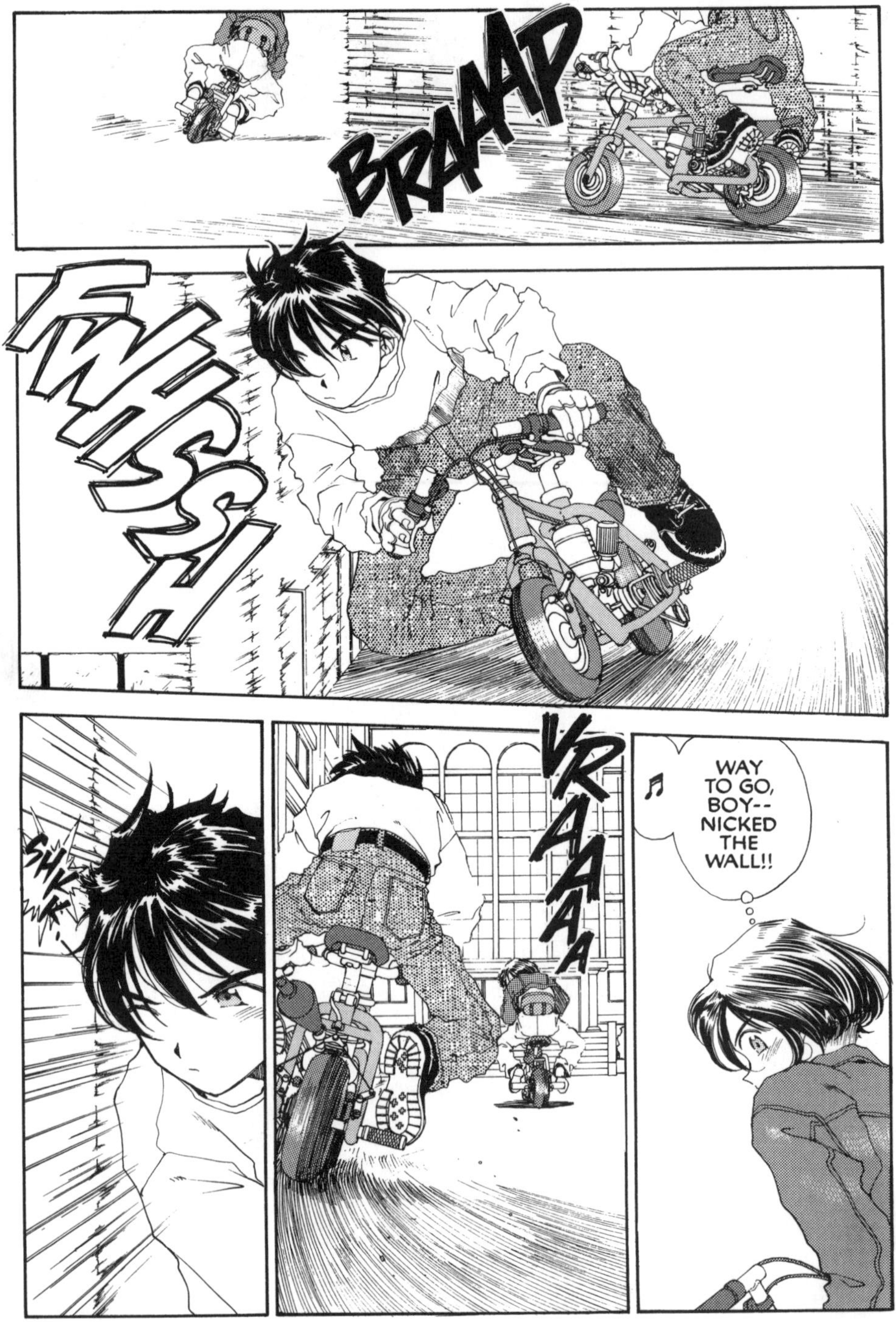
BRAAAP
FWHISSH
SHKR.
VRAAAAAA
WAY TO GO, BOY-- NICKED THE WALL!!

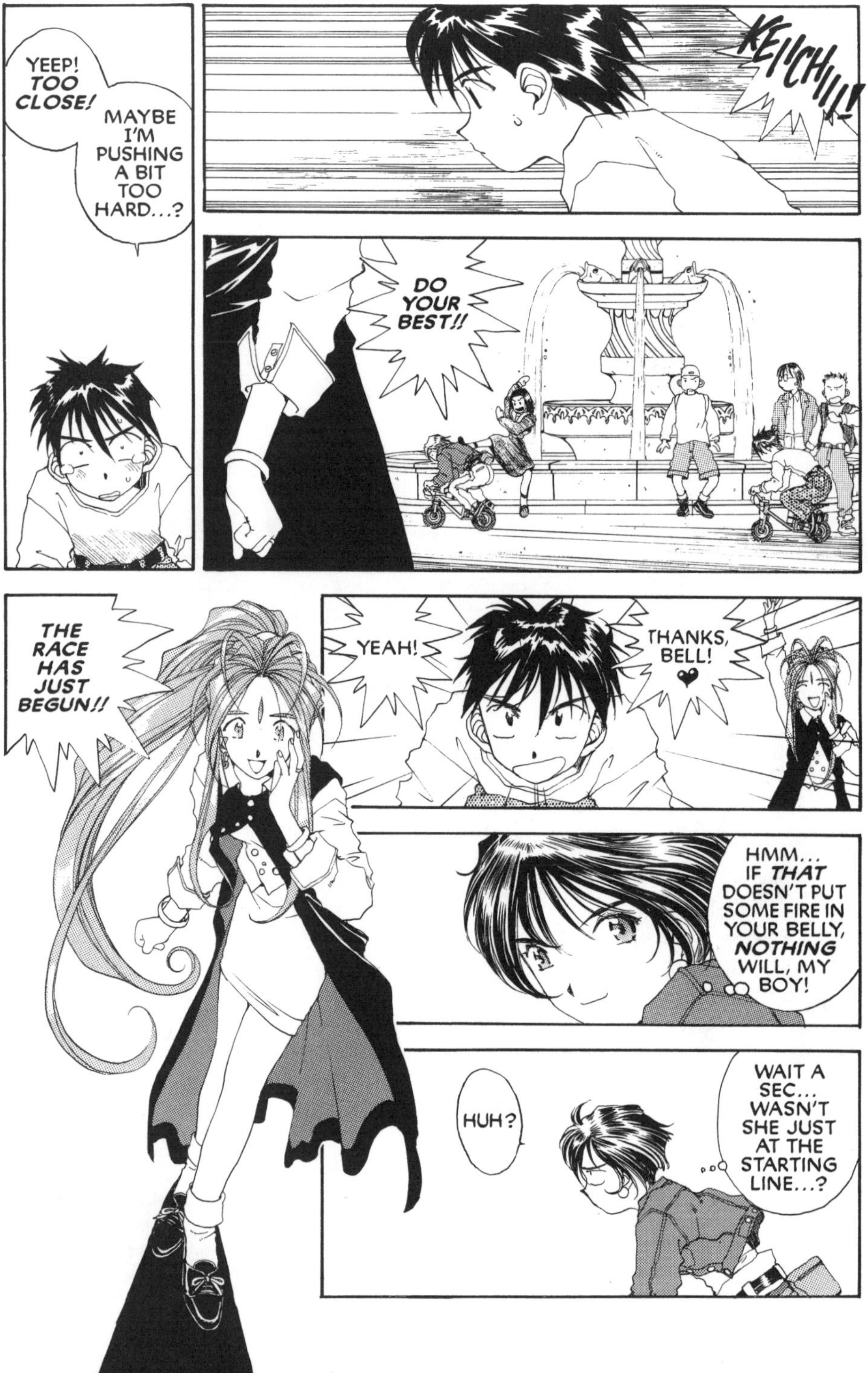
YEEP! *TOO CLOSE!*
MAYBE I'M PUSHING A BIT TOO HARD...?
KEIICHIII!!
DO YOUR BEST!!
THE RACE HAS JUST BEGUN!!
YEAH!
THANKS, BELL! ♥
HMM... IF *THAT* DOESN'T PUT SOME FIRE IN YOUR BELLY, *NOTHING* WILL, MY BOY!
HUH?
WAIT A SEC... WASN'T SHE JUST AT THE STARTING LINE...?

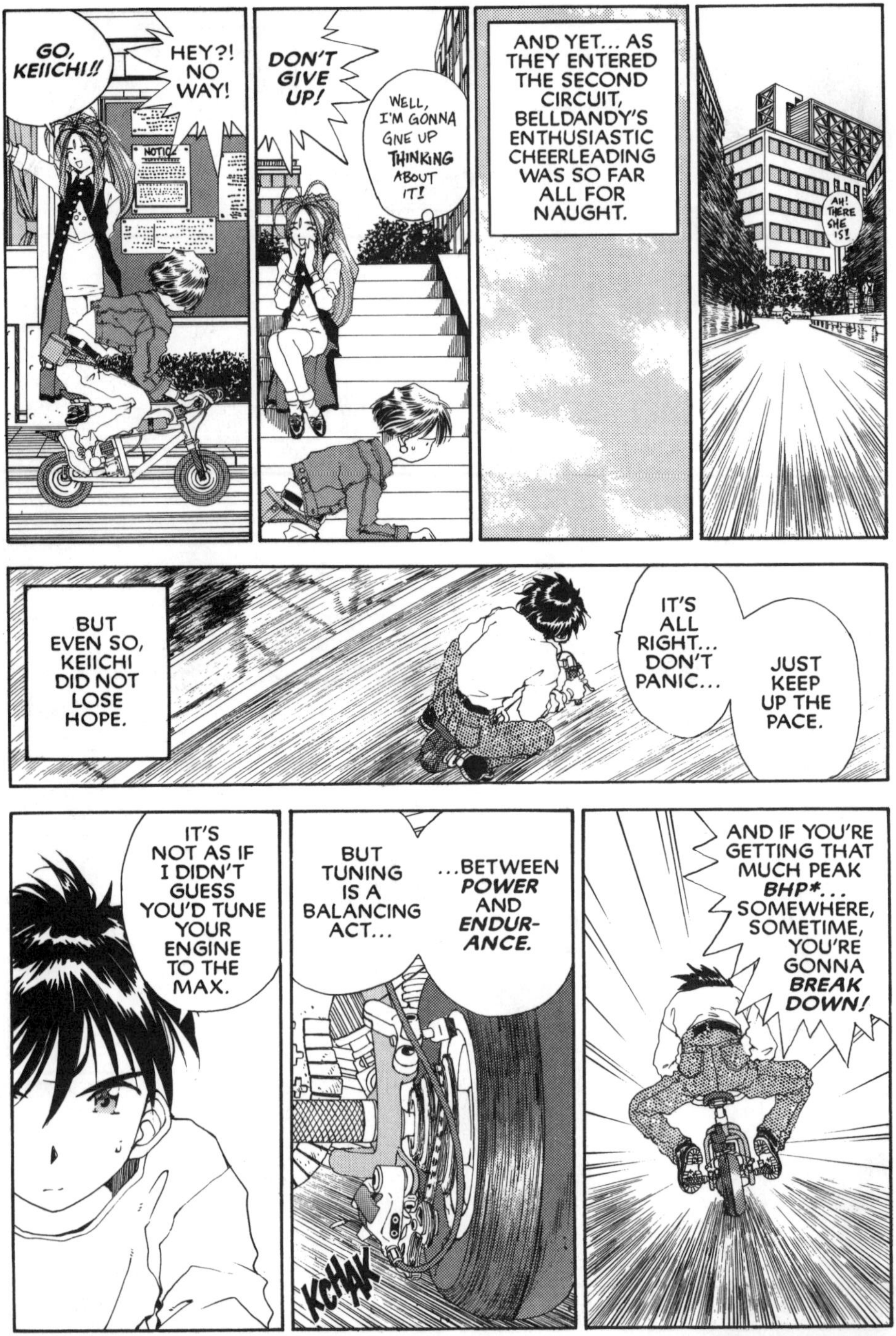
GO, KEIICHI!!
HEY?! NO WAY!
DON'T GIVE UP!
WELL, I'M GONNA GIVE UP THINKING ABOUT IT!
AND YET... AS THEY ENTERED THE SECOND CIRCUIT, BELLDANDY'S ENTHUSIASTIC CHEERLEADING WAS SO FAR ALL FOR NAUGHT.
AH! THERE SHE IS!
BUT EVEN SO, KEIICHI DID NOT LOSE HOPE.
IT'S ALL RIGHT... DON'T PANIC...
JUST KEEP UP THE PACE.
IT'S NOT AS IF I DIDN'T GUESS YOU'D TUNE YOUR ENGINE TO THE MAX.
BUT TUNING IS A BALANCING ACT...
...BETWEEN POWER AND ENDURANCE.
KCHAK
AND IF YOU'RE GETTING THAT MUCH PEAK BHP*... SOMEWHERE, SOMETIME, YOU'RE GONNA BREAK DOWN!

*: BRAKE HORSEPOWER

ABSOLUTELY!

WELL, PROBABLY...

RRG... HURRY UP AND *BLOW,* ALREADY!!

HAH! *GOTCHA!*

HUH?

NO WAY!

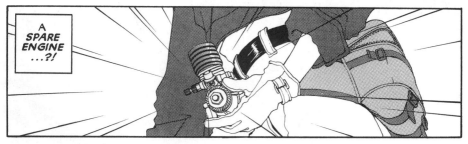

A *SPARE ENGINE* ...?!

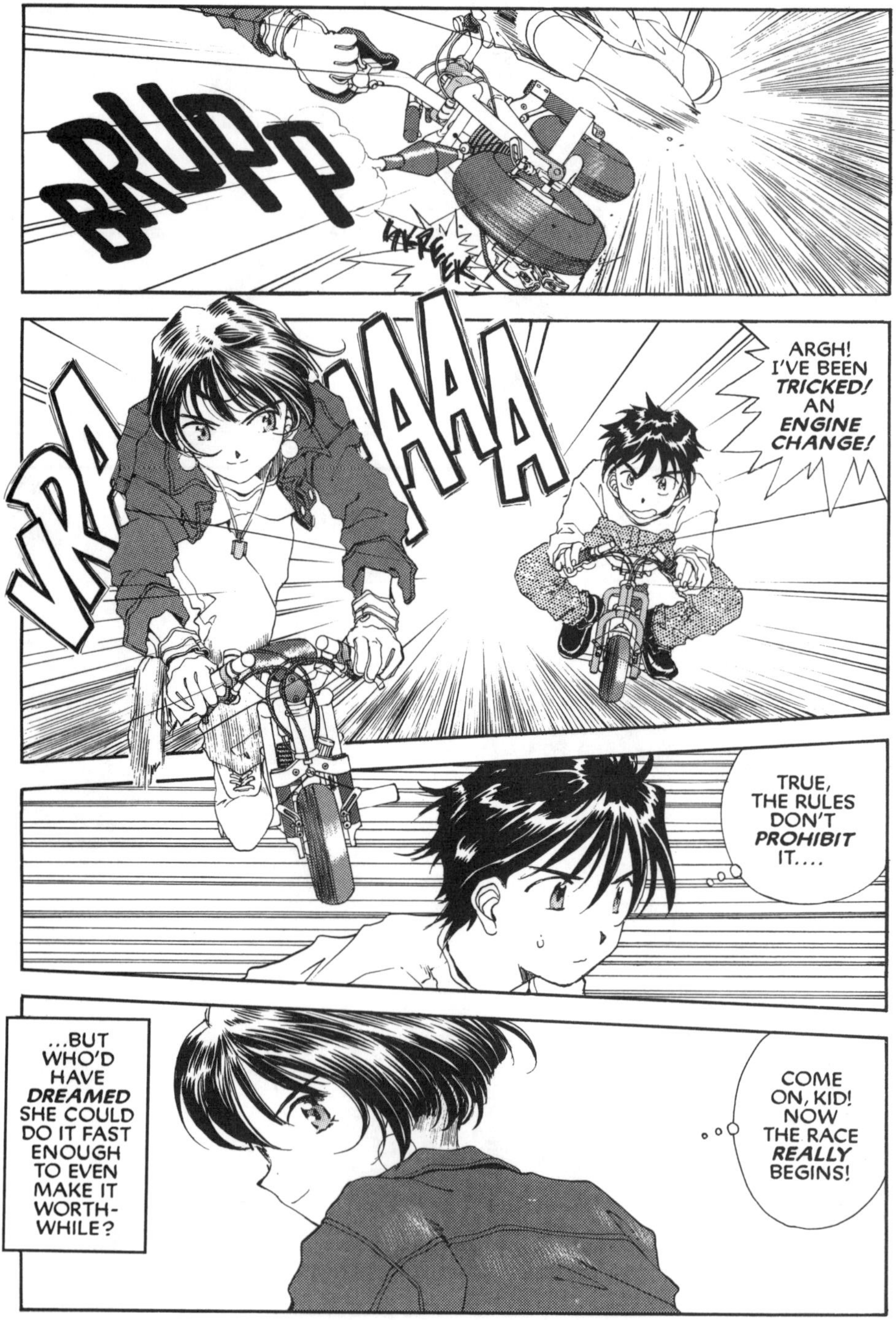
BRUPP
VRAAAAA
ARGH! I'VE BEEN *TRICKED!* AN *ENGINE CHANGE!*
TRUE, THE RULES DON'T *PROHIBIT* IT....
...BUT WHO'D HAVE *DREAMED* SHE COULD DO IT FAST ENOUGH TO EVEN MAKE IT WORTH-WHILE?
COME ON, KID! NOW THE RACE *REALLY* BEGINS!

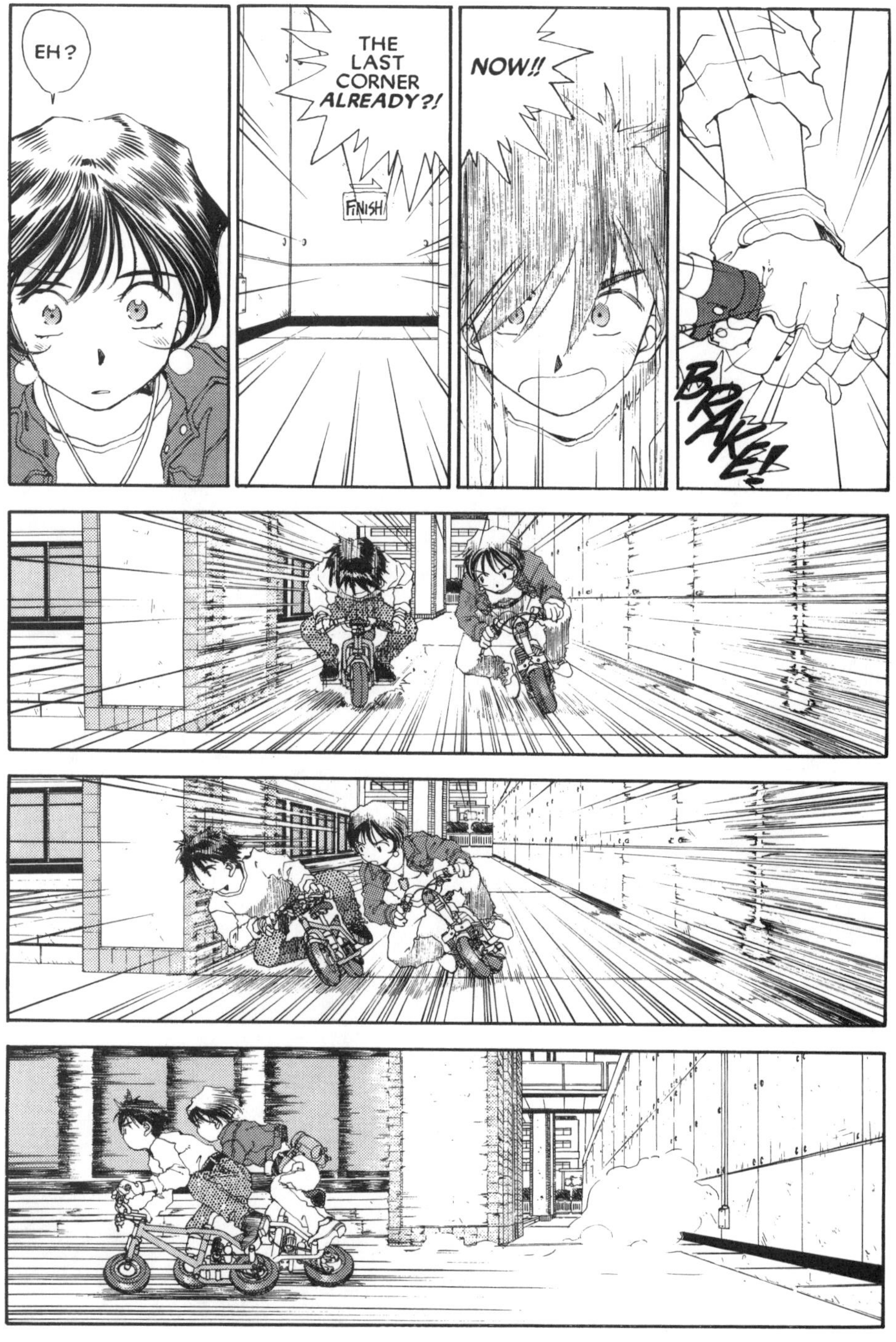
EH?
THE LAST CORNER ALREADY?!
FINISH
NOW!!
BRAKE!

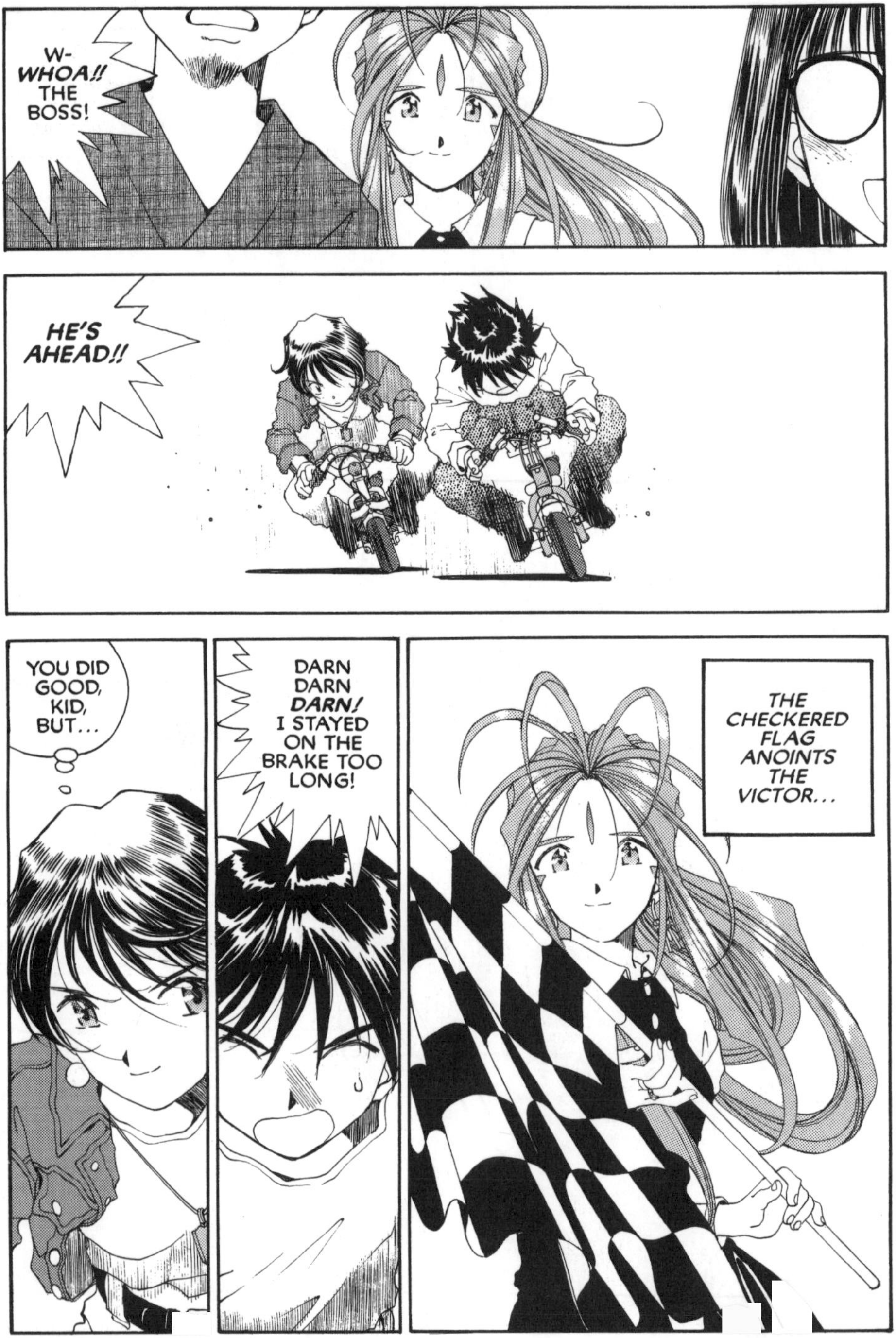
W-
WHOA!! THE BOSS!
HE'S AHEAD!!
YOU DID GOOD, KID, BUT...
DARN DARN DARN! I STAYED ON THE BRAKE TOO LONG!
THE CHECKERED FLAG ANOINTS THE VICTOR...

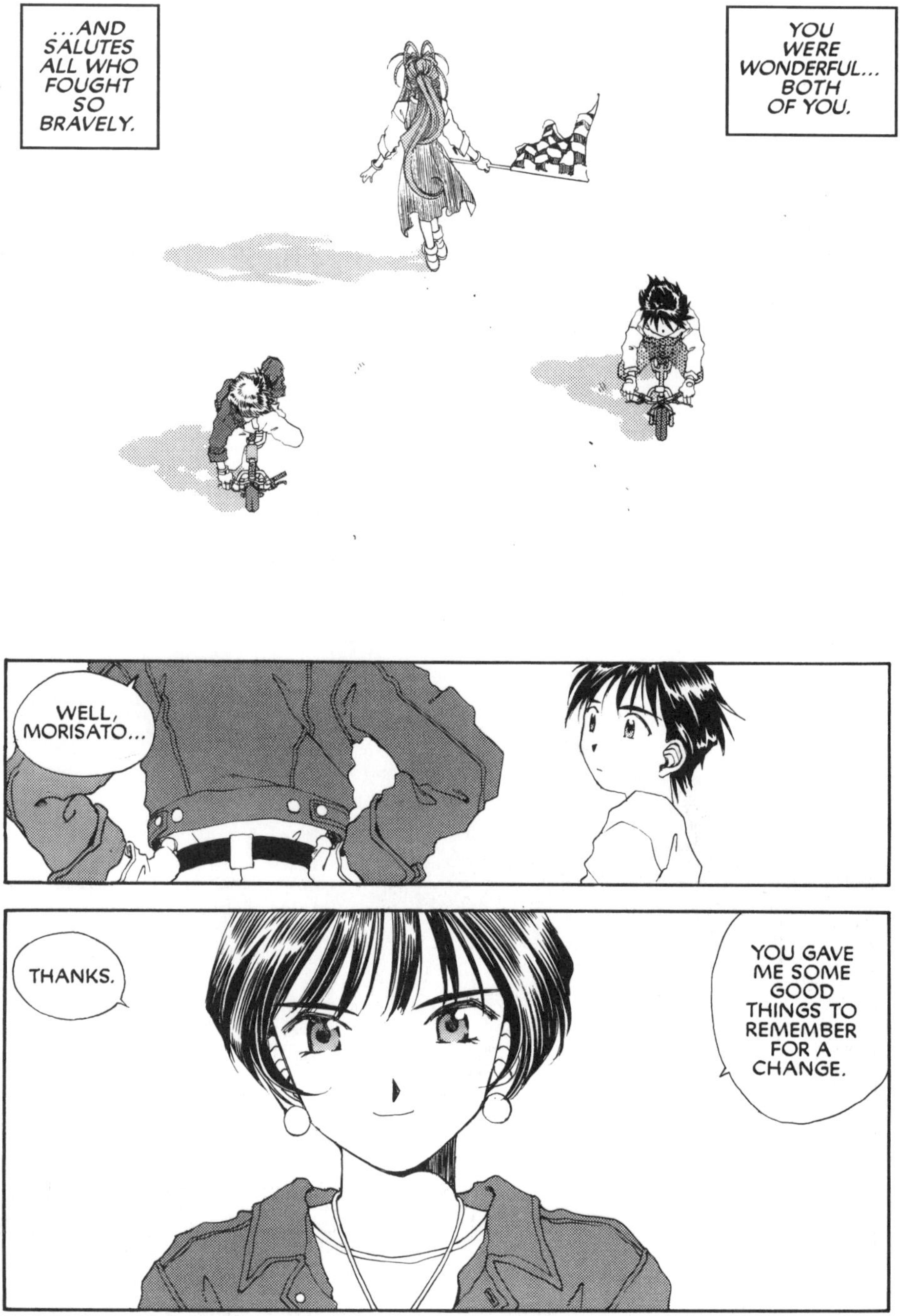
...AND SALUTES ALL WHO FOUGHT SO BRAVELY.
YOU WERE WONDERFUL... BOTH OF YOU.
WELL, MORISATO...
THANKS.
YOU GAVE ME SOME GOOD THINGS TO REMEMBER FOR A CHANGE.

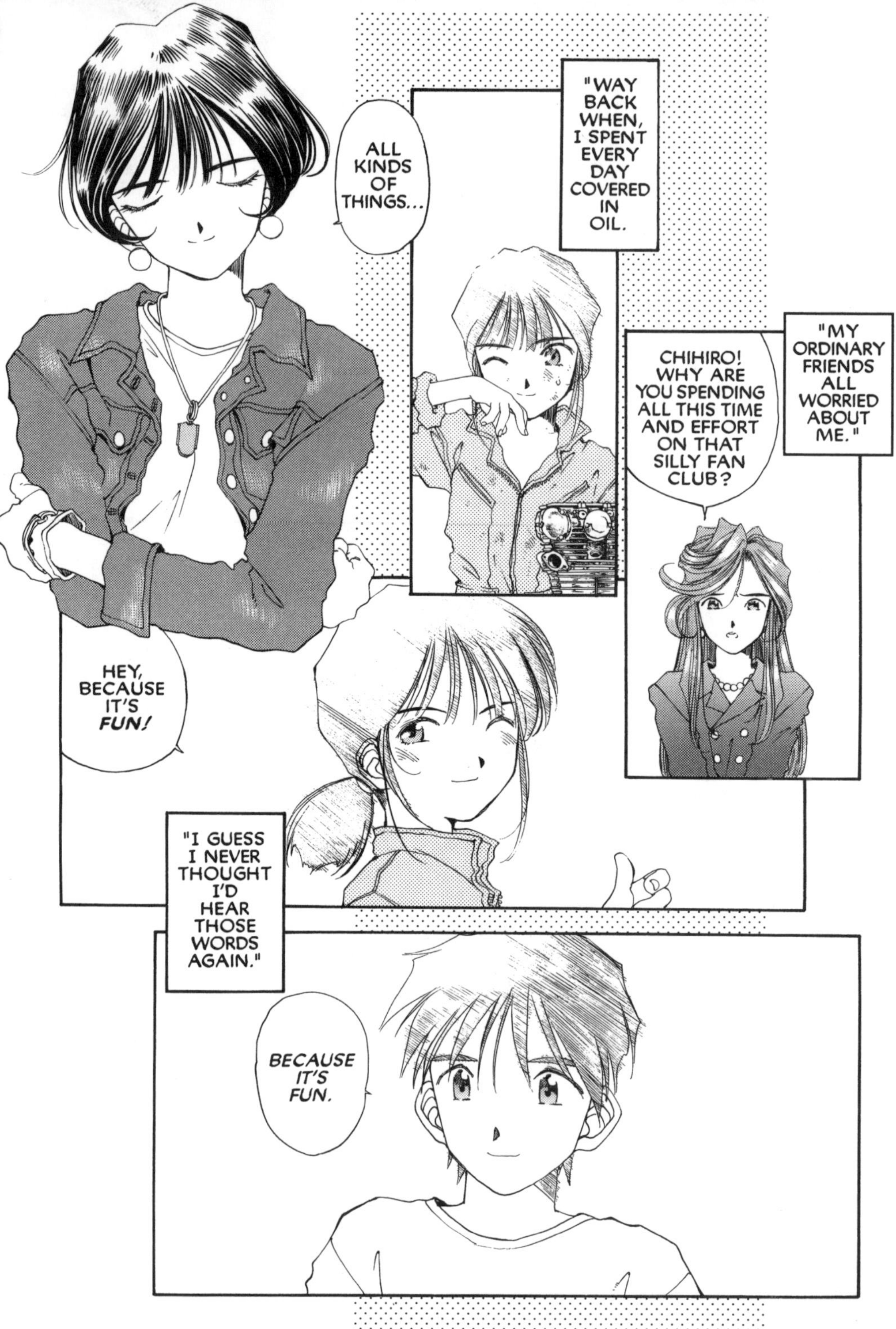
ALL KINDS OF THINGS...
"WAY BACK WHEN, I SPENT EVERY DAY COVERED IN OIL.
"MY ORDINARY FRIENDS ALL WORRIED ABOUT ME."
CHIHIRO! WHY ARE YOU SPENDING ALL THIS TIME AND EFFORT ON THAT SILLY FAN CLUB?
HEY, BECAUSE IT'S *FUN!*
"I GUESS I NEVER THOUGHT I'D HEAR THOSE WORDS AGAIN."
BECAUSE IT'S FUN.

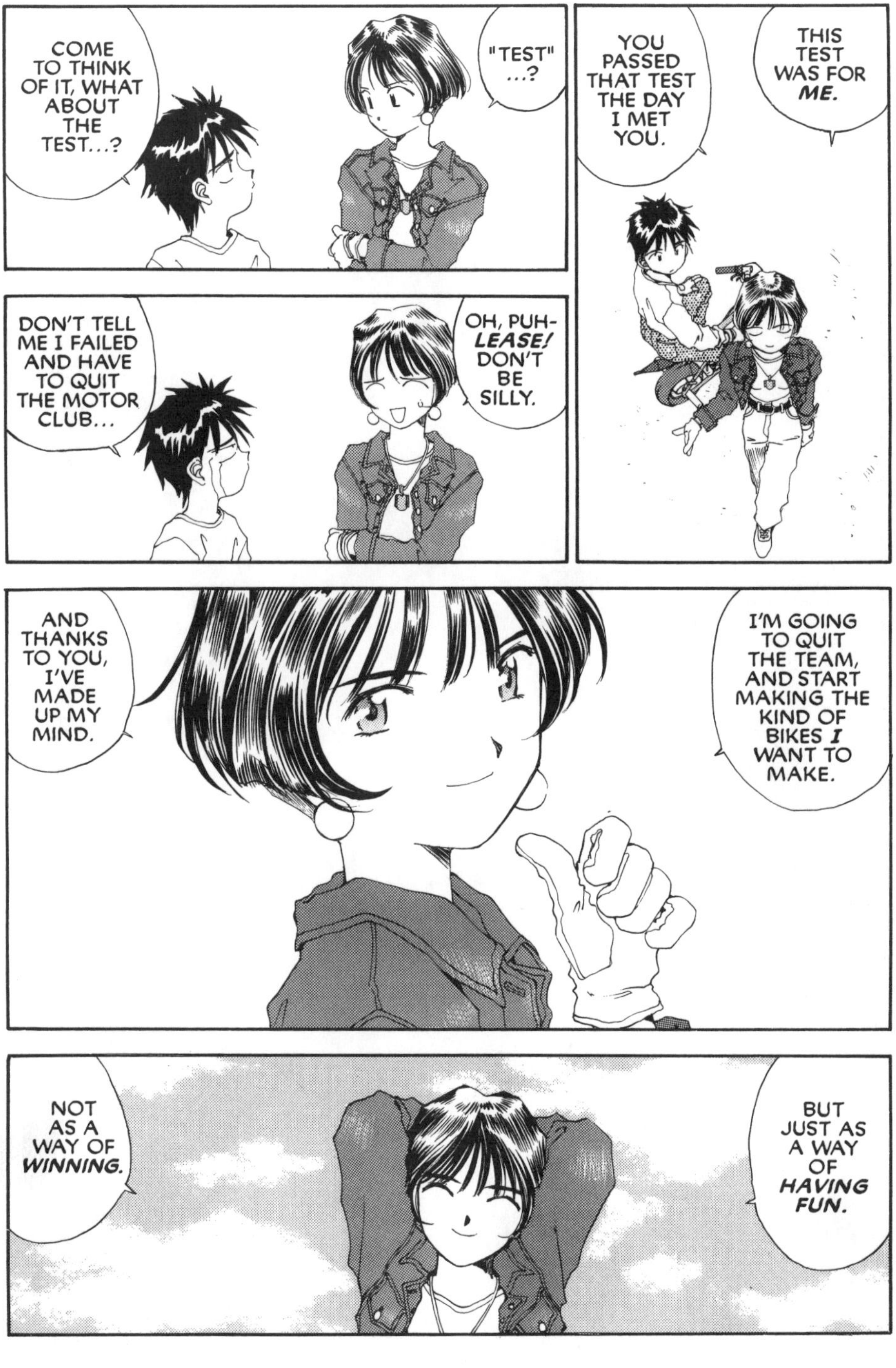
COME TO THINK OF IT, WHAT ABOUT THE TEST...?
"TEST" ...?
DON'T TELL ME I FAILED AND HAVE TO QUIT THE MOTOR CLUB...
OH, PUH-*LEASE!* DON'T BE SILLY.
YOU PASSED THAT TEST THE DAY I MET YOU.
THIS TEST WAS FOR *ME.*
AND THANKS TO YOU, I'VE MADE UP MY MIND.
I'M GOING TO QUIT THE TEAM, AND START MAKING THE KIND OF BIKES *I* WANT TO MAKE.
NOT AS A WAY OF *WINNING.*
BUT JUST AS A WAY OF *HAVING FUN.*

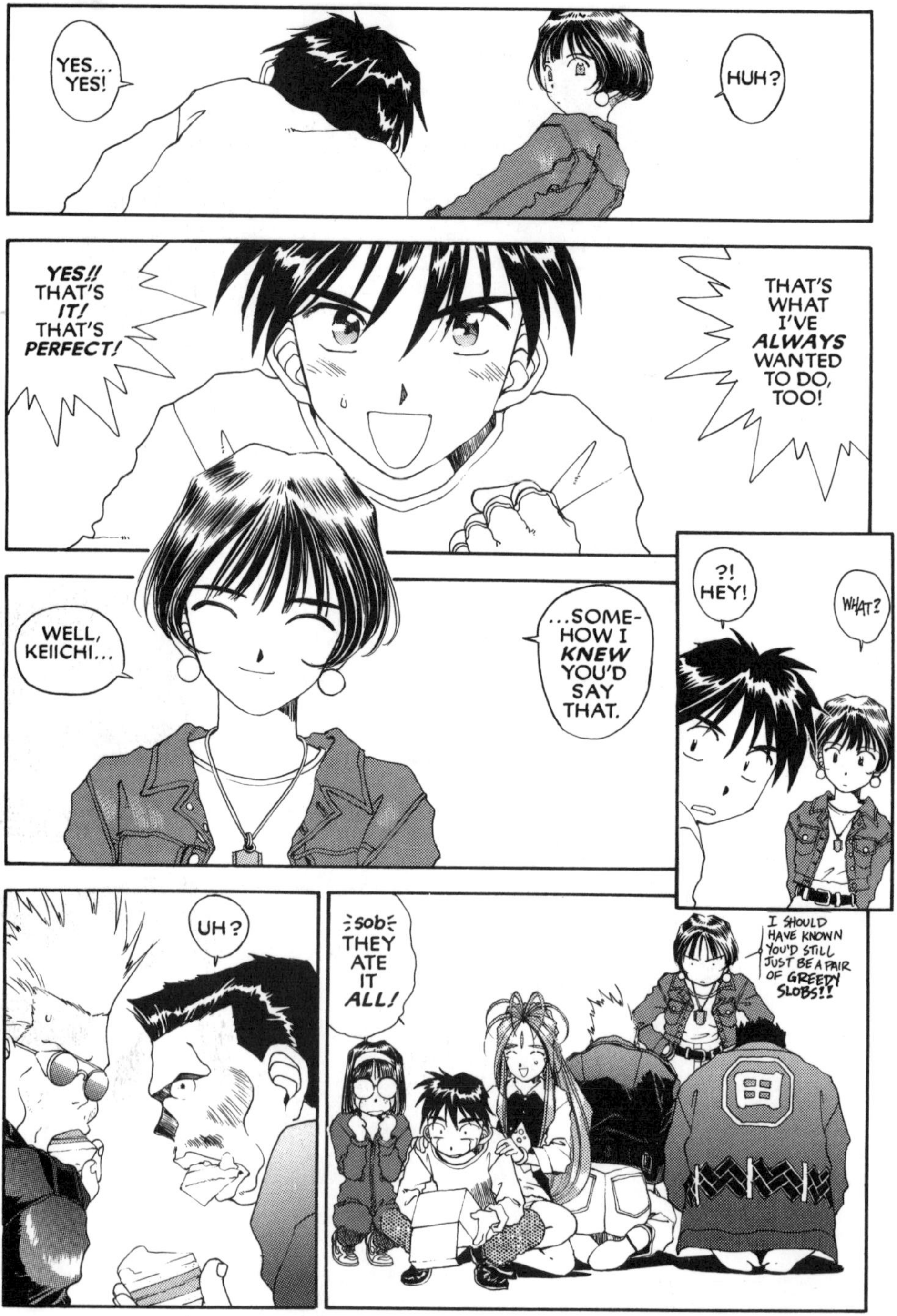
YES... YES!
HUH?
YES!! THAT'S IT! THAT'S PERFECT!
THAT'S WHAT I'VE ALWAYS WANTED TO DO, TOO!
WELL, KEIICHI...
...SOMEHOW I KNEW YOU'D SAY THAT.
?! HEY!
WHAT?
UH?
sob THEY ATE IT ALL!
I SHOULD HAVE KNOWN YOU'D STILL JUST BE A PAIR OF GREEDY SLOBS!!

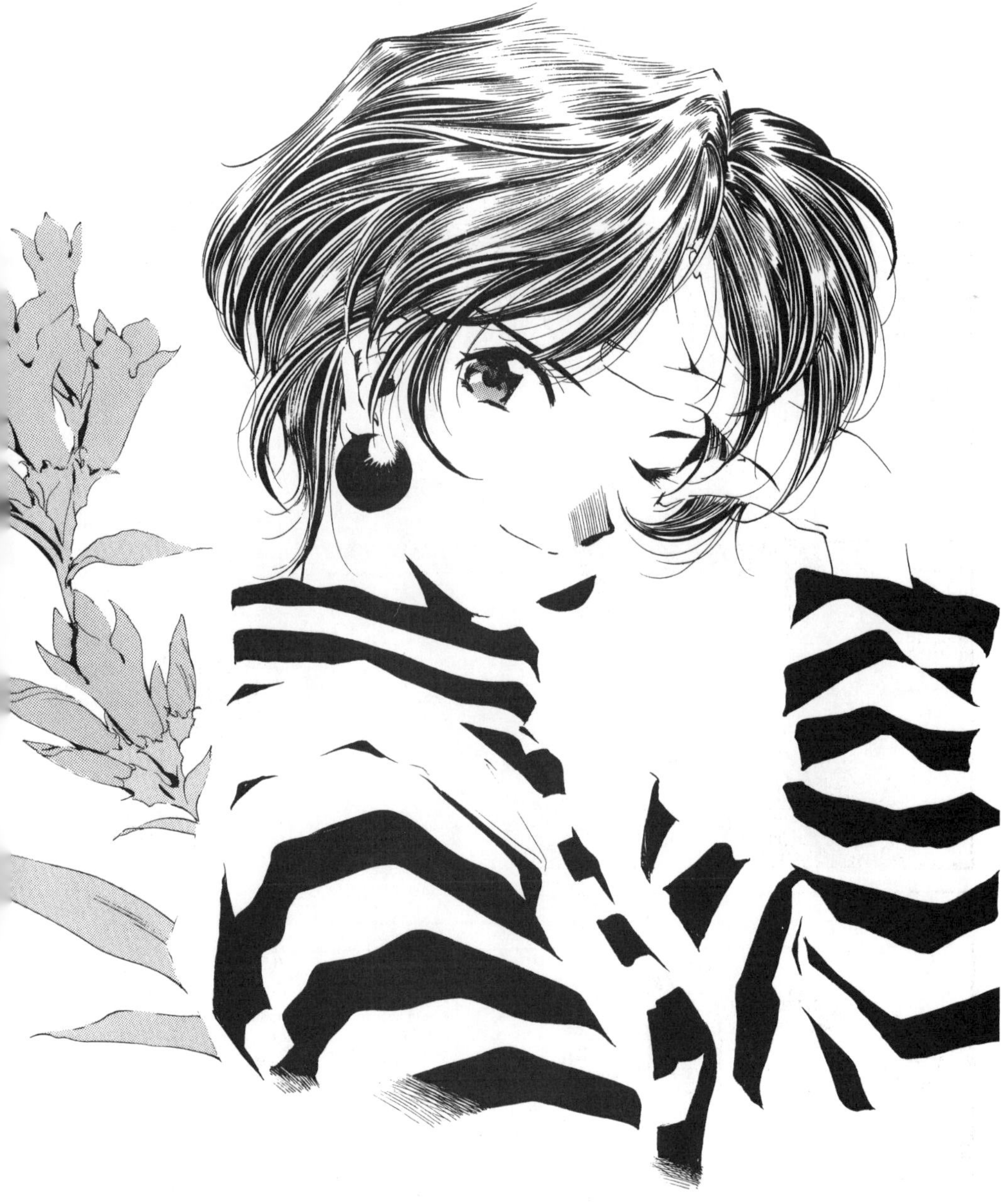

Forever Grrls

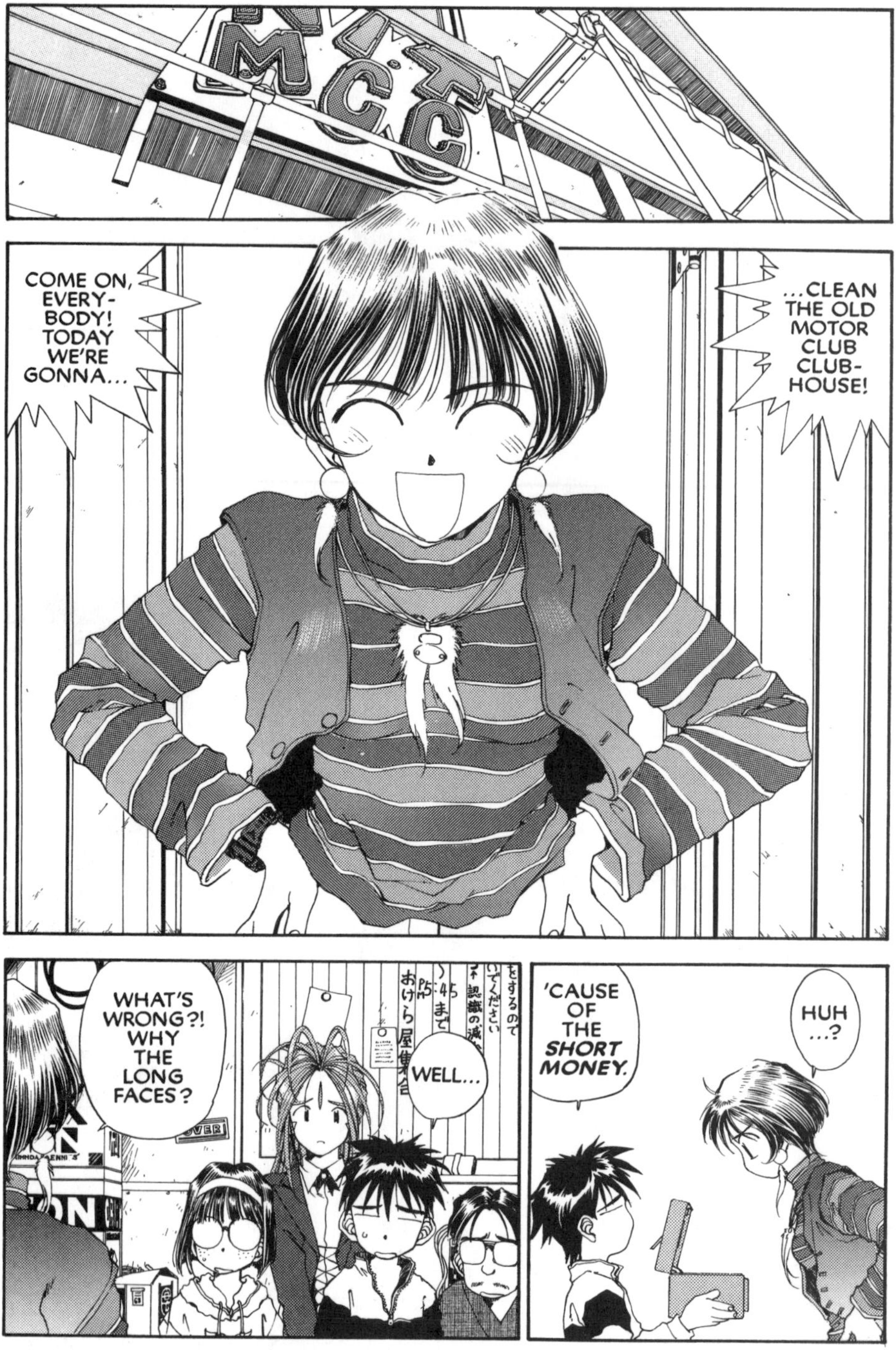
M.C.C
COME ON, EVERY-BODY! TODAY WE'RE GONNA...
...CLEAN THE OLD MOTOR CLUB CLUB-HOUSE!
WHAT'S WRONG?! WHY THE LONG FACES?
WELL...
'CAUSE OF THE *SHORT MONEY*.
HUH ...?

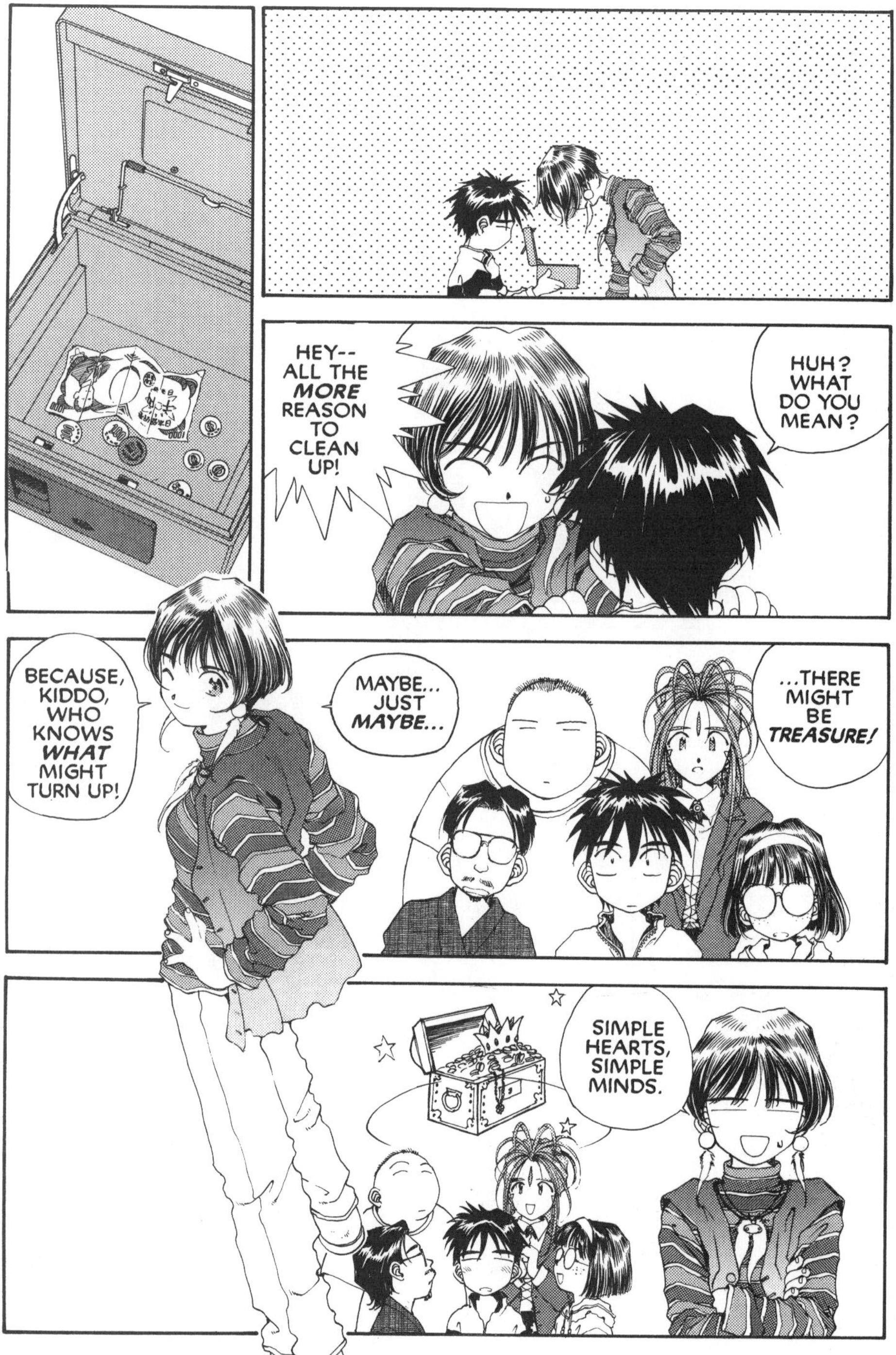
HEY-- ALL THE ***MORE*** REASON TO CLEAN UP!
HUH? WHAT DO YOU MEAN?
BECAUSE, KIDDO, WHO KNOWS ***WHAT*** MIGHT TURN UP!
MAYBE... JUST ***MAYBE...***
...THERE MIGHT BE ***TREASURE!***
SIMPLE HEARTS, SIMPLE MINDS.

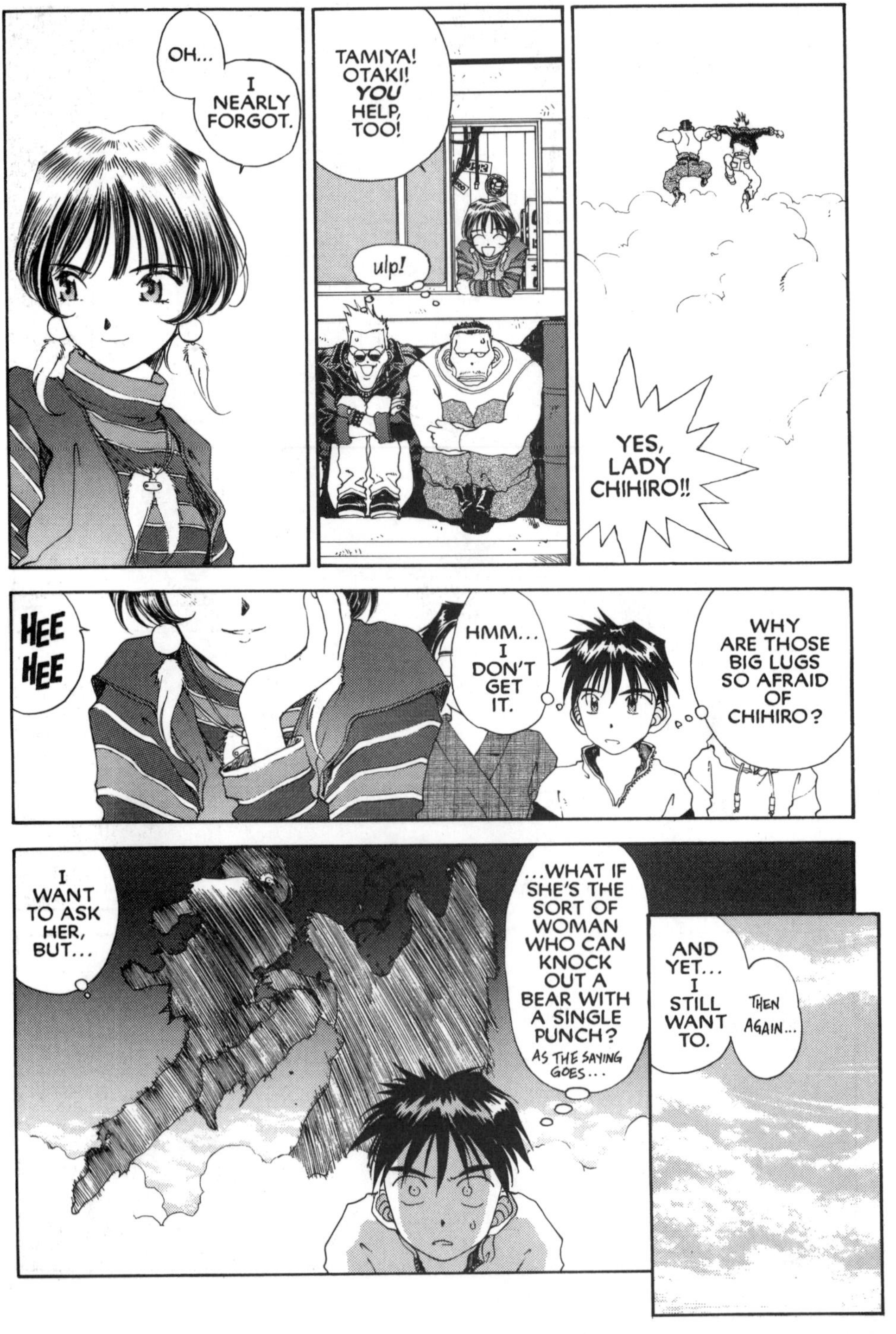
OH...
I NEARLY FORGOT.
TAMIYA! OTAKI! YOU HELP, TOO!
ulp!
YES, LADY CHIHIRO!!
HEE HEE
HMM... I DON'T GET IT.
WHY ARE THOSE BIG LUGS SO AFRAID OF CHIHIRO?
I WANT TO ASK HER, BUT...
...WHAT IF SHE'S THE SORT OF WOMAN WHO CAN KNOCK OUT A BEAR WITH A SINGLE PUNCH?
AS THE SAYING GOES...
AND YET... I STILL WANT TO.
THEN AGAIN...

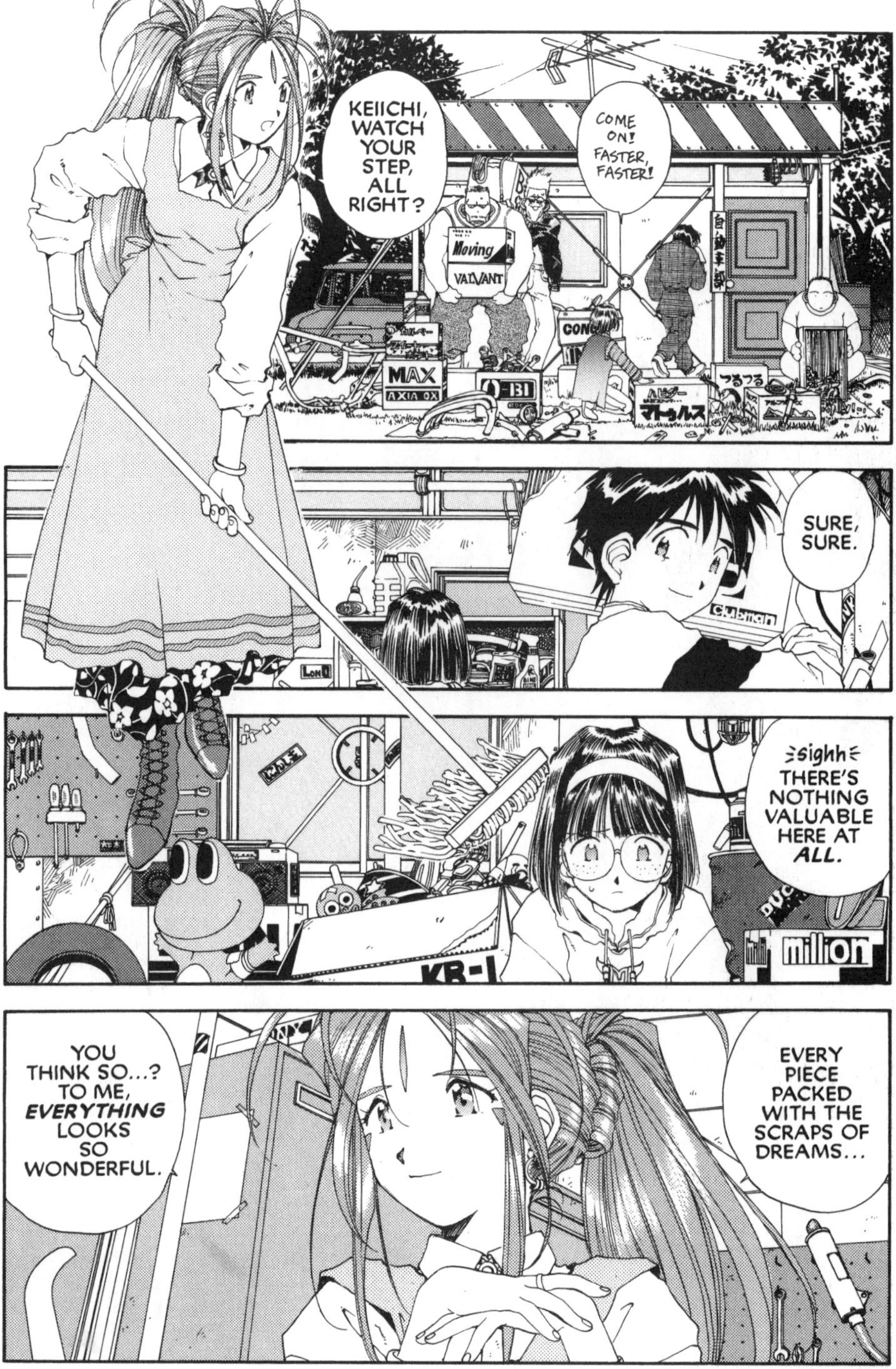
KEIICHI, WATCH YOUR STEP, ALL RIGHT?
COME ON! FASTER, FASTER!
Moving
VALVANT
MAX
AXIA OX
SURE, SURE.
Clubman
≶sighh≷ THERE'S NOTHING VALUABLE HERE AT *ALL*.
million
KR-1
YOU THINK SO...? TO ME, *EVERYTHING* LOOKS SO WONDERFUL.
EVERY PIECE PACKED WITH THE SCRAPS OF DREAMS...

OH, MY ...?

ISN'T THAT ...?

WHAT?! D-DID YOU ACTUALLY *FIND* SOMETHING?!

YES.

KTAK

A PIGGY BANK!

WOW!

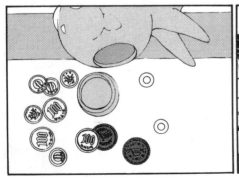

WOW. ¥325.

...

A BIT ON THE LOW SIDE.

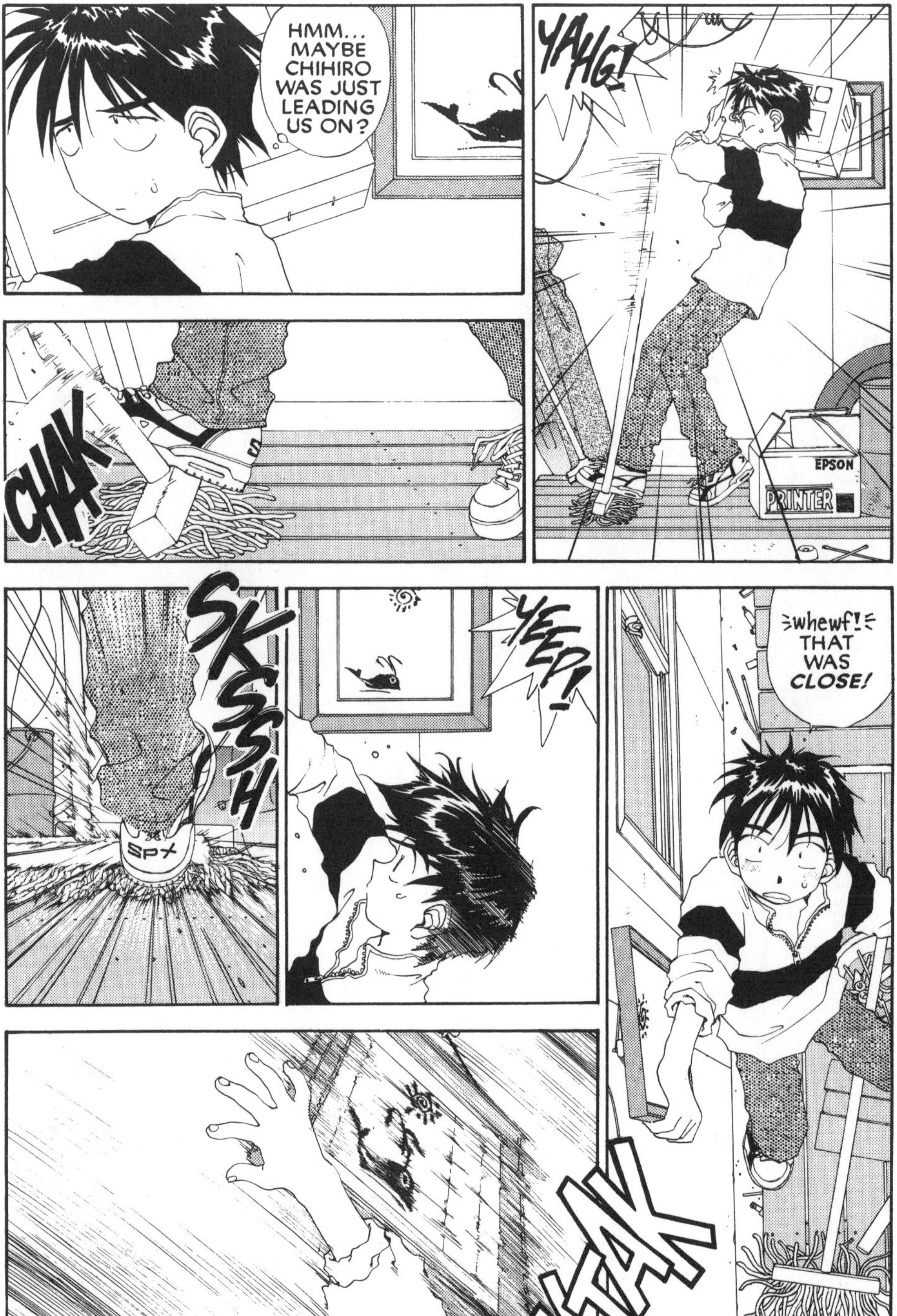

HMM... MAYBE CHIHIRO WAS JUST LEADING US ON?
CHAK
YAHG!
SKSSSH
YEEP!
KTAK
whewf! THAT WAS CLOSE!

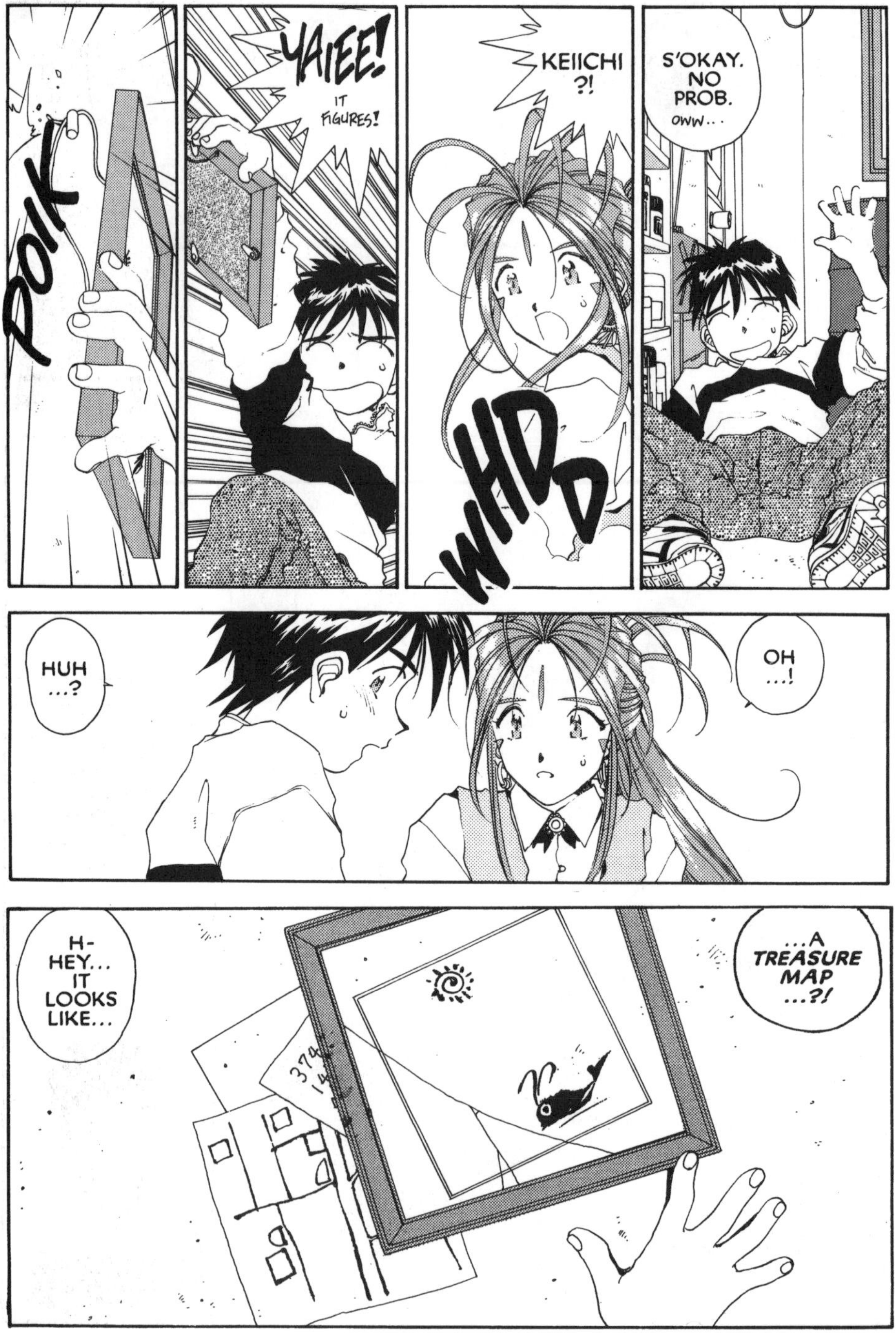
POIK
YAIEE!
IT FIGURES!
KEIICHI ?!
WHDD
S'OKAY. NO PROB.
OWW...
HUH ...?
OH ...!
H-HEY... IT LOOKS LIKE...
...A TREASURE MAP ...?!

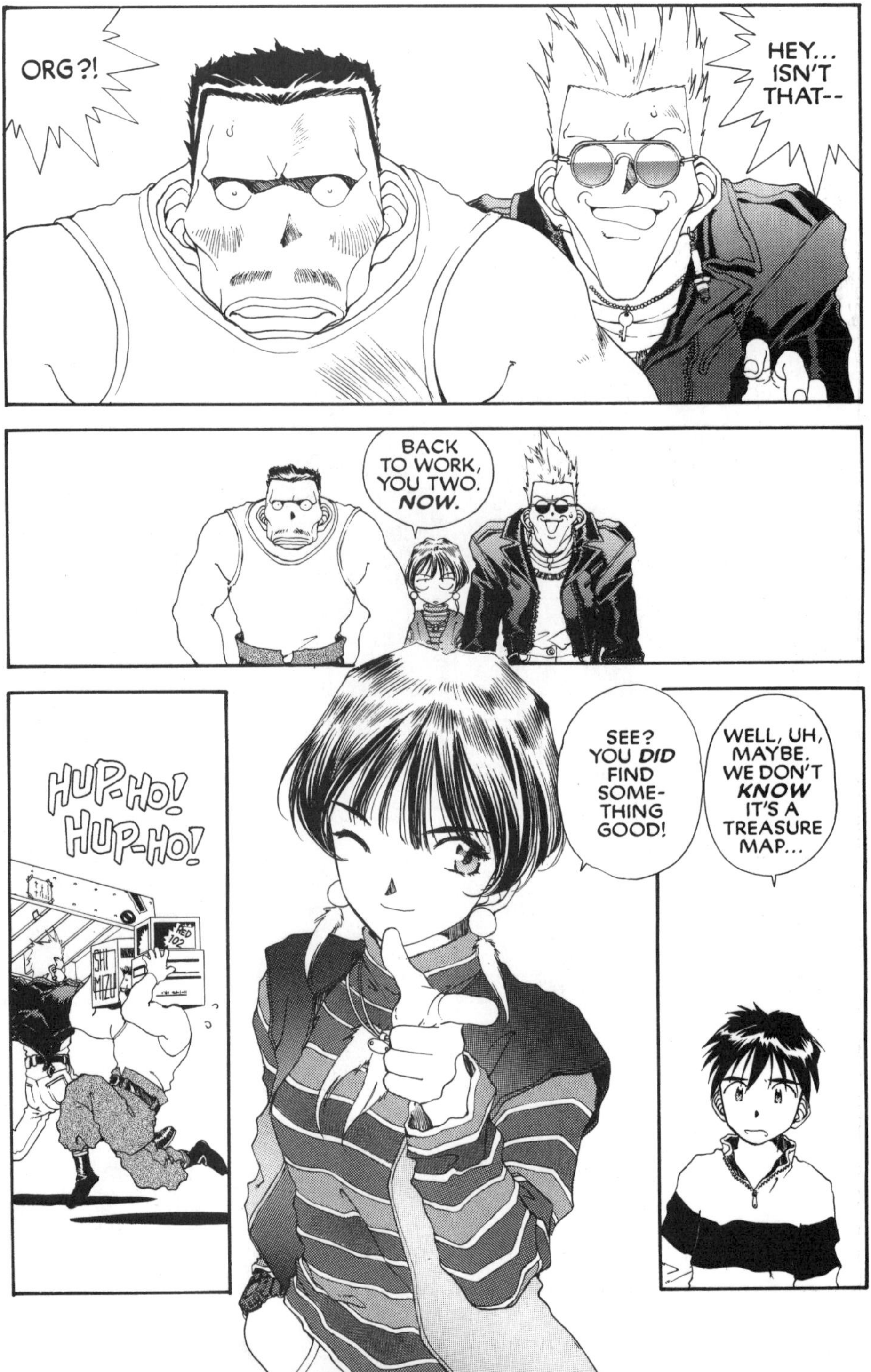
ORG?!
HEY... ISN'T THAT--
BACK TO WORK, YOU TWO. ***NOW.***
HUP-HO! HUP-HO!
SHI MIZU
RED 102
SEE? YOU ***DID*** FIND SOME-THING GOOD!
WELL, UH, MAYBE. WE DON'T ***KNOW*** IT'S A TREASURE MAP...

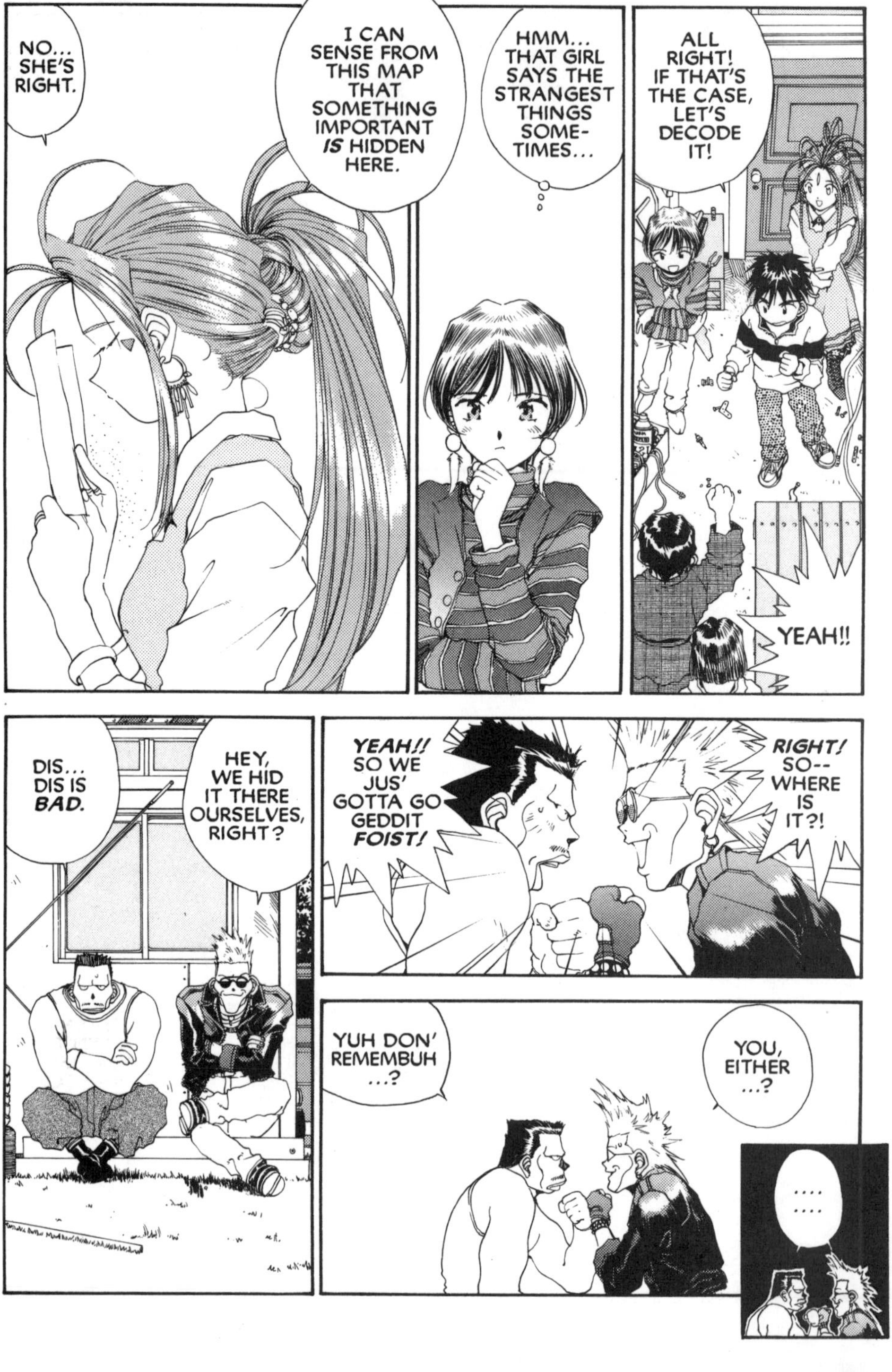
NO... SHE'S RIGHT.
I CAN SENSE FROM THIS MAP THAT SOMETHING IMPORTANT *IS* HIDDEN HERE.
HMM... THAT GIRL SAYS THE STRANGEST THINGS SOME-TIMES...
ALL RIGHT! IF THAT'S THE CASE, LET'S DECODE IT!
YEAH!!
DIS... DIS IS *BAD.*
HEY, WE HID IT THERE OURSELVES, RIGHT?
YEAH!! SO WE JUS' GOTTA GO GEDDIT *FOIST!*
RIGHT! SO-- WHERE IS IT?!
YUH DON' REMEMBUH ...?
YOU, EITHER ...?
....
....

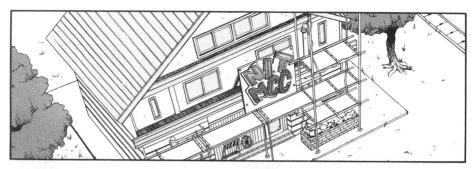

```
37421
143586
451327869
91243876
751439
143586
751439
7216349
58927
143586
```

YEESH ...!

THIS MAP DOESN'T TELL US WHERE TO START, *OR* THE GOAL!

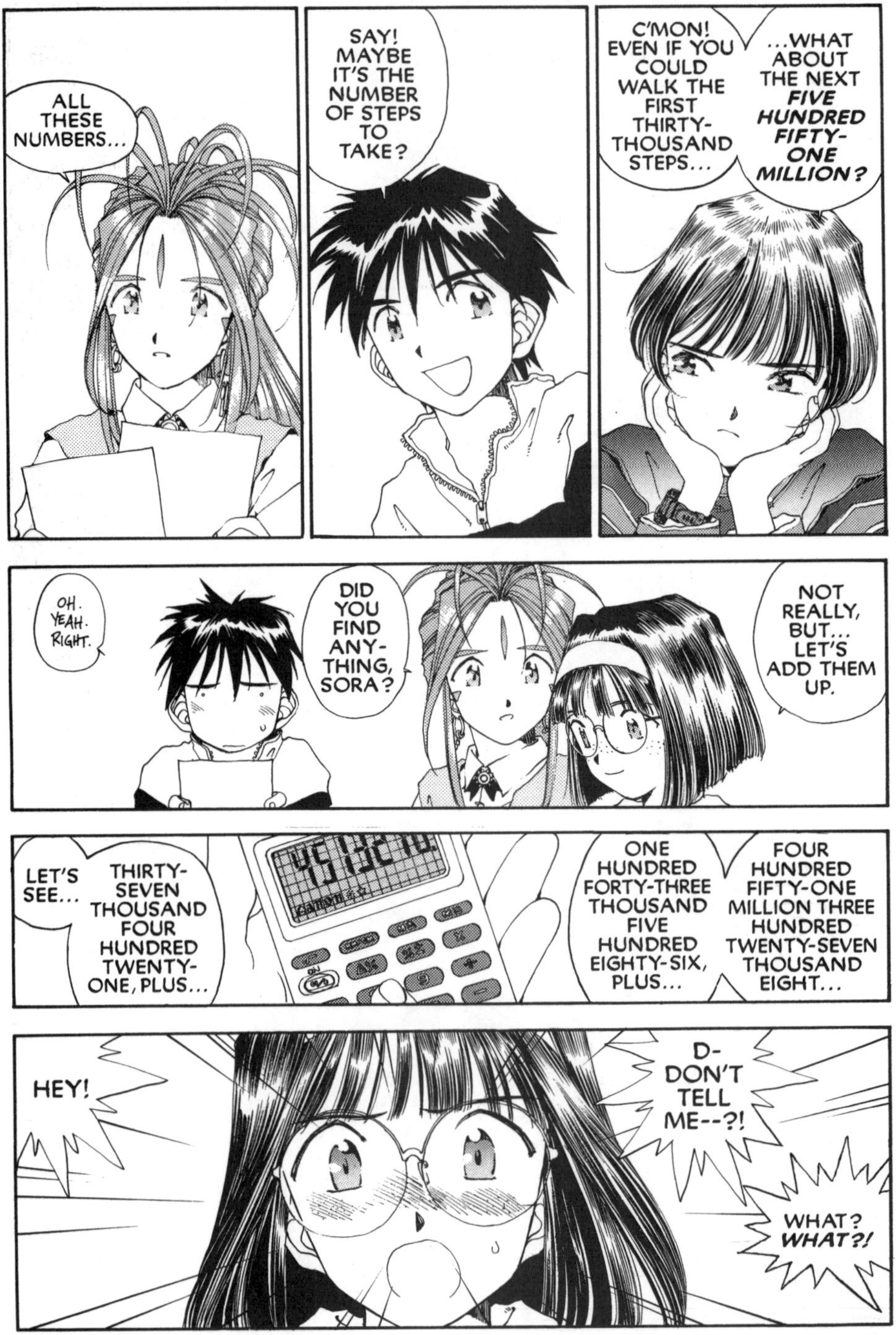
ALL THESE NUMBERS...
SAY! MAYBE IT'S THE NUMBER OF STEPS TO TAKE?
C'MON! EVEN IF YOU COULD WALK THE FIRST THIRTY-THOUSAND STEPS...
...WHAT ABOUT THE NEXT *FIVE HUNDRED FIFTY-ONE MILLION?*
OH. YEAH. RIGHT.
DID YOU FIND ANYTHING, SORA?
NOT REALLY, BUT... LET'S ADD THEM UP.
LET'S SEE...
THIRTY-SEVEN THOUSAND FOUR HUNDRED TWENTY-ONE, PLUS...
ONE HUNDRED FORTY-THREE THOUSAND FIVE HUNDRED EIGHTY-SIX, PLUS...
FOUR HUNDRED FIFTY-ONE MILLION THREE HUNDRED TWENTY-SEVEN THOUSAND EIGHT...
HEY!
D-DON'T TELL ME--?!
WHAT? *WHAT?!*

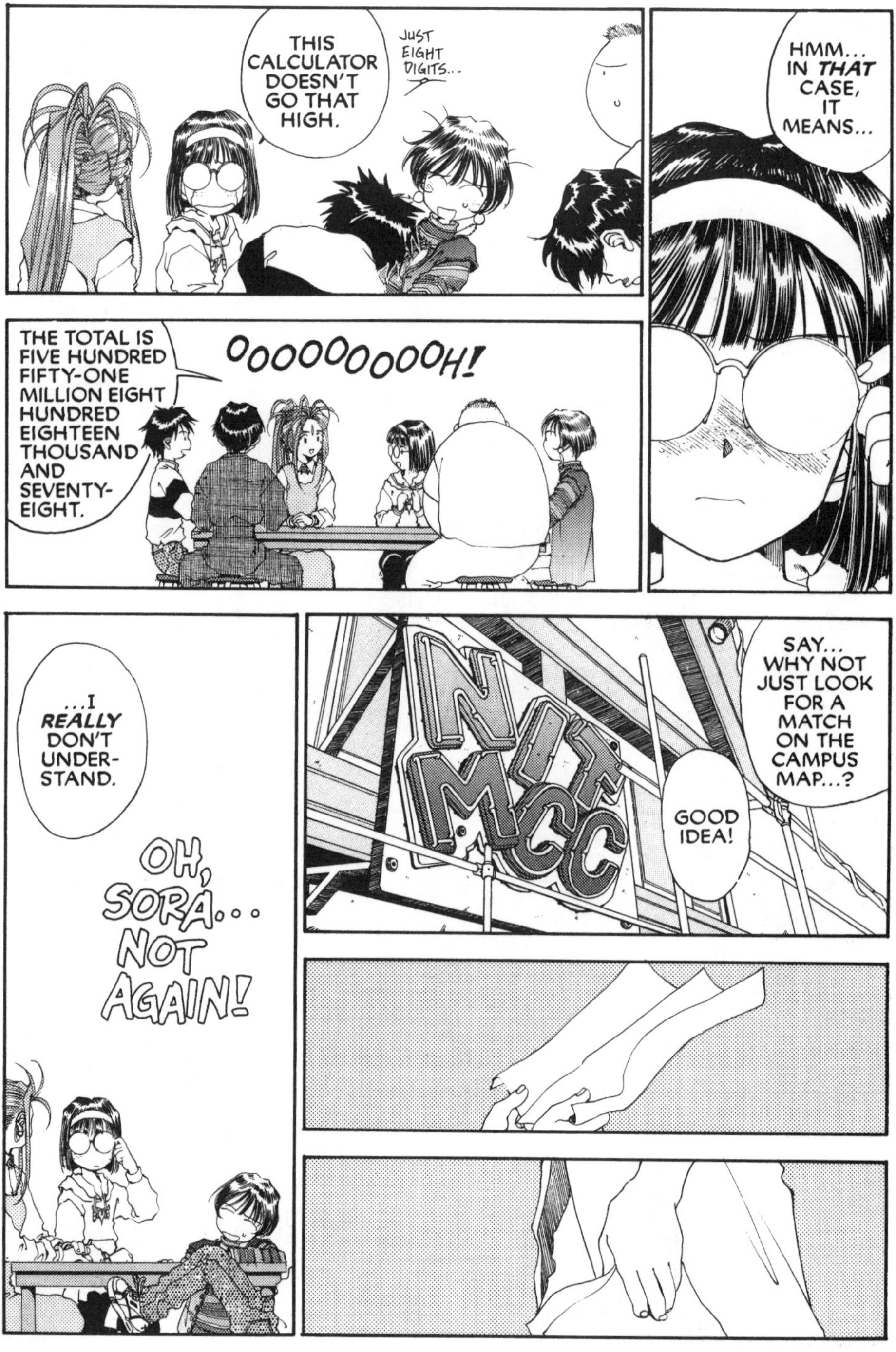
THIS CALCULATOR DOESN'T GO THAT HIGH.
JUST EIGHT DIGITS...
THE TOTAL IS FIVE HUNDRED FIFTY-ONE MILLION EIGHT HUNDRED EIGHTEEN THOUSAND AND SEVENTY-EIGHT.
OOOOOOOOOOH!
HMM... IN THAT CASE, IT MEANS...
...I REALLY DON'T UNDER-STAND.
OH, SORA... NOT AGAIN!
SAY... WHY NOT JUST LOOK FOR A MATCH ON THE CAMPUS MAP...?
GOOD IDEA!

WH...
WHAT THE HECK?!
....
....
WHAT'S THE BIG IDEA? THIS MAP DOESN'T TELL YOU WHERE TO START.
YEAH. AND WHAT DO YOU DO WITH THESE NUMBERS?
IT'S, LIKE, A *TREASURE MAP!*
COOL!
IF WE FIND IT, WE'LL SPLIT IT FIFTY-FIFTY, 'KAY?

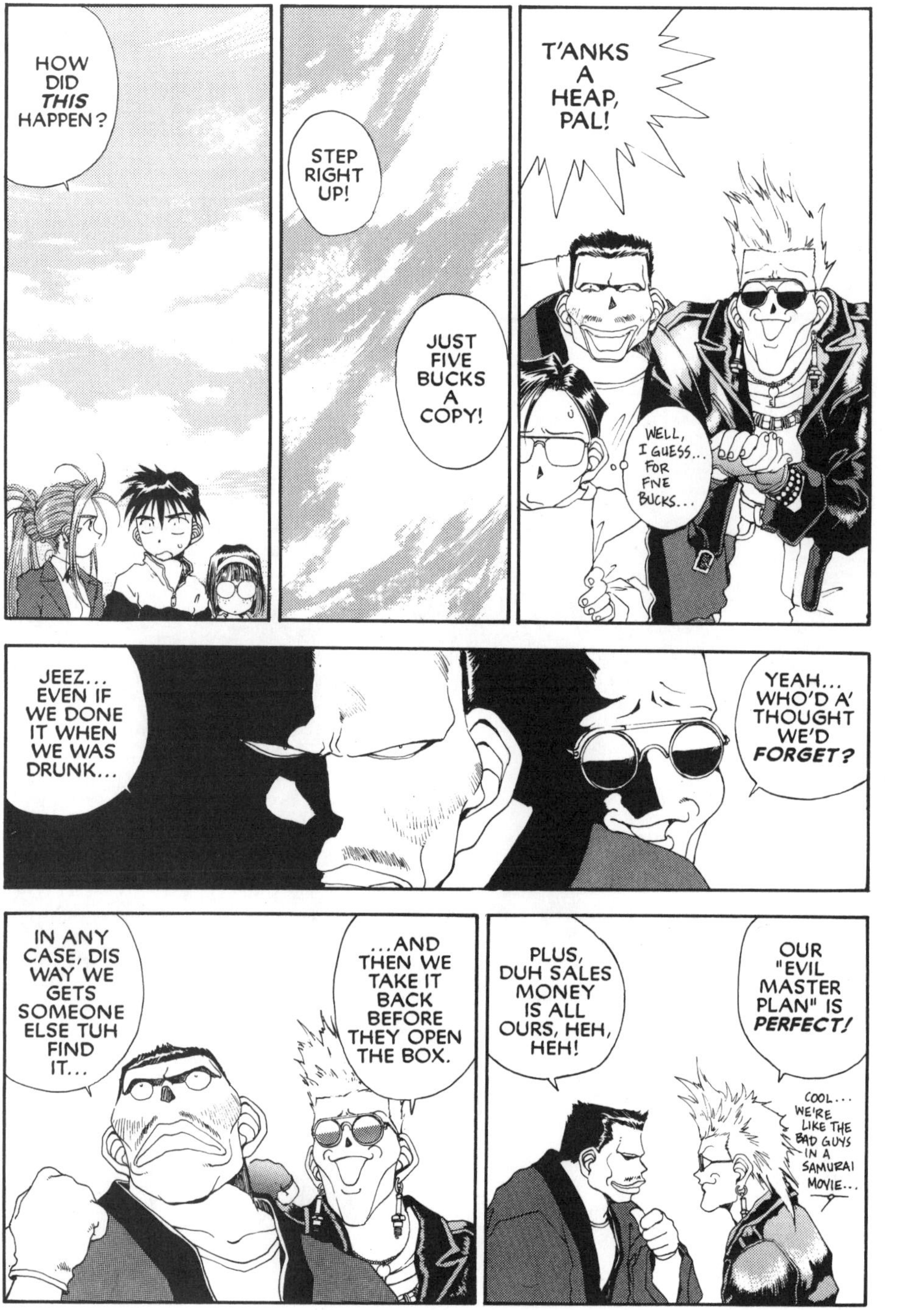
HOW DID THIS HAPPEN?
STEP RIGHT UP!
JUST FIVE BUCKS A COPY!
T'ANKS A HEAP, PAL!
WELL, I GUESS... FOR FIVE BUCKS...
JEEZ... EVEN IF WE DONE IT WHEN WE WAS DRUNK...
YEAH... WHO'D A' THOUGHT WE'D FORGET?
IN ANY CASE, DIS WAY WE GETS SOMEONE ELSE TUH FIND IT...
...AND THEN WE TAKE IT BACK BEFORE THEY OPEN THE BOX.
PLUS, DUH SALES MONEY IS ALL OURS, HEH, HEH!
OUR "EVIL MASTER PLAN" IS PERFECT!
COOL... WE'RE LIKE THE BAD GUYS IN A SAMURAI MOVIE...

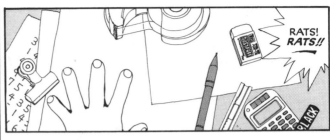

RATS!
RATS!!

NO...
NO...
CALM
DOWN...

HOW ABOUT DIFFERENTIAL CRYPTANALYSIS? IF IT'S SYMMETRIC *DES* ALGORITHMS...

AND NOT IDEA™ OR CAST...

YOU'RE LOSING IT, KIDDO.

NO WAY IT'S **THAT** HARD!

BESIDES, THEY'RE NOT GOING TO FIND IT THAT EASILY, ANYWAY.

WHO EVEN SAID THE MAP SHOWS THIS CAMPUS?

THEN... THEN **WE** CAN'T FIND IT, EITHER ...?

WELL, uh... MAYBE NOT.

HMM... IT MUST BE TAMIYA AND OTAKI SELLING THOSE MAPS.

LATER THEY SHALL REQUIRE... *DISCIPLINE.*

GLEEP! THEN SHE REALLY **CAN** PUNCH OUT A BEAR! **TWO** BEARS!

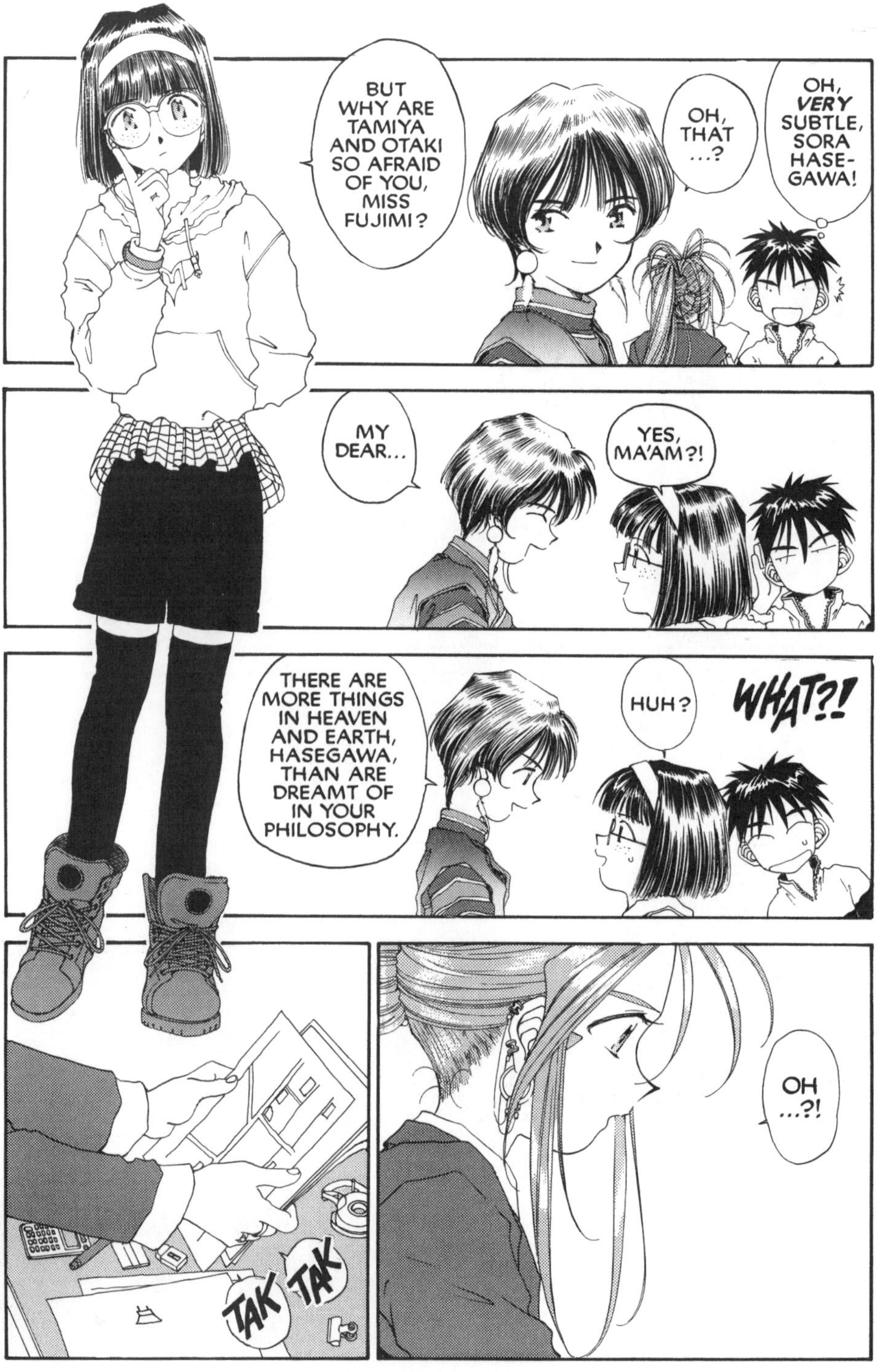
BUT WHY ARE TAMIYA AND OTAKI SO AFRAID OF YOU, MISS FUJIMI?
OH, THAT ...?
OH, VERY SUBTLE, SORA HASEGAWA!
MY DEAR...
YES, MA'AM?!
THERE ARE MORE THINGS IN HEAVEN AND EARTH, HASEGAWA, THAN ARE DREAMT OF IN YOUR PHILOSOPHY.
HUH?
WHAT?!
TAK TAK
OH ...?!

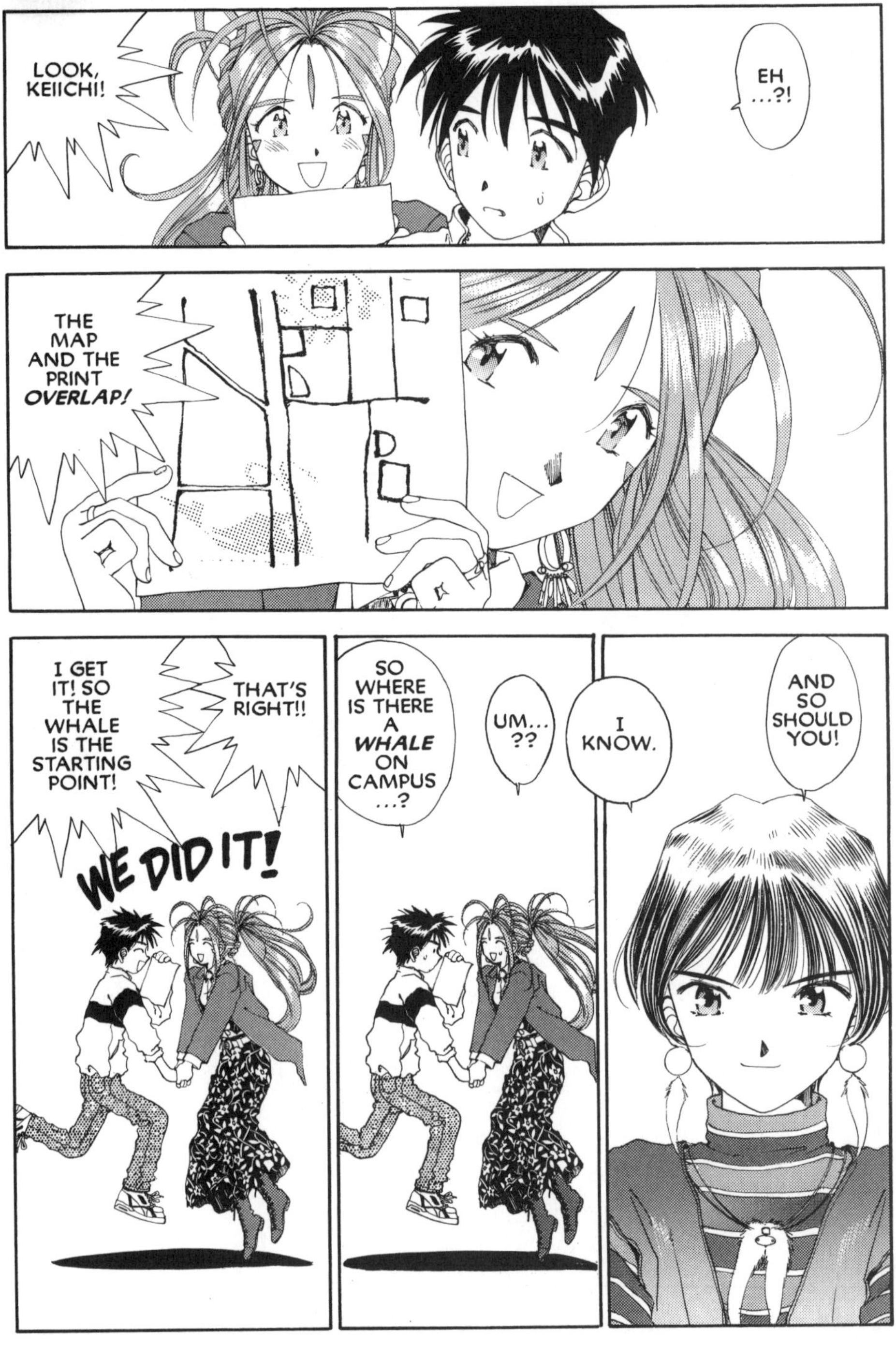
LOOK, KEIICHI!
EH ...?!
THE MAP AND THE PRINT *OVERLAP!*
I GET IT! SO THE WHALE IS THE STARTING POINT!
THAT'S RIGHT!!
WE DID IT!
SO WHERE IS THERE A *WHALE* ON CAMPUS ...?
UM... ??
I KNOW.
AND SO SHOULD YOU!

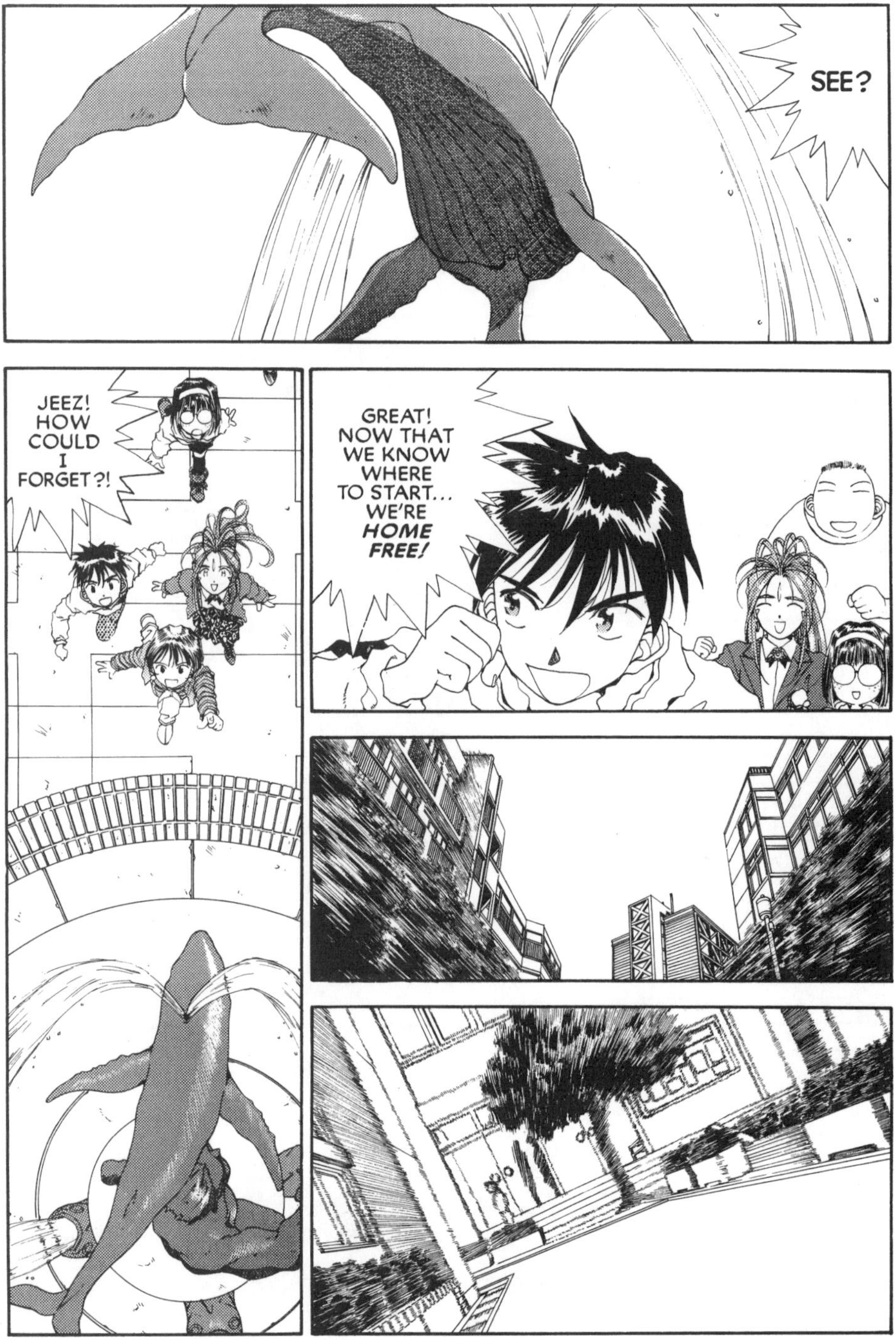
SEE?
JEEZ! HOW COULD I FORGET?!
GREAT! NOW THAT WE KNOW WHERE TO START... WE'RE ***HOME FREE!***

HERE! **THIS BUILDING!**

SO, LIKE... **WHERE** IN THIS BUILDING?

OOP...

THE... THE **NUMBERS** MUST TELL US THAT PART!

AH!

WHAT? WHAT?

WHAT DO THEY SAY?

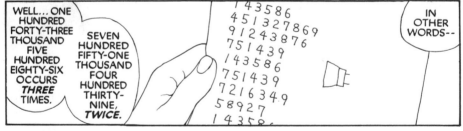

WELL... ONE HUNDRED FORTY-THREE THOUSAND FIVE HUNDRED EIGHTY-SIX OCCURS **THREE** TIMES.

SEVEN HUNDRED FIFTY-ONE THOUSAND FOUR HUNDRED THIRTY-NINE, **TWICE.**

IN OTHER WORDS--

THESE SETS OF NUMBERS HAVE IDENTICAL MEANINGS IN THE CODE.

RRG! THAT'S **MY** LINE!

AH!

OF COURSE!

SMAK

I REMEMBER THIS FROM WHEN I WAS A KID!

LOOK AT THIS, MISTER MORISATO!

WHEN YOU PUT IN 7, 5, 1, 4, 3, 9...

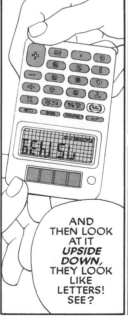

AND THEN LOOK AT IT *UPSIDE DOWN*, THEY LOOK LIKE LETTERS! SEE?

SORA! YOU'RE *INCREDIBLE!*

AHEM

SO HOW DO YOU READ IT?

ER... "GEH... HEE... ZLL" ...? ???

IT DOESN'T MEAN A DARN THING!

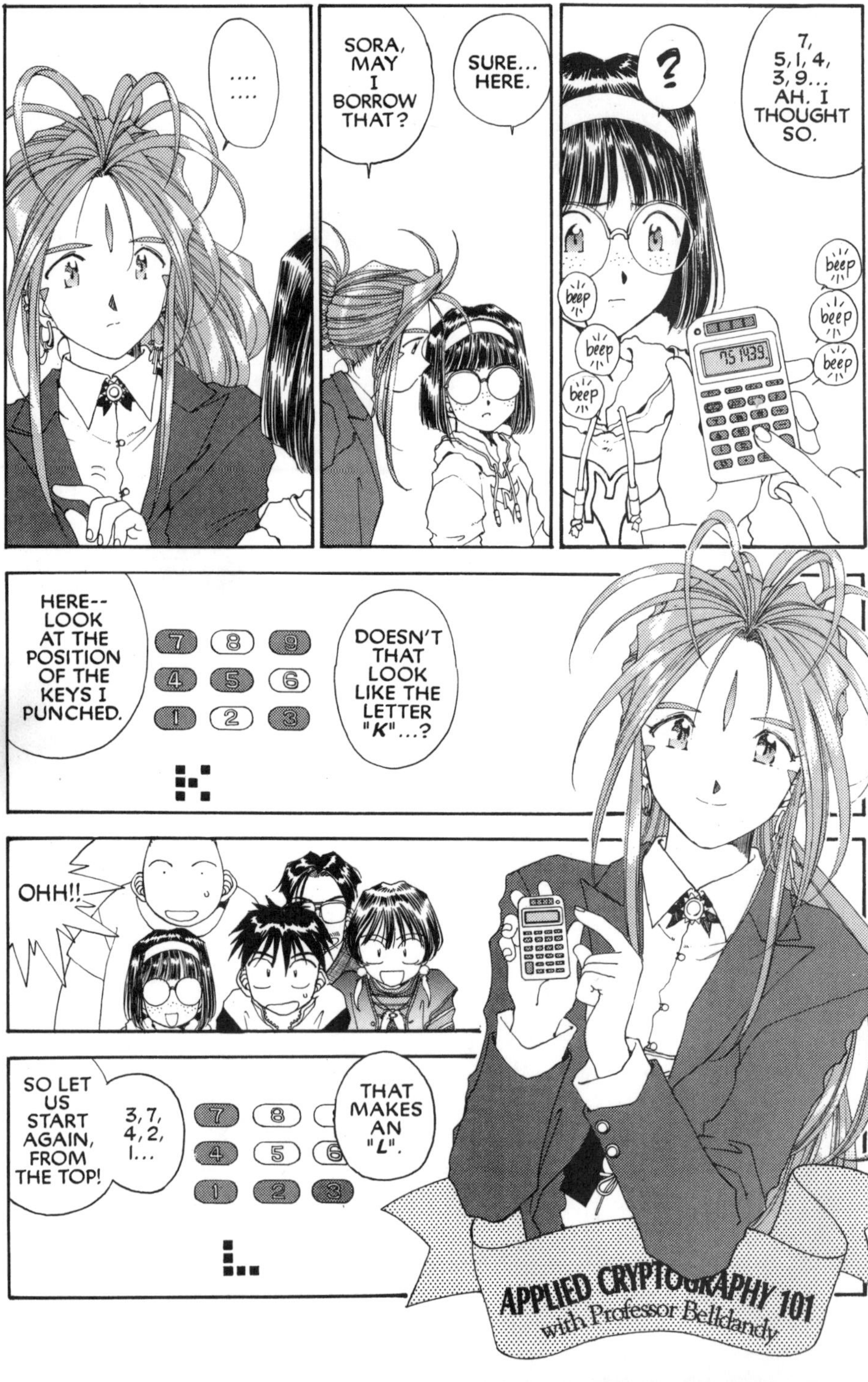
....
....
SORA, MAY I BORROW THAT?
SURE... HERE.
?
7, 5, 1, 4, 3, 9... AH. I THOUGHT SO.
beep
beep
beep
beep
beep
beep
751439.
HERE-- LOOK AT THE POSITION OF THE KEYS I PUNCHED.
7 8 9
4 5 6
1 2 3
DOESN'T THAT LOOK LIKE THE LETTER "K"...?
OHH!!
SO LET US START AGAIN, FROM THE TOP!
3, 7, 4, 2, 1...
7 8
4 5 6
1 2 3
THAT MAKES AN "L".
APPLIED CRYPTOGRAPHY 101
with Professor Belldandy

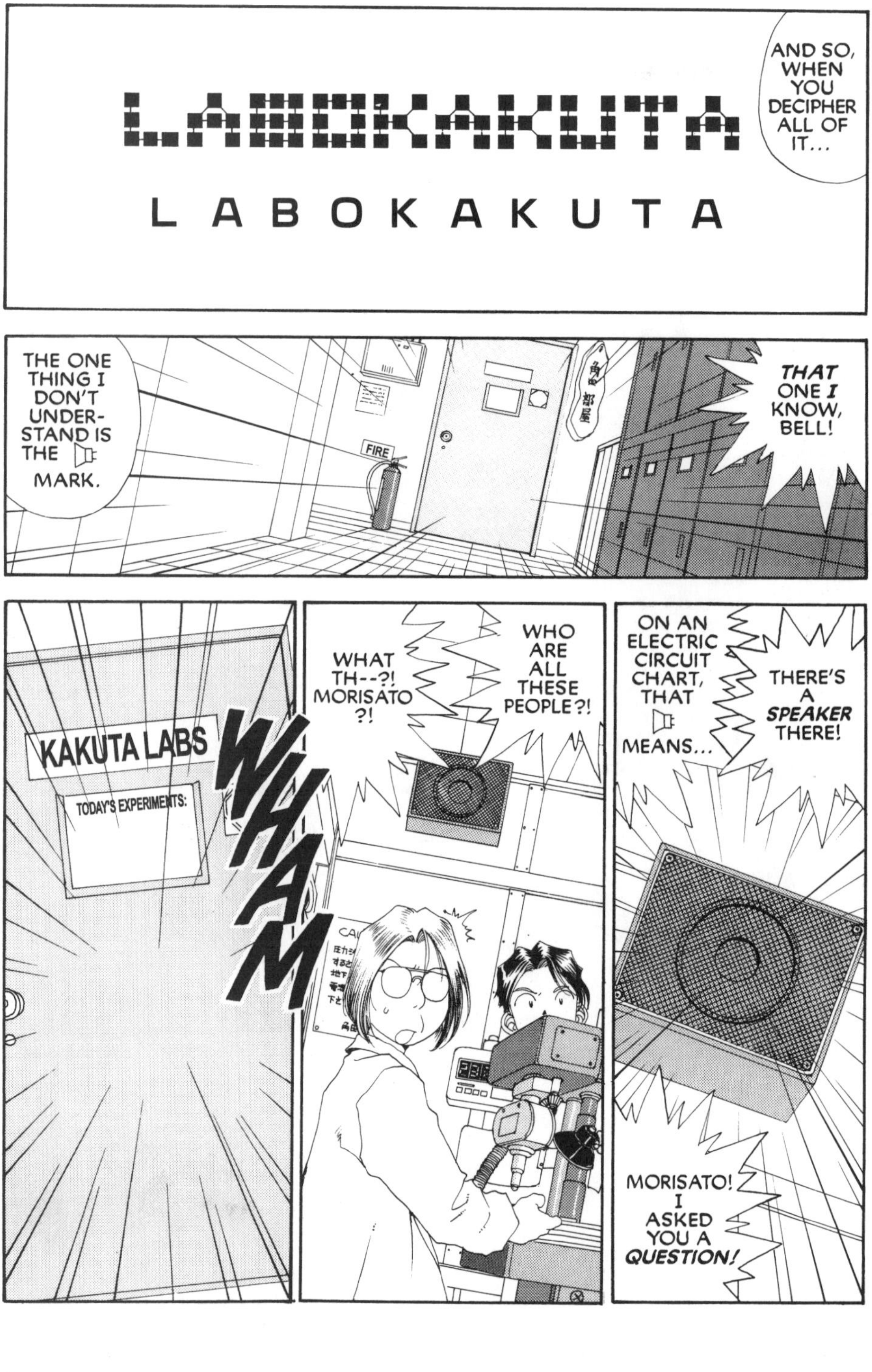

LABOKAKUTA
LABOKAKUTA
AND SO, WHEN YOU DECIPHER ALL OF IT...
THE ONE THING I DON'T UNDERSTAND IS THE MARK.
FIRE
THAT ONE I KNOW, BELL!
KAKUTA LABS
TODAY'S EXPERIMENTS:
WHAM
WHAT TH--?! MORISATO?!
WHO ARE ALL THESE PEOPLE?!
ON AN ELECTRIC CIRCUIT CHART, THAT MEANS...
THERE'S A SPEAKER THERE!
MORISATO! I ASKED YOU A QUESTION!

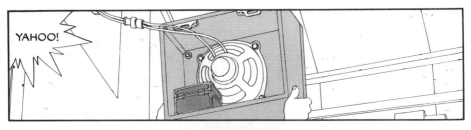

YAHOO!

HERE IT IS!

WE DID IT!

BUT... IT'S *LOCKED.*

UH-OH!

OH...? THIS DRAWING...!

I THINK I CAN OPEN THIS.

REALLY ?!

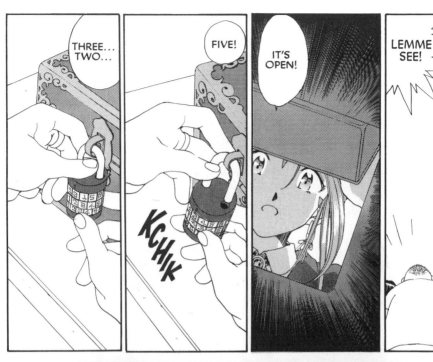

THREE... TWO...

FIVE!

IT'S OPEN!

KCHIK

LEMME SEE!

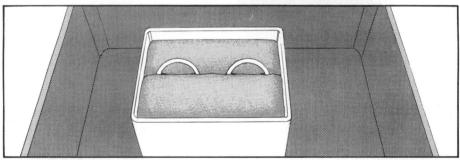

TWO... *RINGS?*

...!

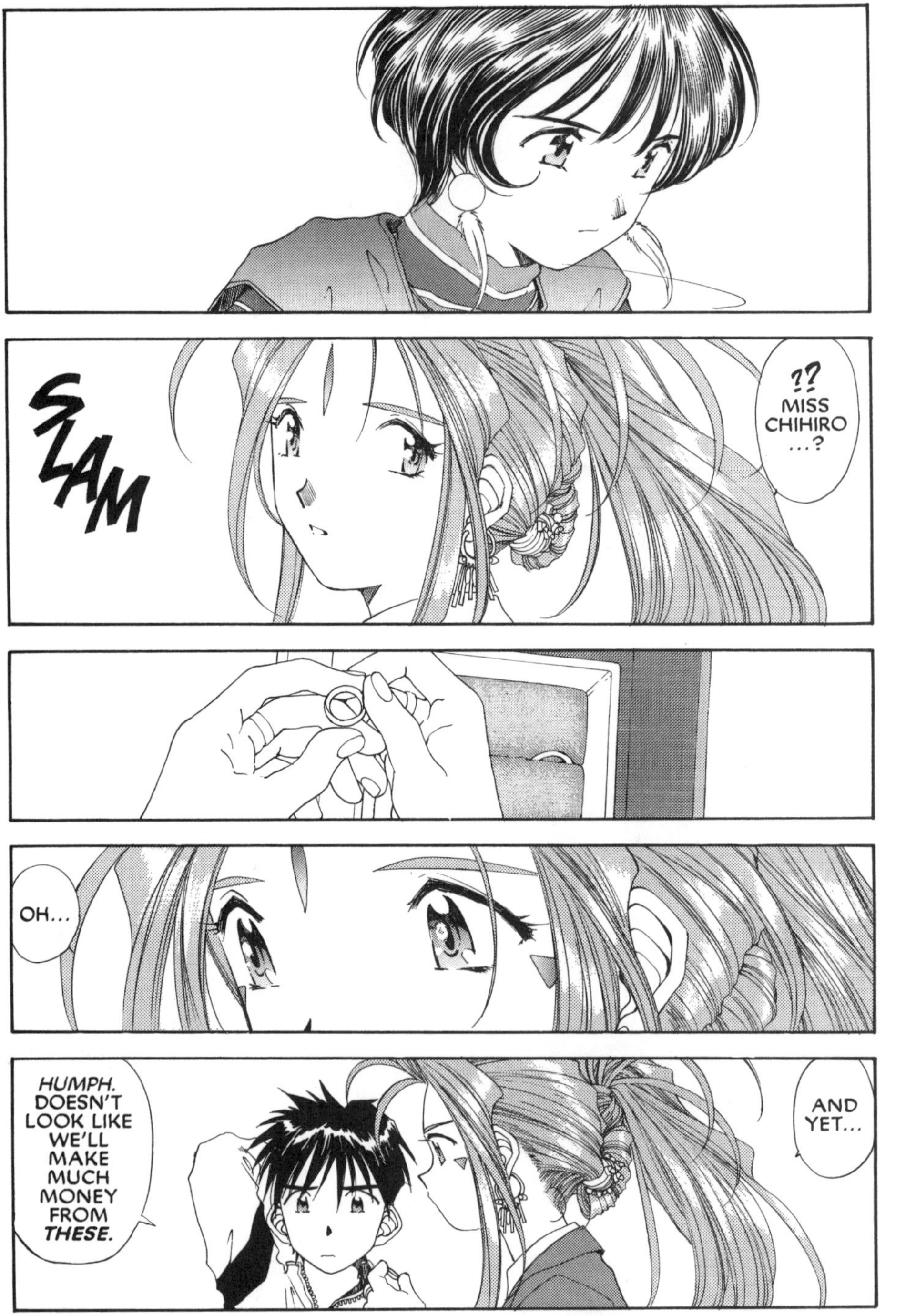
SLAM
?? MISS CHIHIRO ...?
OH...
HUMPH. DOESN'T LOOK LIKE WE'LL MAKE MUCH MONEY FROM *THESE.*
AND YET...

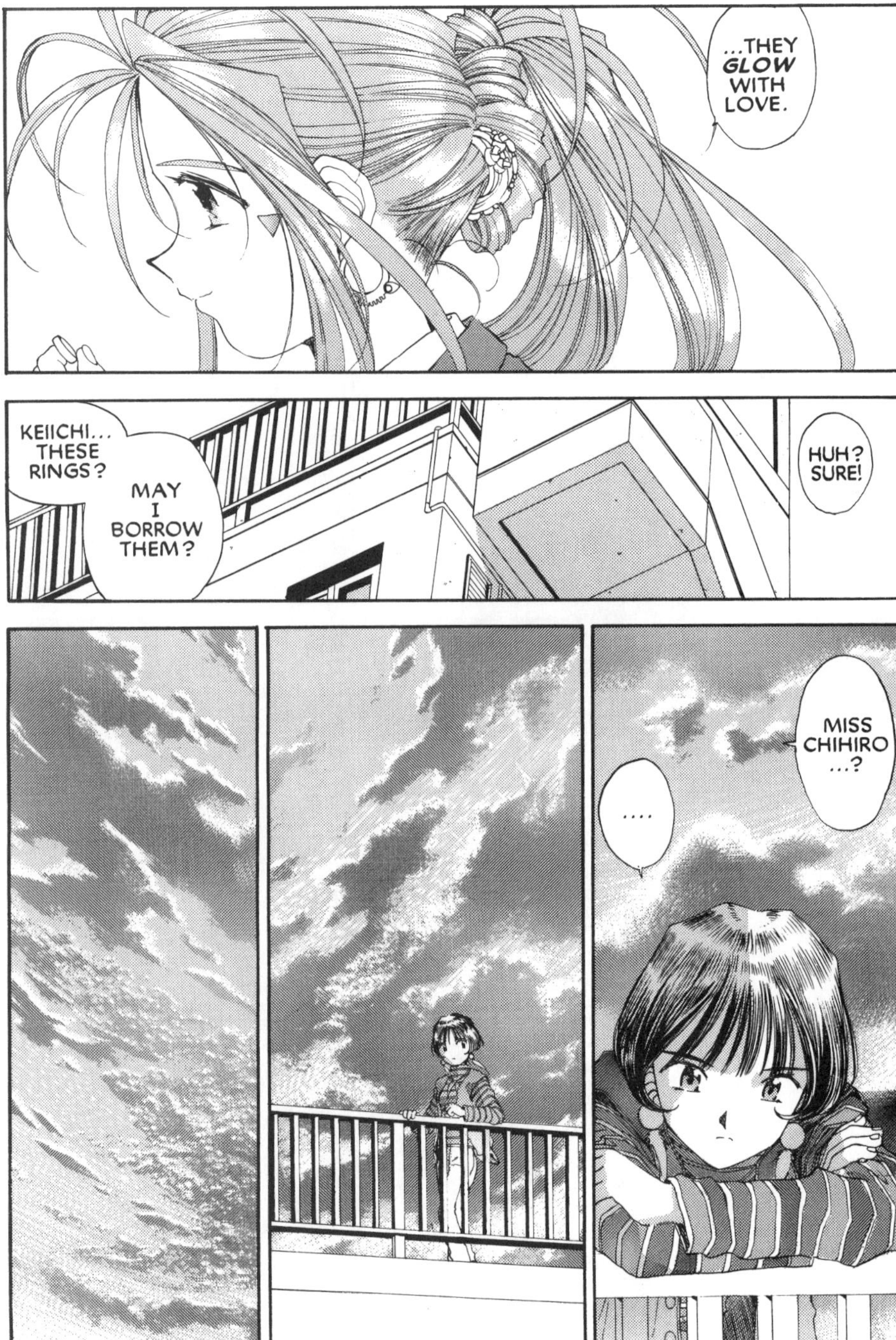
...THEY GLOW WITH LOVE.
KEIICHI... THESE RINGS?
MAY I BORROW THEM?
HUH? SURE!
....
MISS CHIHIRO ...?

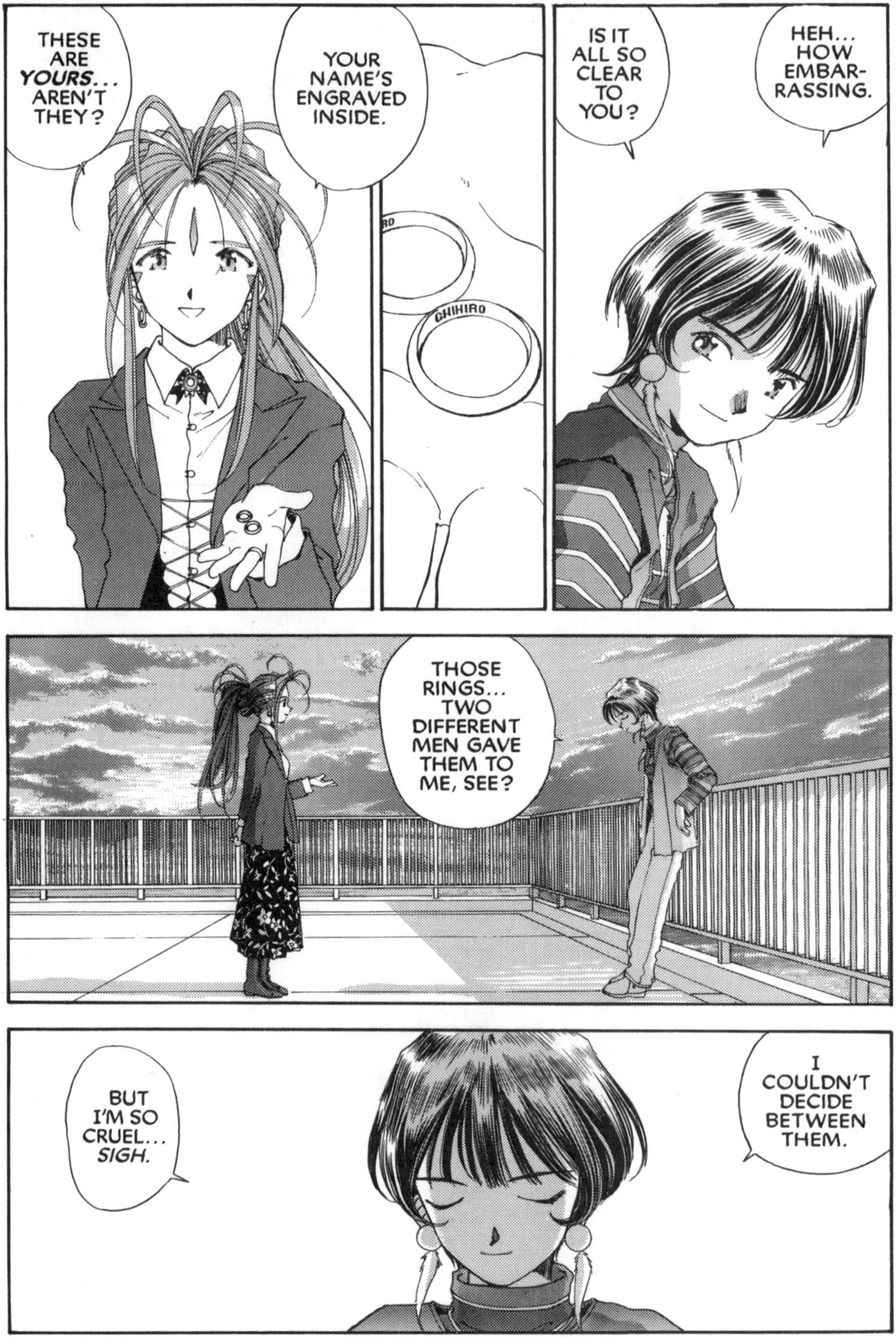
THESE ARE *YOURS*... AREN'T THEY?
YOUR NAME'S ENGRAVED INSIDE.
CHIHIRO
IS IT ALL SO CLEAR TO YOU?
HEH... HOW EMBARRASSING.
THOSE RINGS... TWO DIFFERENT MEN GAVE THEM TO ME, SEE?
BUT I'M SO CRUEL... *SIGH*.
I COULDN'T DECIDE BETWEEN THEM.

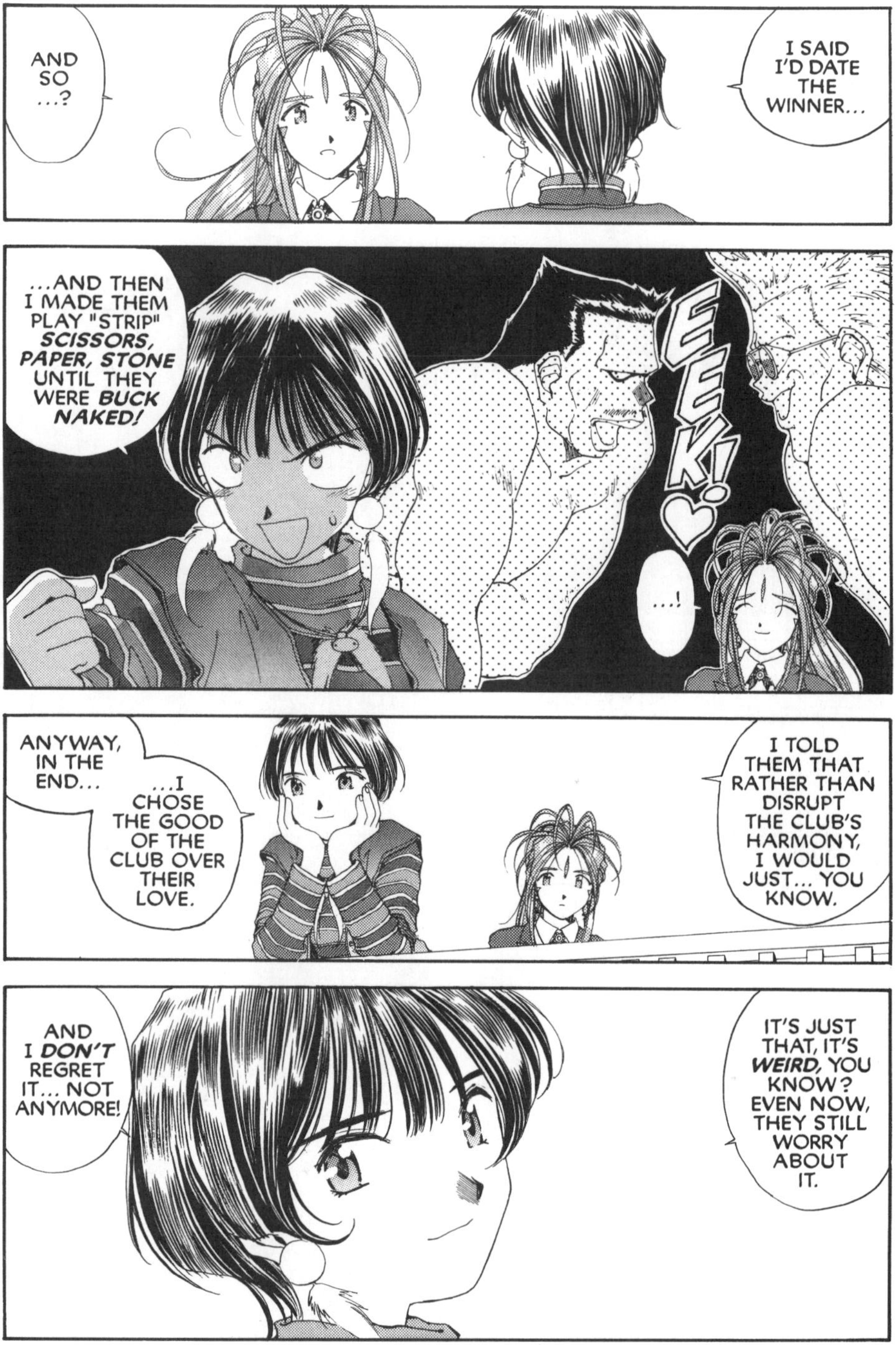
AND SO ...?
I SAID I'D DATE THE WINNER...
...AND THEN I MADE THEM PLAY "STRIP" ***SCISSORS, PAPER, STONE*** UNTIL THEY WERE ***BUCK NAKED!***
EEK! ♥
...!
ANYWAY, IN THE END...
...I CHOSE THE GOOD OF THE CLUB OVER THEIR LOVE.
I TOLD THEM THAT RATHER THAN DISRUPT THE CLUB'S HARMONY, I WOULD JUST... YOU KNOW.
AND I ***DON'T*** REGRET IT... NOT ANYMORE!
IT'S JUST THAT, IT'S ***WEIRD,*** YOU KNOW? EVEN NOW, THEY STILL WORRY ABOUT IT.

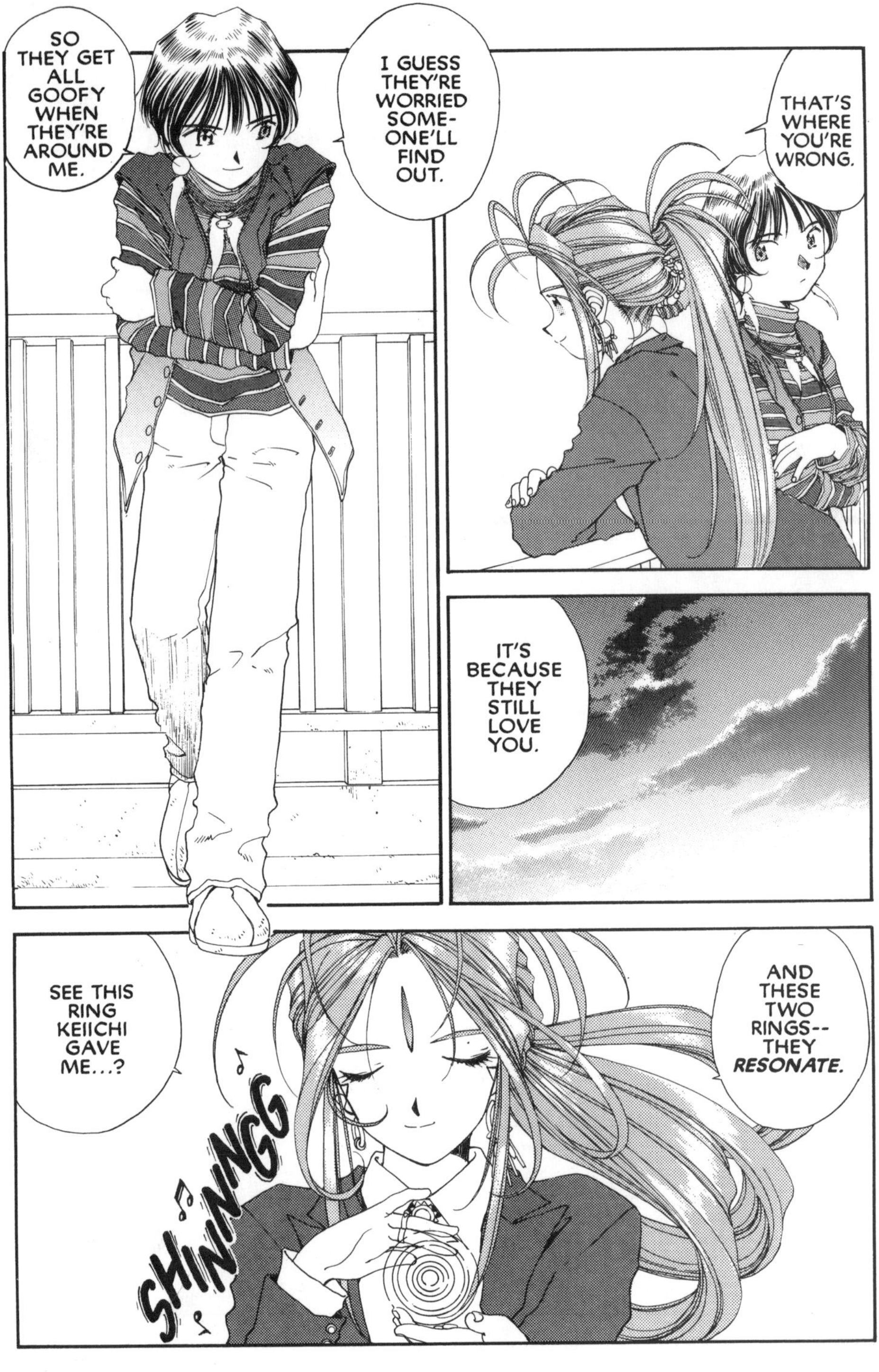
SO THEY GET ALL GOOFY WHEN THEY'RE AROUND ME.
I GUESS THEY'RE WORRIED SOME-ONE'LL FIND OUT.
THAT'S WHERE YOU'RE WRONG.
IT'S BECAUSE THEY STILL LOVE YOU.
SEE THIS RING KEIICHI GAVE ME...?
AND THESE TWO RINGS-- THEY *RESONATE.*
SHINNGG

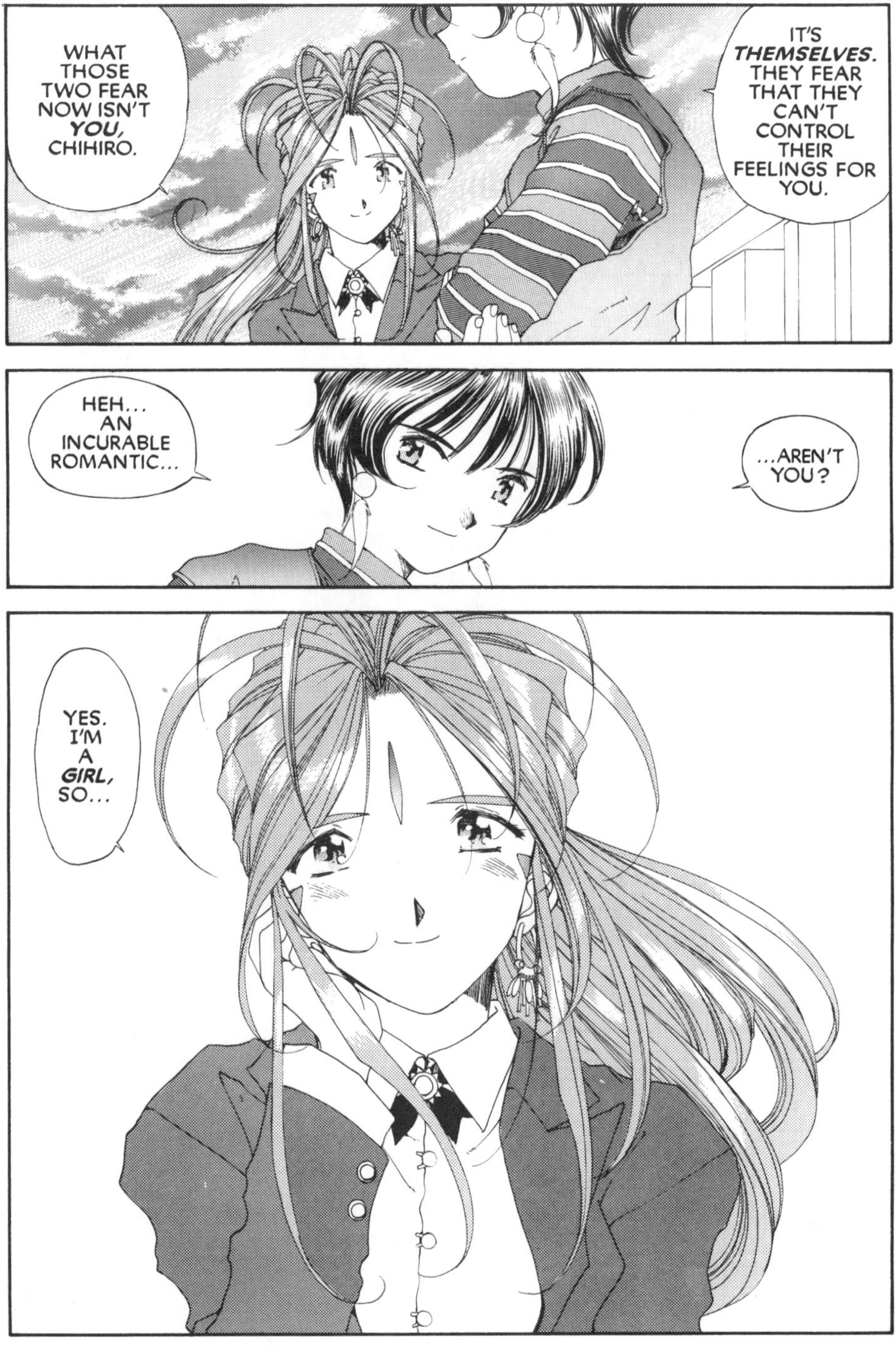
WHAT THOSE TWO FEAR NOW ISN'T ***YOU,*** CHIHIRO.
IT'S ***THEMSELVES.*** THEY FEAR THAT THEY CAN'T CONTROL THEIR FEELINGS FOR YOU.
HEH... AN INCURABLE ROMANTIC...
...AREN'T YOU?
YES. I'M A ***GIRL,*** SO...

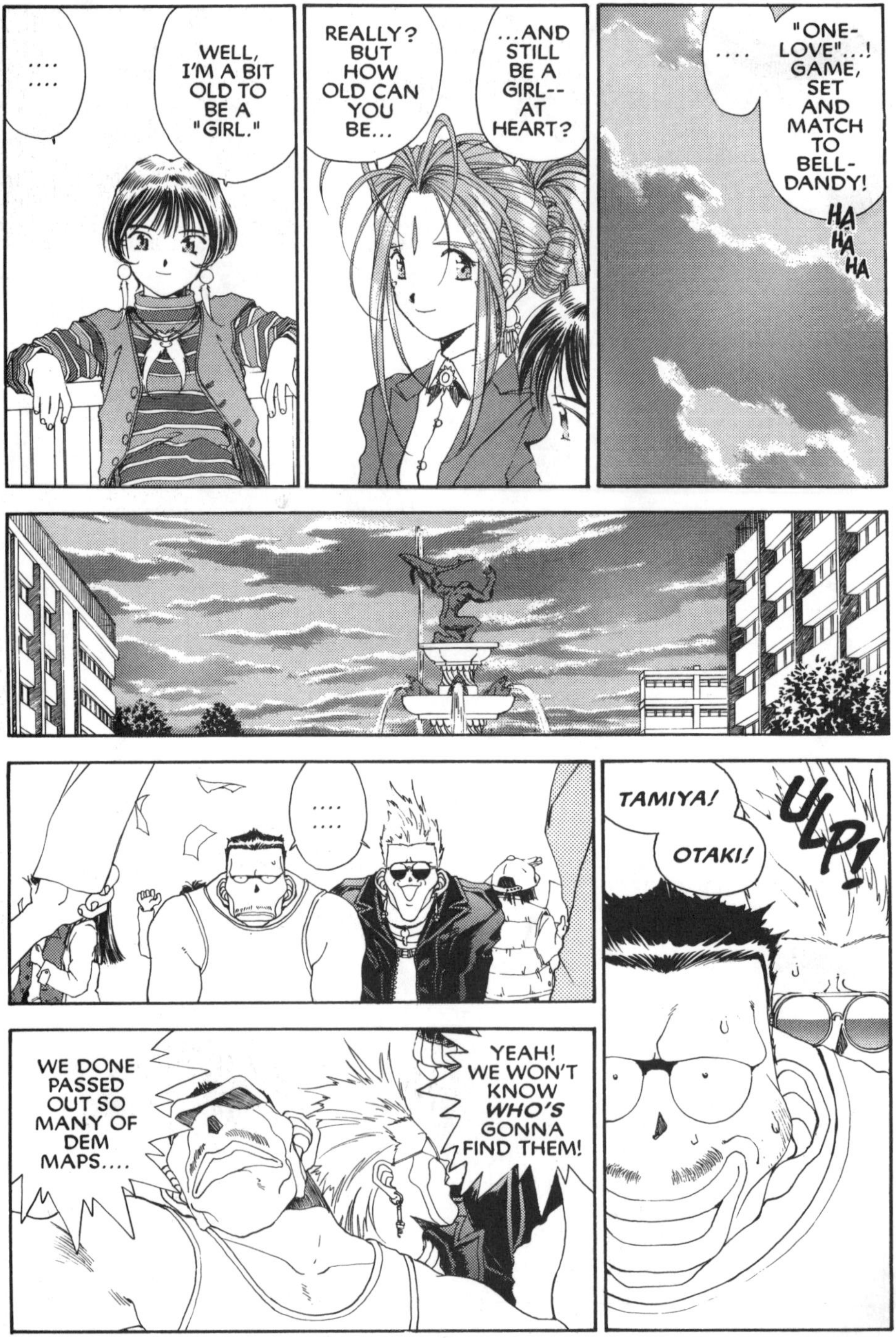
....
....
WELL, I'M A BIT OLD TO BE A "GIRL."
REALLY? BUT HOW OLD CAN YOU BE...
...AND STILL BE A GIRL-- AT HEART?
....
"ONE-LOVE"...! GAME, SET AND MATCH TO BELL-DANDY!
HA HA HA
....
....
TAMIYA!
OTAKI!
ULP!
WE DONE PASSED OUT SO MANY OF DEM MAPS....
YEAH! WE WON'T KNOW ***WHO'S*** GONNA FIND THEM!

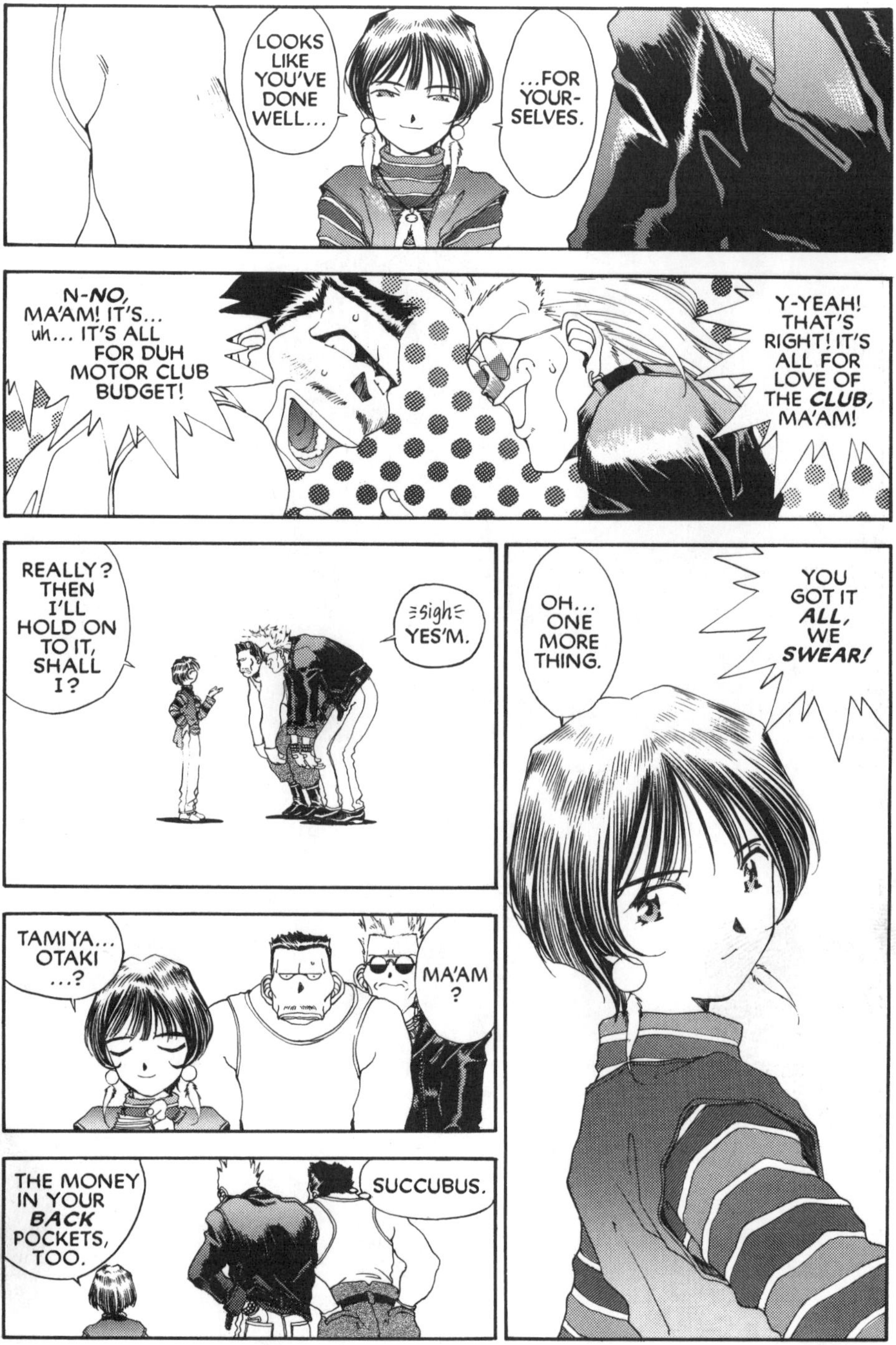
LOOKS LIKE YOU'VE DONE WELL...
...FOR YOUR-SELVES.
N-NO, MA'AM! IT'S... uh... IT'S ALL FOR DUH MOTOR CLUB BUDGET!
Y-YEAH! THAT'S RIGHT! IT'S ALL FOR LOVE OF THE CLUB, MA'AM!
REALLY? THEN I'LL HOLD ON TO IT, SHALL I?
sigh YES'M.
TAMIYA... OTAKI ...?
MA'AM ?
THE MONEY IN YOUR BACK POCKETS, TOO.
SUCCUBUS.
OH... ONE MORE THING.
YOU GOT IT ALL, WE SWEAR!

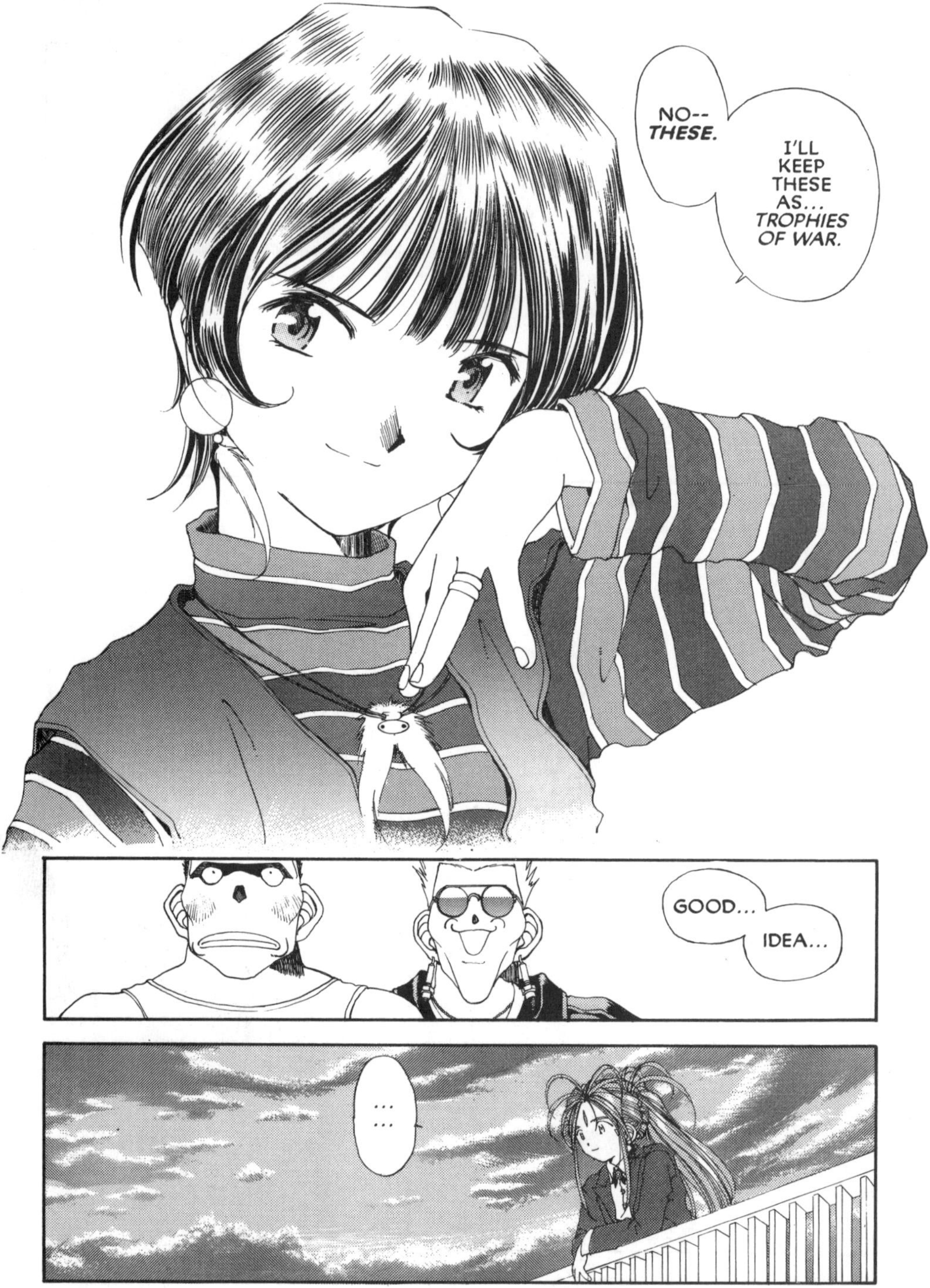
NO-- THESE.
I'LL KEEP THESE AS... TROPHIES OF WAR.
GOOD... IDEA...
... ...

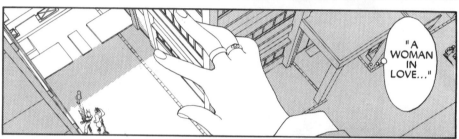

"A WOMAN IN LOVE..."

"...IS A GIRL FOREVER!"

MEANWHILE...

...THE BAFFLED MOB, MAPS IN HAND...

...WANDERED HOPE-LESSLY THROUGH THE NIGHT...

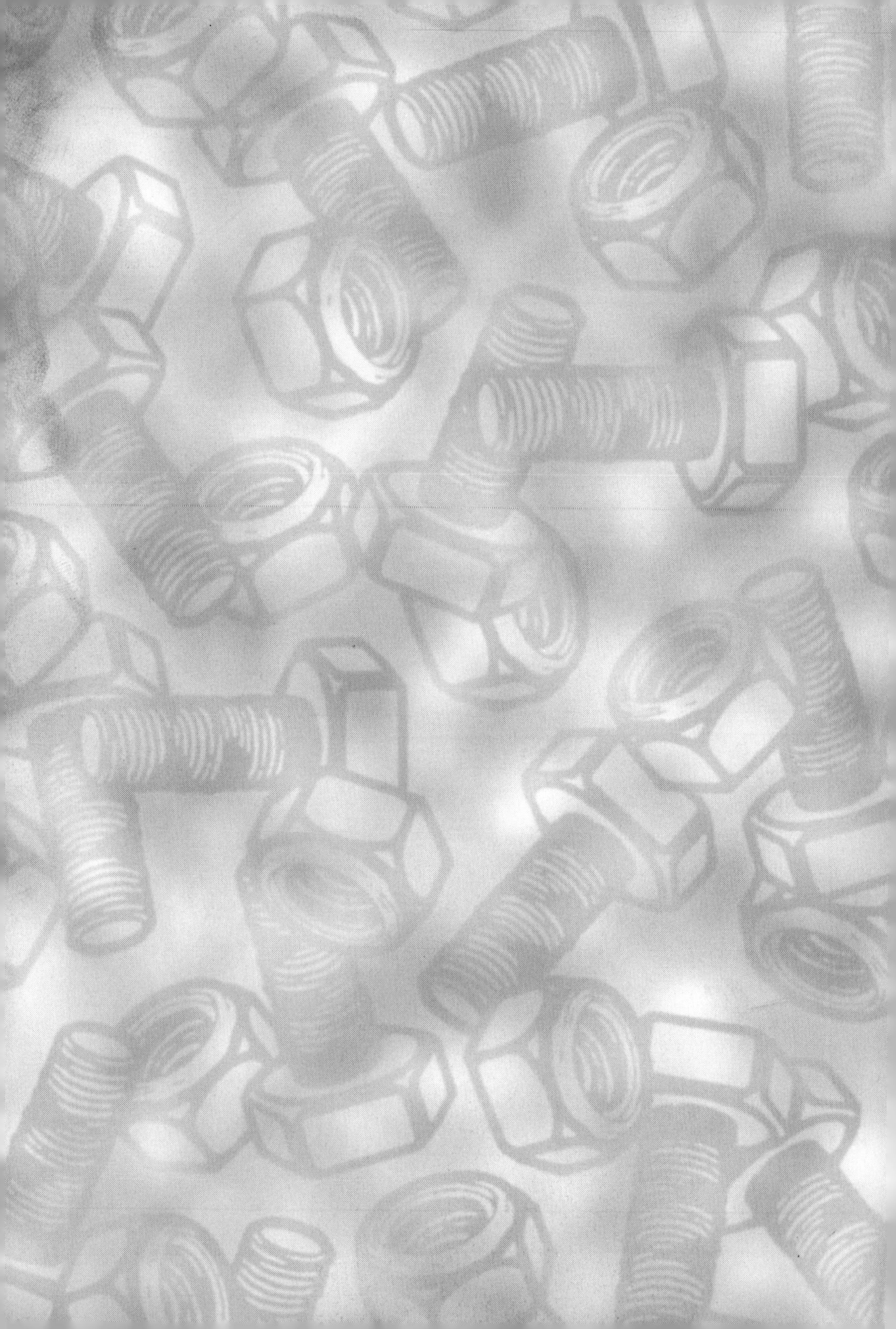

Live to Work, Work to Live!

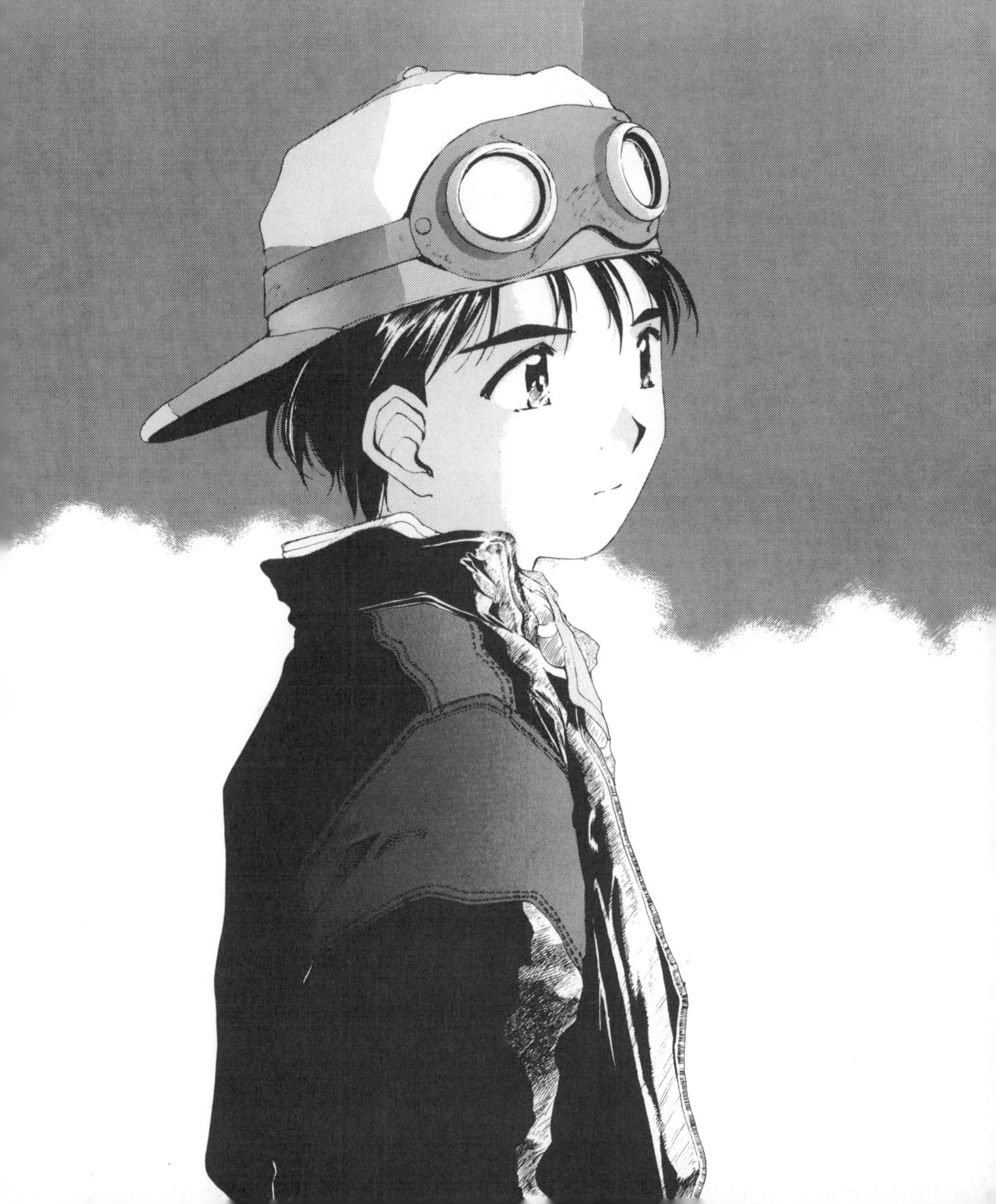

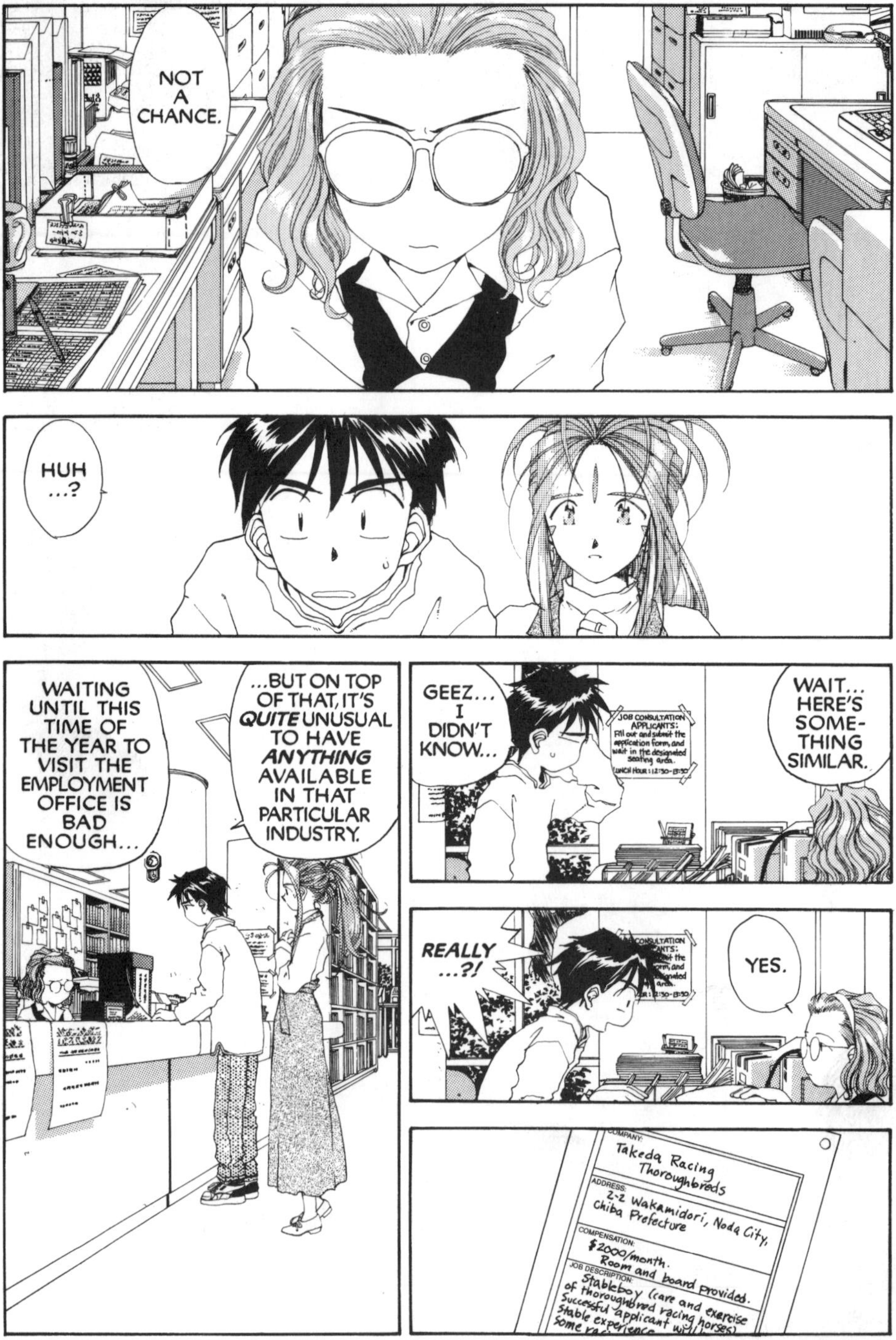
NOT A CHANCE.
HUH ...?
WAITING UNTIL THIS TIME OF THE YEAR TO VISIT THE EMPLOYMENT OFFICE IS BAD ENOUGH...
...BUT ON TOP OF THAT, IT'S *QUITE* UNUSUAL TO HAVE *ANYTHING* AVAILABLE IN THAT PARTICULAR INDUSTRY.
GEEZ... I DIDN'T KNOW...
JOB CONSULTATION APPLICANTS: Fill out and submit the application form, and wait in the designated seating area.
LUNCH HOUR: 12:30-13:30
WAIT... HERE'S SOMETHING SIMILAR.
REALLY ...?!
YES.
COMPANY: Takeda Racing Thoroughbreds
ADDRESS: 2-2 Wakamidori, Noda City, Chiba Prefecture
COMPENSATION: $2000/month. Room and board provided.
JOB DESCRIPTION: Stableboy (care and exercise of thoroughbred racing horses)
Successful applicant will
Stable experience

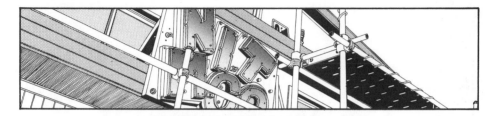

MA'AM...
RACING *HORSES*
IS NOT
EXACTLY "SIMILAR"
TO RACING
MOTORCYCLES.

I SEE.
MY
APOLOGIES,
SIR.

HEYA,
GUYS!

I WAS
IN THE
NEIGHBOR-
HOOD, SO
I THOUGHT
I'D DROP
BY.

....
...?

oh.
hi.

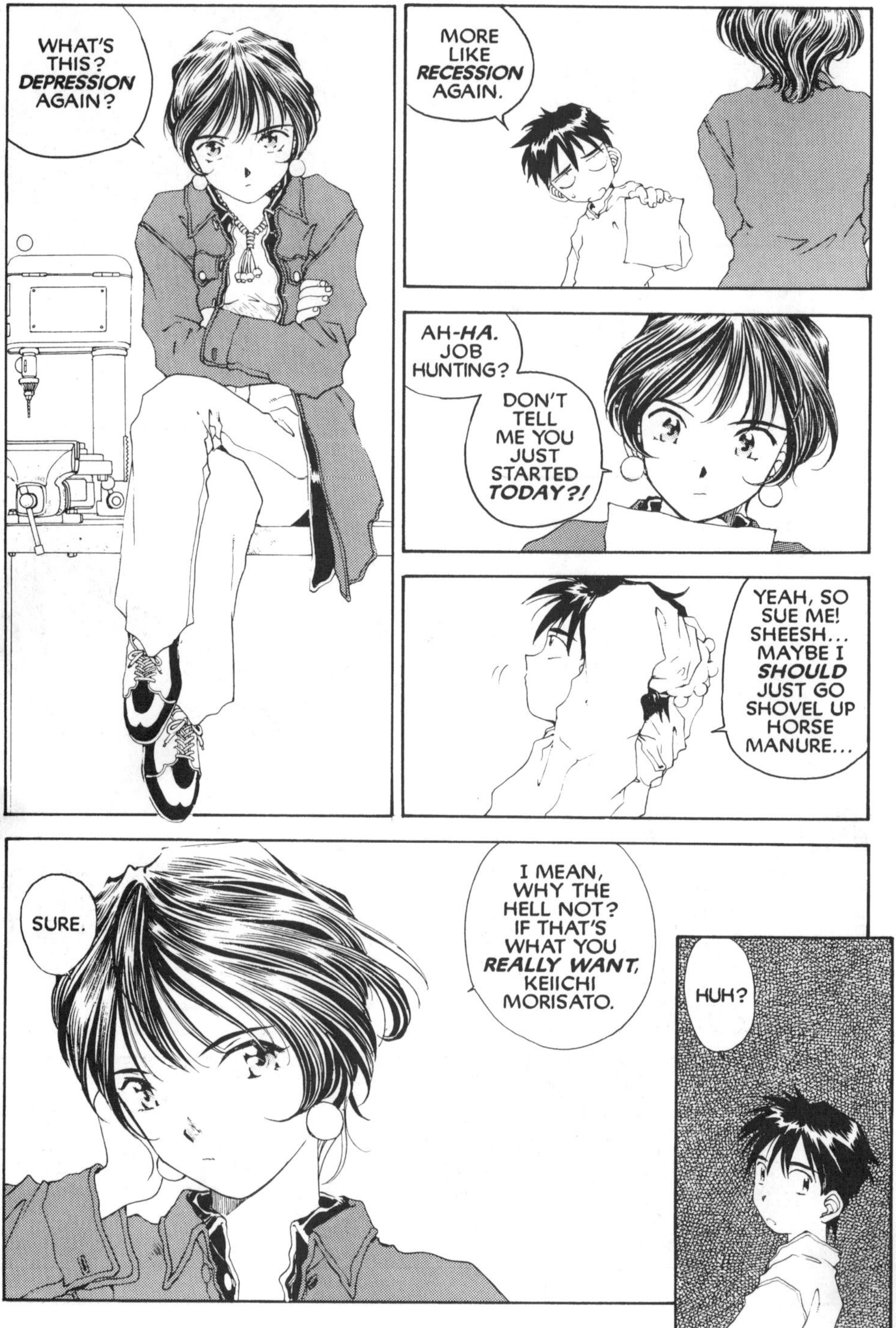
WHAT'S THIS? DEPRESSION AGAIN?
MORE LIKE RECESSION AGAIN.
AH-HA. JOB HUNTING?
DON'T TELL ME YOU JUST STARTED TODAY?!
YEAH, SO SUE ME! SHEESH... MAYBE I SHOULD JUST GO SHOVEL UP HORSE MANURE...
SURE.
I MEAN, WHY THE HELL NOT? IF THAT'S WHAT YOU REALLY WANT, KEIICHI MORISATO.
HUH?

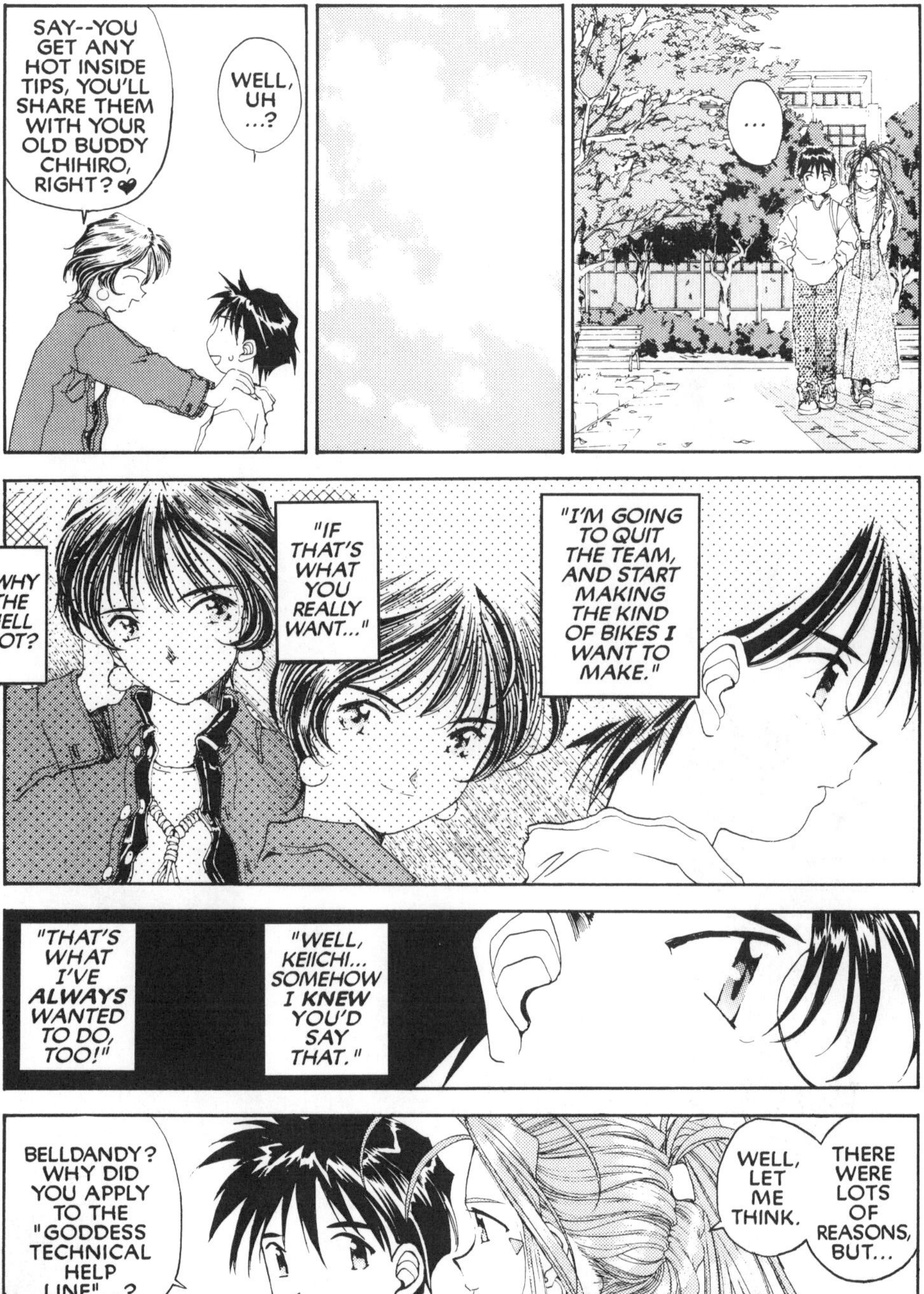
SAY--YOU GET ANY HOT INSIDE TIPS, YOU'LL SHARE THEM WITH YOUR OLD BUDDY CHIHIRO, RIGHT?
WELL, UH ...?
...
"WHY THE HELL NOT?
"IF THAT'S WHAT YOU REALLY WANT..."
"I'M GOING TO QUIT THE TEAM, AND START MAKING THE KIND OF BIKES I WANT TO MAKE."
"THAT'S WHAT I'VE ALWAYS WANTED TO DO, TOO!"
"WELL, KEIICHI... SOMEHOW I KNEW YOU'D SAY THAT."
BELLDANDY? WHY DID YOU APPLY TO THE "GODDESS TECHNICAL HELP LINE"...?
WELL, LET ME THINK.
THERE WERE LOTS OF REASONS, BUT...

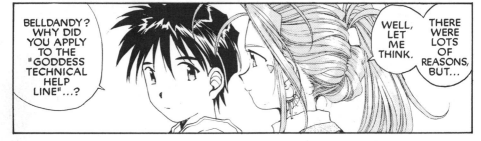

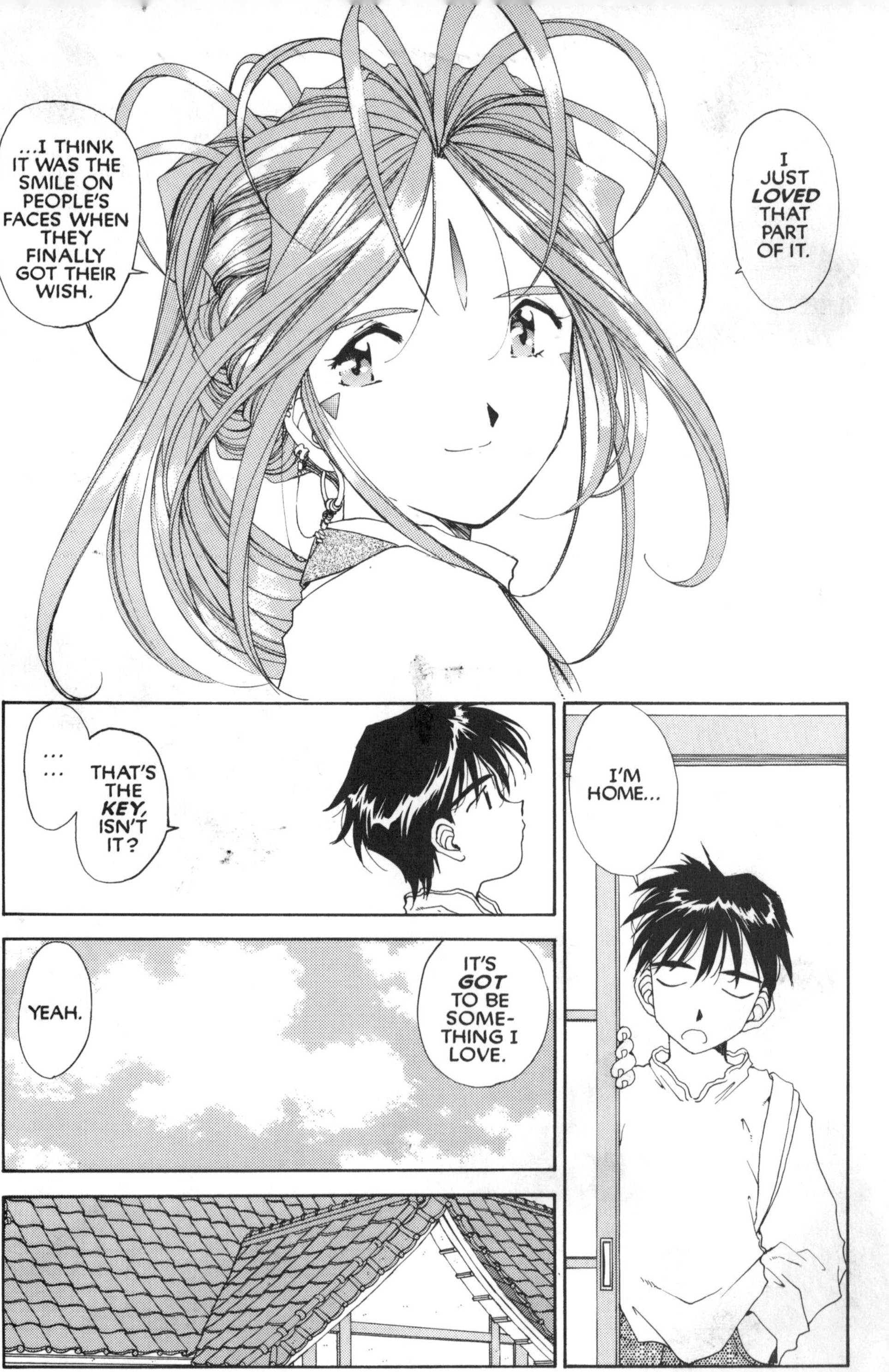
...I THINK IT WAS THE SMILE ON PEOPLE'S FACES WHEN THEY FINALLY GOT THEIR WISH.
I JUST **LOVED** THAT PART OF IT.
... ...
THAT'S THE **KEY,** ISN'T IT?
YEAH.
IT'S **GOT** TO BE SOME-THING I LOVE.
I'M HOME...

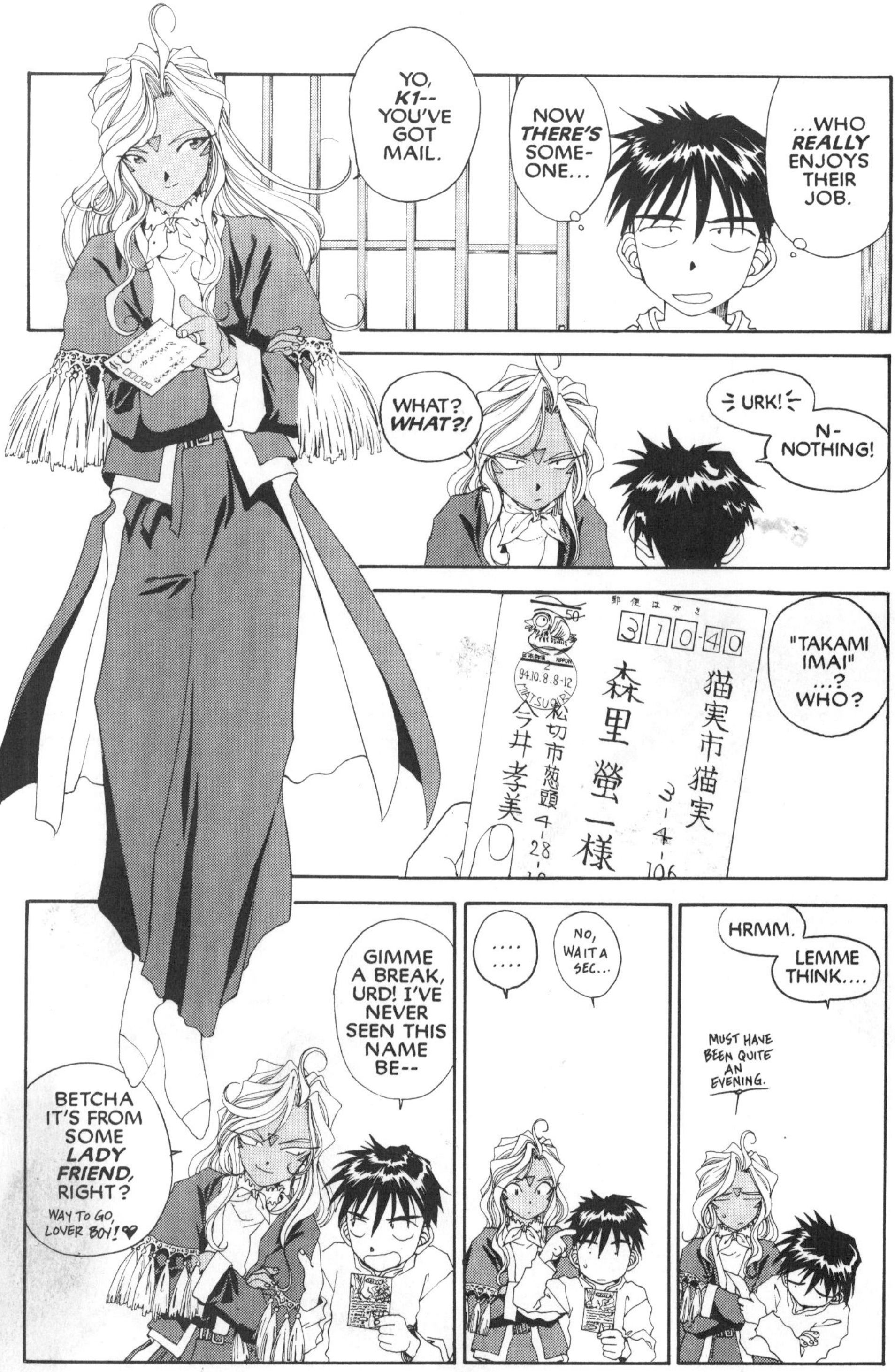
YO, K1-- YOU'VE GOT MAIL.
NOW THERE'S SOME-ONE...
...WHO REALLY ENJOYS THEIR JOB.
WHAT? WHAT?!
URK!
N-NOTHING!
郵便はがき
50
日本郵便 NIPPON
94.10.8.8-12
MATSUGIRI
310-40
猫実市猫実
3-4-106
森里螢一様
松切市葱頭
4-28-
今井孝美
"TAKAMI IMAI" ...? WHO?
BETCHA IT'S FROM SOME LADY FRIEND, RIGHT?
WAY TO GO, LOVER BOY!♥
GIMME A BREAK, URD! I'VE NEVER SEEN THIS NAME BE--
....
....
NO, WAIT A SEC...
HRMM.
LEMME THINK....
MUST HAVE BEEN QUITE AN EVENING.

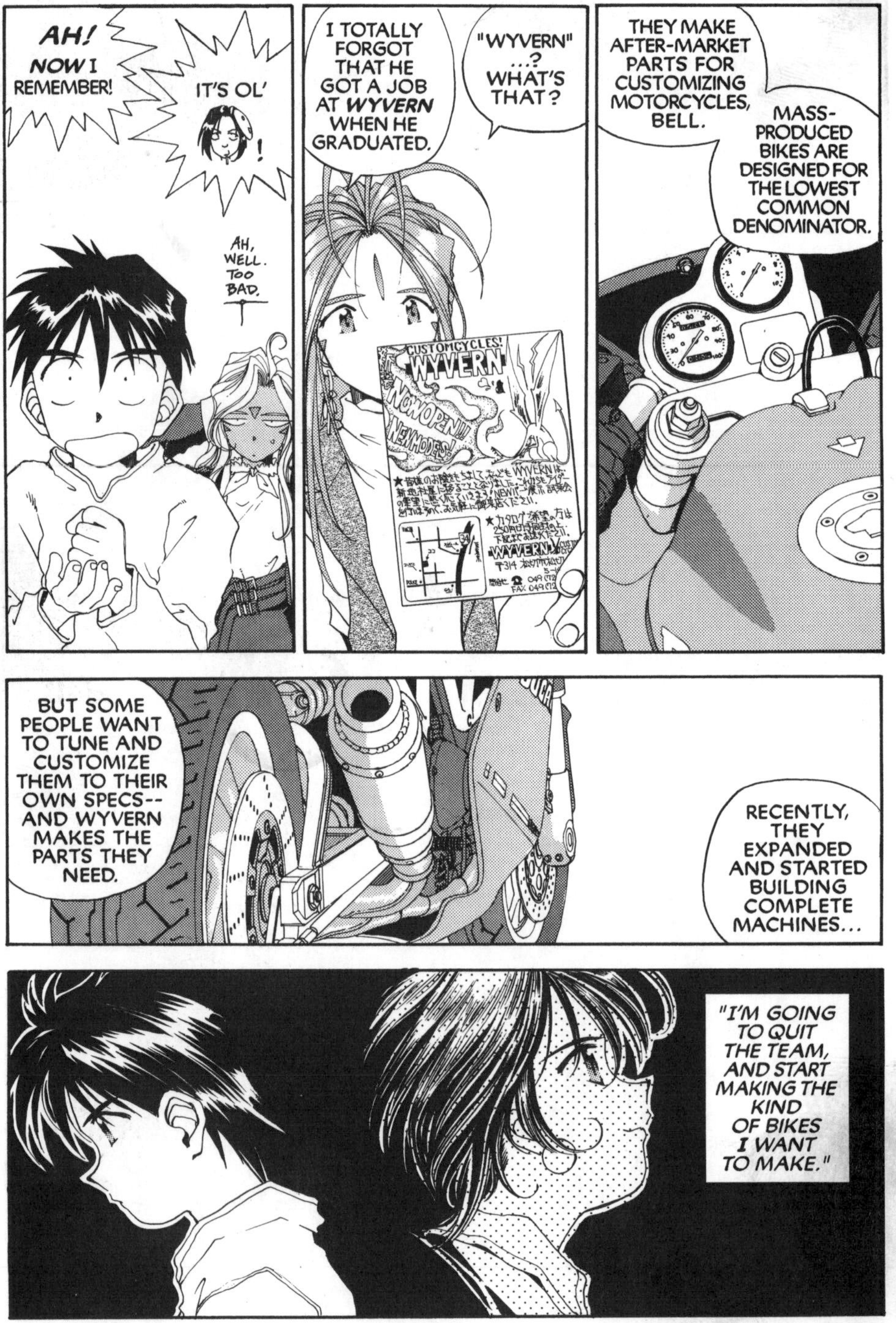
AH! NOW I REMEMBER!
IT'S OL'
!
AH, WELL. TOO BAD.
I TOTALLY FORGOT THAT HE GOT A JOB AT WYVERN WHEN HE GRADUATED.
"WYVERN" ...? WHAT'S THAT?
CUSTOMCYCLES!
WYVERN
NOW OPEN!!
NEW MODELS!
THEY MAKE AFTER-MARKET PARTS FOR CUSTOMIZING MOTORCYCLES, BELL.
MASS-PRODUCED BIKES ARE DESIGNED FOR THE LOWEST COMMON DENOMINATOR.
BUT SOME PEOPLE WANT TO TUNE AND CUSTOMIZE THEM TO THEIR OWN SPECS-- AND WYVERN MAKES THE PARTS THEY NEED.
RECENTLY, THEY EXPANDED AND STARTED BUILDING COMPLETE MACHINES...
"I'M GOING TO QUIT THE TEAM, AND START MAKING THE KIND OF BIKES I WANT TO MAKE."

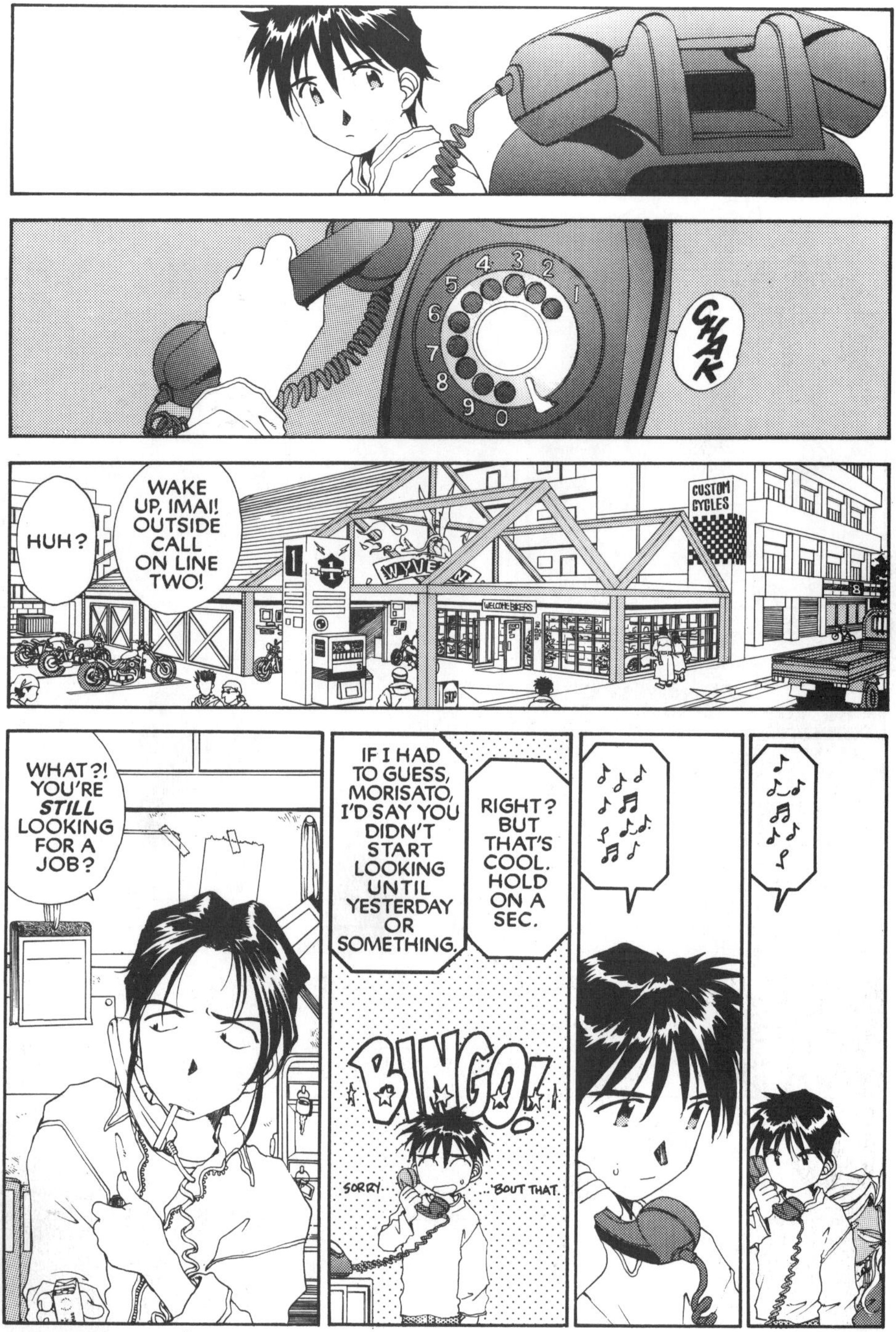
CHAK
HUH?
WAKE UP, IMAI! OUTSIDE CALL ON LINE TWO!
CUSTOM CYCLES
WELCOME BIKERS
WHAT?! YOU'RE STILL LOOKING FOR A JOB?
IF I HAD TO GUESS, MORISATO, I'D SAY YOU DIDN'T START LOOKING UNTIL YESTERDAY OR SOMETHING.
BINGO!
SORRY... ...'BOUT THAT.
RIGHT? BUT THAT'S COOL. HOLD ON A SEC.

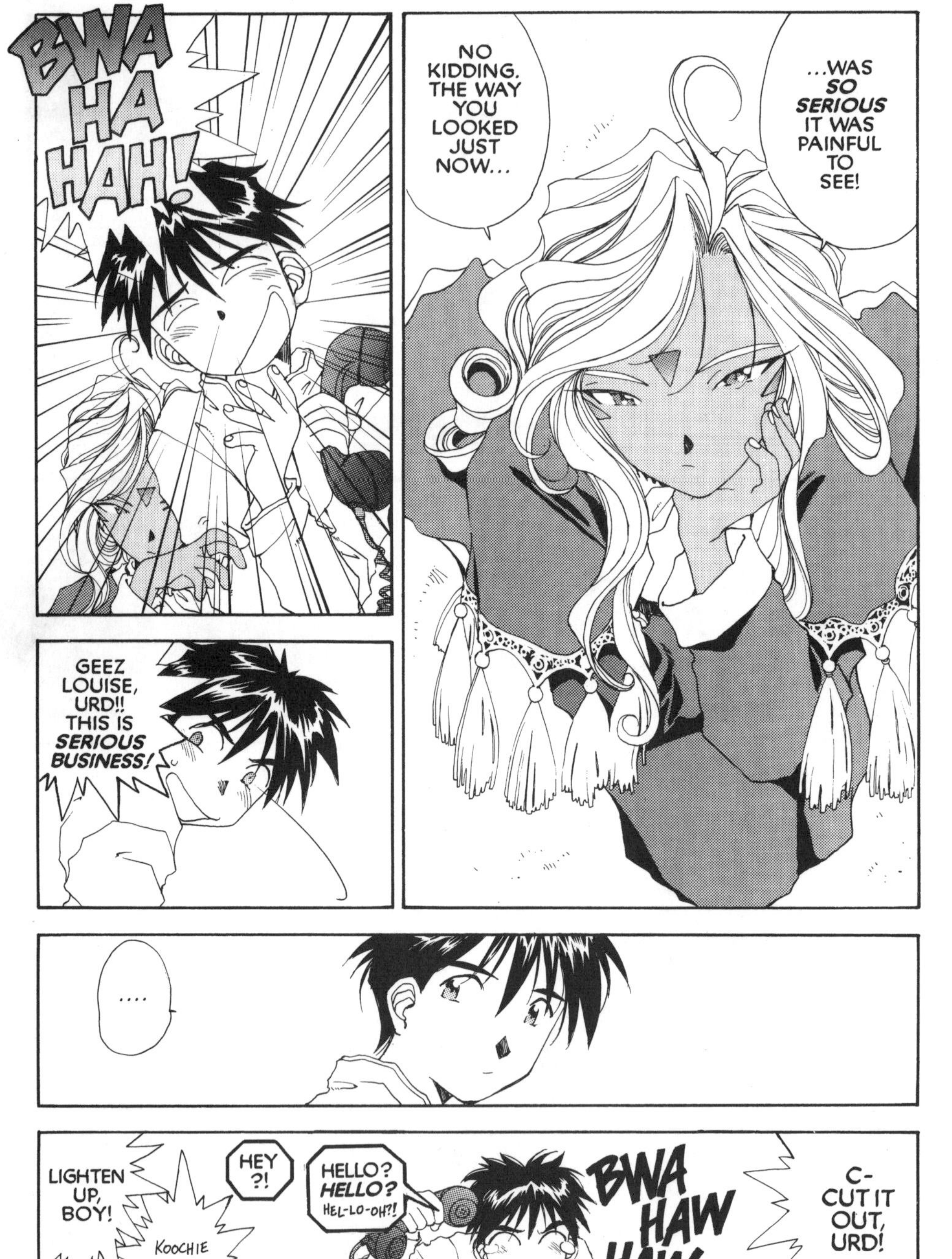
BWA HA HAH!
NO KIDDING. THE WAY YOU LOOKED JUST NOW...
...WAS *SO SERIOUS* IT WAS PAINFUL TO SEE!
GEEZ LOUISE, URD!! THIS IS *SERIOUS BUSINESS!*
....
LIGHTEN UP, BOY!
KOOCHIE KOOCHIE KOO!
HEY ?!
HELLO? *HELLO?* HEL-LO-OH?!
BWA HAW HAW
C- CUT IT OUT, URD!

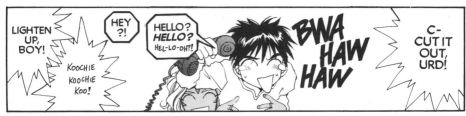

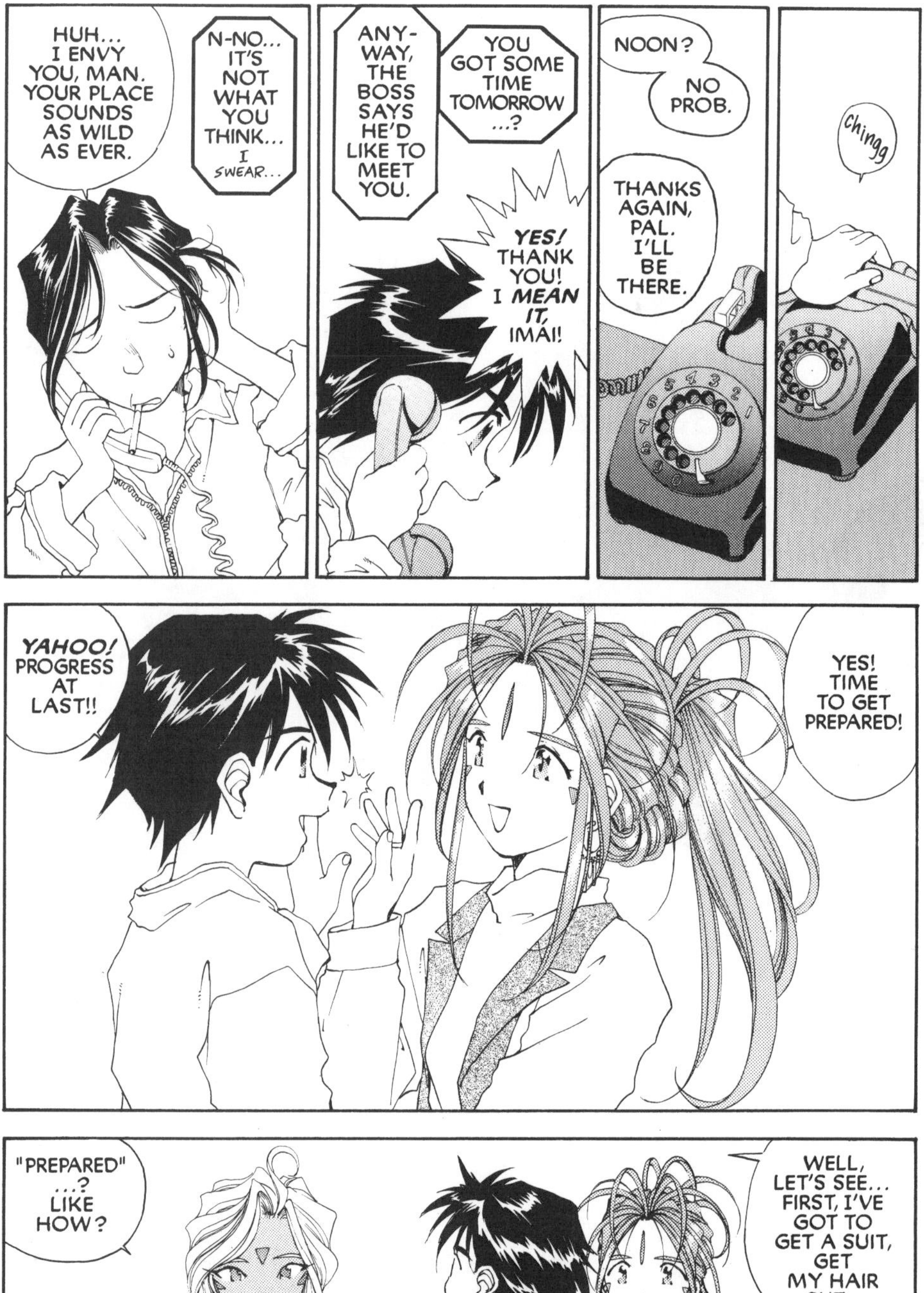
HUH... I ENVY YOU, MAN. YOUR PLACE SOUNDS AS WILD AS EVER.
N-NO... IT'S NOT WHAT YOU THINK... I SWEAR...
ANY-WAY, THE BOSS SAYS HE'D LIKE TO MEET YOU.
YOU GOT SOME TIME TOMORROW ...?
YES! THANK YOU! I MEAN IT, IMAI!
NOON?
NO PROB.
THANKS AGAIN, PAL. I'LL BE THERE.
Chingg
YAHOO! PROGRESS AT LAST!!
YES! TIME TO GET PREPARED!
"PREPARED" ...? LIKE HOW?
WELL, LET'S SEE... FIRST, I'VE GOT TO GET A SUIT, GET MY HAIR CUT--

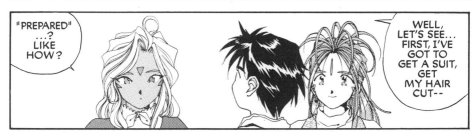

HUH?

OH, *NO!* URD! *WAIT!!*

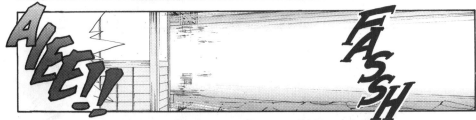

AIEE!!

FASSH

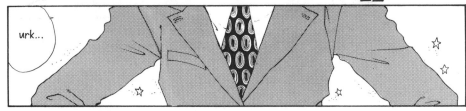

urk...

WELL...? HEH, HEH!

WELL, UH... THE *SUIT* IS GOOD. *VERY* GOOD. BUT...

...WHAT DID YOU DO TO MY HAIR?!

PICKY, PICKY. OKAY, THEN...

TA-DAHH!

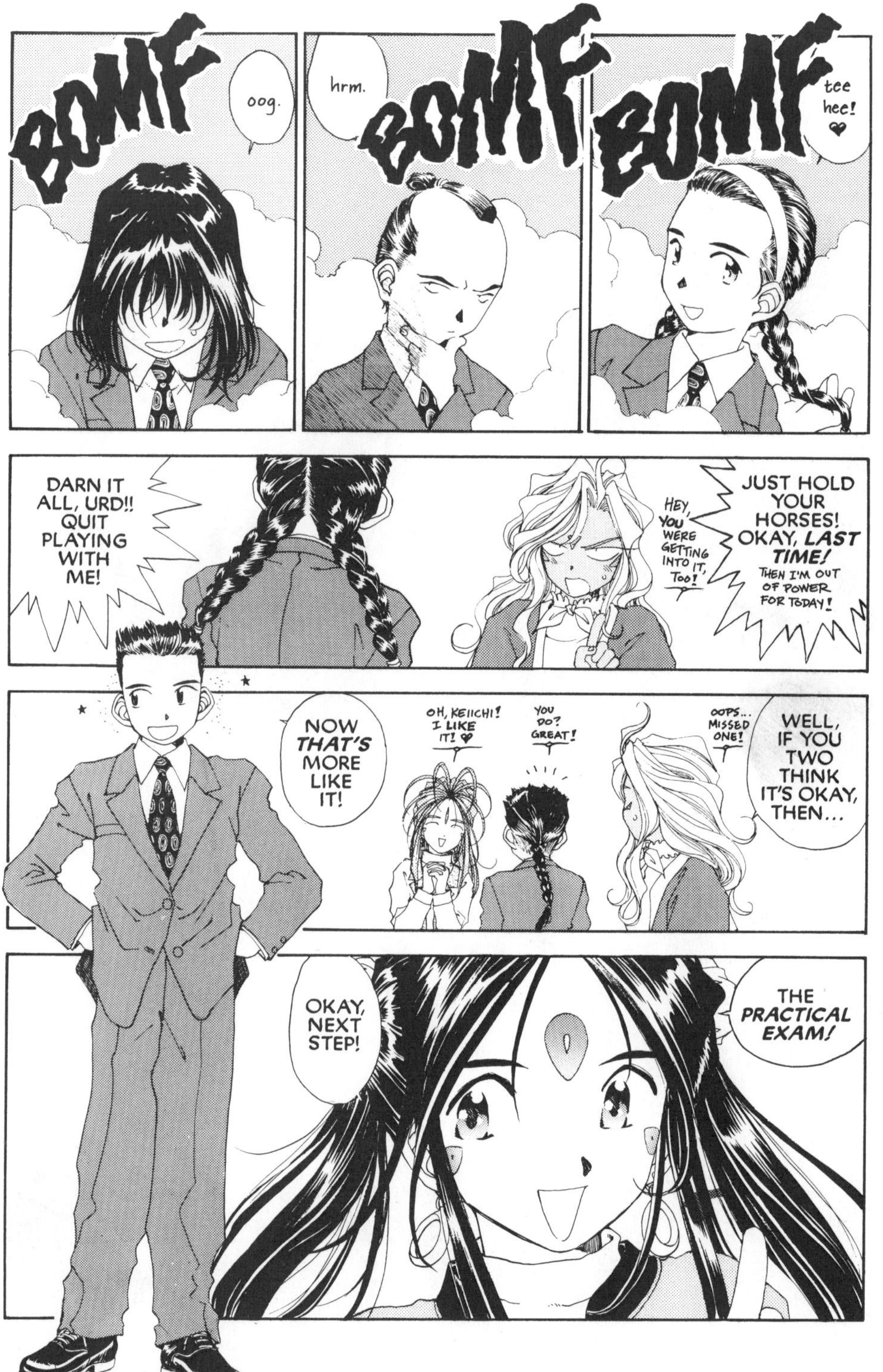
BOMF
oog.
hrm.
BOMF
BOMF
tee hee! ❤
DARN IT ALL, URD!! QUIT PLAYING WITH ME!
HEY, YOU WERE GETTING INTO IT, TOO!
JUST HOLD YOUR HORSES! OKAY, LAST TIME! THEN I'M OUT OF POWER FOR TODAY!
NOW THAT'S MORE LIKE IT!
OH, KEIICHI! I LIKE IT! ❤
YOU DO? GREAT!
OOPS... MISSED ONE!
WELL, IF YOU TWO THINK IT'S OKAY, THEN...
OKAY, NEXT STEP!
THE PRACTICAL EXAM!

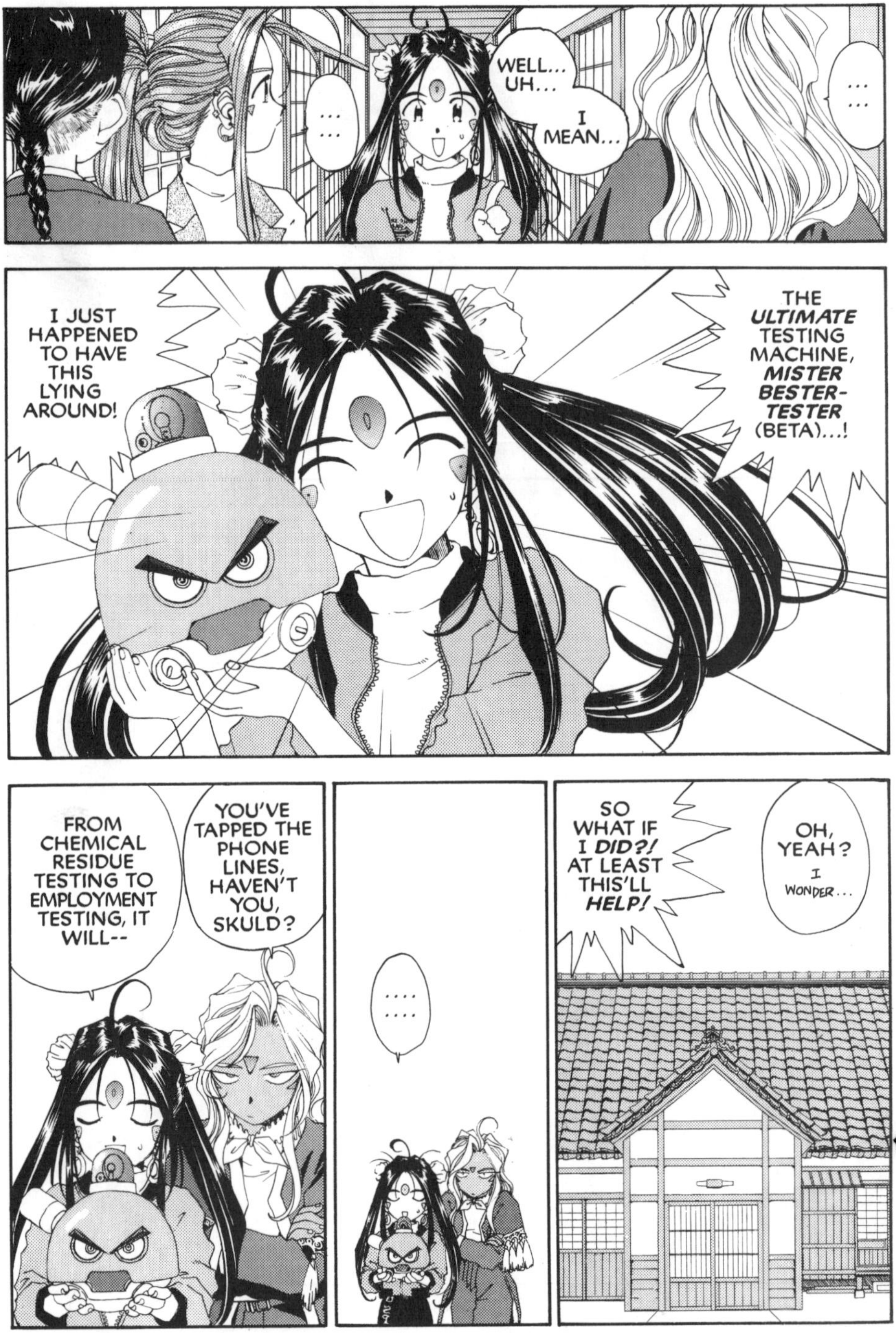

... ...
WELL... UH... I MEAN...
... ...
I JUST HAPPENED TO HAVE THIS LYING AROUND!
THE *ULTIMATE* TESTING MACHINE, ***MISTER BESTER-TESTER*** (BETA)...!
FROM CHEMICAL RESIDUE TESTING TO EMPLOYMENT TESTING, IT WILL--
YOU'VE TAPPED THE PHONE LINES, HAVEN'T YOU, SKULD?
....
SO WHAT IF I *DID?!* AT LEAST THIS'LL ***HELP!***
OH, YEAH? I WONDER...

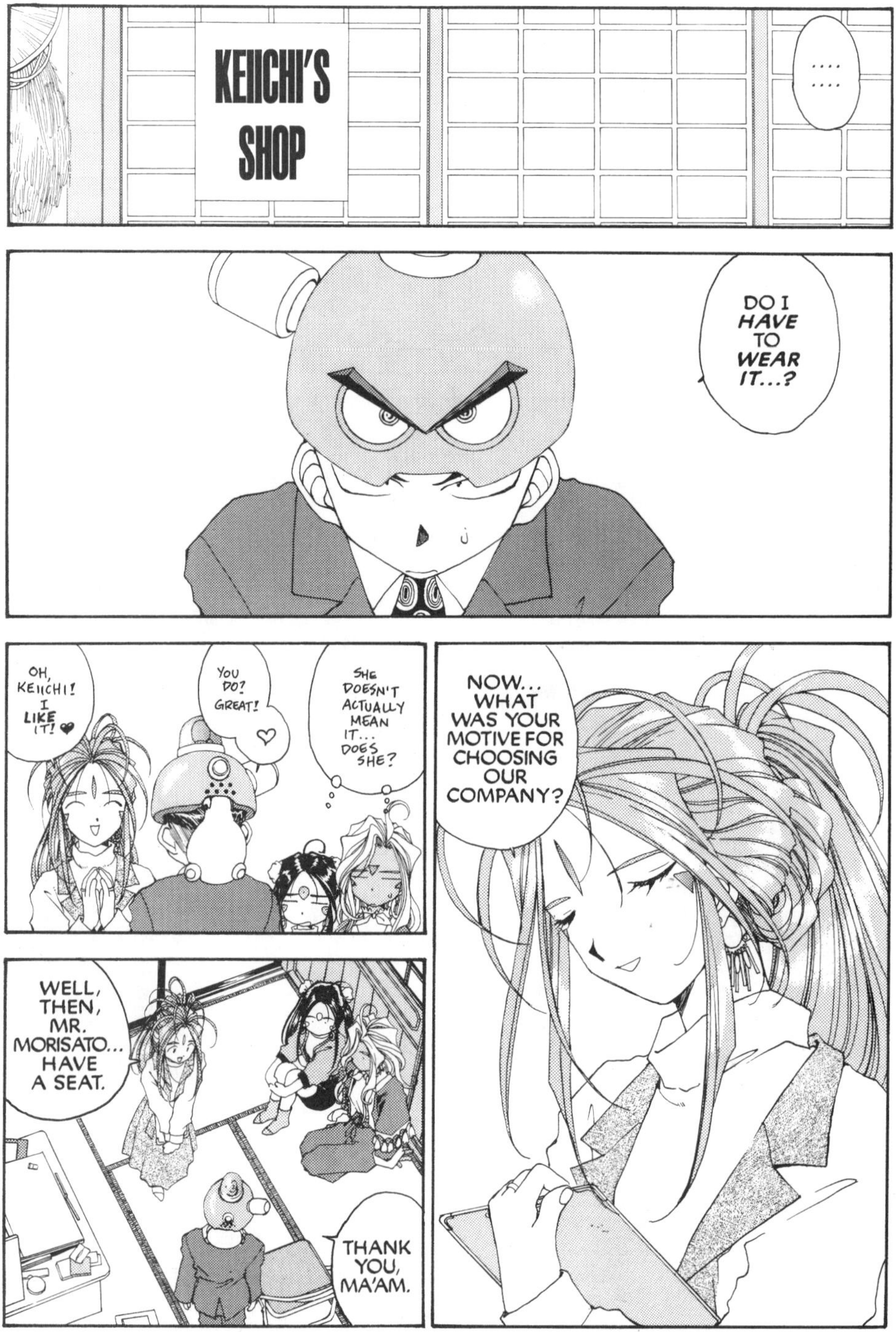
KEIICHI'S SHOP
....
....
DO I HAVE TO WEAR IT...?
OH, KEIICHI! I LIKE IT! ❤
YOU DO? GREAT! ♡
SHE DOESN'T ACTUALLY MEAN IT... DOES SHE?
WELL, THEN, MR. MORISATO... HAVE A SEAT.
THANK YOU, MA'AM.
NOW... WHAT WAS YOUR MOTIVE FOR CHOOSING OUR COMPANY?

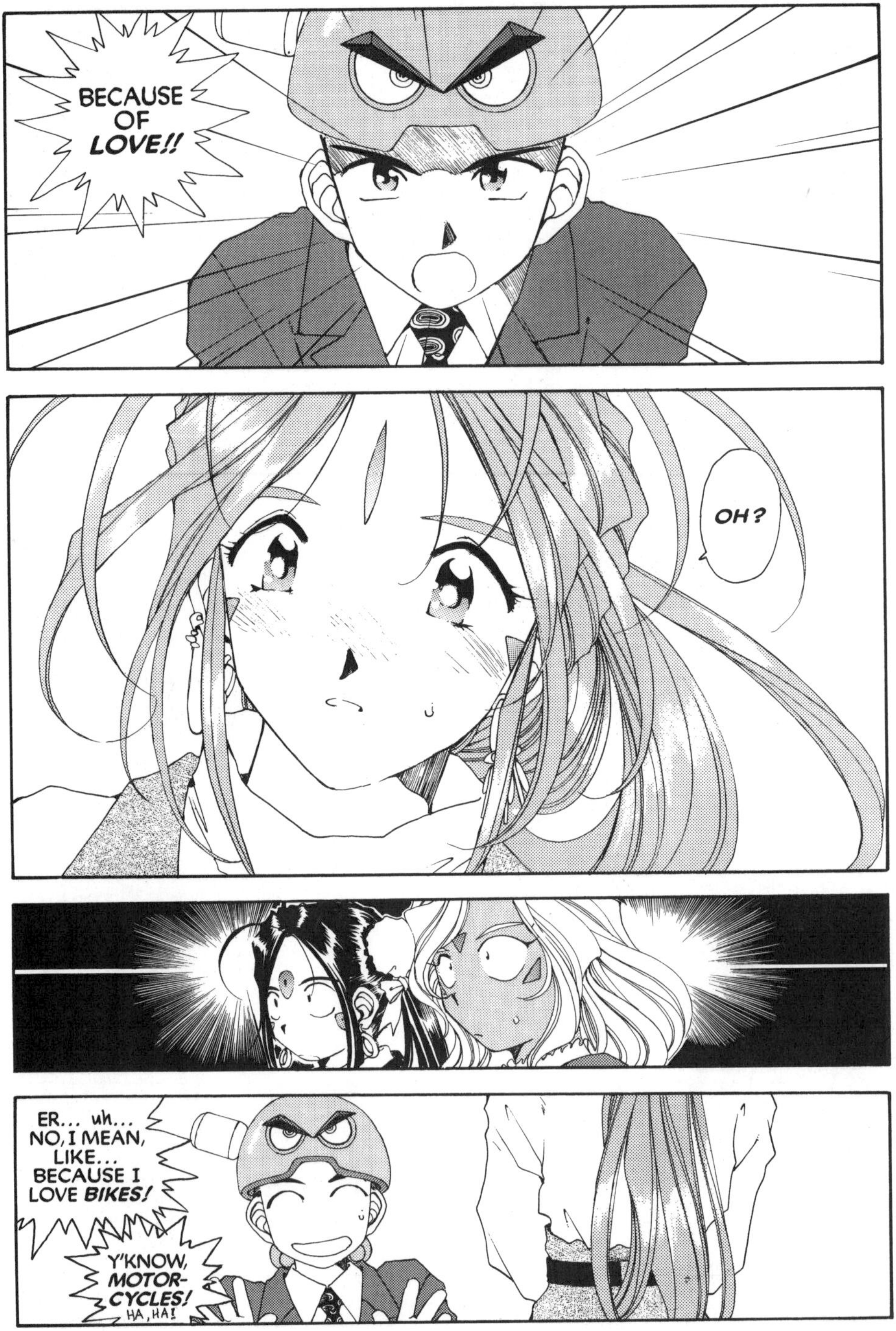
BECAUSE OF ***LOVE!!***
OH?
ER... uh... NO, I MEAN, LIKE... BECAUSE I LOVE ***BIKES!***
Y'KNOW, ***MOTOR-CYCLES!***
HA, HA!

BRZZZT!!

WRONG. QUESTION MUST BE ANSWERED PRECISELY.

PENALTY LEVEL TWO.

FZZZK!

GACK?!

UWAGHH!?!

FRZZK!

OH! K-KEIICHI?!

DON'T WORRY.

IT'S MERELY TRIGGERING MUSCLE CONTRACTIONS BY SENDING A WEAK ELECTRIC PULSE THROUGH HIS BODY.

IT'S THE SAME PRINCIPLE AS *TENS* THERAPEUTIC DEVICES. IT ACTUALLY *RELIEVES* MUSCLE TENSION!

WELL... IF IT'S GOOD FOR HIM, THEN I GUESS IT'S ALL RIGHT...

YEP!

ARE YOU *NUTS*, SKULD?! FORGET--

NNG!

UNG?

SORRY! YOU CAN'T TAKE IT OFF.

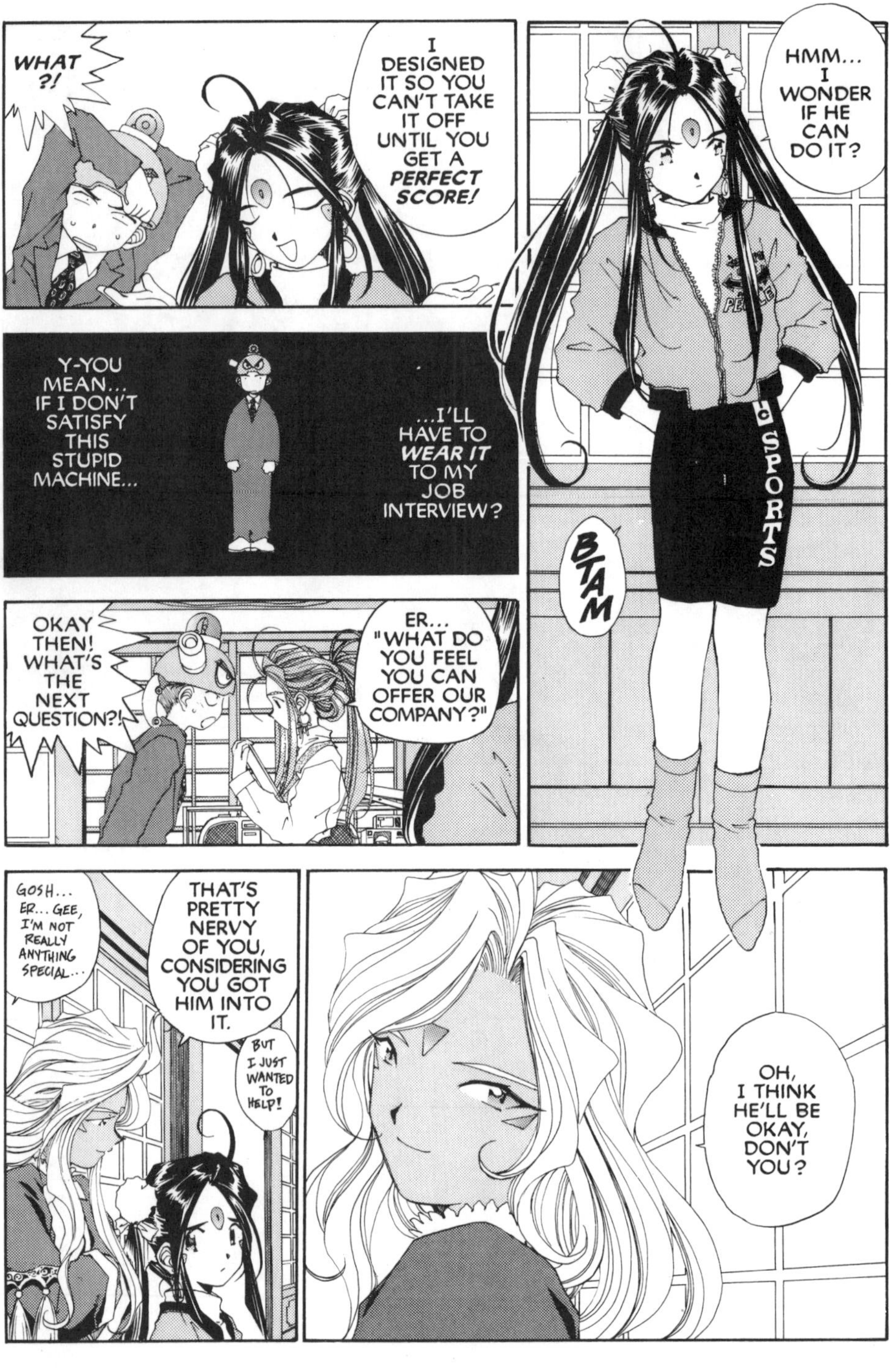
WHAT?!
I DESIGNED IT SO YOU CAN'T TAKE IT OFF UNTIL YOU GET A *PERFECT SCORE!*
Y-YOU MEAN... IF I DON'T SATISFY THIS STUPID MACHINE...
...I'LL HAVE TO *WEAR IT* TO MY JOB INTERVIEW?
OKAY THEN! WHAT'S THE NEXT QUESTION?!
ER... "WHAT DO YOU FEEL YOU CAN OFFER OUR COMPANY?"
HMM... I WONDER IF HE CAN DO IT?
SPORTS
BTAM
GOSH... ER... GEE, I'M NOT REALLY ANYTHING SPECIAL...
THAT'S PRETTY NERVY OF YOU, CONSIDERING YOU GOT HIM INTO IT.
BUT I JUST WANTED TO HELP!
OH, I THINK HE'LL BE OKAY, DON'T YOU?

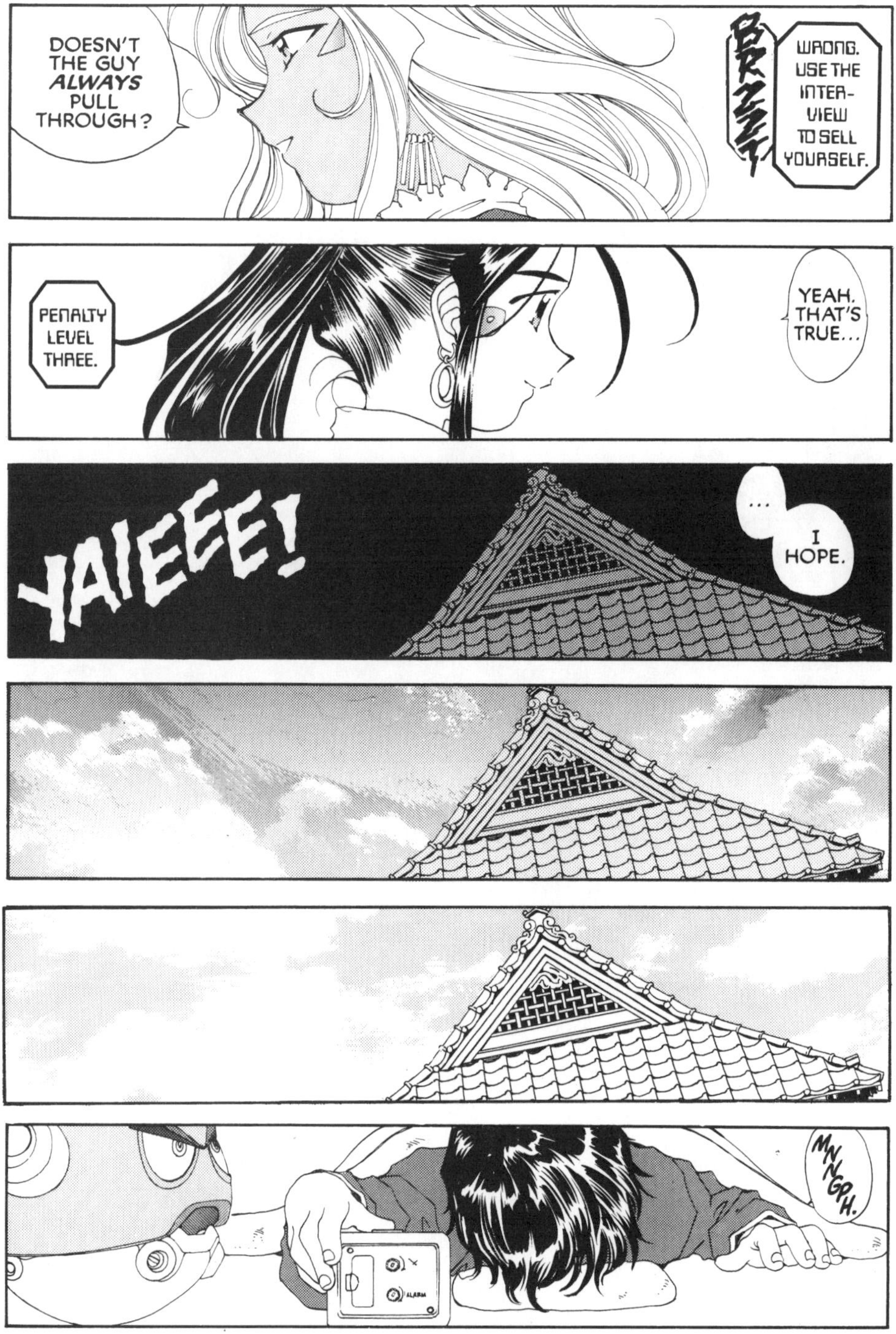
DOESN'T THE GUY ALWAYS PULL THROUGH?
BRZZZT
WRONG. USE THE INTER-VIEW TO SELL YOURSELF.
PENALTY LEVEL THREE.
YEAH. THAT'S TRUE...
YAIEEE!
... I HOPE.
MNNGPH.

AAGH!
I'M *DOOMED!!* I'LL NEVER MAKE IT!!

WHEN WAS YOUR APPOINT-MENT?!

NOON!!

WHY DIDN'T YOU TELL US *YESTERDAY?!*

I DIDN'T DARE SAY *ANYTHING* WITH THAT TORTURE DEVICE ON MY HEAD!

URD! LOAN ME A BROOM! *YOUR FASTEST ONE!*

WELL... I'M NOT SURE I'D RECOMMEND THAT...

JUST *DO IT,* PLEASE!

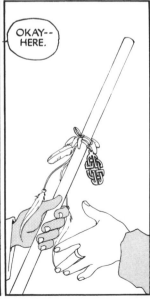

OKAY-- HERE.

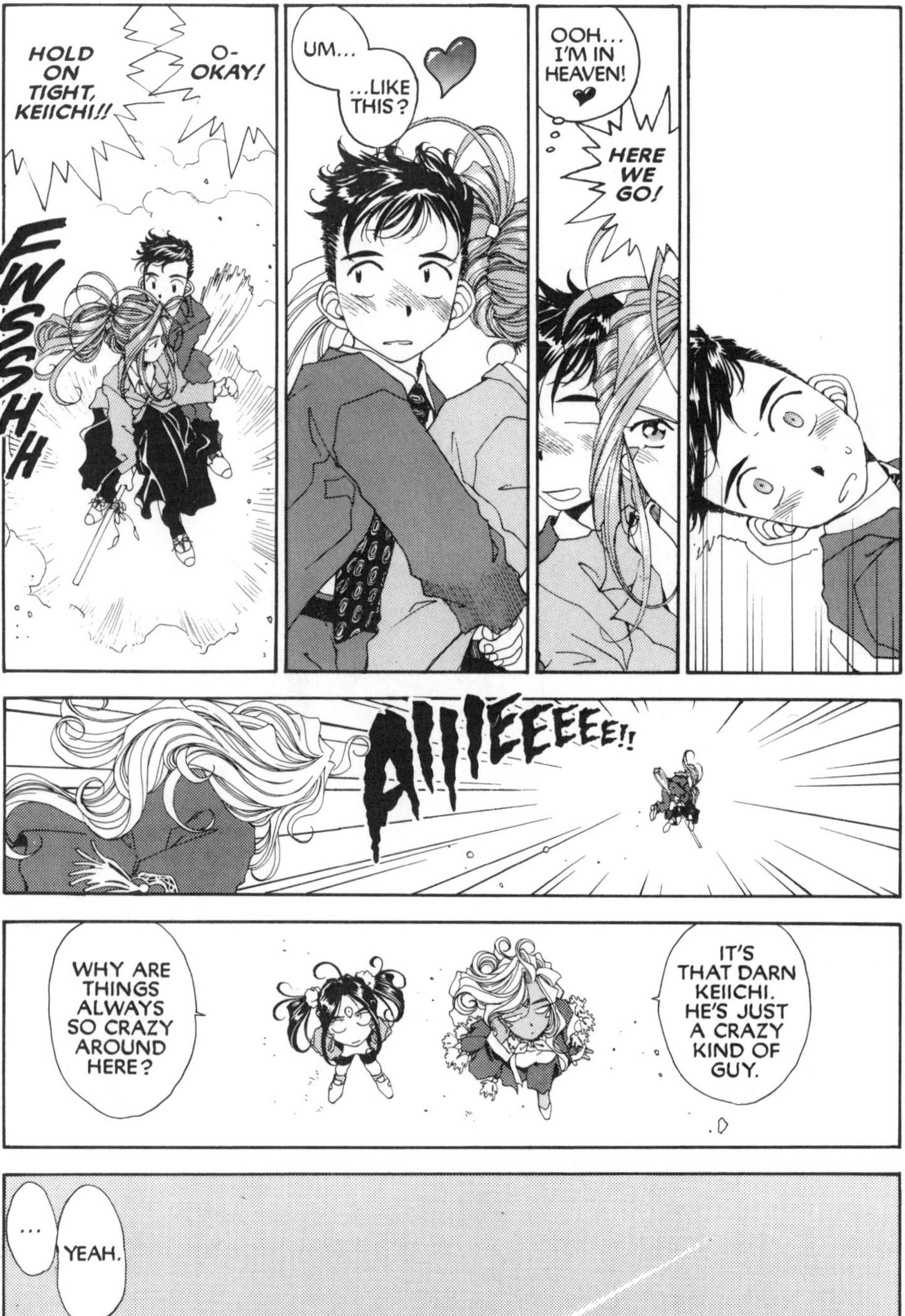
HOLD ON TIGHT, KEIICHI!!
O-OKAY!
FWSSHH
UM...
...LIKE THIS?
OOH... I'M IN HEAVEN!
HERE WE GO!
AIIIEEEEEE!!
WHY ARE THINGS ALWAYS SO CRAZY AROUND HERE?
IT'S THAT DARN KEIICHI. HE'S JUST A CRAZY KIND OF GUY.
...
YEAH.

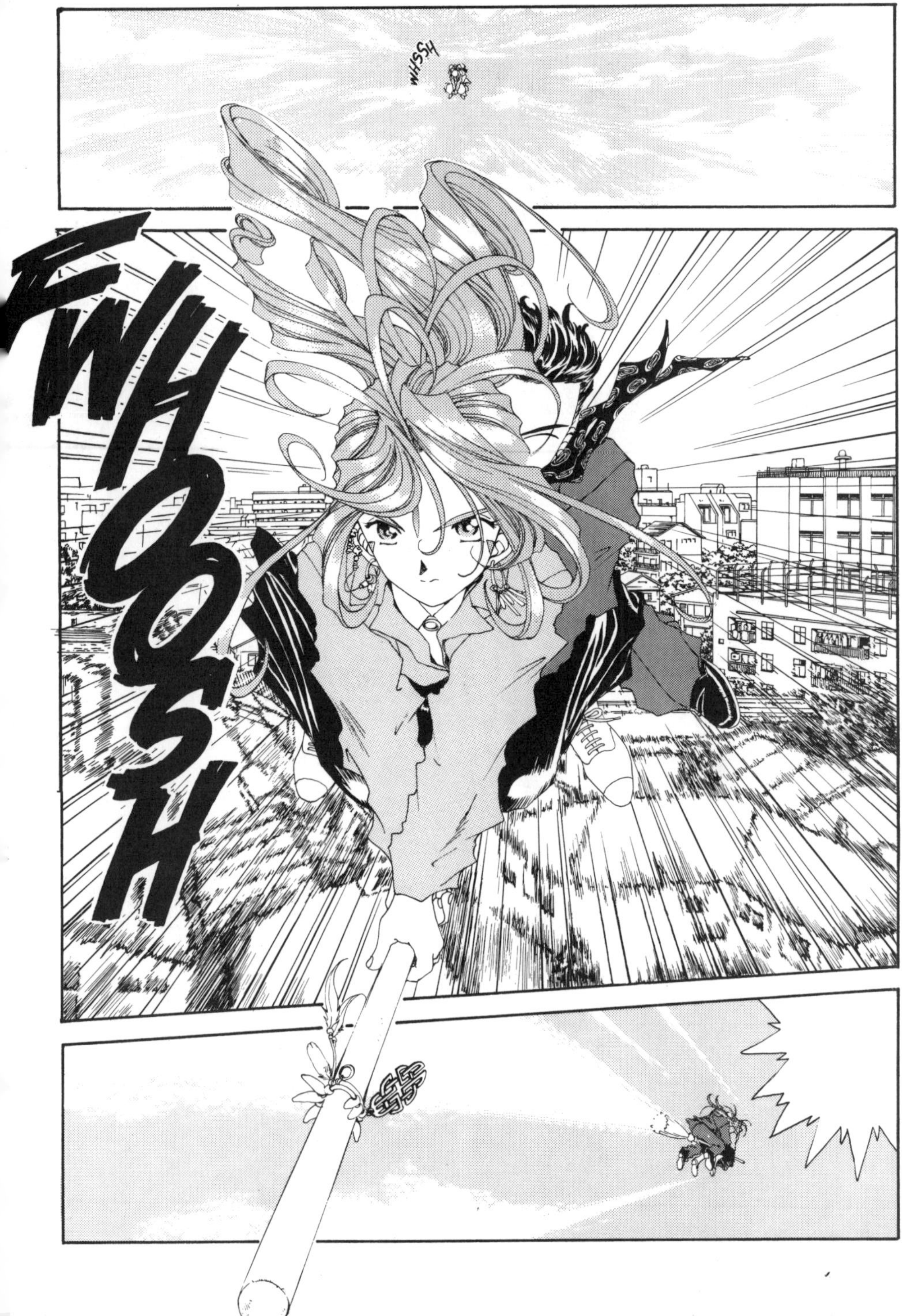
WHSSH
FWHOOSH

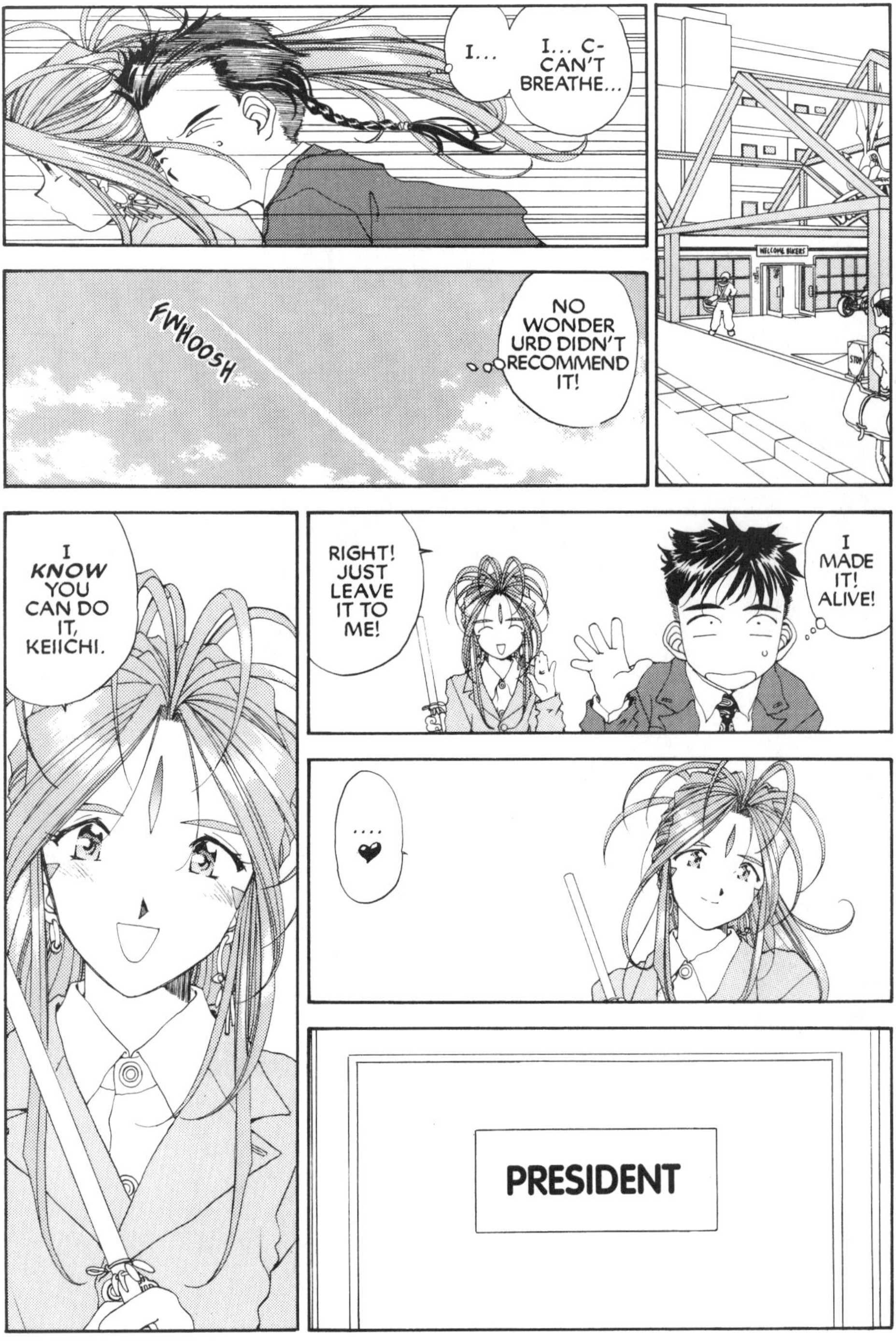
I...
I... C-CAN'T BREATHE...
FWHOOSH
NO WONDER URD DIDN'T RECOMMEND IT!
WELCOME BIKERS
STOP
I KNOW YOU CAN DO IT, KEIICHI.
RIGHT! JUST LEAVE IT TO ME!
I MADE IT! ALIVE!
....♥
PRESIDENT

...!

WELL, THEN.

LET ME SEE YOUR HANDS, SON.

??

HUH...?

ER... YES, SIR.

NO, THE BACKS OF YOUR HANDS.

NOT THE PALMS.

MM!

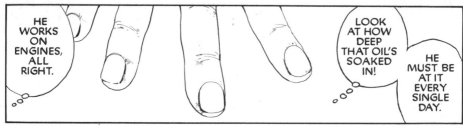

HE WORKS ON ENGINES, ALL RIGHT.

LOOK AT HOW DEEP THAT OIL'S SOAKED IN!

HE MUST BE AT IT EVERY SINGLE DAY.

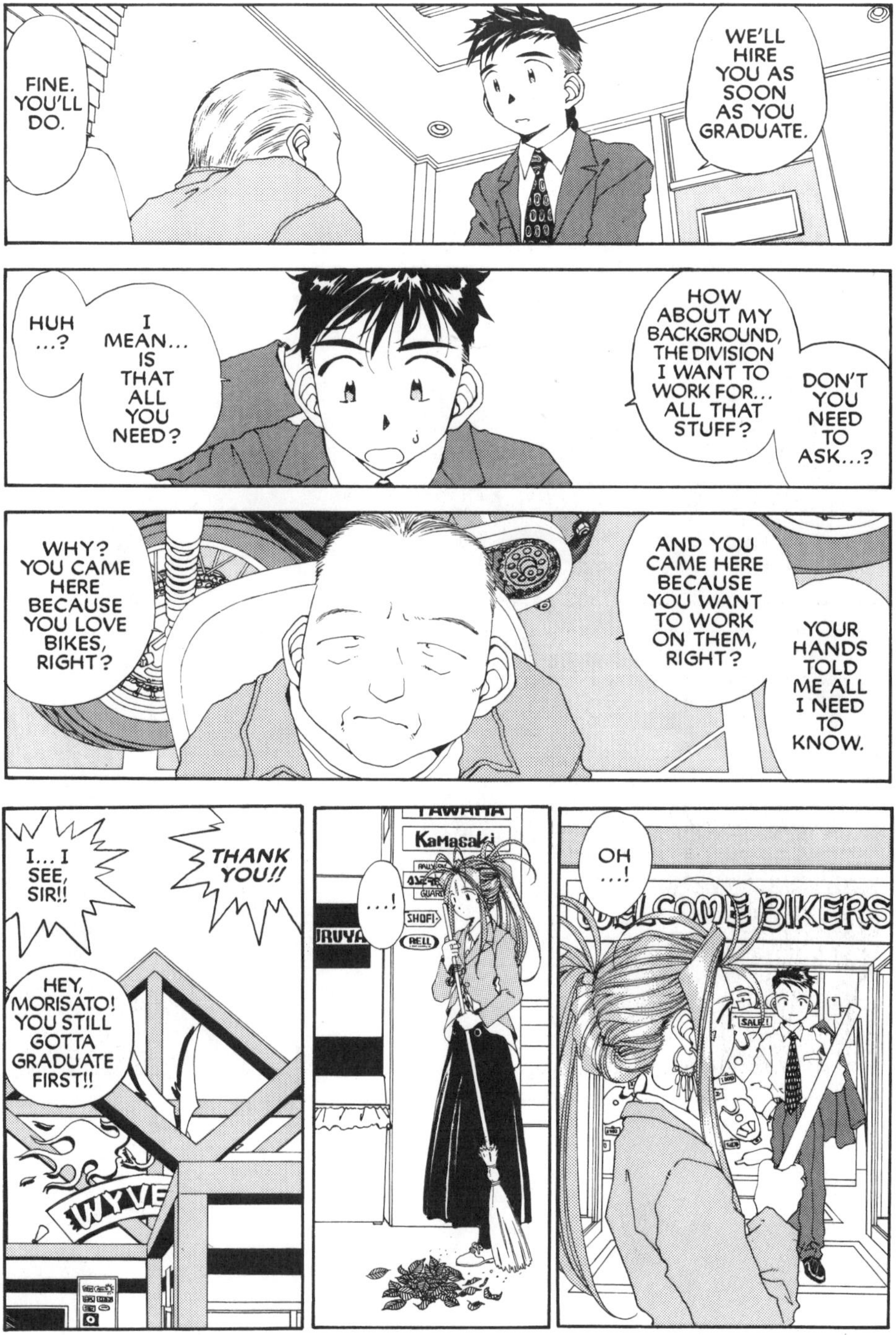
FINE. YOU'LL DO.
WE'LL HIRE YOU AS SOON AS YOU GRADUATE.
HUH ...?
I MEAN... IS THAT ALL YOU NEED?
HOW ABOUT MY BACKGROUND, THE DIVISION I WANT TO WORK FOR... ALL THAT STUFF?
DON'T YOU NEED TO ASK...?
WHY? YOU CAME HERE BECAUSE YOU LOVE BIKES, RIGHT?
AND YOU CAME HERE BECAUSE YOU WANT TO WORK ON THEM, RIGHT?
YOUR HANDS TOLD ME ALL I NEED TO KNOW.
I... I SEE, SIR!!
THANK YOU!!
HEY, MORISATO! YOU STILL GOTTA GRADUATE FIRST!!
...!
OH ...!
WELCOME BIKERS

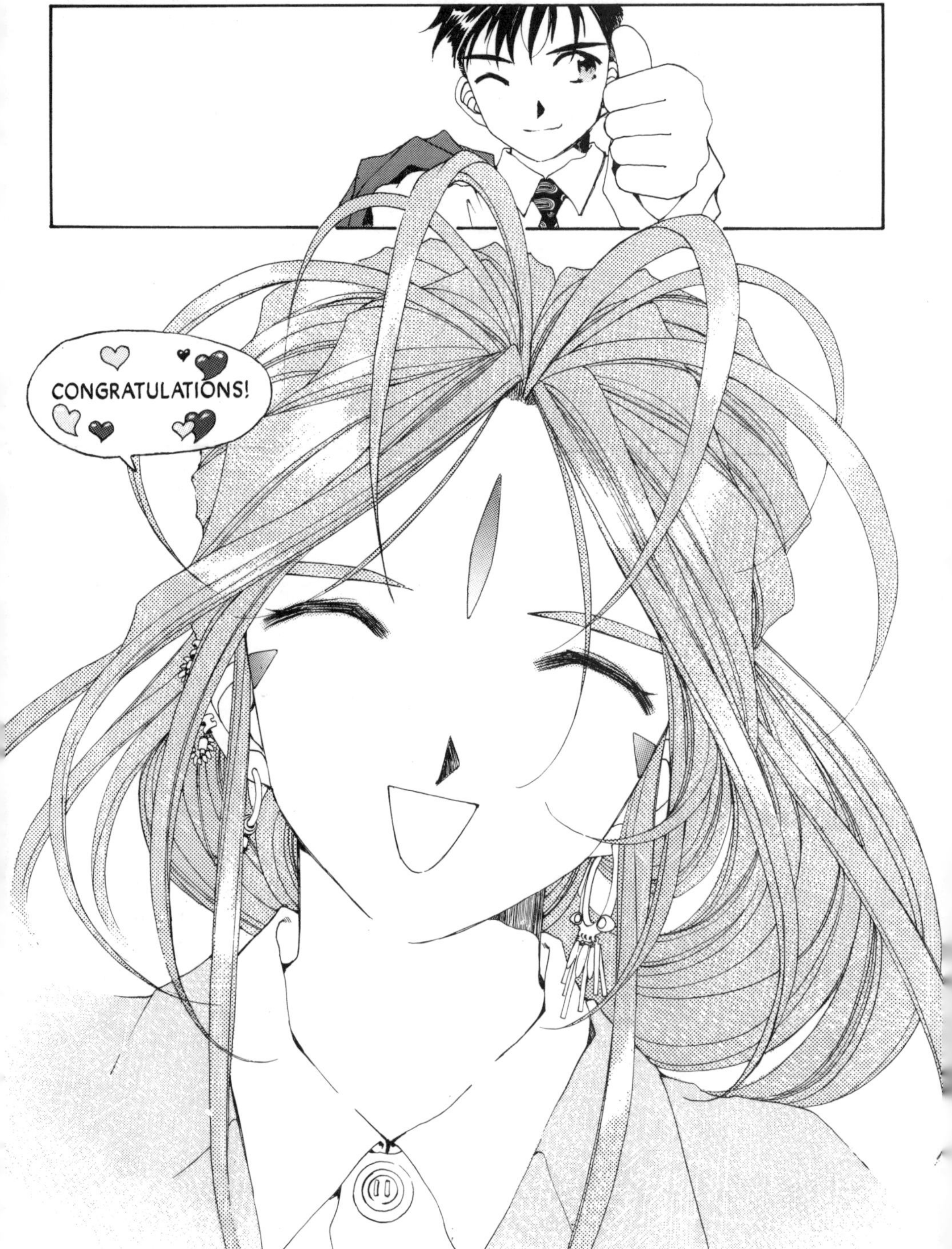
CONGRATULATIONS!

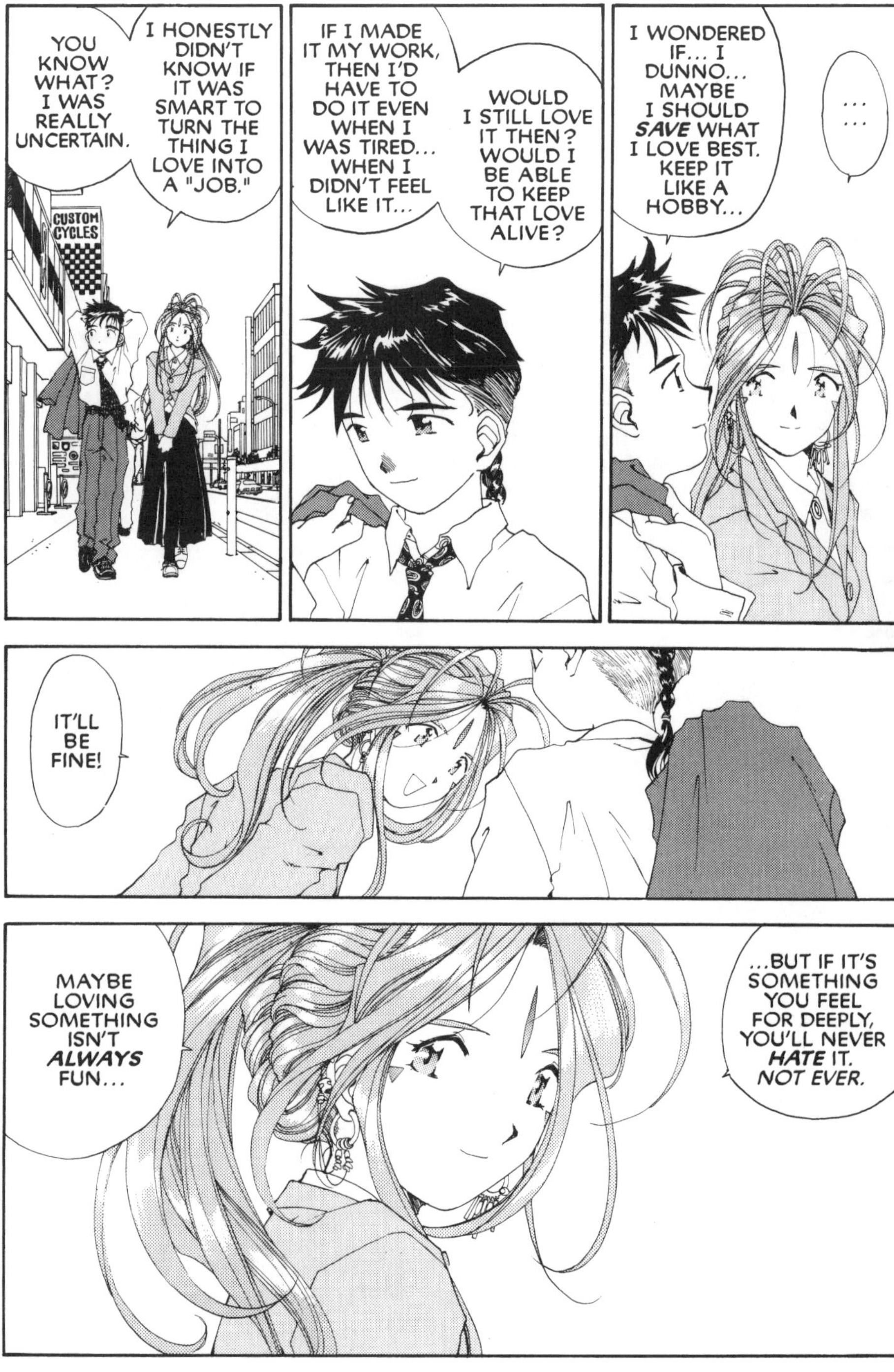
YOU KNOW WHAT? I WAS REALLY UNCERTAIN.
I HONESTLY DIDN'T KNOW IF IT WAS SMART TO TURN THE THING I LOVE INTO A "JOB."
CUSTOM CYCLES
IF I MADE IT MY WORK, THEN I'D HAVE TO DO IT EVEN WHEN I WAS TIRED... WHEN I DIDN'T FEEL LIKE IT...
WOULD I STILL LOVE IT THEN? WOULD I BE ABLE TO KEEP THAT LOVE ALIVE?
I WONDERED IF... I DUNNO... MAYBE I SHOULD *SAVE* WHAT I LOVE BEST. KEEP IT LIKE A HOBBY...
... ...
IT'LL BE FINE!
MAYBE LOVING SOMETHING ISN'T ***ALWAYS*** FUN...
...BUT IF IT'S SOMETHING YOU FEEL FOR DEEPLY, YOU'LL NEVER ***HATE*** IT. *NOT EVER.*

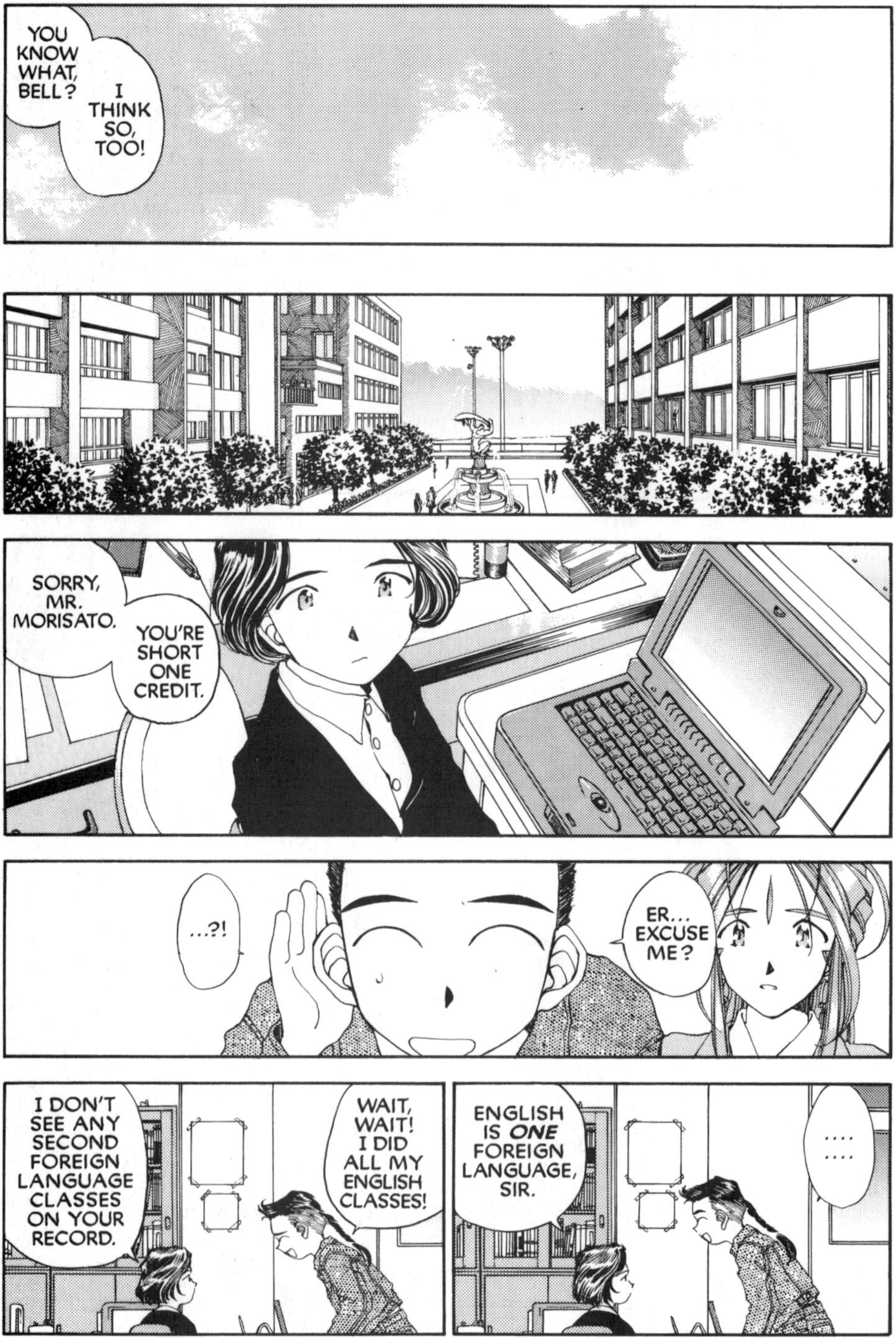
YOU KNOW WHAT, BELL?
I THINK SO, TOO!
SORRY, MR. MORISATO.
YOU'RE SHORT ONE CREDIT.
...?!
ER... EXCUSE ME?
I DON'T SEE ANY SECOND FOREIGN LANGUAGE CLASSES ON YOUR RECORD.
WAIT, WAIT! I DID ALL MY ENGLISH CLASSES!
ENGLISH IS *ONE* FOREIGN LANGUAGE, SIR.
....
....

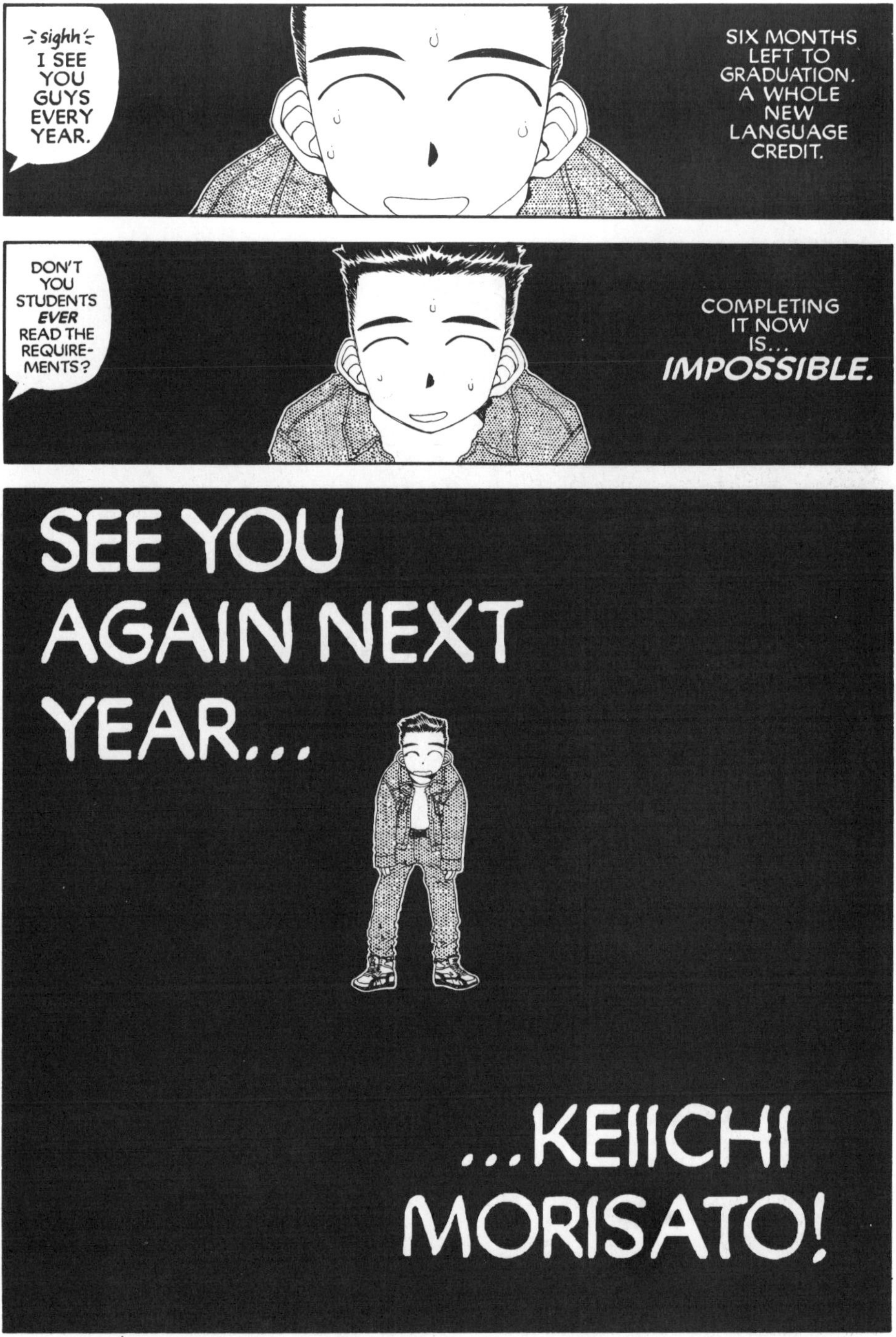

sighh I SEE YOU GUYS EVERY YEAR.
SIX MONTHS LEFT TO GRADUATION. A WHOLE NEW LANGUAGE CREDIT.
DON'T YOU STUDENTS EVER READ THE REQUIRE-MENTS?
COMPLETING IT NOW IS... IMPOSSIBLE.
SEE YOU AGAIN NEXT YEAR...
...KEIICHI MORISATO!

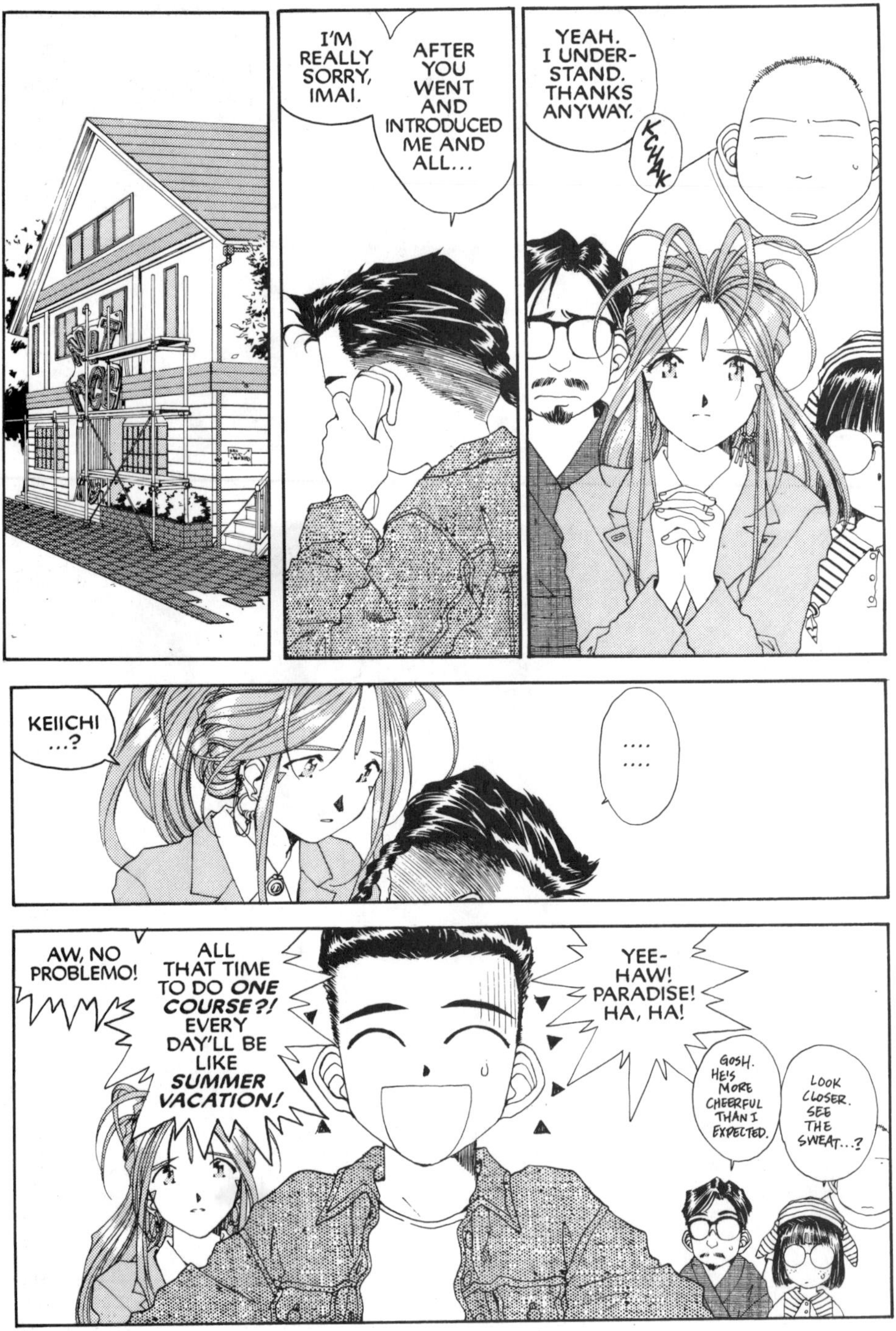

I'M REALLY SORRY, IMAI.
AFTER YOU WENT AND INTRODUCED ME AND ALL...
YEAH. I UNDERSTAND. THANKS ANYWAY.
KCHAK
KEIICHI ...?
....
AW, NO PROBLEMO!
ALL THAT TIME TO DO ONE COURSE?! EVERY DAY'LL BE LIKE SUMMER VACATION!
YEE-HAW! PARADISE! HA, HA!
GOSH. HE'S MORE CHEERFUL THAN I EXPECTED.
LOOK CLOSER. SEE THE SWEAT...?

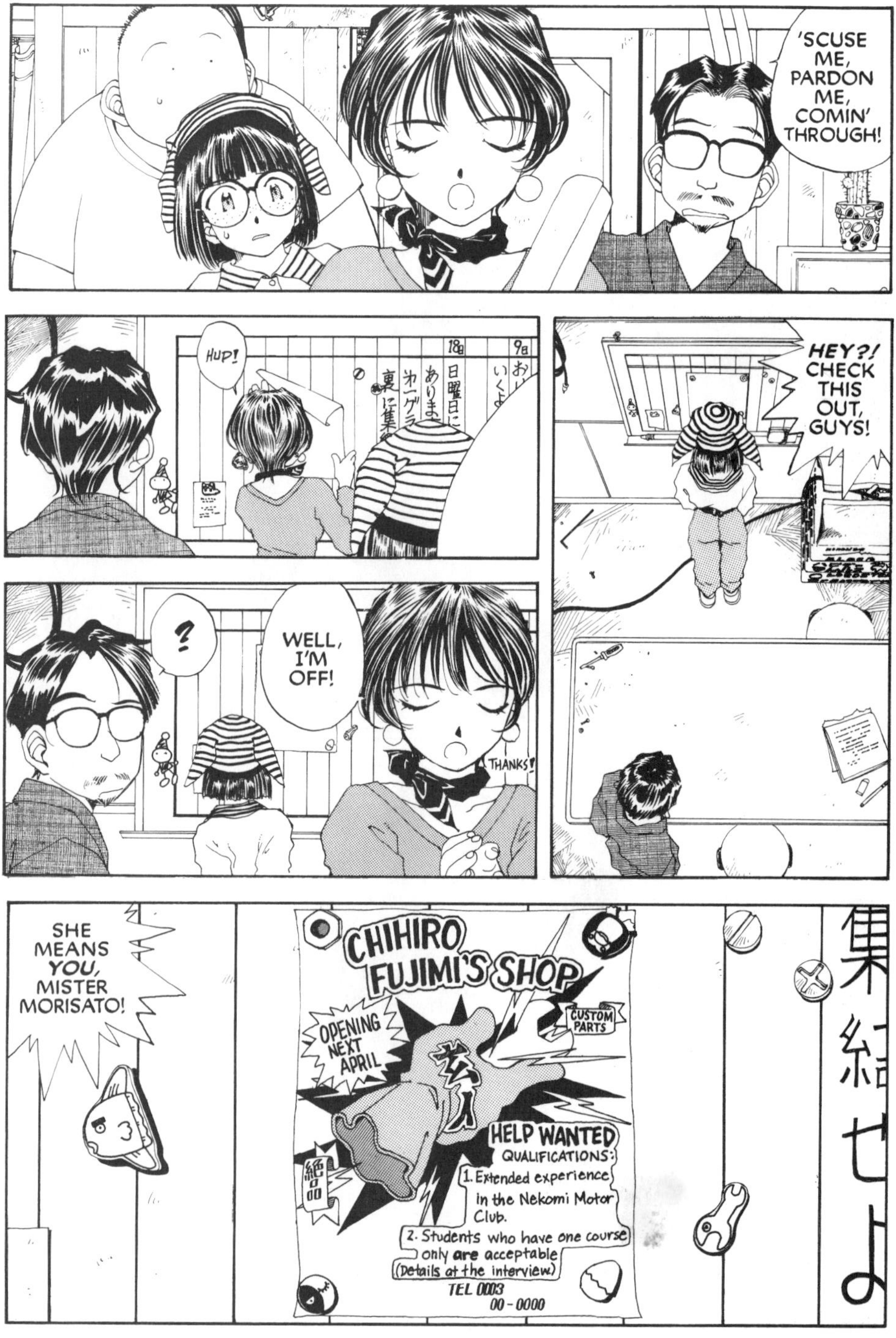
'SCUSE ME, PARDON ME, COMIN' THROUGH!
HUP!
?
WELL, I'M OFF!
THANKS!
HEY?! CHECK THIS OUT, GUYS!
SHE MEANS YOU, MISTER MORISATO!
CHIHIRO FUJIMI'S SHOP
OPENING NEXT APRIL
CUSTOM PARTS
HELP WANTED
QUALIFICATIONS:
1. Extended experience in the Nekomi Motor Club.
2. Students who have one course only are acceptable
(Details at the interview)
TEL 0003 00-0000
集結せよ

YOU'RE RIGHT!

CHIHIRO ...!

THANK YOU! I... I GUESS *EVERYONE'S* TRYING TO SAVE MY BUTT...

YOU'VE GOT IT WRONG, CHUM.

I'M NOT INTERESTED IN SAVING YOUR *BUTT.*

I'M SAVING YOUR *HANDS.*

THAT'S WHAT I WANT, KEIICHI!

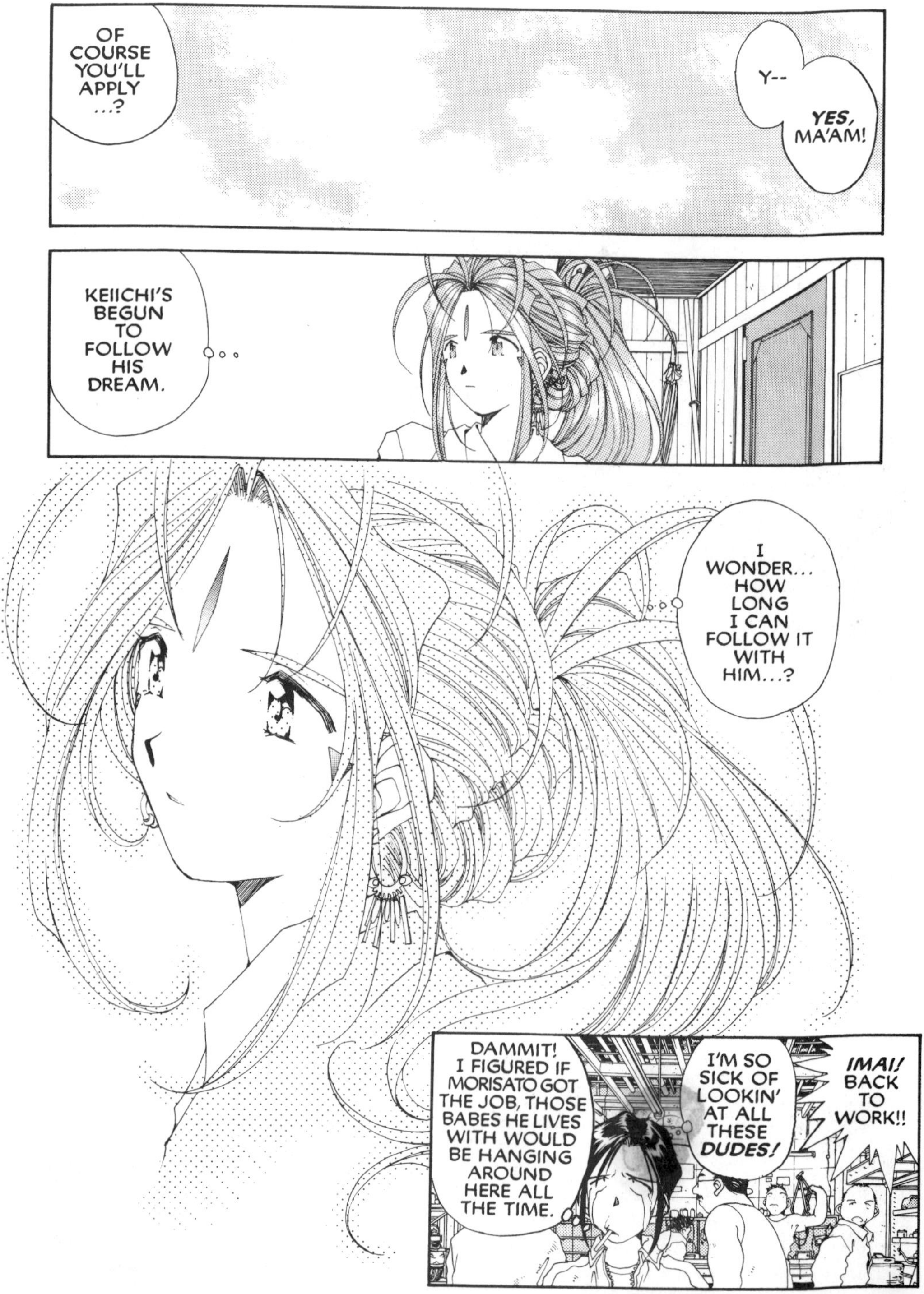
OF COURSE YOU'LL APPLY ...?
Y-- *YES,* MA'AM!
KEIICHI'S BEGUN TO FOLLOW HIS DREAM.
I WONDER... HOW LONG I CAN FOLLOW IT WITH HIM...?
DAMMIT! I FIGURED IF MORISATO GOT THE JOB, THOSE BABES HE LIVES WITH WOULD BE HANGING AROUND HERE ALL THE TIME.
I'M SO SICK OF LOOKIN' AT ALL THESE *DUDES!*
IMAI! BACK TO WORK!!

MANGA! MANGA! MANGA!
DARK HORSE HAS THE BEST IN MANGA COLLECTIONS!

AKIRA
Katsuhiro Otomo
BOOK 1
ISBN: 1-56971-498-3 $24.95
BOOK 2
ISBN: 1-56971-499-1 $24.95
BOOK 3
ISBN: 1-56971-525-4 $24.95
BOOK 4
ISBN: 1-56971-526-2 $27.95
BOOK 5
ISBN: 1-56971-527-0 $27.95
BOOK 6
ISBN: 1-56971-528-9 $29.95
APPLESEED
Masamune Shirow
BOOK ONE
ISBN: 1-56971-070-8 $16.95
BOOK TWO
ISBN: 1-56971-071-6 $16.95
BOOK THREE
ISBN: 1-56971-072-4 $17.95
BOOK FOUR
ISBN: 1-56971-074-0 $17.95
ASTRO BOY
Osama Tezuka
VOLUME 1
ISBN: 1-56971-676-5 $9.95
BLACK MAGIC
Masamune Shirow
ISBN: 1-56971-360-X $16.95
BLADE OF THE IMMORTAL
Hiroaki Samura
BLOOD OF A THOUSAND
ISBN: 1-56971-239-5 $14.95
CRY OF THE WORM
ISBN: 1-56971-300-6 $14.95
DREAMSONG
ISBN: 1-56971-357-X $14.95
ON SILENT WINGS
ISBN: 1-56971-412-6 $14.95
ON SILENT WINGS II
ISBN: 1-56971-444-4 $14.95
DARK SHADOWS
ISBN: 1-56971-469-X $14.95
HEART OF DARKNESS
ISBN: 1-56971-531-9 $16.95
THE GATHERING
ISBN: 1-56971-546-7 $15.95
THE GATHERING II
ISBN: 1-56971-560-2 $15.95
BUBBLEGUM CRISIS
Adam Warren
GRAND MAL
color paperback
ISBN: 1-56971-120-8 $14.95
CARAVAN KIDD
Johji Manabe
VOLUME 2
ISBN: 1-56971-324-3 $19.95
VOLUME 3
ISBN: 1-56971-338-3 $19.95
THE DIRTY PAIR
Adam Warren • Toren Smith
A PLAGUE OF ANGELS
ISBN: 1-56971-029-5 $12.95
FATAL BUT NOT SERIOUS
color paperback
ISBN: 1-56971-172-0 $14.95
DOMINION
Masamune Shirow
ISBN: 1-56971-488-6 $16.95
DOMU: A CHILD'S DREAM
Katsuhiro Otomo
ISBN: 1-56971-611-0 $17.95
DRAKUUN
Johji Manabe
RISE OF THE DRAGON PRINCESS
ISBN: 1-56971-302-2 $12.95
THE REVENGE OF GUSTAV
ISBN: 1-56971-368-5 $14.95
SHADOW OF THE WARLOCK
ISBN: 1-46971-406-1 $14.95
GHOST IN THE SHELL
Masamune Shirow
color/B&W paperback
ISBN: 1-56971-081-3 $24.95
GODZILLA
Kazuhisa Iwata
ISBN: 1-56971-063-5 $17.95
GUNSMITH CATS
Kenichi Sonoda
BONNIE AND CLYDE
ISBN: 1-56971-215-8 $13.95
MISFIRE
ISBN: 1-56971-253-0 $14.95
THE RETURN OF GRAY
ISBN: 1-56971-299-9 $17.95
GOLDIE VS. MISTY
ISBN: 1-56971-371-5 $15.95
BAD TRIP
ISBN: 1-56971-442-8 $13.95
BEAN BANDIT
ISBN: 1-56971-453-3 $16.95
KIDNAPPED
ISBN: 1-56971-529-7 $16.95
MISTER V
ISBN: 1-56971-550-5 $18.95
INTRON DEPOT
Masamune Shirow
INTRON DEPOT
color paperback
ISBN: 1-56971-085-6 $39.95
INTRON DEPOT 2: BLADES
color paperback
ISBN: 1-56971-382-0 $39.95
INTRON DEPOT 2: BLADES CD-ROM
2 CDs with illustrated mousepad
ISBN: 1-56971-485-1 $79.95
LONE WOLF & CUB
Kazuo Koike and Goseki Kojima
VOLUME 1: THE ASSASSIN'S ROAD
ISBN: 1-56971-502-5 $9.95
VOLUME 2: THE GATELESS BARRIER
ISBN: 1-56971-503-3 $9.95
VOLUME 3: THE FLUTE OF THE FALLEN TIGER
ISBN: 1-56971-504-1 $9.95
VOLUME 4: THE BELL WARDEN
ISBN: 1-56971-505-X $9.95
VOLUME 5: BLACK WIND
ISBN: 1-56971-506-8 $9.95
VOLUME 6: LANTERNS FOR THE DEAD
ISBN: 1-56971-507-6 $9.95
VOLUME 7: CLOUD DRAGON, WIND TIGER
ISBN: 1-56971-508-4 $9.95
VOLUME 8: CHAINS OF DEATH
ISBN: 1-56971-509-2 $9.95
VOLUME 9: ECHO OF THE ASSASSIN
ISBN: 1-56971-510-6 $9.95
VOLUME 10: HOSTAGE CHILD
ISBN: 1-56971-511-4 $9.95
VOLUME 11: TALISMAN OF HADES
ISBN: 1-56971-512-2 $9.95
VOLUME 12: SHATTERED STONES
ISBN: 1-56971-513-0 $9.95
VOLUME 13: THE MOON IN THE EAST, THE SUN IN THE WEST
ISBN: 1-56971-585-8 $9.95
VOLUME 14: DAY OF THE DEMONS
ISBN: 1-56971-586-6 $9.95
VOLUME 15: BROTHERS OF THE GRASS
ISBN: 1-56971-587-4 $9.95
VOLUME 16: GATEWAY INTO WINTER
ISBN: 1-56971-588-2 $9.95
VOLUME 17: THE WILL OF THE FANG
ISBN: 1-56971-589-0 $9.95
VOLUME 18: TWILIGHT OF THE KUROKUWA
ISBN: 1-56971-590-4 $9.95
VOLUME 19: THE MOON IN OUR HEARTS
ISBN: 1-56971-591-2 $9.95
OH MY GODDESS!
Kosuke Fujishima
1-555-GODDESS
ISBN: 1-56971-207-7 $13.95
LOVE POTION NO. 9
ISBN: 1-56971-252-2 $14.95
SYMPATHY FOR THE DEVIL
ISBN: 1-56971-329-4 $13.95
TERRIBLE MASTER URD
ISBN: 1-56971-369-3 $14.95
THE QUEEN OF VENGEANCE
ISBN: 1-56971-431-2 $13.95
MARA STRIKES BACK!
ISBN: 1-56971-449-5 $14.95
NINJA MASTER
ISBN: 1-56971-474-6 $13.95
MISS KEIICHI
ISBN: 1-56971-522-X $16.95
ADVENTURES OF THE MINI-GODDESSES
ISBN: 1-56971-421-5 $9.95
THE DEVIL IN MISS URD
ISBN: 1-56971-540-8 $14.95
THE FOURTH GODDESS
ISBN: 1-56971-551-3 $18.95
CHILDHOOD'S END
ISBN: 1-56971-685-4 $15.95
ORION
Masamune Shirow
ISBN: 1-56971-572-6 $19.95
OUTLANDERS
Johji Manabe
VOLUME 2
ISBN: 1-56971-162-3 $13.95
VOLUME 3
ISBN: 1-56971-163-1 $13.95
VOLUME 4
ISBN: 1-56971-069-4 $12.95
VOLUME 5
ISBN: 1-56971-275-1 $14.95
VOLUME 6
ISBN: 1-56971-423-1 $14.95
VOLUME 7
ISBN: 1-56971-424-X $14.95
VOLUME 8
ISBN: 1-56971-425-8 $14.95
SHADOW LADY
Masakazu Katsura
DANGEROUS LOVE
ISBN: 1-56971-408-8 $17.95
THE AWAKENING
ISBN: 1-56971-446-0 $15.95
SUDDEN DEATH
ISBN: 1-56971-477-0 $14.95
SHADOW STAR
Mohiro Kitoh
STARFLIGHT
ISBN: 1-56971-548-3 $15.95
SPIRIT OF WONDER
Kenji Tsuruta
ISBN: 1-56971-288-3 $12.95
3X3 EYES
Yuzo Takada
HOUSE OF DEMONS
ISBN: 1-56971-059-7 $12.95
CURSE OF THE GESU
ISBN: 1-56971-175-5 $12.95
BLOOD OF THE SACRED DEMON
ISBN: 1-56971-735-4 $13.95
WHAT'S MICHAEL?
Makoto Kobayashi
OFF THE DEEP END
ISBN: 1-56971-249-2 $5.95
MICHAEL'S MAMBO
ISBN: 1-56971-250-6 $5.95
MICHAEL'S FAVORITE SPOT
ISBN: 1-56971-557-2 $8.95
YOU'RE UNDER ARREST!
Kosuke Fujishima
THE WILD ONES
ISBN: 1-56971-319-7 $12.95
LIGHTS AND SIREN!
ISBN: 1-56971-432-0 $10.95

*All titles are black-and-white paperback unless otherwise noted

Available from your local comics shop or bookstore!

To find a comics shop in your area, call 1-888-266-4226
For more information or to order direct:
•On the web: www.darkhorse.com •E-mail: mailorder@darkhorse.com
•Phone: 1-800-862-0052 or (503) 652-9701 Mon.-Sat. 9 A.M. to 5 P.M. Pacific Time
*Prices and availability subject to change without notice